ISLES OF THE WEST

D0434108

'. . . a Cobbet-like voyage of discovery into how arrogantly and unjustly the nature quangos run their protectorates in the Highlands and islands.'

Neil Acherson, Book of the Year, *The Herald*

'. . . a complete delight, and a change from the usual kind of book about the Hebrides.'

Chris Dillon, BBC Radio

'. . . a fascinating and important book, which has completely altered my view of that part of the world . . . What, he asks, is a healthy relationship between people and land? To what extent is the love of nature misanthropic? They are harsh questions and in an explosive book with an anodyne title Mitchell attempts to answer them. His questions are, for me, a kind of revelation.'

Adam Nicolson, *The Sunday Telegraph*

'. . . a penetrating and astringent analysis of the state of play in the world of wildlife conservation. No punches are pulled.'

Lord Barber of Tewkesbury, *Country Illustrated*

'It is difficult to fault Mitchell on a single issue. *Isles of the West* is worth reading for its truths and its splendid evocation of island life.'

Ruaridh Nicoll, *The Herald*

'Ian Mitchell has cleverly let the Hebridean witnesses explain their exasperation and despair at the ruination of their islands by the militant conservationists.'

Peter Clarke, *New Statesman*

'*Isles of the West* is an important and fascinating study of present-day island life. It captures the allure of the locale as well as portraying the islanders with warmth, good humour and understanding.'

Hugh Smith, *Oban Times*

'This is a readable, entertaining and well-researched book . . . a penetrating and pertinent analysis. Anyone with an interest in the politics of conservation should read this book.'

Jonathan Bulmer, *Stornoway Gazzette*

'. . . an eye-opening description of land ownership in the Hebrides . . . beautifully written.'

Matt Ridley, *Daily Telegraph*

'I enjoyed this book, its clear lines of argument, its careful documentation, its little anecdotes and its touches of humour. I wonder if Mitchell's sense of the ridiculous is not perhaps what differentiates him from those he criticises, even more than his obvious sympathy with crofters and the Gaelic way of life.'

Jean Hunter, *The Ileach*

'A controversial book, and those who enjoy open criticism of "pure" conservation will find it an enthralling read.'

Colin Shedden, *Shooting and Conservation*

'Ian Mitchell makes some telling points and I confess I found his book deliciously readable.'

Peter Marren, *British Wildlife*

'After this book the politics of land use and land ownership in western Scotland will never be the same again. It exposes the chasm between local people and the RSPB in a way which cannot be ignored by reformists in the Scottish parliament. Mitchell identifies the point never adequately answered: why should local communities in unchanging places be bound hand and foot by new environmental regulations curbing routine behaviour when it was their traditional management that created these environments in the first place? Mitchell's sharp pen has caused a furore in Scotland.'

Michael Wigan, *The Field*

ISLES OF THE WEST

A HEBRIDEAN VOYAGE

IAN MITCHELL

Birlinn

This edition published in 2001 by
Birlinn Limited
8 Canongate Venture
5 New Street
Edinburgh EH8 8BH

First published in 1999 by
Canongate Books Limited
Edinburgh

Copyright © Ian Mitchell 1999 and 2001

Photographs copyright © Ian Mitchell

Ian Mitchell asserts the moral right to be
identified as the author of this work.

All rights reserved.
No part of this publication may be reproduced, stored,
or transmitted in any form, or by any means, electronic, mechanical
or photocopying, recording or otherwise,
without the express written permission of the publisher.

ISBN 1 84158 150 X

British Library Cataloguing-in-Publication Data
A catalogue record for this book is available from the British Library

Typeset in Adobe Garamond by Brinnoven, Livingston
Printed and bound by WS Bookwell

CONTENTS

This book is dedicated to the memory of my father,
who loved the isles, the seas and the folk of the west,
and who helped finance the purchase of *Sylvia B.*

INTRODUCTION

IN 1991 I MARRIED AN ISLAY GIRL and moved to the island from Kintyre, on the mainland opposite. As the distance between the two places was less than 20 miles, I assumed, in my ignorance, that the way of life would not be dissimilar. I could not have been more wrong. Though I had, over the years, visited many of the Hebridean islands and was familiar with the faces they present to the outside world, I soon realised how superficial my impressions were. So, when the publishers of an earlier of book of mine, *The Cost of a Reputation*, offered me the opportunity to write about the islands off the west of Scotland, I accepted the commission with alacrity. If nothing else, the research would be fascinating.

So it was that in the summer of 1996 I made a voyage round the Hebrides in *Sylvia B*, a 21-foot, bermudan-rigged, fibreglass cruising sloop – displacement: one ton – which had been sold as a 'Corribee' by Newbridge Boats of Bridport in Dorset until the firm went out of business in the late 1980s. I have owned her since 1981, and over the years have sailed extensively in Hebridean waters and also round the north and west coasts of Ireland. We are old friends.

My only stipulation to Canongate was that the book concern itself with contemporary issues, rather than the past. Though some history is important if the reader wants to understand the present, I have kept it to the minimum necessary to make sense of the often tangled relations between people and place today.

My particular interest was in wildlife conservation, an issue whose controversial nature I had been almost entirely unaware of before coming to live on Islay. What was the situation elsewhere in the Hebrides? Since I could not go everywhere in a single summer, I decided I would set an itinerary for my trip which would consist of all the islands where the land-owning nature conservation charities – the backbone of the conservation bureaucracy – own land. The list was the National Trust for Scotland, the Scottish Wildlife Trust, the John Muir Trust, the Royal Society for the Protection of Birds and the Woodland Trust. I added to that list the places where Scottish Natural Heritage owns reserves, and included, for comparison, a Ministry of Defence and a Forestry Commission estate, they being the other two large public landowners who have some sort of conservation brief.

My intention, though, was not only to talk to the conservationists and their neighbours, I also wanted to look at the wider issues presented by island life. Thus the Gaelic language, crofting, lairdism, feudalism, economic development and decay, tourism and the problems and possibilities associated with depopulation and incomers are all covered. But conservation and the environment is the one 'political' issue which is common to almost all islands.

I was away from home for two and a half months and, apart from three stormy passages, and a few bouts of homesickness, I enjoyed every minute of it. I love sailing; I love the islands; and I love the independent-minded people of the Hebrides. I had intended to leave while the bluebells were still out and be home before the bracken turned. But my preparations took a lot longer than I had anticipated and I left a month late. Consequently, I did not get back until early October. This was a lucky mistake as the weather throughout the Highlands and Islands in September 1996 was among the best on record. The *Herald* called it 'an Indian summer to remember', noting that Fort Augustus, for example, had enjoyed the second highest total of sunshine hours since records began in the nineteenth century.

But this book is more about people than places. I am grateful to everyone who gave me their views and to the many others who helped in practical ways. In the text I have distinguished between those who talked to me out of common helpfulness and those who did so only in the line of duty, as part of the public relations aspect of their jobs. Unless for reasons of special respect, like age, those in the former category I have referred to in the text by their first names; the others by their surnames. Those whose names are not given at all were people who specifically asked not to be identified.

Apart from the few pub conversations, which I have reconstructed from memory, all quoted words have been transcribed verbatim, from a record made at the time, though I have applied 'Hansard rules' insofar as I have corrected obvious mistakes. In some cases, I have rearranged the sequence of the discussion, and my own contribution to it, to make for more intelligible reading in edited form on the printed page. In three cases, I have added brief subsequent comments in order to illuminate important points. Otherwise, everything printed here is exactly as it was said to me at the time.

This book is a snapshot. I have resisted the temptation to update the record so that the opinions expressed and the facts noted are those of the late summer of 1996. Many things have changed since then, particularly since the announcement of the Scottish parliament and the consequent politicisation of the land debate. Since this book deals with many of the matters which are central to that controversy, I hope that it will make a constructive contribution by giving an accurate, if not comprehensive, picture of how things stood in the Hebrides during the last summer before all the people and organisations with axes to grind had to start watching what they said.

Lagavulin
Isle of Islay
April 1999

GLOSSARY OF ACRONYMS

JMT   John Muir Trust. Formed in 1983 by a group of civilised lawyers to protect 'wild' land from the encroachments of their own civilisation.
        41 Commercial Street, Leith EH6 6JD

NCC   Nature Conservancy Council. This was the government conservation body, formed in 1949. It went through several variants of the name but, for simplicity, I have used the acronym NCC throughout. In 1992 it ceased to exist when SNH (q.v.) took over its functions in Scotland.

NTS   National Trust for Scotland. Founded in 1931 to save grand buildings from the improvidence of their owners. Subsequently it extended its remit to land and became a huge landowner.
        5 Charlotte Square, Edinburgh, EH2 4DU

RSPB   Royal Society for the Protection of Birds. Founded in 1889 to stop the trade in egret feathers. Since that was outlawed it has sought other outlets for its zeal and now purports to protect everything from mountains to the sea, though charismatic bird species are still covered too.
        The Lodge, Sandy, Bedfordshire SG19 2DL

SNH   Scottish Natural Heritage. Founded in 1992 when it took over the functions of the NCC and the Countryside Commission for Scotland. It is the official advisor to government on all matters relating to conservation, and the executive body for all bureaucratic initiatives in this field.
        12 Hope Terrace, Edinburgh EH9 2AS

SSSI   Site of Special Scientific Interest. These are areas of land which owners are no longer free to manage without government supervision. Nothing new may happen on any SSSI without SNH's express permission. There are 1,441 SSSIs in Scotland, covering 12 per cent of the country, or nearly a sixth of all non-urban land.

SWT   Scottish Wildlife Trust. Founded in 1964 as one of the 'County' wildlife trusts, its territory has since become a country and the Trust the main general wildlife protection body in Scotland.
        Cramond House, Cramond Glebe Road, Edinburgh EH4 6NS

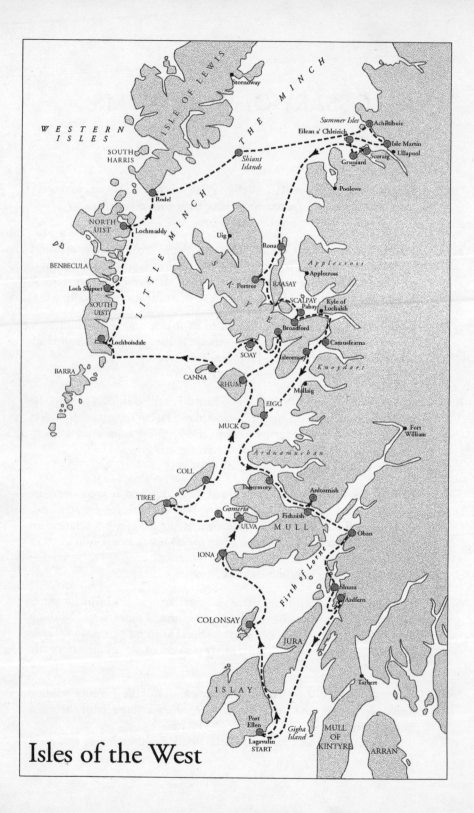

Isles of the West

1

OUTWARD BOUND: COLONSAY, IONA AND THE TRESHNISH ISLES

ALL THROUGH THE LONG EVENING of a Sunday in late July, I sailed north-west from Islay on a burnished sea. Leaving astern the huge lighthouse at Rubha á Mhail, the northerly tip of the island, I had the low mass of Colonsay and Oronsay ahead. A fresh breeze from the south-west brought clouds, through the breaks in which there glowed an amber light which turned large patches of the sea the colour of beaten copper. Gradually Islay shrank and Colonsay loomed. Slowly the light faded until everything around was a choppy, windswept grey, fading to black at the base of the dark island ahead. I made my landfall at dusk, just as a misty rain was beginning to fall. By the time I had cast anchor, made everything snug on deck and gone below to cook, the rain was drumming on the coach-roof. Later over dinner, by the warm light of my two paraffin lamps, I read the material I had brought with me that covered the two islands.

Colonsay is separated from Oronsay only at high tide, and until recently the two islands were bought and sold as a unit. They had passed from the MacDuffies in the Middle Ages to the MacDonalds, then to Campbells who swapped it, in 1701, with the McNeills for part of Knapdale. In 1904 the last of that line, Major General John Carstairs McNeill VC, died and the estate was sold. The purchaser was a Canadian Scot, Donald Smith, by then ennobled as Baron Strathcona and Mount Royal.

Born and bred in Forres, Morayshire, Smith had emigrated in the 1840s and made a fortune in the Hudson Bay Company, initially by cheating fellow shareholders who had trusted him to make a deal on their behalf with the Canadian government over a revised land charter. Smith gambled the fortune he had made by financing the construction – by George Steven, another Scot – of the Canadian Pacific Railroad. The risk was rewarded and Smith went into the Canadian parliament where, despite being nominally a Conservative, he acquired a reputation for supporting whoever was in power. This led to accusations of disloyalty to his own party whose leader, Sir John MacDonald – yet another Scot and the architect of Canadian unity – called him 'the biggest liar I ever met'. The *Dictionary of National Biography* records the allegation that Smith had been 'the man chiefly responsible for the corruption of Canadian public life in the eighties'.

1

Smith came to Britain as Canadian High Commissioner in 1896 where he proceeded to spend his ill-gotten gains buying influence and property. He entertained with immense extravagance and gave away £1.3 million to charity. In 1897 he was ennobled. Two years later the Boer War broke out, and he financed a regiment of rough-riders which he called Strathcona's Horse. In recognition of this last act he was allowed to alter the patent of his barony so that it could be transmitted through the female line. This was important to him since his only child was a girl – that is why the present Lord Strathcona is a Howard not a Smith.

The *Dictionary* says the first Baron was 'a good hater', although it adds, 'He never let animosity get in the way of business.' The circumstances of his purchase of Colonsay illustrated his acumen. He had met General McNeill in Canada in the early 1870s and lent him part of the £80,000 which he paid for the island when he bought it in 1877. The interest payments were a burden on McNeill for the rest of his life. After McNeill's death, his family had to sell the island to repay Strathcona. And who was the purchaser? Strathcona himself. And at what price? £44,000 – little more than half what McNeill had paid for it and the exact amount the family owed him. So no money changed hands. It was a pawnbroker's deal.

At the end of his life, Strathcona gave no fewer than eight addresses in *Who's Who*. Five were in Britain: '28 Grosvenor Square, London W; 17 Victoria Street, London SW; Glencoe NB [i.e. North Britain]; Colonsay, NB; Debden Hall, Newport, Essex.' The present Lord Strathcona is down to only two addresses, Colonsay and a house in Highbury Road, Wimbledon. He is still, however a rich man; at least he is a good deal richer than any of the other inhabitants of Colonsay, a fact he used to advantage in a recent, landmark court case involving a crofter who disputed Strathcona's right to exclusive direction of the economic life of the island. That crofter is a man called Bill Lawson, and I decided I would start next morning by trying to find him and ask about the case.

I drained my glass, put out the lamps and crawled into my sleeping bag. As the rain splashed on deck, the boat yawed slightly on the anchor-chain, rocking a little as it did so – a pleasantly soporific motion.

I awoke to a day of blinding sunshine. Though the wind had got up further, the rain had washed away completely and Colonsay sparkled in the clear air. The sea outside Scalasaig roadstead, where I was anchored, was covered with white. It must have been blowing a good force 6, though still from the south-west. As Scalasaig is on the east coast of the island, this meant that *Sylvia B* was lying in calm water. But the wind was howling in the rigging and the anchor chain was stretched out taut from the bowhead. Everything about me was in motion. It was a day that shouted 'Let's go!'

After a rushed breakfast, I inflated the dinghy and rowed ashore. Bill Lawson was not at home but I was told he would be in the public bar of the Colonsay Hotel that evening. I set out for a long scramble round the rocky east and north-west coasts of the island. Out of the wind the heat was intense, and I ate my lunch sitting on the lush grass above the high-water mark in the completely sheltered Balnahard bay, at the north-eastern extremity of the island. No road reaches it and so it is rarely visited. Below the tideline, the bottom is golden, weed-free sand which reflected a lovely bottle green through the clear water: a magical spot.

By cocktail hour, I was back in Scalasaig, having passed hardly an acre of arable ground the whole day. But in the hotel the bar was packed, mainly with visitors. Clearly there is more money to be made from tourism than agriculture, a fact which lay at the heart of the dispute between the Lawsons and Lord Strathcona. As it happened, Bill had been that day to the funeral of a neighbour who had been known as 'the bard of Colonsay', an irreplaceable, Gaelic-speaking storehouse of lore, legend and song. In an island with so few natives left, this was a grievous loss to the indigenous community. Bill was looking none too happy when I met him.

Three hours and I can't remember how many pints of Guinness later, with Bill looking a little happier – though not much – we made our way up the road, over to Kilchattan where the Lawsons live at 'Seaview'. Bill, a handsome, sandy-haired man with sea-going eyes, is a fisherman, builder and farmer – in that order of priority. Though Kilchattan is one of the few fertile areas on the island, the economics of crofting agriculture are such that he does little more than keep a small flock of sheep. Whereas Bill is from Edinburgh, Annie, his wife, a bustling, friendly woman, is a native of Colonsay. It is she who was the inheritor of the tenancy of the croft, where she runs a very successful bed and breakfast operation. I was shown to a chair at the head of the enormous kitchen table and given a large dram. From time to time, as she came and went with pudding, coffee and other refreshments, I caught a glimpse, through what would once have been the outside door, of a large and opulently furnished conservatory (built by Bill). That evening's guests were finishing what had evidently, from the sound of things, been a very enjoyable meal. It was immediately obvious that even on the arable ground, there was more money to be made from visiting people than resident sheep.

Over the course of the next few hours, the story of the court case was made clear to me. A little bit of background is necessary to understand the full implications for modern Highland landholding generally.

By the end of the Middle Ages, Scotland was for all practical purposes divided (roughly equally in terms of area) between land that was held in feudal tenure, ultimately of the Crown, and land held in a completely different form of tenure under an unwritten law which derived from the ancient usages of Gaeldom – of the Highland chiefs. The next few centuries were a struggle between Anglophone feudalism based in Edinburgh and the Gaelic-speaking world of the autocephalous clans. By means of its hierarchical structure and legally enforceable unity, feudalism slowly got the upper hand. From the seventeenth century onwards, Edinburgh was helped in its struggle by an overwhelmingly powerful ally: the Kingdom of England and Wales. Slowly this early version of the Cold War took on the character of a conflict between a basically commercial way of life and a basically communal one. Thus the Act of Union in 1707 meant that when the final showdown took place – at Culloden in 1746 – the Highland army was opposed by a coalition of English and lowland Scots forces whose overarching strategic goal was to open the Highlands to modern economic development – run of course by the themselves.

The practical outcome was the infamous Clearances of the late eighteenth and early nineteenth centuries when the indigenous way of life was largely destroyed in order to facilitate the expansion of commercial agriculture. Though many Highland lairds remained on their ancestral ground, they were forced to adapt to the new way of doing things. Thus the McNeill family stayed on Colonsay, but as landlords rather than chieftains. They took into vacant possession the best ground on the island – at Kiloran and Machrins, and around Colonsay House – and farmed it themselves with wage-earning employees. The people evicted from this ground either went abroad or were crammed into tiny, uneconomic holdings on the poorer parts of the island, generally near the coast where they could supplement their diet by fishing. Kilchattan is one such community. Annie Lawson's ancestors were among the people thus dispossessed. Since immemorial custom was ignored it is arguably true to say that this amounted to expropriation. As the Clearances were for private rather than public purposes, and as no compensation was paid, it would probably be more accurate to call it theft.

But this gigantic act of ethnic robbery did not happen without protest.[1] A similar process had been going on in Ireland and there a full-scale land war broke out in the mid-nineteenth century. It quickly spread to the Highlands. In 1881 the British government passed the Irish Land Act which partially defused the situation by giving legal effect to many aspects of customary right. Similarly, in Scotland the Crofters Act of 1886 gave security of tenure to all people formally declared crofters on the applicable date in the Highland counties. At that moment, the crofters of Kilchattan became heritors of tenancies, those tenancies being defined as whatever was in practical force at the date of the passage of the Act: a provision which was to become important and highly contentious 100 years later when the case Mrs Annie Lawson, of Seaview and Alister Annie's Croft, *versus*

---

1 In England the Enclosure Acts of the same period similarly dispossessed the traditional peasantry, but there every enclosure of previously common land had to be sanctioned by an individual Act of Parliament and all the dispossessed commoners compensated (though in practice they were usually cheated). In the Highlands neither democratic sanction nor any form of compensation was required. There were two other important differences: in England, people dispossessed of land were rarely evicted from their houses, and most of them were able to find employment either in the increasingly intensive farming operations that replaced communal land-use or in a rapidly industrialising town nearby. Evicted Highlanders had neither cushion. In effect, they were treated as redundant but unsaleable livestock: the intelligent thing to do was simply to get rid of them. As the law forbade slaughtering them, emigration became the preferred solution to the problem of their presence.

The Right Honourable Euan Howard, Fourth Baron Strathcona and Mount Royal, of Colonsay House, came to court.

Crofting law has been modified in detail but not in substance since 1886. Possibly the biggest change was the 1976 Crofting Act which created a right-to-buy scheme. For 15 times the annual rental any crofting tenant has the right to purchase his in-bye land from the landlord. The Lawsons applied to buy their 34-acre croft, as they were entitled to do, from Lord Strathcona, but he disputed their view of the boundaries. This was easy to do because in 1886 definitive lists had been made of the crofts whose tenancies were now protected, but no maps of the extent of these crofts were drawn. Strathcona claimed that the verge between the public road and the Lawsons' croft was not part of that croft and therefore not purchasable under the legislation. The importance of this very narrow strip of land, perhaps 10 feet wide, was that if Strathcona could refuse to sell it, then he would be able to retain the effective right to control what use the Lawsons made of their croft, since he could give or withhold rights of access across 'his' verge on any conditions he chose. What the Lawsons feared was that he might try to limit their bed and breakfast business, which provides the bulk of the family income. Strathcona has a large number of self-catering cottages and apartments of his own in and around Colonsay House. The Lawsons are direct competitors of his in the only viable industry on the island: tourism.

Though the Lawsons were very worried about what a court case would involve, not least the cost, they decided to fight. Early on, they had a stroke of luck when one of their regular guests, an Edinburgh barrister (later a QC; now a Sheriff), declared he was so outraged by Strathcona's claim that he would represent them on favourable terms. Without this, Strathcona's large legal team would undoubtedly have crushed the Lawsons by sheer financial weight. The forum for crofting disputes is the Scottish Land Court, based in Edinburgh. Opening and closing submissions were made in the capital, but the court also came out to Colonsay to take evidence and make a site inspection. All this travelling and time adds to the expense. If the Lawsons had lost, they would have had to pay the whole expense of this for all Strathcona's lawyers as well as their own. It looked like an act of intimidation when, on the first day the court sat, a Monday, Strathcona's advocate stood up to announce that he thought the case would take most of the week. But the intended effect was ruined when the Lawsons' barrister replied that he would not be inconvenienced if the case ran right on into the following week. Despite this bravado, for the Lawsons it was victory or financial death.

Strathcona advanced two principal arguments: first, that the verge was not croft land, and therefore he could refuse to sell it to the Lawsons and, secondly, in the alternative, he should be able to control the Lawsons' activities on their croft for the benefit of the island as a whole, though since he owned 95 per cent of it the distinction between the island's interests and his own was fine, to say the least of it. The Lawsons might establish a picnic area next to the standing stone in the field in front of their house, he warned, or put caravans or holiday chalets

on their ground. 'Could the Court for instance envisage the possibility',
Strathcona's advocate asked at one point, 'that the croft might become a favoured
nuclear waste dump for the Western Isles, and that there would be lorries lined
astern up the road forever and a day putting nuclear waste in a large hole in the
middle of the croft?'

Bill Lawson countered that such matters were for the Planning Department
of the Argyll and Bute Council. As to Strathcona's argument that he should be
able to control all activity on the island for the benefit of the islanders, Bill was
unimpressed. 'When our children went to school here 20 years ago,' he told the
press, 'there were 25 children in the school. Now there are only three. So I don't
think Lord Strathcona always knows what is best for the island.'

In the event, the feudalistic 'beneficial control' argument failed to carry any
weight and the matter was settled entirely on the basis of whether the verge was
legally croft land or not. After a year of deliberation, the judge, Duncan
McDiarmid, gave judgement in the Lawsons' favour. He reasoned as follows: the
key moment in time was 1886 when the area passed from feudal into crofting
tenure. After production of various maps it was agreed that the fence which
today runs along the roadside, next to the verge, would have been preceded by a
stone dyke in approximately the same position. In 1886, there were no tarmac
roads, and hence no such things as verges between the roads and the croft. The
road – more properly a track – would have been as wide as the distance between
the two dykes which ran along either side of it. Thus any crofter would have had
direct access to the road without having to cross a verge. Such tracks needed to
be wide because they were used for driving beasts to and from the common
grazings as well as for all sorts of vehicular, mounted and pedestrian traffic.

> The fact that the width of the road appears wider than is now necessary to
> encompass a single width tarred carriageway should not confuse the issue
> [McDiarmid wrote in his judgement]. This 'verge' did not exist prior to the tarmac
> being laid and quite clearly the crofters concerned have had free access to and
> uninterrupted passage over this area for 100 years. Now the landlord claims that
> on a purchase of a croft adjacent to the public road, the crofter concerned requires
> to approach the landlord for permission to cross what the landlord now terms a
> 'verge' to reach the tarmac . . .
> It is a novel point for a landlord to claim that at that time, although there
> appears to be a dyke or fence on the maps of the day between the croft and the
> road, this line was not a boundary between the crofts and the road, but a limit to
> the extent of the croft, beyond which lay a verge in the landlord's control not
> leased to the crofters and over which the crofters had no access and which separated
> the croft from the road. Similar situations exist in all original crofting townships
> served by a common road since 1886, but it is the first time within our judicial
> knowledge that any such claim to any verges has been made.[2]

In the last point lay the wider significance of the case: if the court found for
the landowner, the whole character of crofting would be altered at a stroke as
lairds all over the Highlands and islands would suddenly be given a stranglehold

2 *Lawson v Strathcona 1992* Strathclyde RN 350, pp. 14, 16, 17.

over any development on crofts bought under the right-to-buy scheme. It would be back to feudalism, whose guiding principle is that the superior can control important aspects of the behaviour of the vassal. Strathcona's desire to assert this level of control eventually cost him £24,000 for the Lawsons' lawyers, plus an unknown, but certainly larger, total for his own. It was a very expensive defeat.

It must have been an unpleasant one too. As we took our second dram in his kitchen, Bill told me an amusing story about a call he had to pay on Colonsay House shortly after the judgement had been given. One of his part-time jobs is reading the island's electricity meters for the Hydro-Electric company. These include all Strathcona's holiday cottages. Hitherto, the laird had given him a key and cheerily told him to wander round and take the readings. This time, Strathcona did not appear, nor was a key handed over. Instead a flunkey emerged from the big house bearing the master key. He escorted Bill round the estate in an atmosphere of surly and suspicious silence.

'What's your impression of the laird on a personal level?' I asked.

'Usually he's very friendly,' Bill said. 'It's come in, sit down, have a dram and tell me what's on your mind. All that sort of thing. But really he's an operator.'

Bill was looking happier now. Sometime shortly after midnight he lifted the bottle from the table and said, 'Come with me'. We walked into the darkness and threaded our way between fences and byres for 50 yards or so until we came to a lighted doorway. Funeral 'eats' were still on the table, and half a dozen relatives of the deceased, including a girl I knew from Islay, were partying full on. One thing led to another and I ended up sleeping on the sitting-room floor after a wild evening which ended long after dawn. I heard more tales than I could possibly remember about Colonsay. My main recollection is of a pleasantly insistent woman saying three or four times, 'Ian, tell me: what is your concept of infinity?'

Next morning I woke to the discreet sound of somebody putting a mug of tea down on the floor beside the cushion I had used for a pillow. I needed that tea badly – as I did the next mug. Tolerably revived after a few of the sandwiches left over from the previous evening, and a third mug of tea, I thanked my hosts for their kindness, bade everyone goodbye and stepped outside into another day of brilliant clarity. Though the wind had dropped a bit, it was still blowing fresh from the west. It was therefore at my back as I started down the road into Scalasaig, with hay meadows down to the right and rougher turf up to the left. With the sun in my face, I was soon feeling quite restored. A mile or two further on, I came to a fork. To the right, Scalasaig direct and, to the left, Scalasaig via Colonsay House. Should I pay a call on the famous laird? Why not?

I walked into the lush policies where the stunted scrub birch, oak and rowans which grow on the rest of the island give way to huge pines and other parkland trees. The house is situated in a hollow and the gardens demonstrate what can be achieved by way of silviculture, even in the Hebrides, with a little care and a lot of shelter. Colonsay House itself is one of the most elegant in the Hebrides, having the look of a French mini-chateau. It is painted a gay primrose yellow with grey-white detailing. The first Lord Strathcona extended and remodelled an existing structure with Montreal in mind, and the result makes a pleasant change from the Scottish baronial style which is so common in post-Balmoral big houses. I rang the bell and Lord Strathcona came out, a tall, lithe, bearded man in a sunhat and slacks. He said he was just about to go in to lunch, but that he would be happy to come down to the harbour at four o'clock for a chat.

Under a blazing sun, I walked the three miles into Scalasaig and had a snack aboard ship, followed by a nap out on deck. Ashore again, I saw, punctually at four o'clock, a tiny Japanese van, of the sort that London flower-sellers use for deliveries, come bouncing down the hill. Strathcona, still in his sunhat, was immediately friendly, telling me by way of greeting that Lagavulin was his 'standard whisky'. I was working, crab-like, round to the subject of the court case, but was foiled when he brought up the much more interesting subject of whelks' penises.

It came about like this: aware that the Royal Society for the Protection of Birds (RSPB) had just moved onto Oronsay, I asked Lord Strathcona about his experience of conservationists in general. He said he had been both a member of the Fishmongers' Company in London and, in the 1980s, Navy Minister in the House of Lords. More than this, he was a keen sailor. Thus he knew about the controversy over anti-fouling paint. These have a dual function, poisoning as much as possible of the marine life which might be tempted to attach itself to a yacht's hull and providing a sacrificial skin under water which makes it easy to clean off things like barnacles which grow despite the poison. Over the years, competition to get the foulest anti-fouling mix meant the paints became more and more toxic, until gross genetic mutations were being observed in the static sea-life in some of the more heavily used yachting havens.

'We had a man from the Plymouth marine biological research place,' Strathcona said, 'who did a fascinating bit of research about female whelks starting to grow penises. It was always on yachting estuaries. So we did a bit of a campaign with yachtsmen saying, surely you don't want to damage the environment you enjoy? Using this very vicious anti-fouling is doing that. The Minister of the Environment then was William Waldegrave, whose sister I happened to be married to at the time, which made it easier. But the paint manufacturers behaved I think absolutely outrageously. They tried to say pooh-pooh, there's no problem. But it wasn't just the whelks: oysters were growing nothing but shell – no meat. And within three years of the Ministry banning the use of TBT [the principal toxic agent], the oysters began to recover. Of course the paint manufacturers discovered a new compound, not perhaps quite as effective but damn nearly as effective, which you, no doubt, use. This was a classic example: some people can be brutally dishonest.'

Moving on to discuss Oronsay, I mentioned that the RSPB had been awkward when I wrote to ask for sight of the management plans of all the Reserves they owned on the islands I planned to visit. I wanted to take as informed a look at them as I could, given the short time available. I had written in similar terms to all the other bodies whose Reserves were on my itinerary, and all had been more or less helpful: the National Trust for Scotland being the most informative. But the RSPB's Public Relations Officer in Edinburgh, David Minns, refused point blank to help me, suggesting in his letter that I had not told him the truth when I had said my purpose was that I was writing a book about a sailing trip. Since the Society had just taken a lease on Oronsay, I was keen to hear Strathcona's reaction to his new neighbour's secretiveness.

'I think you would be perfectly entitled to write to the Charity Commissioners,' he said, 'and say, "I am interested in the activities of the RSPB, I have asked them this question and they have refused to answer it. Don't you think this is rather an odd way for a charity to behave?" My guess is that the Charity Commissioners would not be frightfully amused.'

Overnight the wind dropped, but the rain came back, and on a grey, drizzly morning, I made my way to Oronsay. Lord Strathcona had told me that he had sold the island in the 1970s to raise cash, and that it was now owned by a Mrs Frances Colburn, of Massachusetts, who visits twice a year. She had just given a ten-year lease on the Oronsay farm, which occupies almost all of the island, to the RSPB.

After a long ramble round the coast in the rain, I spent a dry hour examining the principal tourist interest, the ruins of the Augustinian Priory. Founded in the mid-fourteenth century by John, Lord of the Isles, this is, after St Columba's Abbey on Iona, the main ecclesiastical monument in the Hebrides. It was destroyed during the Reformation, though some of the original grave slabs have been recovered and are now displayed in the restored Prior's House. They reminded me of Russian figures – Alexander Nevsky sprang to mind.

I spoke briefly to Donald Coleman, the gardener who is creating what is called the Monks' Garden behind the Priory. Originally from Ireland, Donald used to be a director of an electronics company in Fife, until he took early retirement. He told me that he has a daughter who lives in the Caribbean and that she is always badgering him to go and live there. We stood under the dripping trees as he tried to explain why he prefers this environment. Despite its name, the garden of which he is in charge has no historical reference, being entirely the conception of Penelope Hobhouse, an English garden designer who has a holiday home on the island. Donald is the only full-time resident, apart from the new manager of the RSPB farm, James How.

I called on How and found a man in his mid-20s who comes from Rugby in Warwickshire and had been posted to Oronsay with the aim of increasing the numbers of corncrakes breeding on the island. The corncrake is a small, noisy but physically elusive bird which has become something of a *cause célèbre* in the Highlands due to its local rarity. In Britain, the change from manual haymaking in the early nineteenth century to mechanical silage cutting in the late twentieth has drastically altered its habitat. For perhaps a century, numbers increased dramatically as the introduction of mechanical cutting machines permitted a greatly increased acreage to be used for haymaking. As hayfields are ideal habitat for corncrakes, the result was a density which moved Stanley Baldwin, the 'countryman' Prime Minister, to declare that the sound of the corncrakes in his native Worcestershire was one of the enduring symbols of rural England.

By the time Baldwin spoke these words in the 1920s the decline had already set in. Engineering improvements meant that machines were cutting closer to the ground, and more rapidly. The result of this was that unfledged chicks were caught in the blades. The process was accelerated by the change to silage-making, which meant that fields were cut earlier in the year, so even more chicks were killed. Finally, the dramatic increase of the use of pesticides after the Second World War deprived the adult corncrake of much of its food. Once known as 'the farmer's friend' because of its voracious consumption of damaging insects, the corncrake vanished from most of the British Isles. It survives now only in parts of Ireland and Scotland where agriculture is not so aggressively sophisticated: the prime area is the Hebrides.

The RSPB was founded in 1889, at about the time the British corncrake population was at its peak. For the next 100 years, the Society prospered and the corncrake declined. Some time in the early 1970s the bird became extinct in England, yet the RSPB did absolutely nothing about its plight. It was only in the mid-1980s that articles about the corncrake started appearing with any frequency in *Birds*, the Society's 'awareness-raising' magazine. Revealingly, this coincided with the increase in calls for money to buy land in the Scottish islands.

Appeals were based on the claim that by financing land acquisition, members would be helping 'pull the corncrake back from the brink of extinction'. What the RSPB does not publicise is the fact that corncrakes breed in vast numbers in the former Soviet Union – they winter in south and east Africa – and there is no evidence of globally declining numbers, for the very simple reason that nobody has the faintest idea how many there are. (Even in tame, accessible Britain the bird was not counted until 1978.) Estimates vary from under half a million to well over a million birds, which is another way of saying that the total is unknown. And whether that unknown total was greater last year, or less, it is of course impossible to say. Despite this, the RSPB makes regular, and very successful, appeals for money to help it save what it cynically calls 'this globally threatened species'.[3]

Currently, Oronsay has three pairs of corncrakes and since that is the principal 'target species' on the new Reserve, I started by asking How what sort of increase he was looking for.

---

3   The authoritative *Red Data Birds in Britain* lists all endangered species in detail. There is no mention in the entry for the corncrake of any global threat, for the very good reason that there is no solid evidence to that effect. Despite that, the claim has been repeated so often that it has become received wisdom, even in government. The Scottish Office currently organises a Corncrake Biodiversity Action Plan Steering Group. The Committee's remit statement starts: '1.2 The corncrake is a globally threatened species.'

Postscript: Recent Russian research has revised the total count for that country upwards from 100,000 calling males to 2.5 million. This would give a world autumn population of about 18 million birds. Despite this, neither the Scottish Office nor the RSPB has abandoned their claims about threat levels.

'Any increase at all,' he said, 'even of a single bird, would be good enough for me to say that I think I have satisfied what members of the Society are putting into it. If we get to five calling males within the next few years I'll think we have really done well.'

'And you think that will produce wild cheering from all your paid-up members?' I asked.

'That's what they joined for,' he said.

How will he achieve this? Essentially by reducing the agricultural output of the island, though there are no plans to reintroduce haymaking. I put it to How that creating a vast bird-table for the corncrake was not a very productive use for good agricultural land. Not so, he said, there were other species which would benefit. The chough was an important example, though not the only one. 'I saw a flock of 45 twite today,' How said. 'And this is still summer: that's a lot of twite.'

In the late eighteenth century, Oronsay used to support a population of 40 people on what *The Old Statistical Account* called 'uncommonly rich pasture'. Since How told me he had worked for the RSPB on Islay, where the Society is criticised for damaging rich farmland by encouraging overpopulation by wild geese, I asked him if his experience there had made him sympathetic to the concerns of people, like the Islay farmers, who had to earn their living from agriculture and who saw their efforts nullified by the work of conservationists. He was dismissive.

'Farmers like to moan about something,' How said, in a confiding tone of voice. 'On the mainland they moan about foxes and badgers. On Islay there are no foxes and badgers so they moan about geese. If the geese were all gone, they'd think of something else, and they know it.'

There was something oppressive about Oronsay and I was happy, next morning, to weigh anchor and set sail for Iona, another island of corncrakes and Christians. By that time a thick mist had rolled in. Horizontal visibility was about a mile; vertically it can have been little more than 100 feet. I hugged the coast up to Balnahard bay, then laid a course approximately north-west to take me towards Beinn a Chaol-achaidh, a 400-foot hump near the western end of the Ross of Mull. In clear weather it is conspicuous above the flatter land on either side. It is an important mark as the very treacherous Torran rocks, at the south end of the Sound of Iona, are not far to the west. But not today. I was going to have to keep a very good lookout.

A steady force 3 was blowing in from the west, bringing a long swell, probably five feet from trough to crest. I spent the whole time listening intently for the sound of an approaching vessel that might be on a collision course. After nearly three hours of sailing the visibility had, if anything, deteriorated. I calculated that I must be approaching the Mull coast. I peered into the gloom for the first signs of land. Soon I was distracted by a steady, but seemingly distant, rumbling noise. Was it a ship? It didn't sound steady enough for a marine engine, and it was getting progressively louder, though far too slowly for it to be a passing aeroplane. What could it be? I looked round anxiously. The next thing I saw, rearing out of the mist, directly ahead, at a range of no more than 500 yards, was a sheer cliff face, from the base of which huge explosions of spray shot up into the air at 20-second intervals. I had been hearing the thunder of the surf on the rocks.

The problem was that I could not see much more than 100 feet or so up the cliffs, and so had no idea which part of Mull I was looking at. But wherever I was, I should turn to port and head west. This I did, but I soon found that even if I steered just a little off-shore, the land quickly disappeared into the grey fog and I was without an exact positional reference. The Torran Rocks start less than a mile off the Mull coast, so I headed back inshore. Then, after a while, I suddenly noticed surf breaking over a rock on my *port* bow: ahead, but to seaward of me. Clearly it was a coastal off-lier. I altered course to port. This happened several times as I groped my way westward: a worrying sail.

After a while, the wind died almost completely, though the swell did not go down. I dropped the headsail and started to motor. I weaved back and forth between the cliffs and the off-liers, making consistently west for about an hour, until, looking up from one particularly intense attempt to reconcile the chart with the view, I saw a large fishing boat steaming directly across my path and out to sea. The shocking thing was that he had already crossed my bows, and I had never heard him, so loud was the sound of the surf and my own engine, and so muffling is the effect of thick mist. He cannot have been more than quarter of a mile ahead, but still he passed through my arc of visibility in a couple of minutes and was gone. Nonetheless, it was a relief to see him as he could only have emerged from the Sound of Iona.

Sure enough, it was not long before I noticed the coast beginning to recede to starboard. I edged round perhaps 10°, and soon found I could do so again, then again, and so on until I was steering slightly east of north, and clearly heading up the Sound. Then, just as it became obvious that the danger had passed, the mist lifted. I motored into the anchorage just south of the Iona ferry pier in mild and still conditions. Under a pearly grey-blue evening sky, I fried and ate a delicious mackerel which I had been given by a fisherman at Scalasaig.

Iona was taken from its ancient superiors, the Macleans of Duart, by Archibald Campbell, the tenth earl, third marquess and later first Duke of Argyll, in 1688. The Campbells had traditionally been Protestants and the ninth earl had rebelled against the Catholic King James VII (II of England) soon after his accession to the throne. As a result Argyll's estates had been forfeit. His son was a calculating trimmer. He offered to become a Catholic and to take arms against his outlawed father if only the Argyll estates were restored to him. King James paid no attention to the flexible earl, who then joined the King's enemy, William of Orange, at the Hague and accompanied him to Britain on his mission to make the country safe for Protestantism. Argyll was rewarded with a Privy Councillorship, repossesion of his family's estates and some new grants of land, including the isle of Iona.

The elevation of this powerful turncoat provoked a mustering of many of the Highland clans. In an attempt to enforce obedience, the government in Edinburgh required the clan chiefs to make formal submission to the new regime within a specified time. This they all did with the exception of the MacDonalds of Glencoe, whose chief was 16 days late. The earl then arranged for his own newly raised regiment of Campbells to punish the clan for their chief's tardiness by what has gone down in history as the Massacre of Glencoe. Four years after that the earl was made a Lord of the Treasury, and five years later the first Duke of Argyll in the Scottish peerage. In 1892 that dukedom was elevated to the United Kingdom peerage by the then Prime Minister, Lord Salisbury, as a reward for the eighth Duke's having shifted his parliamentary allegiance from the Liberals to the Conservatives in protest at the granting of rights of secure tenancy to people like Annie Lawson's ancestors in the Crofters Act of 1886.

In 1979 the twelfth Duke indicated that he wanted to sell Iona. Three quarters of the island is held under crofting tenure, and is therefore of strictly limited economic potential as far as the landowner is concerned. Despite this, in April the Duke refused a bid of £600,000 from the National Trust for Scotland. In May he accepted an offer of £1.5 million from the Hugh Fraser Foundation, which immediately presented the island to the National Trust. This was an incredible price for two sets of farm buildings, six leased cottages, the coastal fishing rights and 1800 acres of either sandy pasture or rocky hill. Had it not been Iona, the value would have been perhaps a fifth of that. But the Duke was not just selling real estate, he was selling 'heritage' and that commands a substantial premium.

That heritage is the most famous ecclesiastical site in the Highlands. St Columba established a Christian community on Iona after he fled Ulster in 563 AD. From this base, Scotland was Christianised, and it was here in 690 AD that Columba's successor, Adamnan, wrote his *Life of Columba*, the first extant Scottish book. In the ninth and tenth centuries the island was subjected to repeated Viking attacks. Most of the monks moved to Kells where they completed the famous Book of Kells which, it is now thought, was largely written on Iona.

For all their savagery, the Vikings failed to extinguish religious life on Iona completely. About 1200 AD the Benedictine Abbey, whose buildings stand in reconstructed form today, was founded and for three and a half centuries the Abbey flourished. The island became the principal royal burial ground in Scotland. The cemetery reputedly contains the earthly remains of 48 Scottish, four Irish and eight Norwegian kings, to which were recently added those of John Smith, leader of the British Labour Party.

A thousand years after St Columba's arrival, the Scottish Protestants succeeded where the pagan Vikings had failed and brought religious life at the Abbey to an end soon after the Reformation. They wrecked the buildings, burnt the library and smashed 360 carved stone crosses, dumping the rubble in the sea. As on Oronsay, this was purely destructive, since these soldiers of spiritual enlightenment did not replace the Abbey with anything of their own. For 200 years there was no church of any sort on Iona. The consequences were well described by a Presbyterian minister from Moffat, the Reverend John Walker, who made two fact-finding tours of the Hebrides, 20 years after Culloden, for the Commissioner of the Annexed Estates.

> [The islanders of Iona] are Professed Protestants, but being entirely destitute of the means of Knowledge, they are left in such a State of Ignorance as in a Christian Country is really deplorable. For, of the 200 Inhabitants, there is not one who can either speak English or read the Scriptures, though their little Island was for many Centuries one of the chief Seats of Religion and Learning in Britain . . . They have all of them a remarkable Propensity to whatever is marvellous and supernatural. Every Person has the traditional History of Columba, with numberless Legends, which have been handed down from his monkish Seminary. They are famous for the second Sight; full of Visions seen either by themselves or other; and have many wild and romantick notions concerning Religion and other invisible things. Though they know not what Popery is, the Vestiges of it they suck in with their Milk, which appear in many of their Opinions and Practices . . . The huge Fabrick of artificial Superstition, erected on the spot in which they live, has rendered the very Air of their Island infectious. Their unlimited Veneration for Antiquity supplies the Place of Truth, in the most frightful and marvellous Legends, and the Slender Acquaintance with Religion, is but the Parent of their Superstition, which can only be remedied by a more perfect Knowledge of Divine Things.[4]

Catholicism vanquished, the Abbey began to fall into ruin and after a due interval the ruins began to attract tourists. These have included Dr Johnson, John Keats, William Wordsworth, Queen Victoria and Robert Louis Stevenson – all Protestants. Between Stevenson's visit and my own, the buildings of the Abbey had been restored and a modern religious community established there under the aegis of the Church of Scotland.

The morning after my arrival I woke at 4.30 a.m. and saw clear skies through the main hatch. It looked like a morning for photography. Drinking my tea on deck, I heard a corncrake rasping in the fields opposite the anchorage. I rowed ashore in the chilly air, and walked up past the 'huge Fabrick of artificial Superstition' to the top of Dun I, the summit of the island. There I took some photographs of the dramatic sight of dawn coming up over the Burg area of Mull. Above the massive cliffs, the layered clouds glowed pink, orange and red, shot through with streaks of grey and white, and below them the sea, rippling slightly in the morning breeze, mixed these colours up and reflected a cool amber glow in the path of the sunlight and a rich, dark blue on either side. What wind there was, was in the west, in which direction the sky was cloudless. To the north-east, between the heavy blue of the sea and the light, carefree blue of the sky, lay the long grey mass of Tiree and Coll. Between them and the north-west tip of Mull I could just discern the jagged peaks of Rum, 35 miles away. In the opposite direction I recognised the Paps of Jura, standing out clear in the morning air though they too were almost 30 nautical miles distant. It had the look of a hot day in the making.

---

4 *Report on the Hebrides of 1764 and 1771,* by Revd Dr John Walker, ed. Margaret McKay, John Donald, Edinburgh, 1980, p. 141.

Iona attracts so many visitors that they are threatening to cause problems for the National Trust. Principally, this is due to the weekly pilgrimages organised by the Iona Community for their numerous guests, whom they take to the various points of interest on the island that have connections with its patron saint. The numbers of pilgrims are such that, combined with the heavy hiking boots they tend to wear, even for such short strolls, they are beginning to cause serious erosion on the wet ground. Were they to walk in bare feet, Christ-like, they would not do half so much damage.

These problems are small, though, in the overall context of gross visitor numbers, which are estimated at over 120,000 per year. As there are only two miles of road, it is not hard to appreciate the problem of maintenance this creates, not to mention that of cleaning up after the last ferry has sailed each evening. Iona suffers from another quarter, too. National Trust figures show that only 20 per cent of visitors to the island travelled specifically to visit Iona. The other 96,000 just happened to be in the area, nearly half of them because they were on a coach tour that had the Abbey on the itinerary. Even less appreciative are the 'island baggers'. Later in the trip, in Oban, I heard one such hero boasting to a friend that he had 'bagged' three islands in one day, having crossed to Mull, driven down to Fionnphort, crossed to Iona, taken the boat trip out to Staffa (where Fingal's cave is) and then raced back across Mull to Craignure in time to catch the last ferry back to the mainland. Part of the cause of this madness is the improved roads and ferry services which make it possible. It was only in the 1850s that a road was built along the Ross of Mull to replace the thousand-year old Pilgrim's Way. This year a proposal has been made, by a businessman keen to 'develop' the tourist trade, to build a causeway across the Sound of Iona. That would finally destroy any sense of the island as hallowed ground. My own reaction was to long for the arrival of a new breed of avenging Presbyterian who would wreck the tourist office, burn all the touchy-feeling interpretive leaflets and dump 360 colour-coded way-marked signs in the sea.

As no such epiphany seemed likely to be vouchsafed me in the immediate future, I weighed anchor and motored across the Sound to keep a luncheon appointment I had made with Lieutenant-Commander Robin Tappley R.N. (Retd), the Scottish Wildlife Trust (SWT) representative for Mull and Iona. He collected me at the coach-park next to the ferry pier opposite Iona and drove me up to his house among the lush birch and rowan woods around Loch na Lathaich, near Bunessan.

Though nominally a conservationist, the Commander could not have been more different from the dull, prosaic How. He is one of those cheerful, direct, rather old-fashioned Englishmen who exude what Field Marshal Montgomery used to call 'binge'. (In his command caravan for the battle of Alamein, Montgomery had a sign which greeted all visitors: 'Are you 100 per cent fit? Do you have 100 per cent binge?') Tappley had no Scottish connections until, on retiring from the Navy 15 years ago, he took a job as membership secretary of the SWT at their headquarters in Edinburgh. Neither had he any knowledge of wildlife. 'I can't tell the difference between a daisy and a buttercup,' he told me straight away.

Knowing little of the SWT, I asked him how the Trust came into existence.

'It's quite extraordinary,' he said. 'If you look at all the county Trusts in England and the Scottish Wildlife Trust, which is also under the Royal Society for Nature Conservation umbrella, you'll see they were nearly all started in or around 1965 and were nearly all staffed by ex-pat foresters from Tanzania and similar areas who had all been superseded by their black underlings. Suddenly onto the market came a whole wodge of foresters – dedicated conservationists, though they didn't know it at the time – with experience and with pensions, which meant that they could work virtually for their expenses plus a little pocket money.'

'Where did the members come from?'

'The Scottish Wildlife Trust was set up by a lawyer in Edinburgh and the first members were all his legal friends,' the Commander told me. 'They then got a foot in the universities and we got all of them. Then they got into the cocktail party belt in Perth. I swear that every single member in Perth had been to the same cocktail party. They could afford the £5 a year. In fact when I wrote to them all to turn the subscriptions into covenants, they didn't bat an eyelid. The great thing was,' he said, leaning towards me and lowering his voice, 'they actually didn't know what a covenant was.'

'Nor do I,' I said.

'It's a tax thing,' he said, before changing the subject so quickly that I was left with the suspicion that he was not entirely sure himself. 'Then, in 1981, the Wildlife and Countryside Bill went through parliament and we swept up every single biological and ecological student in the Scottish universities. But that had a backlash because we managed to pick up a lot of nuclear disarmament people and we had a terribly stormy AGM when the audience demanded special subscriptions for the unwaged. The chairman was taken aback. He said to the man who was taking the meeting, "For God's sake just say we'll take it back to Council". Tom Weir, who was meant to lecture, was held up for an hour while all this went on. When it came up at the next Council meeting I looked round the table and said, "Quite honestly, you're all unwaged." The fact was that 90 per cent of them were on pensions of one sort or another and the other 10 per cent were a burden on their fathers.'

'Did that change the character of the Trust?' I asked.

'We certainly had a lot of people who would have been happier with Friends of the Earth. They were what you might call the lunatic fringe. One lot wanted to destroy all landlords and the other lot wanted to play at being landlords themselves: that's why they get Reserves. But it put the membership up quite a bit. It also gave us people for our working parties, for example on Eigg. They used to drive me barmy. I used to send them cheques and they would send them back saying they couldn't afford to put cheques in because the bank manager would just take the money.'

'So you had to send them postal orders?'

'No, pound notes, because they had nowhere to cash the postal orders. I learnt a lot about how the other half lives. I am now renowned for being the man who preaches that under no circumstances should the Trust get involved in Eigg.'

'Why?'

'Because I can see the problems much clearer than they can. All they can see is a lovely bit of land which could be a Reserve.'

'Did you know Keith Schellenberg?' I asked, referring to the recent and very controversial owner of the island.

'Schellenberg I met,' the Commander said. 'He was an awkward customer. He didn't want Eigg to be a proper Reserve. He wanted the Scottish Wildlife Trust to operate in his own interests.'

'In what sense?'

'To give him respectability. My view is – and this is where my heresy comes in – is that when you look at what is living on Eigg, you are not very far away from the Greenham Common peace camps. I am maligning them I'm sure, but many are oddballs, and it is very difficult to run a collection of oddballs on Eigg from an office in Edinburgh. I feel that there are better places for our money than Eigg. And even if we get Eigg, we are only going to get four more members or something. It's not like the Loch of the Lowes [the SWT osprey sanctuary in Perthshire] which brings in a couple of hundred members every year, which is what I think Reserves should be for.'

'You think Reserves should exist for recruiting purposes?'

'Yes, recruiting members and making money. The point of a member is to get a legacy. If you actually add it up, your normal member's subscription just about covers the magazine, the editor of the magazine and, if you're lucky, the membership secretary's salary. If you took all the members out of the Scottish Wildlife Trust and all the subscriptions out of it, the balance sheet would look the same.'

'Is that so?'

'Yup. When I was there I got a tremendously high proportion of covenants and everybody said well done. I said you needn't be so bloody thankful, all I have succeeded in doing is paying my own salary. That is exactly what all the covenants brought in. We weren't making a bean out of the members. On the other hand I opened the post one day and there was a cheque for £20,000. This was from a member in Aberdeen whose mother had left her some money and she didn't want it. Another legacy we got came through a lawyer. We wrote to him and said can you just tell us, please, what made this person leave us some money. He said, "Every lawyer has got a drawerful of good causes. She came in and said she wanted to leave some money to conservation and your magazine was the first one I pulled out of my drawer." '

'Where did the members mostly come from?' I asked, aware of the very precise socio-economic targeting of the RSPB's recruitment policy.

'When I was in Edinburgh, I would say that a good 50 per cent were either ex-pat English or people of a certain class: retired, a little bit of spare cash, a lot of interest in Scotland. All they wanted for their consciences was to pay their annual subscription and to know that there was somebody somewhere doing something.'

'You mentioned their consciences,' I said. 'Do you think there is any comparison with people going to church 100 years ago and putting their shilling in the collection tray and thinking they had atoned for their sins Monday to Saturday?'

'You're not far out,' the Commander replied. 'Of course we do have our workers. They are a different group. That is the difference between us and the RSPB. RSPB members don't do anything, they just pay the subscription and, if they want to, go once a year to a bun fight in London. SWT members, or those who want to be more active, can become much more involved. We always used to impress on the staff that we are there to do what the members want. That is the difference between the two.'

As a newcomer to Scotland, the Commander is alert to the English–Scottish problems that bodies like the SWT encounter. He told me an extraordinary story of English prejudice which concerned an absentee landowner who had asked the Trust for advice about some aspect of the management of his estate. At a meeting of the full SWT committee, this man was given something much more radical than he had expected. He started to argue, implying they were talking 'activist rubbish'. 'Then there was a deathly silence,' the Commander said, 'and everyone looked round. The whole of our executive committee, except the chairman, was English. Then he gave in. Because there were 12 Englishmen in the room, he was prepared to accept that we knew what we were talking about. He was not going to accept it from 13 Scotsmen.'[5]

Over a lunch of soup, bread and cheese and chilled German lager, I asked about his experiences as an incomer in Mull.

'When we came here we kept our heads down,' he said. 'I think the first thing we went to was the AGM of the lifeboats. We then discovered how Mull runs. If you go the AGM you are automatically on the committee. Then my son decided to make an honest woman of his girlfriend and he took one look at the registry office in Tunbridge Wells and thought it was so scruffy and crude he said, "We can't be married here." So he came to Tobermory, and we got him married in church. By the time all that had finished we had discovered where you get

---

5   My own experience confirms the Commander's view. While interviewing staff at RSPB headquarters in Bedfordshire before leaving for my trip, I talked to Bob Scott, the Englishman who was then Head of Reserves, UK. At one point in our conversation he said (knowing I was Scottish), 'The Celtic fringe has been rather slow on the uptake as far as conservation is concerned.' Curious to discover the reason for this prejudice, I subsequently wrote to him. 'I attended a meeting in the late 1970s (or very early 1980) in central Wales,' Scott wrote back by way of explanation. 'The purpose of the meeting was to discuss various aspects of conservation and the environment as it would impact on the area. There were 20+ people sitting round the table, including representatives from government and non-government conservation bodies, local authorities and the Welsh Office. Not one of the people in the room was Welsh, they were all English.' (22 July 1997)

everything from. Pipers turned up without any request from us. The petrol-pump attendant is a photographer and the bus driver took the videos. We suddenly found we knew an awful lot of people.'

Amused, informed and pleasantly nourished, I collected my bags and made to leave. It was a blistering hot day by now, and beyond the Tappleys' verandah the birchwoods glowed in the early afternoon heat. Observing this fact, and being sensitive to the inconveniences of life in small boats, the Commander made a kind offer. 'I don't mean to be offensive,' he said in flawlessly tactful tones, 'but you'd be very welcome to have a bath if you want.'

By mid afternoon, I was back at sea and heading north-north-east to the lovely, sheltered anchorage between Gometra and Ulva, off the north-west coast of Mull. The wind was blowing a lively clip from the west but it was so hot that I sailed with my shirt off. Fully canvassed and well heeled over, *Sylvia B* had 'a bone in her teeth', as the saying goes. With foam rushing off her bows, she surged through the swells, making the helmsman very happy. We left Staffa to port. I have visited the island twice and, thinking of Iona's problems, I felt it better to pass respectfully by.

As evening came on, the wind began to die. By the time I ghosted into the little cove, I was able to search for a suitable anchoring spot in almost completely calm water. After coming to anchor, I spent a fascinating hour or so drifting round in the dinghy looking at the sea-bed through a glass-bottomed box which attaches to the stern. Beneath *Sylvia B* the sand was largely clear, with long, grass-like fronds of weed growing in scattered clumps. Their tops bent this way then that, with the gentle surge and return of the tide. Between the clumps scuttled black crabs, darting sideways at unpredictable intervals, looking, it struck me for no apparent reason, as frightened British soldiers must do in Bogside alleyways when seen from a patrolling helicopter. Two crabs had a fight: a most peculiar spectacle given the number of limbs involved. I found myself trying to imagine how frightening it would be to find yourself in the ring with a six-armed Mike Tyson who could, between rounds, remove his gumshield, gurgle the water-bottle, scratch his groin and towel himself down simultaneously.

Shoals of tiny fish swam past, swerving and turning with the precision of flocks of starlings. Fascinated, I dropped slowly astern of *Sylvia B* until, as suddenly as the hump of Staffa rises out of the sea, a rocky reef reared up from the bed of sand. Covered in floating tendrils of kelp, and here and there glowing a raw, quartzite red, it created a savage, awesome impression. I thought I could see some larger, dark shapes moving sinisterly among the fronds, but I could not be sure.

Next morning the weather was quite still. Scattered patches of layered cloud gave some shade under a hot sun. Beyond these the earth baked.

Over breakfast I read about Ulva, which is owned by James Howard, a cousin of Lord Strathcona's, and has a tiny population. The island suffered some of the more brutal of the nineteenth century clearances, its population dropping from 360 to 51 between 1849 and 1851. The landlord at the time simply sent his men round, without warning, to set fire to the thatched roofs of the houses of the crofters he wanted rid of for the expansion of his sheep farm. In the years before the Irish land war broke out, that was acceptable – though technically illegal – behaviour, provided it was done by a landowner to the landless. The other way round it was called fire-raising and punished with savage ferocity

Gometra suffered a similar fate. Its population of 168 in 1837 had dropped to 30 by 1881. By 1981 it was down to four. Today it is zero.

I took my coffee on deck in the sunshine and watched two eagles soaring in the thermals above the cliffs that surround the anchorage. I packed my camera and some lunch and rowed over to the Gometra shore. Above the deserted settlement which lies in the hollow behind the ruined boathouse, I came upon a rather moving graveyard. Amid almost impenetrable, shoulder-high bracken, there were three newish-looking graves. One read: 'Sailor of the 1939–45 War, Merchant Navy, found 27 November 1940. Known unto God.' The other two varied only in the dates.

The empty island's single farm worker lives ten miles and a ferry ride away on Mull. Drowned sailors washed up on Gometra today would be eaten by eagles rather than buried by islanders.

I had decided to visit two other small islands before my next major landfall on Tiree. Cairn na Burgh Mor and Lunga are uninhabited parts of the Treshnish Isles, a small chain which stretches south-west from the north-western tip of Mull. At about 7 a.m. on another brilliant, still day, I made a landfall on Cairn na Burgh, having motored the five miles from Gometra. The tide flows fast around these islands, so it is important to select an anchorage out of the main stream, given that my dinghy cannot be rowed at much more than a knot. Having 'prospected' for a while, I anchored in a spot which also seemed to be a favourite swimming place for a vast colony of puffins. For an hour or so I rowed around as quietly as I could trying to take pictures of these impish-looking birds.

Cairn na Burgh is an island in two parts, Cairn na Burgh Mor and Cairn na Burgh Beg (big and small castles on the rock). Together with the nearby island of Fladda, they command the passage between Coll and Mull. They were thus of great strategic importance throughout the thousand years during which the sea was the main highway in this area, roughly from the eighth century when the Vikings arrived to the eighteenth when General Wade started the Highland road-building programme which brought metropolitan control, followed by trade and tourism, to the west of Scotland. The principal remaining fortifications can be seen on Cairn na Burgh Mor, and they are very impressive. It is obvious that the island was easily defensible, rising sheer out of the sea for over 100 feet. On the east side there is a little grassy ledge, perhaps half an acre, from which a steep and narrow cleft gives access onto the flattish top. The whole island is about 300 yards long and more than 100 yards wide. There is a well and, on Fladda, an abundant supply of peat. It is a self-contained mini-archipelago.

The earliest surviving record of this stronghold dates from 1249, when it was said to be held by the Lord of Lorn from King Haakon of Norway. After the Treaty of Perth, in 1266, by which the Hebrides were ceded by the Norwegian Crown to the Scottish one, Cairn na Burgh came to be regarded as a royal castle. By the sixteenth century, it was in the hands of the Macleans of Duart. In 1549 Dean Monro, the first visitor to the Western Isles to have left an account of his travels, wrote of Cairn na Burgh that the two islands were 'strenthie craigis . . . lyand in the middis of it great stark streams of the sea.' The Reverend Walker says that, when the Protestant reformers destroyed the library of the Iona Abbey, the few documents which were saved were conveyed to Cairn na Burgh, where they lay in safety for over 100 years until the Civil War, during which they were destroyed by fire.

The Royal Commission on Ancient and Historical Monuments in Scotland thinks some of the fortifications to be seen today should probably be attributed to General Alexander Leslie, the famous Covenanting soldier; certainly the island was impregnable to the Duke of Argyll's forces 30 years later. The Macleans came out for King James in 1715, after which the island was taken over by government forces and garrisoned. When the great events of 1745–46 passed Cairn na Burgh by, it became clear it had ceased to be of strategic importance. The castle was abandoned and the fortifications allowed to fall into ruin.

Today it is a lovely spot. Its insular situation may have ceased to be of use to human beings, but, as I discovered after clambering up onto the plateau, it still represents security to our old friend the corncrake. I heard one rasping away amidst the matted grass. Back on board, I ate a late and doubly relished breakfast. For an hour I sat on deck in the sun watching the seagulls and shags jockeying for position on the rocks and listening to an immense number of eiders cooing the middle distance. A seal drifted round *Sylvia B*, clearly curious at this unusual intrusion. A mile or so off-shore, a clam-dredging boat trundled back and forth, methodically raking the seabed. It kept this up for the rest of the day, slowly moving east of the beat where it had started.

Towards lunchtime I raised the anchor and motored the two miles south to Lunga, the largest of the Treshnish Isles. Preferring to keep out of the 'great stark streams of the sea', I anchored south of the spot recommended by the Clyde Cruising Club, which notes, 'The islands are interesting but the area is studded with rocks and requires great caution.' I chose a spot away from the skerries, in deep water, just beneath a dramatic cleft in the eastern rock face which looked as if it would give access to the plateau on top. An eagle soon appeared, gliding back and forth in front of the cliffs. Over a cup of coffee I sat and watched as it perched on a ledge, part way up, for a while. Then it spread its wings, lunged forward and dropped off, falling 10 or 20 feet before picking up speed and lift. It struck me that the motion was not unlike that of an aircraft being catapulted off a carrier.

By the time I had finished my coffee, it was nearly noon. The day was so hot, I thought I would go below for an hour or so before attempting the climb up onto the top of Lunga. I opened the forehatch to let the air move through the boat, poured myself a glass of cider and settled back to read the material I had brought with me on the man who had put Lunga on the map, so to speak, the famous pioneering conservationist, Frank Fraser Darling: the father of modern conservation practice in Scotland.

'Frank Moss —' as his birth certificate had it, giving no surname, was born a bastard in Devon in 1903. His mother, Harriet Darling, was a genteel Yorkshirewoman who defied the convention of the time by bringing up her son as a single mother. Frank took her surname and called himself Frank Moss Darling until he married Marion Fraser in 1925 and changed his name to Frank Fraser Darling. All his life, Darling's mother exercised an extraordinary influence over her son, who never established complete emotional independence from her. Writing in middle age of his rejection of religion in his youth, Darling said, 'The Lord was not my shepherd in those days; my mother was enough for me.'[6] Darling's daughter thought her father saw his first wife as very much an extension of his mother.[7] Darling himself wrote that his wife and he made 'excellent comrades in work and as long as we kept working together and not being man and wife and mother and father together.'[8]

Darling dropped out of school at the age of 15 and went to work as a farm labourer. He then enrolled at an agricultural college in Yorkshire, after which he took a job as a Clean Milk Advisor with the Buckinghamshire County Council. But he was ambitious and managed to wangle a place in the Edinburgh University PhD programme, studying the fleece of the blackface sheep. This was followed by a job with the Imperial Bureau of Animal Genetics in the same city. For some reason Darling now started to claim, completely bogusly, that he was half Scottish. Restive in the unglamorous job in Edinburgh, he applied for a Leverhulme Fellowship to study red deer, which he wanted to do on the Isle of Rum. But he was refused entry by the laird, Sir George Bullough, and had to work on the mainland, in Dundonnell, south of Little Loch Broom where his wife's father had connections through the Freemasons with the local laird, Lord Tarbat.

In 1937 Darling published *A Herd of Red Deer*, after which he moved on to a study of the birds on Eilean á Chlerich (Monk's Island) in the Summer Isles and of grey seals, first on North Rona and latterly here on Lunga. He wrote about this in *Island Years*, published in 1940. In that book he describes the moment when his private, escapist fantasy came true:

> I had reached the ideal kept in my mind since childhood, a tiny house with presses and shelves for everything, set down in your own fairy country beyond the reach of an external world. I had played and pretended this bit of escapism all my life, and here it was, as good as the pretending.[9]

6 *Island Years*, Frank Fraser Darling, Pan Books edition, London 1973, p. 243.
7 *Fraser Darling's Islands* by John Morton Boyd, Edinburgh University Press, Edinburgh 1986, pp. 19, 233–4 *et passim*.
8 Letter to Frank Kendon, quoted in *Fraser Darling's Islands*, pp. 187–8.
9 *Island Years*, Frank Fraser Darling, Pan Books edition, London 1973, p. 114.

The outbreak of the Second World War saw Darling running a croft on the Isle of Tannera in the Summer Isles, at the mouth of Loch Broom. He was a pacifist, and rationalised his position by claiming he had, 'something of the seer' in him. This, he claimed, gave him 'a very special responsibility at this time...[to write] of the things of peace and the good life . . . To love universally and not selfishly is the hardest of all things to learn – and in a wave of nationalism it passes for treason.'[10] His obituarist in *The Times* saw it differently: 'The Second World War found him badly out of touch and out of sympathy with the main currents of national life.'[11] Darling's wife's view was more personal: she thought he did not join the army because he did not relish 'the rough and tumble of sharing life with his fellow soldiery.'[12]

Up to 1943, Darling's contribution to the war effort amounted to nothing more than feeding himself on Tannera, and to writing a self-congratulatory book about how he had done so, called *Island Farm*. He told a pacifist friend, 'I depend on writing for money, and spend it on pulling this place from its dereliction. In that I am doing a social service with my pennies and I believe the artist in me is a better artist for the wholeness which this work of my hands gives. But I don't think being monetarily poor really suits an artist because he has to deflect too much energy wondering where the next penny is coming from.'[13] Within five years Darling was driving a Rolls Royce.

This change of fortune happened when the wartime Secretary of State for Scotland, Tom Johnston, asked him to publicise his advice for the better management of crofts. Darling was appointed Director of the West Highland Survey, which launched him into the career of bureaucratic authoritarianism which has had such a profound effect on the modern Highlands. He never went back to the simple crofting life he had said so many times previously that he loved so dearly. Perhaps significantly, he quickly lost the stammer which had plagued him since boyhood.

Once in a position of power, there was no more talk of universal love. Darling announced he was treating his project as 'a problem of human ecology [which] involves the states of men's minds.' He was going to change the way the people he had come to live among thought and behaved. He was the first to see the Highlands as a 'great, outdoor laboratory', and the Highlanders as subjects of his experiments. Not surprisingly, Darling achieved nothing positive. Crofters scorned his panaceas and the scientific establishment disregarded his writings. The book he published as a result of his researches, *Natural History in the Highlands and Islands,* exposed his patchy grasp of the subject. The Regius Professor of Natural History at Aberdeen University savaged it in a review which included the

10 Quoted in *Fraser Darling's Islands,* pp. 170, 173.
11 19 November 1979. The obituarist is thought to have been Max Nicholson.
12 *Ibid.*, p. 172.
13 *Ibid.*, p. 185.

memorable comment on Darling's theory about the migration of herring that it had been, 'the latest thing in the days of Thomas Pennant's *British Zoology* (1761–66)'. Darling had little algebra, no calculus and only a shaky knowledge of basic physics. He was less a scientist than a skilful self-promoter. Darling was a driven man who, in the view of at least one colleague, never fully overcame 'the stigma of his bastardy'.

As a bureaucratic authoritarian, Darling was exultant when, in 1949, the Nature Conservancy was founded by Royal Charter. Now crofters could not ignore his prescriptions. The Scots would have to do as they were told:

> The establishment of the Nature Conservancy, is the most considerable event in British natural history in this century; especially so for Scotland, and most especially for the Highlands and Islands . . . [It] operates throughout Great Britain; Scotland having a headquarters in Edinburgh but with *little autonomous power. Nevertheless, Scotland can have no valid grumble* over the degree to which her wildlife, vegetation and land is being conserved and brought into National Nature Reserves.[14] (Emphasis added)

The authoritarian tone has been perpetuated with enthusiasm by Darling's successors.[15] This centralised approach is inevitable, since no bureaucracy can be so flexible as to take account of every situation in every locality in so varied a country as Scotland. Nature is infinitely changeable and bureaucracy can only operate by rules, standards and general procedures: arguably the two are inherently incompatible. If so, the whole idea of managing nature by civil servants, Darling's basic legacy to Scotland, is a dead end; the great, outdoor experiment a complete dud.

With a chill feeling, despite the heat, I sweated up the gully onto the main plateau of Lunga. Thinking about what I had read, I remembered that Morton Boyd, ex-Director in Scotland of the Nature Conservancy Council, wrote in *Fraser Darling's Islands* that after a visit to Lunga by way of research into the mentality of his friend and mentor he felt he had 'that day trodden hallowed ground'. The language is that of a cult; the emotion that of a disciple.

Above the cliffs, the ground is flattish and fertile-looking, though much of it is covered with bracken. Sheep graze it, so the grass is short, too short to tempt the lazy walker to lie in it and snooze in the sun. Being grazed, it had a rich display of wildflowers and the air was thick with butterflies. I climbed to the summit of the island and sat for a while on the warm rocks of the Cruachan, enjoying the spectacular views in all directions. I took a long circuit down, walking south onto the rich, level pasture of the plateau which stretches out towards the Dutchman's Cap, the southerlimost point of the Treshnish Isles. Turning back north, I passed under the shadow of the Cruachan and the warmth had gone from the air.

---

14 *Highlands and Islands,* F. Fraser Darling and J. Morton Boyd, Collins, London 1964, pp. 291–2.

15 The office which administers the Highlands and Islands has its headquarters in Inverness, in a building called Fraser Darling House.

Back aboard ship, I made a restorative cup of coffee, then weighed anchor and drifted in very light airs round the south of the island. In a mood of pleasant anticipation, I laid a course for the densely populated crofting island of Tiree, the highest points of which were just visible due west. It was a beautiful evening for a sail, particularly after the wind picked up a bit. Halfway across, I got a fine photograph of the leonine form of the Sgurr of Eigg, couchant yet grand, lying grey upon the northern horizon.

Later, outside Gott Bay, the wind got up further and I sailed into the wide open anchorage at a chilly clip. Inflating the dinghy as quickly as I could after anchoring, I packed a bag with clean clothes and a book and rowed ashore. I walked the mile and a half round to the hotel on the north-western edge of the bay, where I took a pint of Guinness upstairs into a steaming hot bath, and lay and read for an hour. Afterwards I had another, more sociable, pint in the crowded bar downstairs. In the 1930s Fraser Darling wrote, 'I find truth in wilderness. In my view humanity spoils when it packs.' Looking at the cheery faces round the bar and listening to the noisy evidence of a new island and an unexplored community, I could not have disagreed more.

By the time I left the pub, the wind had gone down and the whole island seemed quiet. I had been told that the forecast for the morrow was good. With a sense of pleasurable anticipation, I walked back round to the boat across the hard, moonlit sand. It occurred to me that I had just bagged my third island that day.

2

TIREE

TIREE IS SEPARATED FROM COLL by less than a mile of clear water. Despite being so close, the two islands are quite different in character. Coll and Tiree illustrate – though not uniquely because there are many similar cases – just how varied the Hebrides are. The foundation of their differences is the nature of the land. Tiree is low-lying and fertile. In the Middle Ages it was known as the granary of the Isles. Reverend Walker describes it as 'champaign' and notes that 'Tiree is the highest Rented Land in all the Western Isles.' Coll, by contrast, is rocky. The *Old Statistical Account* notes, 'The coast is bolder. Not above a sixteenth part is arable. Though rugged and unfriendly to the plough, it affords excellent shelter to cattle.'

Historically, the differing productivity of the soil of the two islands has meant significant differences in population. Though their area is much the same, the census of 1841 recorded 4,391 people on Tiree and only 1,442 on Coll. Having more than doubled in a century, this was the high-water mark of population growth for both islands. In 1846 the potato blight struck and there was famine in the Highlands, just as there was in Ireland. By the time of the 1851 census the population of Tiree had dropped by 15 per cent and of Coll by 20 per cent. By 1951, the population of Tiree was down to 30 per cent of the figure a century earlier and that of Coll to 20 per cent. Since 1951, a further drop of about a quarter has been registered on both islands.

The similar rate of reduction conceals a significant difference: the people of Coll really have gone away, almost totally. Of the 160 who live on the island today, only 16 of them are native Collachs, whereas of the 800 people who live on Tiree, the vast majority are Tiree folk. More than that, most of the few remaining natives of Coll are old, whereas the Tiree population has an age structure much like that of any other Highland community. There is no likelihood that they will all be replaced by incomers. Being less populous, Coll has no bank, no supermarket and no policeman; being more cosmopolitan, it has a bistro, a telecottage and an RSPB estate. Tiree, by contrast, has no RSPB-owned land, no bistro and no telecottage; but it does have a bank, a supermarket, a policeman, a High School, an airport and a proper scruffy pub. In short, Tiree has a much more 'lived-in' feel than Coll, an island in whose main street more than half the houses are holiday homes.

The reasons for this state of affairs are themselves interesting. Essentially, Tiree was saved by wet ground and violence. The wet ground helped 200 years ago, when sheep first started displacing people in the Highlands and Islands. The *Old Statistical Account* comments, 'Though in other counties a most beneficial stock, [sheep] are most destructive [on] Tiree. There is not a sufficient range for them. They do not thrive in summer owing to certain weeds; nor in winter on account of the wetness of the pasture. They lodge in the hollows for shelter, and so break the sward, and expose the sand to be driven by the winds, whence whole fields are ruined, becoming white banks.' Tiree was left to corn and black cattle. Although people emigrated for economic motives, there were no mass, forcible clearances for sheep as happened on Coll after the island was bought, in 1856, by John Lorne Stewart from its traditional owners, the Macleans.

If, by the late nineteenth century, the crofters of Tiree were safe from sheep, they were still not safe from their laird, the Duke of Argyll. In 1880 William Gladstone and the Liberal Party came to power at Westminster, committed to an attempt to find a solution to the Irish Land War. As noted above, the Irish Land Act was the result. In 1883, Gladstone decided to apply a similar policy to Scotland and appointed the Napier Commission to look into the land problem in the Highlands. Lord Napier spent a year taking statements from landowners, their factors and crofters. His Report formed the basis of the 1886 Crofters Act. The Duke made a submission to Lord Napier which, unusually, he decided to publish in the form of a short book, *Crofts and Farms in the Hebrides*.

The Duke's essential argument was that he had been a good landlord, making no evictions, but that there were too many people on Tiree for the agricultural potential of the island to support. This was a problem which would be compounded if they were given security of tenure. Furthermore, he argued, improvements to the agriculture could only come about as a result of the proprietor's being able to organise and finance them, and force them through 'by the authority of ownership'. The Duke dismissed the 'irrelevant complaints' about him which crofters and cottars on Tiree brought before Lord Napier by saying they were merely parroting the words of agitators and propagandists who played on the islanders' 'passive credulity'. The Duke compared this process with a performance he had seen in Edinburgh where a man was 'made to believe he was at a market and that a piano in the room was a horse for sale.'

On one point, though only expressed in a footnote, the Duke was strikingly prophetic. He foresaw the rise of popular tourism, and even birdwatching, in those days almost unknown as a recognised leisure activity.

I fully expect that 'far on in summers which I shall not see' the Island of Tiree will be a great resort of health. Its strong yet soft sea air – its comparative dryness – its fragrant turf, full of wild thyme and white clover – its miles of pure white sandy bays, equally pleasant for riding, driving or walking, or for sea bathing – and last, not least, its unrivalled expanses for the game of golf – all combine to render it most attractive and wholesome in the summer months. My own tastes would lead me to add as a special recommendation its wealth of sky ringing with the song of skylarks, which are extraordinarily abundant.[1]

---

1 *Crofts and Farms in the Hebrides, being an Account of the Management of an Island Estate for 130 Years*. The Duke of Argyll, David Douglas, Edinburgh 1883.

All of these, with the exception of golf courses, have come to pass in recent years. But in the 1880s, the concern of the government was not so much the promotion of genteel tourism as the quenching of rebellious sentiment on the part of the rural poor. The Duke could see that the government was likely to change the law to grant secure tenancies to the mass of his crofters (which is what it did). That would be disastrous. If he were not to be saddled with what he considered an overcrowded island, the Duke would have to act quickly and remove as many people as possible before the new law came into force. In 1885 he arranged for a force of 50 policemen and 250 Marines to be sent, on two warships, to make evictions from the island.

A combination of stout physical resistance by the crofters and a certain amount of sympathy for their plight from the law officers meant that there were no evictions. The following year the Crofters Act became law and the moment for the Duke had passed; six years later though, as noted earlier, his resistance to change was rewarded with the elevation of his dukedom to the United Kingdom peerage by Gladstone's opponent Lord Salisbury. Twice the dukes of Argyll have tried to sell Tiree, first in the 1900s and then in the late 1940s. On both occasions the inability, as a result of the Crofters Act, to offer vacant possession frustrated the Duke's hopes of a substantial cash injection.

Not only has Tiree been lived in, it has also been died for. This thought is hard to escape when looking at the little war memorial which stands on the knoll between the ferry pier and the settlement at Scarinish. It was my first stop on the morning after my arrival as it is only a step up from the anchorage. Those who complain about crofters' rights would do well to ponder the blood sacrifice the people of this island – and Tiree is not untypical of the Hebrides – have made in defending their country. The basic social contract of the clan was that clansmen had the right to try and wrest some form of subsistence from the land in return for the responsibility to help defend it in time of war. By degrees that right was taken away from them, though they were still expected to discharge the once-corresponding duty. This they have done with a will.

Reverend Walker noted in 1771 that Tiree 'has about 1681 Inhabitants . . . It sent 57 Men to the late War, and of those only 12 returned.' A quarter of a century later, the *Old Statistical Account* said, 'In the time of the last American war, in one twelvemonth 120 youths, and in this spring above 100, left this island for the service of their country. Does not this merit attention in many respects?' In the Napoleonic Wars the regiments which, after amalgamation, are now the Argyll and Sutherland Highlanders served with distinction, as they did in the Crimean War where their unbreakable discipline earned the semi-official army nickname, 'The Thin Red Line', a term so evocative of the fundamental military virtue that it has been hijacked by the British Army as a whole.

The habit of sacrifice continued this century. In the First World War, 6442 men of the Argylls were killed. In the Second World War the regiment again won many battle honours. One in particular stands out: the Second Battalion's retreat on Singapore in January 1942. They were the last troops to cross into the so-called fortress. So fiercely had they fought the rearguard action that only 100 of the original 800 men emerged from the Malayan jungle. More generally and more recently, it will be remembered that the memorial service after the 1991 Gulf War was held in Glasgow because nearly 40 per cent of the British fighting contingent had been Scottish, though less than 10 per cent of the British population is – and Highlanders were over-represented, proportionally, within the Scottish total. In short, it can hardly be said that these people have stinted their blood in defence of their country.

A glance at the Tiree memorial shows the impact this made on the small community. The memorial records the names of 65 men of the island who died in the First World War, from a total population of about 2000. Applied to Britain as a whole, that proportion would have meant total national casualties of 1.5 million, when in fact they were about 650,000. It is worth reflecting on the endlessly repeated claim that it was the 'young officer class', the 'flower of the nation', which alone bore the heaviest brunt of the national sacrifice. This is not true: Highlanders gave their lives in equivalent numbers, *pro rata*. The First World War memorial in School Yard at Eton records 1157 names. At that time, there were about 10,000 Old Etonians alive in the world. This is an 11 per cent (fatal) casualty rate, approximately double that of the country as a whole, but equivalent to that suffered on Tiree. If you assume that about a third of the population of Tiree at the time were men of more than school-leaving age, the 65 Old Tireans who died represent about the same proportion of the available manpower within their community as the 1157 Old Etonians represent within theirs.

Contemplating this in brilliant sunshine, I looked round at the smiling face of this lovely island. Full of flowers, the fields rolled gently away to the south and west. To the east was the sea, with the little fishing boats beached on the sand in the tiny and very shallow harbour at Scarinish. Looking north, the miles of beach sand around Gott Bay glowed a brilliant white. I could see some people in the distance flying kites with long, colourful tails snaking behind them in the fresh breeze. There was a palpable sense of freedom. Much of the land is unfenced, and there was not a Keep Out, Private Property, or Trespassers Will be Prosecuted sign anywhere in sight. The houses are built wherever a crofter in years past wanted to, almost all being on sites in use since long before the Town and Country Planning Act of 1947. They are therefore scattered over the island with a delightful lack of regimentation. Today, these would be classed as 'isolated rural dwellings' and subject to a presumption of refusal of planning consent unless the applicant could show practical necessity for agricultural or similar use. The Darlings of the modern nature bureaucracy have a statutory right to object to any proposed development on conservation grounds. 'Herb-rich grasslands', with which Tiree is so abundantly blessed, is a commonly used one. The freedom is far from safe.

The principal 'political' drama on Tiree today is the conflict between the wildlife conservationists and the crofters over the rising numbers of greylag geese. I visited the Duke's factor, Ian Gillies, and asked him what the background to this problem

was. A quietly spoken, down-to-earth man, Gillies told me that Tiree has long
had a wintering population of this species of goose, which has never caused any
problem until, 20 years or so ago, they started breeding on the island. A summer
presence was very damaging since the geese eat the crofters' grass and trample
their silage. Numbers rose steadily until, a couple of years ago, a Goose
Management Committee was formed to deal with the problem. Its first practical
action was to hire a gun to shoot some of the geese. The hired gun was Angus
Maclean, a retired crofter, and he was my next call.

Angus lives in quiet comfort in the middle of the herb-rich grasslands of
Scarinish. He is a calm, dignified man who looks happy that he still has some
outdoor work to do. In his sun-filled sitting room, to the quiet ticking of the
clock on his mantlepiece, I asked him what, in round terms, the size of the goose
problem was. The only figure I had been able to find was a statement by the
RSPB that 380 greylags winter in this area.[2]

'I've been shooting geese since I was the height of a gun barrel,' Angus said,
'and I can safely say that that is a lot of nonsense. There were nearly 3000 greylags
in Tiree last winter.'

'How many breeding pairs do you have in the summer?' I asked.

'About a thousand,' he said.

'The RSPB quote a figure of 90 pairs.'

'Och, a lot of tosh, that. No, for heaven's sake, if you went out on that moor
there,' he said, gesturing out of the window, 'and that's only a very small portion
of the whole area on Tiree where they nest, you'd get hundreds of nests. And
each one will hatch probably four eggs, of which the hoodie crows will get one
and the black-backed gulls another. So on average two is what they will get away
with, every year.'

Numbers started to rise about 15 years ago, as far as Angus remembered. Before
that, there were perhaps a couple of hundred of the birds wintering on the island
and none breeding. Now the effect of protective legislation, improved grass on
reseeded fields and what he called 'a slight change in the weather pattern' has
brought about a sudden explosion. The first two factors were easy to understand;
I asked about the third.

'For some unknown reason we seem to get more northerly winds now in
April,' Angus said. 'Long ago the weather was balmy and the wind from the
south, then. Sensible geese won't migrate against a headwind. They wait and
they wait. In some cases in the last few years I think they waited until it was too
late. Now they've sort of lost the instinct for migration. In less than 20 years they
have changed their way of life completely.'

As goose control officer, Angus reckons that he shot 133 geese the previous
year. Very few crofters still shoot for the pot, as most used to. Argyll Estates,

---

2 *Important Bird Areas in the United Kingdom* ed. Pritchard et al. RSPB, Sandy 1992, p.
   208. The area covered is not clearly defined, but the figure used is for proposed
   protection areas for both Coll and Tiree. The figure is quoted as a minimum.

which still retains shooting rights, also has a goose shoot once a year. He estimates that a total of possibly 500 birds are killed – but the population keeps on rising.

The conservationists' response has been to try scaring the geese. A couple of years ago they provided crofters with large kites which they were supposed to fly above any grazing flocks. The kites were intended to suggest, in the mind of the goose, a bird of prey. But it turned out that the mind of the goose is subtler than the conservationists thought. Once they realised that these new objects in the sky did not swoop down and snatch their goslings, they started to ignore them. Now they are equally unconcerned at shotguns fired over their heads in the close season: they have worked out that bangs do not mean death as long as the weather is warm. There is, Angus says, no other option but shooting for real.

In 1993 the RSPB leased 850 acres of ground around the airport, on the large plateau known for centuries as The Reef. With low-lying, very sandy soil, it is famous for what the *Old Statistical Account* called its 'beautiful carpet, variegated with flowers'. I asked Angus what the Society's attitude to shooting was.

'I don't know,' was Angus's answer. 'For many years I had the goose shooting on The Reef. The RSPB still say I can go and shoot, but I have nothing in writing and they won't put anything in writing, so I don't.'

Part of the RSPB's purpose in renting The Reef is to promote corncrake breeding on Tiree – their publicity goes on endlessly about the island's hay meadows – so I asked Angus for his views on the threats this bird faces. He was quite definite: the biggest is feral cats. 'I'm quite sure, this year, that they have done away with 50 per cent of the corncrakes on Tiree. Nobody will listen to that, but I have seen them.'

Next morning it was raining hard. The wind was gusting in from the south-west bringing those surges of rain – they never quite stop, but vary in intensity – so familiar to anyone who lives in the Hebrides. It was cosy sitting down below on *Sylvia B* eating breakfast and reading, with the rain lashing on the deck and the wind moaning in the rigging. I had decided I would pay a call on the RSPB *rezident* Clive Mackay and ask for his views on geese and corncrakes. As he lives nearly five miles from the anchorage, I waited for the weather to lift a bit before setting off.

When I did, it was still cold and wet. As I plodded past the Scarinish Hotel, I wondered whether or not it would be sensible to wait inside, in the public bar, for the weather to clear a bit more. Happily, another squall passed over at just that moment and I had the excuse I needed. Soon my jacket was drying over a chair in front of the coal fire and a pint of Guinness was gleaming on the bar counter.

There were a couple of other folk in, all islanders. We discussed the traditional (but now illegal) custom of collecting seagulls' eggs from the cliffs on the west of Tiree. Men were let down by ropes, which frequently chafed through with fatal results. In those days, the eggs were part of the staple diet of the islanders.

'Would you eat them now if the law were changed?' I asked.

'To tell you the truth some people still do – not very many, but a few,' one man said. 'I have tried gulls' eggs and they're disgusting, absolutely disgusting. When you think of what the birds eat, sewage and everything, you couldn't even imagine the eggs tasting good.'

'It's the same with the gannets,' another said. 'You know they still catch the young ones in Lewis. They pickle them, and box them up and send them out to Australia, to their relatives. Well, I've tried those, and I couldn't eat them. Not at all. I'd sooner have a chicken from the Co-op.'

Towards the end of the third pint of Guinness the gloom outside started to lighten. I forewent an offered fourth pint, although I did accept a quick dram. Then I gathered up my now-dry gear and set off. Almost immediately a lady stopped to give me a lift. As the suburbs of Scarinish consist of three converted blackhouses, the school and the Argyll Estates office, we were soon out in the 'champaign' country, bowling along between the hay meadows, chatting happily.

I was dropped within a mile of Mackay's house and had a very pleasant walk up through other hay meadows. The Norse influence in the island's past is very apparent in the names of the townships. Mackay lives between Heylipol and Barrapol, in the middle of yet more hay meadows. It is not hard to see why he is here.

'My job on Tiree is primarily to do with corncrakes and the corncrake initiative,' Mackay told me, as he rattled a spoon in a mug of coffee. His father, he told me, had been an impoverished Irish immigrant to Yorkshire. Mackay grew up in Sheffield, the same town as Fraser Darling's mother.

'The corncrake scheme,' he went on, 'is open to anybody who has a corncrake on their land or is within 250 metres of a singing corncrake. For any field that is hay or silage, we pay £60 per hectare for cutting the grass in a corncrake-friendly fashion. Tiree is the corncrake capital of Britain. I count the corncrakes, I draw maps of where they are and draw a circle with a 250-metre radius around every one and speak to every crofter within that radius if they've got any silage fields. Then there's all the paperwork which follows on from that. That takes from May to September. It's just corncrakes all the way.'

I was curious to learn how much all this corncrake activity on Tiree costs. I had already been told that the whole scheme, nationally, costs over £300,000 per annum, most of that public money. The RSPB claim to have 'at least 35 people directly involved in corncrake work'.[3] The result of all the expenditure has been a national increase of the total British corncrake population from 480 (calling males) in 1993 to 584 in 1996. That increase, of 104 birds, has been bought at a cost of over £900,000, or £8653 per bird. I asked Mackay how he justified this extravagance, but he said that financial matters should be raised with head office, in other words, David Minns, the man who refused to let me see the Reserve Management Plan. All Mackay would say was that on Tiree, payments direct to crofters totalled £30,000 per annum.[4]

---

3   *Birds* Spring 1996, p. 66.

I asked Mackay if he agreed with Angus Maclean's point that the biggest
threat to corncrakes on the island was cats.

'Cats do eat corncrakes,' he said, 'but we don't know the level of the problem.'

'You don't?'

'No idea.'

Apparently Angus's impressions do not count as 'knowledge'.

'You spend £30,000 a year giving money to crofters to protect the corncrake,'
I asked. 'Do you spend any money trying to abate the cat problem?'

'No.'

'Why not?'

'We don't know the scale of their predation. There are all sorts of other threats
to the birds. They get knocked down by cars, they fly into fence posts, and get
caught in barbed wire.'

'Which of these is the most serious threat?'

'We don't know.'

'In 1995 you recorded 140 calling males,' I said, 'and this year only 117. Do you
have any explanation for the decline?'

'No. There's lots of possible theories, but to actually know the answer to that
question is not easy, possibly just normal population fluctuation. It may just be
a little blip. The other possibility is that we had a lot of south-easterly winds
during the migration season when they were coming up from Africa and it is
possible some birds overshot Tiree. With a good tail wind they ended up going
further north to the Outer Hebrides, where numbers seem to have gone up.
That's the only logical explanation that I can think of, otherwise it's just
guesswork.'[5]

Mackay's last explanation is probably close to the truth. Research has established
that corncrakes are not particularly 'site-faithful', so the fact that there are more
or fewer birds on Tiree really is meaningless.[6] Similarly for the British total. It
expanded in years when the population in the north of Ireland declined sharply.

---

4   Total numbers on Tiree in all years which have been censused: 1978: 85 calling males;
    1988, 101; 1989, 89; 1991, 106; 1992, 97; 1993, 111; 1994, 126; 1995, 140; 1996, 117. The
    RSPB reserve sometimes has one pair of corncrakes; most years it has none. The
    Society manages 4.5 per cent of the island (3.56 hectares out of 7.134) yet attracts less
    than 1 per cent of its corncrakes, despite the fact that Item 2 of the RSPB's Main
    Management Policy reads: 'To increase the number of corncrakes on the
    reserve . . .' (*The Reef, Tiree: Management Plan*, Gwen Evans, RSPB 1995, p. 3,
    unpublished – one of the documents David Minns refused to let me see).

5   In 1997 Mackay moved to the RSPB reserve on Islay and the following year corncrake
    numbers there were down by 60 per cent, despite an increase on Colonsay. In the
    official report, he offered no explanation, except to say, 'We can't help thinking that
    some Islay-bound birds must have missed their target and ended upon Colonsay and
    Oronsay.' *Fieldworkers Corncrake Reports 1998*, RSPB/SNH p. 13.

6   'The Recent Decline of the Corncrake on the Isle of Canna' R. L. Swarm, *Bird Study*,
    1986, Vol. 33, p. 203. Swann says that of the 150 corncrake chicks ringed on Canna,
    only two ever returned to the island, a third being found on Islay. The rest were never
    seen again in Britain.

It is entirely possible that the whole British increase has nothing to do with the expenditure of all those hundred of thousands of pounds but simply to the fact that the birds in northern Ireland, for some as yet unexplained reason, flew on to Britain. They might fly back again next year. But since the RSPB regularly appeals for funds to buy land for corncrakes, this factor tends to be downplayed. Money talks.

On the other hand, Angus may be right and the decline due more to cats than any other factor. I did not take Mackay's apparent ignorance of the cat problem at face value. Cat predation of birds is a touchy subject with the RSPB. Pet food manufacturers' statistics show that there are about 10 million domestic cats in Britain. Independent zoological research has shown that the average cat kills about 10 birds per year. Thus domestic cats – that is not counting feral or wild cats – account for a staggering 100 million birds every year. Yet the RSPB does not publicise this threat. Why? Because so many of its actual and potential members are cat lovers. Once again, money talks.

Finally on the corncrakes, I asked Mackay about the fact that RSPB research – research which the Society keeps very quiet about – has shown that the real threat to the corncrake is the Egyptian quail netters who catch an estimated 10,000 birds every spring on their migration from Africa to Europe and Asia.[7] The corncrake eats very well – Mrs Beeton gives a recipe for them – and they are an important source of food. But they are small birds, weighing about 150 grams, or three to a pound. If all the corncrake scheme money were given to the quail netters to release corncrakes, the 10,000 birds would be valued at £30 each, or £90 per pound. Since they probably only command a few pence in the markets of the Nile delta, the commercial logic of spending the money in Egypt rather than in Britain is obvious. But proposals for a corncrake-efficient use of funds runs into one insuperable obstacle: Egyptian quail netters are not people the RSPB membership wants to spend money on. I put this to Mackay.

'The RSPB is a British organisation,' he said. 'It could be that the British birds go nowhere near Egypt.[8] Anyway, we're working with crofters on Tiree, and that bit of money helps support the community here to some extent. Crofting is not a 100 per cent viable pastime; it is no way of making a living.'

'But you're supporting the corncrake, not the crofters, surely?'

'We're doing both at the same time, which is the beauty of the system. Corncrakes are dependent on crofters, so it is in the RSPB's interests to work with crofters, and that's why we do it. The proportion question is a big question,

---

7   'Trapping and shooting of Corncrakes on the Mediterranean coast of Egypt' *Bird Conservation International*, RSPB 1996, pp. 215–27.

8   The RSPB's *Species Action Plan 0421* Corncrake – another document Minns refused to let me see – comments about the north African slaughter, 'This source of mortality seems unlikely to contribute much to the decline of the corncrake in the UK. There is no direct evidence that the corncrakes for the UK pass through Egypt.' (p. 12) The important thing, therefore, is not to save corncrakes but to raise money for appearing to save the few that fly to Britain.

but what can you do outside your own country? You have to start on your own ground. We tell people they shouldn't be cutting down their own forests; we talk globally, but within Britain, we're not acting globally, are we?'

Changing the subject, I asked Mackay if he liked living on Tiree. He said he liked working in small communities. 'I try and enrich their lives a wee bit,' he said. 'I try and enrich everyone's world a wee bit, by ensuring they have a nice environment.'

Since the greylag geese were doing exactly the opposite of enriching the lives of the Tiree crofters, I asked him about them. Mackay started by saying he thought Angus Maclean's figures were inaccurate, but he did concede that numbers had been rising sharply and that the birds were now breeding on the island.

'Why?' I asked.

'I've no idea.'

'What is the solution to rising numbers?'

'It's hard to say,' he said, 'hard to come up with a solution. There are no simple solutions with geese.'

'Surely shooting's a pretty simple solution?'

'Well that sets lots of precedents, doesn't it? On Tiree there are two species of totally protected goose, barnacle and white front. One has to be careful about setting precedents about controlling numbers by shooting.'

'Why?'

'Well, precedents are precedents. If you allow shooting one day, the species could be extinct in a year's time, if there isn't a careful control of it.'

In the light of that conversation, it was a shock to learn, within an hour, that Mackay sits on the committee that actually *organises the shooting of greylag geese on Tiree!* In a sense, he is Angus Maclean's employer. I discovered this because my next call was on Donnie Campbell, chairman of the Goose Management Committee.

After leaving Mackay, I got a lift up to Kilmaluig, where Donnie lives, in what looked like an 'ex-fleet' Ford Sierra with a family from the west Midlands of England who described themselves as 'green tourists'. To put it mildly, they did not seem to be enjoying their holiday. They had not heard a single corncrake on the island, they told me, and had not had much luck counting earwigs either. *Earwigs!?!* Yes, indeed. They showed me the Ordnance Survey map on which they were recording earwig sightings.

'Why do you go bird-watching?' I asked the driver, a sad-eyed man in a beard and 'Bill Oddie' hat.

'Because I'm too old to watch women,' he said, without a flicker of expression.

They said they found the people on Tiree unfriendly, and did not like the digs they were in because the landlady had 'no blarney'. They were happy to take me right to Donnie Campbell's door, going well out of their way. 'We're not pushed for time,' the driver said. 'There's nothing to do when we get back to the cottage except listen to the radio. We're just driving round, really, to use up the time till tea.'

Donnie Campbell turned out to be a sharp-witted and voluble man who bears more than a passing resemblance to Donnie Munro, the Runrig singer and aspiring parliamentarian. He is a native of the island, a Gaelic speaker, crofter and deputy headmaster of Tiree High School. Until recently he was also District Councillor for Coll and Tiree – his successor is Ian Gillies – and chairman of the Crofters' Union branch on the island. Today, he is also chairman of the Greylag Goose Management Committee, as well as being a board member of the Scottish Environmental Protection Agency. In short, he is both an islander and a politician.

Sitting in his stockinged feet in the warm kitchen of his large, modern house, Donnie told me about the politics of conservation on a small but 'lived-in' island. The realisation that it had become necessary to cull the breeding greylag geese had come quite recently.

'One could argue', Donnie said, 'that the Estate has been in dereliction of its duty to some extent in that it has not kept down what some would regard as vermin, especially in the summer. Anyway, one day at the Crofters' Union we had a grousing session and said, it's time we stopped talking and did something about the greylag geese. So we had a meeting with the NFUS [National Farmers' Union of Scotland] and formed an interim joint committee and that then asked all the interested bodies to come along and form a Goose Control Committee.'

They invited the Estate, all the conservation bodies and all the agricultural committees, advisory boards and departmental representatives. Everybody came. 'The most difficult political aspect was keeping everyone on board,' Donnie said. 'We had RSPB and SNH [Scottish Natural Heritage, the successor in Scotland to the Nature Conservancy Council], to some extent, over a barrel because they didn't want to be seen rejecting a grass roots movement which was born of a lot of frustration and which was obviously going to be set up responsibly. We were not a lot of hotheads who were going to go around shooting geese left right and centre. We did not want to get rid of them all.'

The aims of the committee were clearly stated in the Constitution, which he showed me. All members had to put their names to it. 'The principal object is to bring about a substantial reduction in greylag goose numbers within a period of three years . . . through a range of measures *including shooting.*' (emphasis added)

'The RSPB didn't jib at that?'

'Oh yes,' Donnie replied. 'They jibbed at quite a lot. But ultimately they did not want to be seen outside a grass roots, respectable body, though our objectives were not particularly politically correct: shooting lots of birds. We made some concessions, for example we changed the name from the Goose *Control* Committee, which the crofters very much wanted, to the Goose *Management* Committee, which the RSPB felt more comfortable with.'

'Why was it important for you that the RSPB were kept on board?' I asked.

'Just the whole corporate, public body scene: very difficult to explain. If you're involved in conservation management and you have either the RSPB or SNH outside your ring fence, you are perceived by powers looking at you to give you money, or looking at you to take you seriously, as maybe being a bit off the wall, maybe as being a bit politically incorrect. It's just jumping through the correct hoops. The problem was we'd get stick from folk around here who would say, you've been employing a goose officer since September and we see so many geese around. The average member out there does not want to see me sitting in meetings, he wants to see me shooting birds.'

'I can imagine that,' I said, thinking of the goose problem on Islay.

'But I'm trying to push the line that it's going to take three years and we're getting there,' Donnie went on. 'We cannot go out and shoot a thousand geese tomorrow, it would be all over the papers for a start. It would be politically incorrect, and we'd get no more money from the AIE [Argyll and Islands Enterprise, who pay part of the costs]. So we're playing the political game. The RSPB know that we need them and we know that they need us, and SNH to a certain extent. It's classic partnership, grass roots, coalition building *et cetera*. So we are regarded as respectable. Two years ago the feeling was not respectable: it was the killing of as many geese as possible.'

I asked Donnie why he thought the RSPB were prepared to lend their name to a bird shooting project, particularly when there was no conservation purpose to be served.

'I think that the greylag geese are expendable as far as the RSPB are concerned,' he said. 'What they are really worried about is the corncrake, and the red-throated divers, and the other rare birds here. Greylag geese are dirt common. What they want to do is to not alienate themselves from the crofting community of Tiree because they want to promote the corncrakes. They want conservation to have a good name. It is relatively easy for them, as long as the shooting does not get too greatly publicised.'

'You've kept quiet about it?'

'Not exactly,' he said. 'I've been on the radio several times about this – though in Gaelic right enough.'

An intriguing thought: bad publicity is not bad publicity to a Bedfordshire-based organisation if it is in Gaelic and therefore incomprehensible to the target market for membership subscriptions.

Donnie told me how they had convinced the local Enterprise company to pay for Angus's services. 'We did a very detailed breakdown on what a goose costs. In the old days with the souming[9] there was a relationship between how many domestic geese you had and grazing. And from that I was able to work out the grazing pressure of all our geese.'

That relationship was five geese to a single beast – geese are voracious eaters. Taking Archie Maclean's 2000 breeding greylags, that is equivalent to 400 beasts.

---

9 A 'soum' is the unit of pasturage used when a crofting township decides how much land a single cow, sheep or other animal needs for support. The souming is the allocation of the common grazing amongst those crofters who have a right to it. In the souming there is an accepted relationship between different types of animal, as in one beast is equivalent to five geese. A shareholder in the common grazing is allocated non-specific units at the souming and is free to decide, species by species, the make-up of his or her own portfolio.

'If you take a gross margin of £200 per beast,' Donnie went on, 'that comes to a fair economic pressure. AIE were convinced by that.'

That 'economic pressure' amounts to £80,000 per annum. The nett cost to Tiree of 'green economics', then is £80,000 less the £30,000 which is paid in by the RSPB and SNH for corncrakes, or £50,000. As there are 70 crofters on Tiree, this averages out at £714 per crofter per annum. Mackay said that the conservationists are subsidising the crofters, but the truth is exactly the opposite: the crofters are subsidising conservation.

More broadly, Donnie told me he was worried by the extremely close relationship between the RSPB and SNH. SNH, being the government's official conservation advisor in Scotland, has a duty to be independent of all pressure groups. He did not blame the RSPB for being activists, rather he criticised SNH for allowing their ears to be so easily bent by an activist political body.

'Maybe I'm just too used to dirty politics,' he said, 'but I expect the RSPB to do that. I expect them to have a political viewpoint. The members pay for a certain line to be taken, and they represent their members' political viewpoint. My grouse is against SNH, who are the statutory body, that they're getting into bed a bit with the RSPB. I've had letters from SNH that have been copied to me to do with goose committee business and at the bottom it says "cc RSPB", not to the other agencies, just the RSPB.'

Donnie explained that, for an orderly reduction in breeding goose numbers, it is first necessary to have an authoritative figure for the scale of the problem. The Goose Management Committee decided it would be best for 'political' credibility if SNH were asked to organise a census that August. Incredibly, SNH were so strapped for cash, that they had to ask the crofters to pay for the counting.

Donnie got a bigger shock when he was told that SNH were not going to carry out the count themselves but were going to subcontract it to none other than the RSPB. This surely bears out Commander Tappley's point about the conservation world that it helps to be English if you want to be taken seriously in Scotland.

Donnie had been both annoyed at the news and sceptical. 'I said to SNH, "Can you trust the RSPB to give such sensitive baseline figures honestly?" SNH say yes, but it's a huge political issue. We must be very, very sure that RSPB are using good, objective science. There's a real danger there.'[10]

'What,' I asked finally, 'do the Tiree people as a whole think of the RSPB?'

'There hasn't been an anti-RSPB backlash here particularly,' Donnie told me. 'They are maybe suffering a little bit from an anti-conservationist feeling because of the geese generally. But certainly I still hear of people finding dead corncrakes and taking them to Clive Mackay. So the RSPB are not ostracised to that extent, though, goodness gracious me, they do not talk to the ordinary crofter, or socialise with the ordinary crofter.'

---

10 Postscript: the count was conducted as arranged at the end of August 1996. In the event, Angus Maclean's much derided figure of 1000 pairs proved to be much closer to the mark than the RSPB's figure of 90: the count was 1108 pairs

'Is the problem purely a social one?' I asked.

'No, Clive's an evangelist. I don't want to denigrate the man personally, but it's also to do with somebody parachuting in to the island that doesn't know anything about it, and presumes to know something about the place and its people and how they operate. For example, SNH say that at the goose count one of the people we will use is Clive Mackay's wife. She's had experience of this kind of thing, having worked on Islay, they say. But I'm going to resist that because our two counters, who have done all the other counts in the past, are basically ordinary people from the island who needed the money and got the job. It is not going to go down too well amongst the crofters, who are paying for the count, that this person should simply parachute in and take their jobs.'

As I gathered my bags and notes together, I found a piece of paper I had meant to show Donnie, but had forgotten in the torrent of words. It was a page from an RSPB internal document, written by Andy Knight, Mackay's predecessor, reporting on his 'fieldwork' on Coll and Tiree in the summer of 1991. Every crofter was listed and comments were made about their farming practices and their attitude to corncrakes.

Donnie was shocked to see it. He could accept that it was legitimate for the Society to gather material on the working practices of those people who took money from them in the corncrake initiative, but the idea that every crofter should have his attitudes investigated and recorded without his knowledge or consent was 'quite unacceptable'. One named crofter, Knight noted, was 'unlikely to be helpful'; while another was 'a conservationist at heart'; of a third he had written: 'Difficult to broach subject of the corncrake, feels I might get at him for his income from drainage work.' With every succeeding name Donnie's face darkened, until he saw his own: 'D. Campbell, Councillor/Crofter, Difficult to extract an opinion on anything,' he read, and burst out laughing. ' "Difficult to extract an opinion"? What's he talking about? That's not me!'

Outside again the weather had cleared. The wind had dropped, the rain washed away and a low, evening sun was shining a dull platinum through a slight haze. I sauntered down the hill to see Peter Isaacson, Angus Maclean's part-time assistant goose shooter, where I was entertained to an informal supper of crab, stilton and red wine.

I had had enough of geese and corncrakes for the day so, I asked Peter about island living. He is 40-ish and has recently moved to Tiree from Inverness-shire, where he had been a full-time stalker for many years. He was here because his wife, Jane, had decided to start a riding school and pony-trekking centre on the island. After a doing a degree in Agricultural Economics at Edinburgh University, Peter had spent a couple of years abroad. Coming back to Scotland, he did not want to go into the commercialised world of farming and ended up on the hill. Since there is no stalking on Tiree, he is now a part-time grave-digger, part-time grass-cutter for the Council and part-time goose control officer. He also does a bit of fishing.

As he had no prior connection with the island, I asked Peter how he found life on Tiree.

'I think there's an acceptance of people here,' he said, 'though within a classification system. Right from "the bloody English", as you get anywhere in Scotland, though more so in Edinburgh and Glasgow than anywhere else, through to, "Oh well, they've come from the mainland, they're always a bit unusual there." It goes on to, "Ah well, he's from the east end of the island, you can't be too damn sure about him." Ridiculous! The island's the size of soup plate and they're talking about the east and the west end.'

'It's the same on Islay,' I said. 'It depends whether you're south or north of the big bridge, over the Laggan. "See Bowmore folk," they say in Port Ellen. "They do things differently." I imagine in Bowmore they say the same things about Port Ellen folk.'

'I believe there's a part of Skye,' Peter said, 'where they're worried about the number of Harris people that have moved in. They're worried about this blood influence. "They're a bit different and they certainly don't have the same accent and habits as us." Where do you draw the line?'

'I quite like it,' I said. 'There is such a thing as the spirit of place. It makes a difference if people have real roots. There's nothing fake about it, or bad – so long as it does not become negative.'

'I've not found that here,' Peter said, 'not to my face anyway. If you come from Edinburgh and you go anywhere you tend to be the odd man out. It was the same when I married into a Highland family.'

'I imagine in Edinburgh that's considered something of a moral lapse.'

'Again,' he said, laughing, 'that depends on which side of the city you're from.'

At about midnight it was time to stop. As the weather had turned foul again, Peter kindly drove me back to the boat, from the west side of the island to the east. In the dark and the sluicing rain, it was difficult to tell which end of the soup plate was which.

3

COLL

IT IS NO MORE THAN 12 miles from Gott Bay to Loch Eatharna (loch of the small fishing boats) on Coll. Next morning the 5.50 a.m. forecast for both Malin and Hebrides was for gales from the south-west. Outside I could see that it was windy, though it looked as if it was far from blowing a gale. I was aware of the need to keep moving if I was to get round the circuit I had planned before autumn, and did not want to be gale-bound on Tiree for a couple of days. So I thought, I'll go right now and chance it. It will be downwind anyway and there is a wide entrance to the anchorage on Coll. After tea, oatcakes and an apple I hoisted sail – a reefed main and the working jib – hauled in the anchor and stood out to sea. The clouds were scudding by and there was a long swell running in from the Atlantic. It was blowing perhaps force 5 and, with the wind on the starboard quarter, *Sylvia B* creamed off the crests of the waves with a lovely surge, giving a healthy kick from the tiller.

We passed the Oban ferry, steaming on an opposite course and butting into a head-sea with great explosions of spray from her bow. By nine o'clock the wind had died slightly and Loch Eatharna was just ahead of the port beam. Seeing what looked like quite a fierce squall coming up astern, I gibed the boat. We were about a mile out when the wind suddenly increased, bringing a flurry of rain in huge droplets and an intense but short-lived shrieking of the wind in the rigging. I eased the sheets, but it was past almost as soon as it had arrived. Composed, but purposeful, *Sylvia B* reached into the loch at a civilised four knots or so.

By 10.30 I had a lump of gammon frying down below, a pint-mug of coffee in my hand and a selection of jams arranged on the saloon table for afters. Unfortunately, in snugging the boat down I had broken the rivets that fix the boom to the gooseneck. This is a hinged casting which sits in a track on the mast. The track allows it to move vertically, while the hinge lets the boom swing laterally. I had tightened the uphaul at the gooseneck before slackening off the vang, a diagonal downhaul for off-wind sailing which is fixed a third of the way out on the underside of the boom. Result: a huge shearing force on 18-year-old rivets as the gooseneck wanted to rise but the boom to stay still. *Crack!* Two days before departure, while putting the finishing touches to a home-made boom-tent, I had broken my rivet gun. Such tools cannot readily be bought in Port Ellen, so I had been compelled to sail without one. A superstitious sailor would not have been surprised that that was the first tool I actually needed on this trip.

41

After a leisurely breakfast, I rowed ashore. The little hamlet of Arinagour, the only one on Coll, lies to the west of Loch Eatharna. The Isle of Coll Hotel dominates the loch from the north. My first call was to the grocer's shop where I asked if there was a mechanic on the island from whom I might borrow a rivet gun. I had not finished explaining my problem to the lady in the shop when a shopper standing behind me invited me round to her house where, she explained, I could have a cup of coffee while waiting for her partner to return: he was, she said, related to almost every native islander. If there was such a thing as a rivet gun on Coll, he would know who owned it, whom he had just lent it to and where that person was working with it at the moment. Her name was Lynn and her partner was Alistair Kennedy. Alistair was as good as Lynn's word and within an hour, I had not only a gun, but a handful of rivets and the loan, unasked, of a battery-driven power-drill to bore out the old ones. When I returned everything in the late afternoon, with the repairs completed, I was offered a bath and dinner, both of which I gratefully accepted.

Shortly before the meal was served, a neighbour, Hugh Mackinnon, came in for a dram. Hugh is one of the last remaining Gaelic-speaking Collachs. He grew up on a croft on the other side of the island. He was 11 years old, he said, before he had been as far afield as Arinagour. Serving in the Argylls in the war, he had been captured at St Valéry in June 1940 when Churchill had sacrificed the 51st Highland Division to the hopeless cause of Anglo-French co-operation in the chaotic aftermath of Dunkirk. Hugh spent most of the rest of the war in captivity, escaping five times, and being recaptured four.

Since the war, Hugh has lived quietly on Coll. We discussed the changes he had seen in his lifetime. Increased prosperity was the most noticeable development, he thought. I asked him if he thought people preferred the modern prosperity to the discomforts of the past.

'I don't think they were uncomfortable at all,' Hugh said, denying my premiss. 'There was ten of us and we were quite happy, as long as we had plenty of fish and potatoes and porridge and oatcakes and scones. What more can you want? Nowadays, they've thousands of pounds and they're not happy. I think they were happier then. I'm sure they were. Every house was lived in and you got a laugh at every door.'

We had another dram and got onto the subject of religion. Hugh said that, like most of the rest of the island, he had been a member of the Free Church, but now he was saddened to see there were just ten left in the congregation.

'But there is more than that in the Church of Scotland,' Alistair said.

'Aye, but they're incomers.'

I asked if there had ever been any Catholics living on the island.

'I don't think there was,' Hugh said. 'But if there was, they were made friends the same as anyone else. The only lady I remember coming to Coll – she was a very good-living Catholic – used to come down and give us a hand to clean out the Free Church. She still phones me up and asks me about Coll, and is dying to get back to Coll. I never thought anything of it. Why not? I think the one lot's as good as the other. That's the way I look at it.'

A third dram and we were onto the evergreen subjects of farming and nature. In the past, Hugh said, there were many more birds on Coll, despite the fact that every crofter had a gun. 'They had to, that was the only way they had to live,' he said, 'to shoot geese. You didn't murder more than what you wanted, you just shot a goose and that was it. There was always enough. You never carried on shooting birds for sport. It was the barnacle that we mostly went after.'

'I've been told they don't eat very well,' I said.

'No, but they make a lovely pot of soup,' he said, grinning. 'Actually in Coll it was the cormorant that people mostly went for, and eider ducks. There was plenty of them flying about.'

'But there's not so many now?' I asked.

'No.'

'Why?'

'I'll tell you why: because there is no feeding for them. The fish are gone. That's why cormorants used to be round the village here, but you never see one now because they've gone away somewhere else to try and get a feeding. They eat sandeels, and the young saithe, what we call cuddocks, and they're not there now.'

I asked if he used to collect gulls' eggs.

'I did.'

'I gather they don't taste very nice,' I said.

'Oh they're lovely, especially the young ones. Not the older birds, but the young gull lays a lovely egg, as good as any house hen. Lovely. My father was a fisherman and we used to go over to the islands and collect so many eggs and come home and have a great feed, but then we left them alone to breed.'

'What about corncrakes? Were there many on the island when you were a boy?'

'There used to be plenty of corncrakes on Coll. You used to hear them at night in the field up by the hotel. You couldn't hear anything but corncrakes. Up at the doctor's, that was another place. Every field in Coll had them. I think what happened to the corncrake on Coll, like the other islands, too, was when the mowing machine came in, it was either smashing up the eggs or killing the young chicks. And they definitely weren't so plentiful as the years went on. Before that the fields were cut with a bailer and horses, a very slow machine, and the birds had plenty of time to escape. I looked out, if I knew there was a corncrake in the field I was mowing. I used to be very careful.'

'Presumably that slowed you down?' I asked.

'Aye. '

'So why did you bother?'

'Because I loved them. I didn't like killing the corncrakes, you know.'

'Why did you love them?'

'Just because they were birds. I still love birds. I like their life in this world. Why murder birds that's doing you no harm? I would have a look and if I saw a nest I would circle round it and leave that bit. It was only two or three bites of a cow that you would lose. And why not? Why kill half a dozen poor young birds?

I'm pretty sure that these birds were just as sorry when they lost their young ones as what we were if we lost children. I'm sure they were. So I took good care that if I could help them at all I did help them. And I wasn't the only one. A lot of the farmers in Coll did that, took care of the birds. They've got as much right to live as what we have. I wouldn't harm any bird at all if I could.'

I asked about the corncrake Reserve which the RSPB established in 1991 at Totronald at the west end of the island where they bought 3000 acres. I asked Hugh if he thought the acquisition a good thing.

'To a point, yes,' he said. 'But I don't think they should waste so much ground for the sake of the corncrake. If they wanted to work the ground, they could work it with horses and the corncrake would still be there.' He paused. 'But they won't ask me what I think. I think it's a waste of time because they could do it in a better way.'

Next morning I was up early as I had arranged to pay a call on Major Maclean-Bristol. A famously irascible character, he was until recently *gymnasiumsführer* of the Project Trust, a charity which selects and prepares 18-year-olds for a year of voluntary service overseas, or language teaching abroad, between school and university. Supporters say it is a toughening and broadening experience for town-bred youngsters; critics call it a cheap way for the Major to get his dykes rebuilt. Nonetheless, the Project Trust is by far the largest employer on Coll.

The Major is a larger-than-life figure who, though English, is reported to wear a kilt all year round, only switching to trousers when travelling abroad. 'Don't want to get touched up by poofters on the aeroplane,' he recently told *The Independent.* He had not been keen to meet, being busy preparing his sheep for the Coll show, and had said to me, with a briskness which I took to imply military menace, 'If you are here by nine o'clock, I'll give you half an hour.'

It is seven miles over a hilly, twisting road from Arinagour to Breacachadh Castle, the Major's GHQ. Alistair Kennedy had kindly lent me a mountain bike, so I set off at about a quarter past eight, thinking I had plenty of time. Foolishly, I had not taken a map with me, thinking that with only one road on that side of the island it would be hard to lose my way. Well, I was wrong.

I presumed the track leading down to Breacachadh would not be hard to spot. Getting on for nine o'clock, one such track appeared, leading down a steep hill. I turned off and raced down, only to find that it led to a farm house. I knocked intending to ask if I might telephone to warn the Major of my lateness. But there was no one at home. Now the question was, do I sweat back up to the road, or cut across the hill? The next bay must surely be the one I want and, after all, this is supposed to be a cross-country machine.

Within 15 minutes I was sweating like a pig, as every succeeding rise in the hill was breasted only to reveal another empty dip in the ground, or bay with no castle at its head. I ended up carrying the bike nearly three miles over bog and brae, going as fast as I could. It was after ten o'clock before I staggered, exhausted, into the keep of Breacachadh Castle like some particularly useless VSO cadet.

Being an hour late, I fully expected to be slapped on defaulters and told to bugger off until I could learn proper timekeeping.

But the Major was understanding. This might have been due to the fact that he is now a full-time writer. A year ago he handed over the swagger stick to his wife, Lavinia, who now runs the Trust (wearing trousers). The Major's subject is the history of the Macleans. The previous year he had published the first volume, *Warriors and Priests*,[1] of a projected trilogy. His current work-in-progress, the second volume, centres round Sir Lachlan Maclean, the sixteenth-century harasser of the MacDonalds of Dunyveg on Islay.

Breacachadh Castle was built, he said, by 'my thirteenth great-grandfather in 1400' and was, until 1750 the seat of the Macleans of Coll. It stands amidst a beautifully flower-carpeted expanse of machair – Breacachadh means speckled field – leading down to a wide, sandy and gently shelving beach. In the days when galleys were the main form of communication among the isles, Loch Breacachadh was the principal port on the island. Modern ferries, which need deep water, come into the rocky, fjord-like Loch Eatharna, which is why Arinagour is today the capital of the island.

The visual impact of the castle is increased by the fact that it has no artificial gardens round about it, nor much in the way of a road leading to it. A hundred yards further up from the sea stands a second castle which was built by the Macleans in the 1750s in the neo-classical style. A hundred years later the family went bankrupt and sold the island to the Stewarts. John Lorne Stewart extended the eighteenth century castle making a large, ostentatious building, part Saxe-Coburg baronial and part Anglo-Irish neo-classical, which the Major describes as 'a monster' and which is now uninhabited.

The Stewarts allowed the older castle to fall into ruin, and in the late 1960s the Major bought it for £500. Consequently, he says, 'nobody has ever lived in it apart from my own family.' The success of the Project Trust has enabled him to restore it so that today it makes a beautiful and very unusual home. The Major's study is a circular room at the top of the tower. Light floods in through windows in the roof, and narrow slits in the walls give peeping views of the sea, the machair and the hills. As artists' garrets go, it is majestic.

All the land surrounding Breacachadh is now owned by the RSPB who have started putting up fences and gates, erecting signs and generally destroying the free, Hebridean feel of the place. This was the first subject we discussed.

'I *cannot* see their justification for owning land,' the Major said. 'As far as corncrake numbers are concerned – and there is a certain amount of mystery surrounding the way they play the numbers game – they could have achieved the same result with a great deal less money by coming in with £X and giving grants to the farmers, saying, right, cut your hay like that, save the corncrakes and here's money to make you do it. No buggering about owning land and things like that.'

---

1   *Warriors and Priests* by Nicholas Maclean-Bristol, Tuckwell Press, Edinburgh 1995.

'What is the problem with their owning land here?' I asked.

'They have no commitment,' he said. 'Somebody else could have bought the estate, which would have meant another family who had financial involvement in the island and would therefore make a go of it. The RSPB don't do that. They are short-term young men coming in before they properly know what they are doing. They're making decisions, like cutting across rights of way which they've done in several cases, and they don't see the broader picture. There's not the commitment as when you own land. We're here forever; we'll be buried here.'

The subject of burials is a sensitive one with the Major as the tombs of the Macleans are located in a mausoleum on the RSPB Reserve. The Major wants to restore it, but apparently the RSPB will allow him access only on condition that he asks them for permission every time he wants to take a vehicle there. Since the Society's officers presumably know that tomb restoration involves the transport of heavy materials, the Major has taken this as a 'No'. As a result, the monument – a roofless, walled, pseudo-castellar quadrangle – is being slowly destroyed by the cattle which graze that ground.

The Major had another point to make. 'I asked if we could rent land round here. The answer was no. We were told we were the wrong socio-economic group.'

'What on earth does that mean?' I asked. 'That you're too rich?'

'Well, that's what they think.'

'Is that a specific term they have used?'

'Correct. By two of them, yes. They want people who will do as they are told, or, more precisely, who cannot afford not to do as they are told.'

The Major told me that Coll has a similar, though smaller, problem to Tiree as far as geese are concerned. 'Because of their fund-raising, the RSPB can't be seen to shoot things, so the greylag geese are increasing and I'm chairing the goose and rabbit control committee. Rabbits have gone berserk as a result of the RSPB and SNH's policies. But the main problem is the geese. I like geese, there's nothing pleasanter than having geese about the place, but they've got to be in balance.'

Like Donnie Campbell, the Major had applied to the Argyll and Islands Enterprise for funding for a goose shooting programme. 'At first they said yes, now they've said we've got to justify, on scientific grounds, the amount of grass that is being used. Well, I haven't got the time, nor the expertise to put up a case, so immediately you're in the realms of bureaucrats with red tape who say, "Well, can you actually *measure* the amount of grass?" Bloody silly question, you can *see* what they're eating. But once you've got these sort of people moving in on the thing you've had it. Unless you are another organisation, and you can afford to pay for somebody to do a survey with equal knowledge to them, you're up a gum tree. It's the bloody cult of the expert: a lot of balls.'

The request to measure grass, I discovered to my amazement the next day, should be taken quite literally. In the 1996 edition of the *Coll Magazine*, I read the following sentence written by Charlie Self, the RSPB Warden: 'Some aspects of conservation work can seem a touch exotic – I certainly feel a bit removed from reality on approaching my 3000th grass-height measurement in a day!'

The absurdity does not stop there. Not only does grass height have to be dealt with statistically, but so does grass density. In order to satisfy the conceit that their knowledge is 'scientific', the RSPB uses a machine called a penetrometer to measure the force required to insert a 150 mm diameter shaft 500 mm into a given clump of grass, 100 mm above the ground. A 'sward penetrability quotient' is arrived at, which helps the professional ornithologist decide if that clump is densely matted or not. Since corncrakes are supposed to prefer loose grass, like hay, the penetrability quotient of a given field, measured clump by clump, is supposed, quite fancifully, to give some indication of its likely corncrake-hosting potential.

The Major ended our interview by making a very interesting general point. 'I feel quite strongly,' he said, 'that it is a dangerous thing to have any multinational organisation with very large funds owning land in such a small community as this. Nobody can compete with them financially. If they want to buy something they get it. My basic disagreement with the RSPB is that they are a single issue body, where everything in a place like this has to be balanced. You've got to take all the things into consideration. The community is very vulnerable. They are playing with things they don't know anything about.'

I cycled round to the dunes on Totronald, the RSPB Reserve, where I had previously arranged to meet Colin Kennedy, who owns a large farm abutting the Reserve. Colin also rents grazing on part of Totronald. He was there putting his sheep back out after the summer layoff which the RSPB insist upon in the cause of bird protection. By now it was noon and the sun was beating down. Puffy white clouds were making huge, gleaming castles in the sky. While waiting for Colin, I lay on my back on the dunes above Crossapol beach watching the fantastic sight above me. The light was so intense, the clouds almost seemed to be glowing.

My reverie was interrupted by the solid tread of a bluff, bearded, 40-ish man in a flat hat and blue needlecords. Even before he had introduced himself, I was in no doubt that this was Colin Kennedy. He sat down beside me while his two collies ranged back and forth, Colin shouting at them ferociously from time to time. I started by asking him about this piece of ground. Apparently, the RSPB had originally tried to buy a large farm on the north-east part of the island, but had been out-bid. So when they came down here, they were particularly aggressive purchasers.

'This bit we are sitting on,' Colin said, 'was offers over £70,000. I offered £120,000 to buy it: nowhere near it. The other bit was also offers over £70,000 and they paid £281,000 for both together. They doubled the asking price and added a thousand.'

I asked how the island had reacted to the news of the purchase.

'No bugger on Coll knew about the RSPB,' he said. 'Myself included. We didn't know what they were about. I knew they had Gruinart on Islay but I never, ever realised they were such a massive, powerful organisation. It's only since they've got their teeth into Coll that we've realised.'

'Has that changed people's attitude?' I asked.

'Hard to say. There's a queer bunch of folk living on Coll. There's not many local folk left. There's a lot of incomers and they all think they're massive fish in a little pond. I've discussed this with various people. They reckon that if you go for a job with the RSPB, and SNH up to a point too, you've got to have a certain degree of sleaze about you. You know, you look at them and you can say, "They're RSPB".'

'What do you mean by sleaze?'

'I don't know, it's just a word I'm using: yes-men. You never know exactly where you stand with them. So I've got a great game: they never know where they stand with me. Every time they're speaking to me I'm always laughing and joking and saying silly things. A lot of them haven't got two ha'pennies to their name. They'll get the hire of a tractor off the warden and other favours. RSPB are sort of buying their popularity in a roundabout way. But the ones that run after them on Coll, I don't see hellish many of them that are actually members of RSPB.'

In his corncrake opus, Andy Knight had commented on Coll farmers as freely as he had on the Tiree crofters. I asked Colin for his reaction to the entry about him. Knight noted that he had had three 'contacts' with 'Kennedy', no initial given. 'Father and son with two separate farms,' Knight had written. 'Both father and son can be difficult but could respond to dosh.' The word 'dosh' had been crossed out and 'financial inducement' substituted. Colin couldn't have cared less about the slighting reference, though he, like Donnie Campbell, thought it quite wrong that this sort of material should be collected about private individuals going about their lawful business. Colin's objection was more straightforward. 'That man Knight *never* spoke to me or my late father.'

'Really? Are you sure?'

'Never spoke.'

At that moment the RSPB Land Rover cruised up, with a dark-haired, thin-faced man at the wheel.

'Hello there, how are you,' shouted the unsmiling face behind the wheel.

'Never been better!' said Colin, beaming almost to the point of parody 'How's yourself?'

'OK,' the officer said, dully.

'First of August's here today,' Colin went on, brightly 'The stock are happy; the farmer's happy; everything's going great. How about yourself?'

'Oh, we're fine, yeah. The sun's come back out.'

'You're enjoying your trip to Coll?'

'Aye,' he said. There was a short silence, then he said, 'OK, see you around.'

'No problem, sir. We'll see you later.'

The gears of the Land Rover crunched and Colin wiped the inane grin off his face. 'Andy Knight never spoke to me in my life,' he said without pausing. 'Certainly never spoke to my father.'

'Are you sure? This would have been the summer of 1991.'

I turned up the first page which gave the dates of Knight's visits to Coll: the first was on 27 April and the last on 7 September.

'Listen, my old man died in October 1991 and he was in hospital from April, lambing time, that year. And the Knight fellow never spoke to me. The first time I ever spoke to an RSPB man in my life was when Ian Illingworth and Jack Fleming came and knocked on my door and asked me if I would be interested in renting land. I knew who Andy Knight was, but never once did he speak to me. I suppose that's what I'm getting at: that's the standard of sleaze they operate by.'

I asked Colin about corncrakes. 'The best farmer that ever was on this island in my lifetime was a man who farmed at the east end. He had every field in a rotation and all ploughed and seeded, wonderful. And he told me, "There's only one thing wrong with Coll, I cannot sleep at night for the bloody corncrakes." He had turbo mowers; he had silage in about 20 June; he had two cuts of silage; he was working the place better than a mainland farm. That man left Coll, now there's no reseeding, no ploughing, nothing. The corncrakes have died out.'

'Why's that?'

'Because the ground's not getting worked. Now there's old grass, weeds, lack of insects, there's no dung getting spread on the ground. The other major contributory factor that I see is vermin. You're no longer allowed to poison hoodies, black-backs [seagulls] and so on. They had a gamekeeper on Coll 30 years ago, the last gamekeeper here, and there wasn't a hoodie on Coll. Over the last 30 years the hoodies have multiplied and the corncrakes died out. The vermin have got to live on something.'

'I suppose so.'

'I'll give you another scenario, down at my own place,' Colin said. 'There's been no corncrakes there for the last number of years, since we had stopped putting in corn. I put in a field of corn and this year there was a corncrake there. It's no RSPB management, no late cutting. It's just a field of corn. Go to Tiree what have you got? Corncrakes in the corn. Maybe that's got nothing to do with it, but it strikes me that they were called corncrakes because they were found in corn.'

'But down in England they grow corn all over the place,' I said, 'Why are there no corncrakes left there?'

'Because there'll probably not be enough habitat alongside the corn. It'll be corn, corn, corn and corn forever and they're spraying it with pesticides. There's not a field down there that's not sprayed with pesticides.'

'So you were not spraying your field?'

'No, not a drop of spray went onto the field, and I think you'll find the same on Tiree. But spray, and everything's killed out. There's no weeds with seeds on them in the fields in England. So I would say it's lack of feeding and the pesticides. And the other thing here is they're shutting off fields in January for birds nesting, but in my younger days there were fields with dung spread all winter, and the grass would be that high and those bloody birds were living in the dung, getting hay seeds out of it when they landed here. Nowadays there's nothing. Where are they going to land?'

Though on Totronald the corncrake is, as on Oronsay, the 'target species', the

RSPB's literature also mentions the 'incredible richness of flowers . . . on the machair several hundred species of flowering plant have been identified.' Colin is no botanist, but I still thought it worth asking him about the flowers.

'The RSPB are on here about what they're doing and their achievements,' he said, 'but two years ago, I jumped off the tractor in that field over there, the day before the Coll Show, and gathered pushing 60 species of flowers, all kinds: it was a wonderful scenery of flowers. There was half the flowers last year, and this year there isn't a flower to be seen.'

'Why's that?'

'Well I think they've got the whole damn thing wrong. This shutting the place up and keeping all the sheep off the ground for the whole summer is choking things out. And they're not grazing it off properly in the winter time so there's old matted grass. Two years ago that place had been grazed to buggery and the flowers just peaked. Now they're not grazing it hard enough and they're not allowing the weaker plants to come through. The grass is just killing them out. But they won't agree with that. They say they've got the balance right. It's found its own level. Well it's found its own level, and that's nothing.' Colin snorted in disgust, roared at his collies and adjusted his cap. 'So for the benefit of the corncrake the flowers have gone. They don't give two hoots about the plants and flowers here, it's the corncrake. But out in my territory, where it's just machair and there's no arable fields with corncrakes, it's flowers. "We want the flowers." They want the best of both worlds. Here the flowers don't matter. Out there my sheep don't matter.'

Finally I asked Colin about the broader picture. What did he think was the overall effect of the RSPB's ownership of Totronald?

'The place is going backwards,' he said. 'This is the best bit of the island by a mile. The rest is a wilderness. They are just ruining the island. Without the farming the ferries will be fewer, and the services on the island will be less. I think the day may well come, if their funds allow it, that Coll will end up like Rum. There'll be nobody left.'

On the bike again, I started heading back towards Arinagour. The breeze was behind me and the sun at its hottest. In shirt-sleeve weather, the Hebrides must be the most beautiful place on earth. It was early afternoon and all nature, including the people, seemed to be asleep. I had the world to myself. My last call was on a Mrs Pat Graham, a middle-aged English lady who, after her husband had been made redundant from a job in Luton, had bought 24 acres of the Stewart estate at the 1991 sale. Pat is a keen birder, having kept detailed records all her adult life. Though a Life Member of the RSPB since the early 1970s, she has become very disenchanted with the Society since watching their performance on Coll.

She runs a bed and breakfast operation at the Garden House, while her husband farms in a small way. We sat in her sunlit sitting room while I lunched hungrily but gratefully on a mug of coffee and two plates of biscuits. 'I first got involved with the RSPB when I was very young,' Pat told me, 'in Buckinghamshire where

I was brought up. We had great crested grebes on some local gravel pits which developers wanted to fill in. The RSPB fought to get these birds saved, and I supported them. I still support their principles, but I sometimes get angry when I think about how they have changed.'

'How do you see them now?' I asked.

'The RSPB's principles are wonderful; they are brilliant. But somehow or other, they have turned into an elitist organisation where politically – and it is a big political banner they are now holding – they now say, "We will not be argued with. We will not be countermanded. We will not be criticised." Members cannot go back to the RSPB and say, now look, we don't like what you are doing. They're not interested. We've been to the offices in Glasgow: they don't want to know. They're all in a little clique of their own. I think it's sinister, very sinister. That's the best word I can use for it. They seem to say, only we know about birds. We are the experts. You, the general public, know nothing.'

'That's because you haven't got a penetrometer,' I said.

'How do you know I haven't got a penetrometer?' Pat said, with a mock leer.

I asked what in particular had caused her to change her mind. Maltreatment of corncrakes was her surprising answer.

'The corncrake is a very shy bird,' she said, 'and for the first three years this warden was in, that bird was actually hounded. It was picked up. It was weighed. It was ringed. It had a radio tracking device put on it. The noise the direction-finding device makes is deafening if you happen to get it pointing at you. Everywhere the poor little thing went it was followed. They're very keen on publicising themselves, so they had television cameras down here filming them, with lights and noise. They had researchers down looking at them. It was terrible.'

It got worse. Pat told me that she, like some other people on the island, believe that the RSPB has been uplifting corncrakes and moving them around to make the numbers look good in support of their claim that they know what sort of habitat the bird likes. Though it should be stressed that Pat has no facts to back up this suspicion, it is indicative of the animosity that the Society has created on Coll that some people believe this amazing allegation.

However, Pat did have facts to support another allegation. In 1993 she and her husband had applied for a Woodland Grant in order to plant 14 acres of their ground with 3500 trees, a carefully planned mixture of birch, maple, cherry, hazel, hawthorn, beech, walnut, juniper, crab apple, poplar, oak, willow, elder, rowan, holly, ash, hornbeam and wild pear. This would be the most diversified and species-rich plantation on the island. However, Pat had the RSPB as a neigh-bour and it objected to the plan. David Sexton, the Reserves Manager, wrote to Pat saying that it had done so because of the presence of a corncrake in the area:

> the conservation benefits of the woodland scheme would be outweighed by the loss of the area for corncrakes . . . It looks like 'Shorty' [the corncrake] did actually use the whole area. The various bleeps from his radio transmitter showed that he foraged down the whole length of that piece of ground . . . If only corncrakes used woodland on a regular and long-term basis they would be much better off!

Unfortunately, a young woodland – even a native one – develops into a habitat that corncrakes cannot utilise.[2]

Pat was shocked, but in a way not surprised, to learn from SNH a few years later that 'research in Poland has shown that corncrakes utilise woodland edges as early cover areas.' But by then her grant application had been formally refused.

Back in Arinagour, Loch Eatharna was like a mill-pond. I dined aboard ship and then went ashore to see Robert Sturgeon, a Collach who had grown up on the island but spent most of his adult life working abroad as an agricultural adviser, mainly in Africa. Some years ago he retired and now runs a guest-house overlooking the harbour.

Robert is a prominent campaigner against what might be called the conservationisation of the island. I asked him who the main culprits were. 'Scottish Natural Heritage,' he said. 'They more or less do what they like. They make arrangements with farmers and the next thing you find that where you've walked for years you can't reach because the bloody place is covered with fences and barbed wire. I think this is wrong. People have been living in these parts for years. I don't know why this sort of thing is creeping in. They're treating people with contempt. As you know, there are fairly hefty subsidies handed out. I think there should be more strings attached. For these people to try to impede the ratepayers and taxpayers of this country, to prevent them from getting to areas where they've been going for years, I think is quite wrong. Who pays the subsidies?'

'Does all this conservationism bring in the tourists?' I asked.

'Not very many, I would say, no. There are more people coming to use the beaches and do a bit of fishing than coming to see the birds. Anyway people have always come to this island to look at the birds. There's not been any great increase.'

Robert was saddened by the new confrontational atmosphere which has invaded Coll. 'This was always a very friendly island. I think in these parts we should attempt to work together as we did years ago. We should try to retain some of the customs that are being pushed out. The way of life is one of the main reasons that people have come from outside to settle here. I can't see the justification for people coming here and then, some of them at least, trying to impose a way of life that they are used to where they came from. It defeats the whole object.'

After offering me a dram, Robert presented me with two interesting paradoxes. The first concerned the housing. When he was a boy every house was lived in, but many of them were not really what we would now consider habitable. Public

---

2 10 November 1993. In fact some of the corncrakes on Coll call from the woodland around Arinagour, though the RSPB does not publicise this fact. The shallowness of the RSPB's knowledge of this bird is illustrated by the fact that the great Russian writer, Sergei Aksakov, wrote in *Notes of a Provincial Wildfowler*, published in 1852, that 'The corncrake is equally at home in the steppe, amid grain crops, wet pastures and *at the edges of forests*'.

money was spent on council housing and private money on converting many of the old houses into comfortable holiday homes for owners who live on the mainland. As a result the situation has changed from one in which the houses in the island's main street were uninhabitable but inhabited, to one in which they are habitable but uninhabited.

Looking out over the sunlit harbour, with the boats swinging idly on their moorings in the evening calm, Robert went on to put a second paradox to me: the sad story of the demise of the once-famous Coll cheese. Apparently this was such a delicacy that, up until the Second World War, it was a permanent feature on the menu in the dining rooms of both Houses of Parliament in London. Most of the farms on the island produced milk which a substantial force of workers converted into cheese. McLelland's in Glasgow were the agents and they sold the product worldwide. In modern marketing terminology, it was a brand with substantial equity.

But cheese-making is a labour intensive activity, and in the bright new world of the late 1940s, that was considered a Bad Thing. Industrial production was the new Grail and labour was needed in the cities. The politicians in London decided that the subsidy which had hitherto gone to the cheese-making should be transferred to the production of beef and mutton, both of which needed far less labour. The cheese-making stopped and large numbers of people had to leave their island, many of them going to the Central Belt, to find the work which paid for the holiday homes they own in the main street. In little more than a decade the island lost a quarter of its population.

Then, just as the shakeout had been completed, the government in London decided it had to do something about rural depopulation. In the mid-1960s the Highlands and Islands Development Board was founded. The HIDB, as it was known, was given the brief of subsidising the start-up of enterprises which would export from this area to the wider world outside. From aluminium smelters to fishing boats, money was poured into the Highlands. By the 1980s the smelters had gone bust and the owners of many of the fishing boats were being paid yet more money to take their vessels out of commission. The buzz phrase was now 'adding value' to local resources. Instead of just producing commodities, the aim was to process them in their place of origin. Salmon were no longer just caught in the Hebrides, they were cured there too in government-funded smokehouses. Milk was no longer shipped to the mainland, it was made into butter and, yes, cheese in government-funded creameries.

But few of these enterprises showed signs of fledging financially, so the HIDB started pouring money into 'marketing initiatives', paying for attendance at international trade fairs and the like. Grants were available for the design of logos and for attendance at Total Quality Management seminars. The aim was to promote Scottish merchandise as a 'quality product', or, in marketing terminology, to create brand equity, just what had been destroyed by the bright ideas of the 1940s. Today government subsidy policies are devised, in effect, to undo the damage done by previous government subsidy policies.

Next morning, Friday, was the Coll Show. I had decided to stay for this and leave on Saturday. If the Islay Show is anything to go on, I thought, this will be good fun. Also I hoped to catch up with the RSPB Land Rover driver – the warden was on holiday – to give him an opportunity to answer some of the criticisms which had been made of his organisation. I had phoned the office perhaps a dozen times over the past couple of days but the phone had never been answered. Twice I left a message asking whoever was manning the office to look out for me at the Show.

On my way up to the field where the Show was to be held, I called in at the Coll teleservice centre to get some photocopying done. Teleservice centres, or telecottages, are one of these new initiatives aimed at providing 'added value' employment in the Highlands. They have been tried widely (including on Islay) and the idea is that a computer, fax and photocopying bureau is established with public 'seed money', from which will grow an electronic revolution.

The Coll telecentre was housed in an unfriendly, modern-looking hut; I found a friendly but not quite so modern-looking man behind the counter. Sporting a beard and slightly frayed jeans he introduced himself as Martin Lunghi. A chatty Londoner, he said he had moved to Scotland many years ago to work in psychology and medical sociology at Edinburgh University. Subsequently, he had moved with his family to Coll to work a smallholding, but had divorced and now found himself living, penniless, in a caravan. He had two daughters, one of whom was away at college in the Borders and the other working in the Coll Hotel and desperate to get off the island. Martin told me he was equally keen to move, but found he was stuck here. 'It's a fairly common problem once you have sold a house on the mainland,' he said. He could not earn enough money to move anywhere he might be able to earn more money. His skills were not very marketable on Coll. 'Most people here are generalists; there is no scope for specialisation,' he said. 'A larger island like Mull is totally different. It has a micro-economy.'

I asked him what he had thought of Coll when he first arrived.

'You think islands are remote and have a very small population,' he said, 'but what you don't realise is that they have a very *cohesive* population. You get assimilated into it and become very much part of the community. Here everyone knows everyone else and everyone knows you. It is quite nice in a way, but if you're from the city, you miss the pleasures of anonymity.'

'Surely you expected that?'

'I'd lived in small communities before, but you could keep yourself to yourself a lot more.'

'Where was that?'

'Villages outside Edinburgh. You are in a small community but you have the option to leave it. I hadn't realised how pleasurable things like going off for a run in the car on Sunday afternoons were. Here I don't have that option to travel anymore. I miss that quite a lot.'

'Have you never thought of getting a boat?'

'It's the economy again, I can't afford it. You can only afford things like that if you've got a job on the mainland.'

I asked him what future he saw on Coll.

'This island only supports one full-time fisherman now. When you look at the future, the island will have to focus on tourism, or conceivably become a conservation area like Rum. Or it will just empty.'

'Like Rum.'

'Yeah.'

Not for the first time on this island, the subject of the RSPB came up. Although he said he was not a birder, Martin seemed keen to talk about the Society – actually I got the sense he was keen to talk about *anything* to somebody new. I asked what impact he thought they had had on the island.

'Apart from annoying a few people,' he said, 'they have been quite well received. Their arrival has coincided with a restriction of the freedom to roam which existed about ten years ago. At the same time a number of owners came to the island who have put up fences all over the place. You're getting this feeling of territoriality.'

'Do the RSPB contribute much to the community?'

'Not a lot, really The community does not benefit in a direct way from the use of the land like that. It's as if part of the island has been lopped off by a private owner and, though it is in principle accessible, it is not a lot of use to the islanders.'

'Why, because it is not farmed?'

'Yes, I suppose so. You know if somebody comes in and buys a new estate you think, oh there's going to be work there maybe, something's going to happen there, a business or a trade is going to be attempted and some sort of financial spin-off will occur. But a big purchase by the RSPB, or any similar body, does not seem to have similar implications, financially. We were trying to get a bit of business from the RSPB here at the telecentre, but really they are quite self-contained. They don't need anything that we have. You can imagine that if the east end of the island went the same way, there would be the feeling that there is less and less room for a vital working community. Perhaps there never will be a community like that here again. But it's managing just about to get along. People are coming in who are turning their hand to this and that. '

'Where do they tend to come from? Are they good-lifers from down south?'

'No, they come from Fife – good working stock.'

'Do you find as an English person there is any hostility to you?'

'Very little, it's a good island like that. It's a bit like Mull, very cosmopolitan.'

'Do you mean, there's lots of other English people?'

He laughed. 'I suppose so.'

I asked Martin what he liked about living on Coll. He told me how nice it is to greet and be greeted in the street, though he thought it wasted a lot of time, and he had got tired of 'the banality of day-to-day clichés'. Then he went off at a tangent. 'One thing a number of people have commented on is that when you go to the mainland, or even across to Mull, you come back feeling emboldened, in other words you come back with ideas, things that occurred to you, things people have suggested to you and you come back feeling quite excited, thinking oh, that's possible, or, isn't that great, then you start sinking into the miasma of being back here again. There tends to be a resistance to innovation here, a feeling of automatic mild antagonism, very little interest in supporting new ideas. Not even in supporting this centre.'

Once again, I asked, 'What would you say you enjoy most about Coll?'

He thought hard, then said, 'One of the advantages which I have come to like is that people have confidence in you, in a way that they don't on the mainland. It's quite flattering, you feel more significant. But at the same time, I have to say, nobody acknowledges you for any training you've got or background experience you've had. Nobody has ever asked me about, nor expressed the slightest interest in, what I've done in the past. So when you come into a community like this you've got to start from the bottom again, and establish yourself. You can't bring in your past achievements, or status or interests. It's not relevant here. My own background in counselling and psychotherapy isn't relevant here. For a start there is no confidentiality on this island – except for financial matters, of course.'

'What would you say is the worst thing about Coll?'

'The sameness of the community, the feeling of small-mindedness, which is affecting me so that I feel I am becoming more parochial, narrow in outlook, less ambitious; the horrible feeling that time is passing and I'm going to get stuck here for the rest of my life: that's a little bit frightening.'

I paid for my photocopying, which included the *Coll Magazine* cutting about Self's 3000 grass-height measurements. I had another Selvian gem, this time from the 1995 edition:

> Corncrakes are the reason the RSPB is on Coll [the warden wrote]. They have spin-off benefits. Coll and its corncrakes have been featured on TV, radio and a dozen or more newspapers and magazines from *The Times* to *Woman and Home*. Even Dorito's Corn Chips, the product that will revolutionise the UK's snacking habits, burst onto the market place in an imaginative PR surge on Coll. 'Corn Chips for Corncrakes' was the punchy slogan, grinning wardens accepting packets of product for a photo-opportunity and a live radio link-up was beamed through the ethers (*sic*) to Radio Leicester.

By the time I got up to the Show, the sheep judging was in full swing. I had a dram with a Mrs Kirsty Macleod whose family have a large croft at the east end of the island. Though she now lives and farms in Inverness-shire, Kirsty is in close and continuous contact with Coll. She took the opportunity of rehearsing an argument which I had not heard before, namely that the RSPB and SNH should be looked at together as far as the designation of land of so-called conservation value is concerned.

Donnie Campbell on Tiree had emphasised that, for an activist pressure group and a supposedly independent government quango, the RSPB and SNH have a suspiciously close relationship. What might the reason for this be? Kirsty's answer was that the RSPB benefits when SNH imposes restrictive designations, like

Sites of Special Scientific Interest (SSSI), on ground the Society might one day want to buy. Any such designation reduces the landowner's freedom of operation and therefore reduces the value of the land. It also makes it more likely to come on the market since over-designated ground has limited attractions for conventional landusers. Kirsty believes the RSPB has its eyes on the east end of Coll and is encouraging its designation by SNH. If she is right, this is a form of bureaucratic corruption which ought to be addressed at the highest level. She laughed cynically when I suggested this process might be described as a 'protection racket'.

After the livestock judging, there were games, races and a mini-marathon, all to the background noise of a well-filled beer tent and a non-stop barbecue. There was a large produce, flower and art show in the hall, which was packed for the prize-giving at four o'clock. Despite the crowds, I never caught sight of my friend with the penetrometer. I did, however, catch a glimpse of the Major and noticed, to my surprise, that he was wearing trousers: could there have been a connection?

Saturday dawned grey and blowy. There were gaps in the cloud but the forecast was not for sunny weather. There was a stiff breeze blowing from the south-west and it seemed like time to weigh anchor and lay a course for Rum. Distance-wise, there was no hurry, as it is no more than 30 miles, or seven hours' sailing with a fair wind. I ate a monster breakfast and then, at about 10.30, hoisted sail. In a brief period of sunshine, *Sylvia B* raced briskly down the loch. We tacked close under the CalMac pier, while passengers disembarking from the Oban ferry waved. In a flurry of hands and sheets, I waved back while settling the boat on its new heading. Then we stood out to sea. Directly ahead, though as yet invisible in the thickish weather, was the precipitous mass of what used to be called the Forbidden Island.

4

RUM

Symbolically, the key to the mystery of the 'Forbidden Island' of Rum lies in the orgy room in Kinloch Castle. Nominally a ballroom, it is where Sir George Bullough and his gang of Edwardian ex-army high-lifers indulged the fantasies that they used to keep boredom at bay. As ballrooms go it is not exceptionally large, though it is well equipped. It has a sprung floor and an enormous crystal chandelier. Between the white-painted wood panelling and the white, neo-Jacobean plasterwork of the ceiling, the walls are covered in gold damask. The effect should be light and airy, but it is not. The room has a curiously cooped-in feeling, deriving partly from the fact that the few windows are all set high in the walls, deliberately so in order that the servants could not look in. For the same reason, the only access from the staff side of the castle is through a serving hatch, possibly three foot square, which itself was hidden by a screen. More bizarrely still, the minstrels' gallery is laid out like an elevated stage with curtains which were usually drawn: the dancers should not be subject to the vulgar gaze.

The fascination of Kinloch Castle derives partly from the fact that when the Bulloughs got bored of it, they simply shut up the house and walked away. Everything was left untouched. There was wine in the cellars, estate papers on Sir George's desk, and the instruments of his private orchestra lying beside the chairs in the minstrels' gallery. They are still there, just as they were left after the last dance of the last ball held by the last laird of Rum. The castle is a time-warp.

The Isle of Rum is now the property of the people of Scotland, being owned by Scottish Natural Heritage in perpetuity. It is a vast museum to the follies and failures of human management of the Highlands. The whole history of Rum is interesting, though by far the most colourful period was the 71 years it was in the hands of the Bulloughs of Accrington. Accrington is a small mill town in north-west England where the first and second generations of the family made a fortune as machine builders for the cotton-spinning industry. The island was one of the private playgrounds bought by the second generation, and enjoyed by the third. There was no fourth.

Rum contains one of the oldest known sites of human habitation in Scotland. Dating from 6000 BC, it is situated on the slope which overlooks Kinloch Castle to the north. More recent finds suggest continuous occupation since that time, though never in great numbers as the island has very little fertile ground. When it was advertised in 1886 Messrs Watson Lyall described it thus: 'The extent is about 27,000 acres, of which about 300 are arable, 150 acres lochs and rivers, 530 acres foreshore and 26,000 forest and moorland.' In this context 'forest' does not imply the presence of trees, of which there were hardly any, but deer forest: hill and moorland. It was not always so bare. The *Old Statistical Account* (written in the 1790s) notes,

> In Rum there were formerly great numbers of deer; there was also a copse of wood that afforded cover to their fawn from birds of prey, particularly from the eagle. While the wood throve, the deer also throve; now the wood is totally destroyed, the deer are totally extirpated.

The mountains on Rum are among the highest in the Hebrides, exceeded only by Ben More on Mull and the black Cuillin on Skye. The names of the places around the coast are Gaelic, but the peaks all have evocative Norse names: Barkeval, Hallival, Askival, Ainslival, Ruinsival, Trollaval. 'Val' was the Norse for hill, from which the English word 'fell' is derived. This seems to have been due to their height: the Vikings being seafarers, such prominent navigational reference points would have been very important to them.

After the forfeiture of the Lordship of the Isles, Rum belonged, first, to Clanranald and then to the Macleans of Coll who forced a mass conversion of the inhabitants to Protestantism. There are several extant accounts of this event. In 1771 Reverend Walker gave this version:

> The Inhabitants of Rum adhered strictly to the Popish Religion till about the beginning of this Century, when, in one Day, they were all converted from Popery. Maclean of Coll, their Chieftain, being himself a Protestant, insisted that they should renounce the Roman Catholick Religion. He came to the island with a Protestant Minister, and ordered all the people to appear at a certain Place, on Sunday, at publick Worship. They came to the Place, but refused to go into the House where the Protestant Service was to be administered. The Chieftain reasoned with them, but they became more Refractory. At last, he seized the most resolute Man among them, and having drubbed him heartily with his Cane, drove him into the House. Upon this, they all followed, without any further Opposition and so the Reformation of this Island was accomplished. From that Day, they have ever since continued staunch Protestants. Their neighbours, however, in the Popish Islands of Eigg and Canna, still continue to call the Protestantism of Rum *Credivk Chall Vuy*, that is, the Faith of the Yellow Stick.[1]

In the early nineteenth century, the island was let to one of the laird's cousins, a Dr Lachlan Maclean, who thereby acquired the right of disposal, or dispersal, over the inhabitants. Maclean realised that he could increase the island's rental value from £300 per annum to £800 by substituting sheep for people. The only expense in doing so would be the passage money to Canada. At £5/14/– per adult, the total came to about £500. As this was the difference between the old and the new rental values for the island, the investment required to destroy the indigenous community would be recouped in the first year: thereafter it was pure profit for Dr Maclean. In all about 400 souls were forcibly depatriated in

---

1   *Report* on *the Hebrides of 1764 and 1771*, by Reverend Dr John Walker, *op. cit.*, p.197. I am informed by Mrs Kirsty Macleod that the correct Gaelic for 'Faith of the Yellowstick' is Creidamh a' bhata bhuidhe.

order to make way for 8000 blackface sheep. In Canada, North American Indians were pushed off their land to make room for the palefaces who had arrived in order to make room for blackfaces.

But there were red faces on Rum when Maclean realised that the only family he had allowed to remain on the island were totally incapable of herding all 8000 sheep by themselves. Modern hill-farmers, utilising motorised off-road equipment, consider a ratio of one man to 800 ewes about the realistic maximum. Dr Maclean soon found he had to import people to replace those he had evicted. Over 100 souls, who were being evicted by their own lairds on Skye and Mull, were settled on Rum in the 1830s.

This was the start of the period which the current Reserve Manager, Martin Curry, described to me as one of 'incredibly intensive land punishment through sheep and deer'. The 8000 sheep quickly ate their way through the island's reserves of herbage, so numbers had to be cut. The total was down to 5000 within 20 years. Soon, this proved to be too much for the increasingly exhausted land to support. The only remaining way for Maclean to extract cash from the ground was to sell it to someone who might want to use it as an adventure playground. Thus in 1845, Rum was sold to a sportsman, James Brownlow Gascoyne-Cecil, 2nd Marquis of Salisbury.[2]

Though he retained most of the sheep, Salisbury reintroduced deer to the island. He also tried to improve the fishing by increasing the flow of water in the Kinloch burn. In this he was none too successful. He built a dam on the Kilmory burn with the idea of diverting some of the flow down to Kinloch. The dam took two years to construct, but stood for only two days after filling up. The not unusual occurrence of a heavy fall of rain brought the burn down in spate and burst the wall, the ruins of which can be seen to this day. The water which cascaded down to the sea at Kilmory gorged out a gully so deep that it permanently altered the course of that stream.

Later, another attempt was made to improve the fishing by diverting the flow of the Harris burn, through construction of an aqueduct from the Long Loch, on the saddle of the island, into the Kinloch burn. Once again, the project did more harm than good. The water now flowed so fast that much of the gravel in the river-bed was washed away, and the spawning grounds for the salmon were ruined.

Lord Salisbury had used local labour to build his dam, but when it was completed, there was little other employment for many of them. Those people on the island who were not either shepherds, ghillies or domestic servants were left without any means of supporting themselves, Maclean having abolished all the original smallholdings. Salisbury hated the sight of paupers, so in 1852 he organised another forced depatriation which brought the population down to a more manageable 70 or so, an adequate human reservoir, he felt, for his foreseeable staff requirements. To protect his sporting interests Salisbury closed the island to outsiders.

---

2 He had been born James Brownlow Cecil, but had extended his name in 1821 after marrying the daughter of a Mr Bamber Gascoyne.

Lord Salisbury died in 1868 and his son, the 3rd Marquis and future Conservative Prime Minster, had no use for Rum. He was an ambitious politician who had already tasted power as Secretary of State for India in Disraeli's short-lived administration of 1867-8. He had bigger fish to fry than the few remaining salmon in the Kinloch burn. In 1869 he sold the island to Mr John Campbell of Ormsary. Campbell used the island as a sheep farm and let out the sporting rights. From 1885, the tenant was one John Bullough (pronounced 'Boolla') from Accrington, who bought the island three years later.

Bullough was by then married to the daughter of a Stornoway banker and infected with a romantic view of Rum. He wrote innumerable poems about the island. These are the opening and closing stanzas of one of them:

Is't the home of giants hoary,
As we read of in child's story,
Giants of such dread and wonder
Glancing lightning and speaking thunder,
Whose elves from caves and corries swarm
To torment men who've done no harm?

No! When city life we're freed from,
And we learn to live in freedom,
'Tis no giant monster frights us
But old Nature that delights us.
. . .

And year by year, as round we come
To greet our grand old Father Rum,
He'll o'er and o'er renew his blessing,
Well pleased to see us to him pressing.

Astonishingly, the man who composed this childish doggerel was one of the foremost industrialists of England. John's father, James Bullough, was a clog-wearing Lancastrian who had started work at the age of seven in a cotton-spinning mill. James was endowed with gifts for both mechanical engineering and business. He invented so many labour-saving devices for cotton-spinning that he was run out of Blackburn by enraged workers who claimed he was destroying their jobs. In 1856 he set up in Accrington in partnership with John Howard. It was not long before Howard and Bullough, of the Globe Works, was one of the largest loom manufacturing companies in Britain. It is said that, despite the change from cloth cap to top hat, James Bullough continued to wear clogs – ostentatiously painted ones, admittedly – until the day he died.

James educated his son, John, at a Quaker school in Hampshire and at Glasgow University. John was, if anything, more gifted than his father and built the firm up until in 1891, when he died, it was the world's largest producer of ring-spinning frames. He took an active interest in politics, making innumerable speeches on behalf of the Conservative Party, though without any public reward, at least not in the form he craved: a knighthood. As was fashionable at the time, Bullough had a very contemptuous view of crofters. He expressed his views in a letter to *The Times* in 1888, two years after the passage of the Crofters Act: 'The well-clad, well-fed, pampered crofter continues to loaf away his time while his wife does the work, reserving his small stock of energy for attacks on his neighbour's property and demonstrations against the officers of the law . . . It would be well for the country if we had less of [them].'

At his death, John Bullough's estate was valued for probate at nearly £2.5 million (possibly £200 million today), making him one of the dozen or so richest men in the kingdom. Appropriately, he had sent his son, George, not to a Quaker academy, but to Harrow. With that, the family gift for making money died, to be replaced by a remarkable talent for spending it. For most of his adult life, George occupied the post of chairman of Howard and Bullough with handsome grace and little else. Apart from a brief flourish as an arms manufacturer in the First World War, Howard and Bullough slowly sank into oblivion, finally being sold in the 1960s to Messrs Mather & Platt, who closed the Globe Works.

George seems to have grown up a rather unhappy boy. He was tyrannised by his successful and domineering father who divorced his mother – a Swiss lady he had 'got into trouble' – in very acrimonious circumstances, banishing her from the estate for life. George never afterwards managed to form a contented, long-term relationship with a woman, though he is said, as a teenager, to have had a protracted affair with his Scottish stepmother.

George devoted much of his life to ensuring that the world at large paid attention to him. Like Fraser Darling who had no father at all, George developed an outsize ego which demanded satisfaction of its various desires. But these desires were very different from those of the seer of Tannera. No tiny houses on remote islands for him! At the age of 21, George bought himself a 221-foot twin-screw, steam-powered yacht, the *Rhouma,* which was one of the largest and most luxuriously equipped of its type in the world. He then rounded up a gang of boon companions, hired an orchestra, and set off on a two-year round-the-world cruise.

Out east, George spent money like water, on one occasion even outbidding the Japanese Emperor for an ivory eagle the Mikado especially coveted. Today the eagle reposes in the Royal Museum in Edinburgh, but visitors to Kinloch Castle can see a good substitute: a monumental Japanese bronze study of an eagle, its wings outstretched, cast with monkeys clambering on an ivy-covered gnarled wood stump – to quote the inventory prepared by Phillips in 1992 (they valued the piece at £120,000). Another acquisition, which reposes today in George's study, is a bound collection of photographs of oriental torture victims. Chinese coolies being trussed, whipped and beaten in a variety of situations provide the context for the star attraction, a series of close-up pictures of a beheading. It is gruesome stuff. The only consolation for the tender-hearted is that, unlike Fraser Darling and his seals, George did not go so far as to eat the objects of his morbid curiosity.

Back in Britain, George found that he was not treated with the deference he had become accustomed to on his travels. Lord Salisbury, the former owner of Rum, was Prime Minister and engaged in the last serious campaign in British history by old, landed money to put new, industrial money in its place. Lord Salisbury was one of the richest of the old-style peers. When he died in 1903 he left a personal fortune of £300,000, a vast sum in those days, but less than an eighth of John Bullough's. Like his father, George Bullough hoped for a knighthood. But Lord Salisbury was dead set against the proliferation of titles, remarking late in life that in London 'you cannot throw a stone at a dog without hitting a knight.' With no hope for a political honour, George appears to have set his sights on Royal patronage. At any rate, he decided he would build a huge, ostentatious house on Rum where he would be able to entertain the future King Edward VII and his circle.

George commissioned Leeming and Leeming, the fashionable London architects who had recently built an extension to the Admiralty, to produce a design. The end result was a two-storey, mock-Tudor structure, on a square plan, surrounding a large courtyard. At each corner there are turrets and a taller turret is set off-centre in the east front. From this yet another turret, higher and thinner, is corbelled out on the south-east side. The tops of all the walls are castellated, as are all the turrets. On three sides, the ground floor is surrounded by a verandah. This, too, is castellated. Externally, the effect is of unrelieved frivolity.

Inside, the keynote was convenience. The house is full of gadgets, some ludicrous to modern eyes, like the orchestrion which is said to be the only functioning one left in Britain. Others were more practical. There was a telephone intercom system, central heating, and an electricity supply driven by a mini-hydro-electric generator, all of them very innovative in their day. Even the plumbing had its features, notably a shower in George's bathroom which blasted jets of water at all angles to the body, including one shooting directly up between the bather's legs. These gadget were so expensively specified that they are all in full working order today, nearly a century later. Both the shower and the orchestrion are regularly demonstrated to visitors.

The whole edifice is set upon thousands of tons of soil which was transported from Ayrshire. It was built with almost as great a weight of red sandstone which was shipped in from Arran. The construction labour was brought from Lancashire. (The men were given an additional daily allowance for wearing kilts when visible to the laird.) Outside there was an aviary with humming-birds, a heated turtle pool – it may have been a mock-Tudor building, but George liked real turtle soup – an alligator pit and a nine-hole golf course. There was also a squash court complete with a gallery from which the staff, who were commanded to attend when the laird was playing, could watch and applaud whenever Himself hit a sizzling winner down the side wall.

The whole ensemble cost about £250,000 – close to £20 million at current prices. According to the SNH guide, the building was utilised for about five weeks a year for 12 years, between its completion in 1901 and the outbreak of war in 1914. After the war, it was used even more rarely, and much less grandly, for about ten years until 1929 when it was shut up. Thus the Bulloughs got little more than a hundred weeks' use from the house. This works out at about £2500 – approaching £200,000 at today's prices – per week for the building alone. On top of that the staff costs were vast. The estate employed about 40 people, most of them on the payroll for 12 months of the year. Fourteen gardeners, for example, were needed to tend the ornamental gardens, the huge walled vegetable garden, the greenhouses, the orchards and the golf course.

Kinloch Castle was a perfectly absurd establishment. But then it was conceived for a perfectly absurd purpose: to give a boost to the social ambitions of an emotionally dysfunctional, unemployed millionaire bachelor. In its own terms, though, it seems to have worked. King Edward VII enjoyed the rackety society he met on Rum and visited regularly.

The SNH guide who conducted me round the house told me how George Bullough finally acquired a title. In 1906 King Edward asked George to help him with a ticklish matter: he, the King, was about to be cited as respondent in a divorce case and he needed help. The deal was that if George agreed to marry the woman concerned, an illegitimately pregnant French aristocrat, and the scandal was thereby diverted from the royal family, the King would see to it that his friend's loyalty did not go unrewarded. In due course a baby girl was born and George Bullough created a baronet: the implication of royal corruption, though unstated by my guide, was obvious.

I checked up on this colourful story after getting back from the trip. In fact, it was nonsense. George Bullough was knighted in 1901 for having fitted out the *Rhouma* as a hospital ship and lending it to the government during the Boer War. He was married in 1903 and his only child, Hermione, was born in 1906. The knighthood was elevated to a baronetcy in 1916, six years after King Edward's death, in recognition of the war work done by his employees in Accrington. The implication of corruption cannot be sustained. SNH should stick to nature.

Sir George's marriage appears to have brought him little joy. Monica, being French, aristocratic and a Catholic, had little time for her husband's plutocratic Lancastrian philistinism. She is said to have bossed him about mercilessly and to have used his wealth for her own social advancement. This may well be so, as portraits of George show a gentle, almost sad-looking individual. The one in the great hall of the house, painted by Hugh Rivière in 1909, makes him look like Anthony Eden on a rainy Saturday when the tennis had been cancelled. The handsome but slightly weak-looking face has a limp, disappointed expression, as if gazing into an unappealing future.[3] Not much else happened in Sir George's life, apart from the commercial cancer in Accrington which weakened, and finally destroyed, his ability to use the castle. In 1933 he refused permission for a Mr Darling to use the island for deer research and in 1939, while on a golfing holiday in France, he died.

Lady Monica lived until 1967 and was buried alongside John and her husband in the other bizarre building on Rum: the mausoleum which George had built at Harris, on the south-west coast of the island. It is a huge, pseudo-Doric temple containing three enormous table tombs. John's is in red sandstone and Sir George's

---

3 According to Simon Green, the expert on the castle at the Ancient and Historic Monuments Commission, Sir George did not occupy the bedroom next to his wife's, as visitors are told, but lived separately in a self-contained apartment where the building manager now has his flat. It was Monica's side of the house which got the sunshine.

and Lady Monica's are in pink granite. For all his execrable verse, John clearly loved Rum. But his son and daughter-in-law seem not to have done. At any rate, as soon as their sojourns on the island lost their social purpose, they more or less stopped coming. So why did they choose to be buried on Rum?

One glimpse at the absurd edifice supplies the answer: egotism. John had himself buried in more modest accommodation in a tiled structure nearby, but when a guest said to the socially insecure Sir George that it looked like a public toilet, he had it dynamited, and the present one designed. In a cemetery in Accrington, or in London or Herefordshire or Newmarket, where Sir George had other houses, Doric temples, however vast and vulgar, do not stand out in the same way as they do at the top of Hebridean cliff-faces. The Rumachs may all have gone to ordinary graves, if any, in Canada, not one of them remembered by name on their native island, but the incomer, 'Sir George Bullough Bt of the Isle of Rhum',[4] to use the style on his tomb, will be remembered for as long as it takes the Atlantic westerlies to erode the quarter inch-deep incisions on the pink granite – a thousand years?

In 1957, Lady Monica made a partial act of restitution for what many would consider the theft of Rum from the Scottish people by selling the island, 'with all and singular houses, biggings, mills, woods, fishings, parts, pendicles, forests and pertinents', to the Nature Conservancy for the trivial sum of £23,000, less than £1 per acre. More than this, she gave Kinloch Castle and all its contents to the nation. If Lady Bullough had been as mercenary as the Duke of Argyll, she could have secured a much higher price for the island. Rum is as much a shrine for British nature worshippers as Iona is for Scottish Christians. It is also 12 times the size, has a huge castle, legendary sporting opportunities and not a single registered crofter. It is not known why Lady Bullough acted as she did, the only clue being her stipulation in the deed of gift that the island be used as a nature reserve 'in perpetuity'. Excluded from the sale were only the mausoleum, which stayed in the Bullough family, and the large stock of old madeira in the castle cellar, which was sold.

The conservation bureaucracy now had its chance. In his Foreword to *Rhum, the Natural History of an Island,* Dr Morton Boyd described the opportunity in the terms the new owners saw it.

> The vision of Rhum possessed by the founding fathers of nature conservation was the great outdoor laboratory and demonstration area, stemming from the original idea of Frank Fraser Darling . . . The purpose of the Rhum National Nature Reserve [is] based on high scientific ideals and endeavours and set upon a steady course of continuous evolution of the environment towards stated goals in nature conservation . . . Rhum is a symbol of the inspired optimism of the 1950s for the

---

4   The name is Gaelic and implies an enclosed space. Properly it is pronounced as in the English 'room'. The addition of 'h' as the second letter was an affectation of George's, imposed, according to Dr John Lorne Campbell, on the Post Office and Ordnance Survey in 1903. SNH officially changed their spelling to 'Rum' in 1991. The correct Gaelic, though, is Rùm.

future of nature conservation . . . Rhum is symbolic of a society conscious of its achievements in civilisation and enlightenment.[5]

The Nature Conservancy takeover of Rum attracted considerable public protest when it was realised that this public body intended to continue the 'closed island' policy which had been initiated by Lord Salisbury and reinforced by the Bulloughs. Max Nicholson, the Director-General of the Nature Conservancy, wrote in the 1957 Annual Report that as 'the primary purpose of the acquisition is scientific research' it would not be possible to permit public access. 'The work requires a permanent open-air laboratory, and scientists working in the open air need no less protection from avoidable interruption and disturbance than scientists working at a bench inside a building . . . Unless scientific research is adequately protected from interference the community will be deprived of the assistance which science can give in this field of human welfare.'[6] Nicholson told the *Glasgow Herald* that Parliament had given his organisation a job to do, 'to find out information about the vegetation and animal life of the island', and so Rum 'cannot be made into a hikers' playground'.[7] The grazing tenant on the island left, declaring he could not work alongside the conservationists. The protest grew and the *Herald* gave editorial authority to it, saying, 'The scientist must learn sooner or later to deal with the farmer and crofter as working partners.'[8] But in those days London could ignore Glasgow with impunity and Nicholson got his way. Rum remained the Forbidden Island. Science was given free rein.

Not only has Rum been a National Nature Reserve since 1957, it was also designated a Biosphere Reserve in 1976 by UNESCO. In 1978 the whole of the Small Isles, in which it is included, was designated a National Scenic Area by the Countryside Commission for Scotland (a body later subsumed into SNH). In 1982, Rum was designated a Special Protection Area under the European Community (EC) Wild Birds Directive. In 1987 it was notified by the NCC as a Site of Special Scientific Interest (SSSI). Most recently, it has been proposed as a Special Area of Conservation under the EC Habitats Directive and the sea area round about a Marine Nature Reserve. With so many acronyms and designations, the international wildlife bureaucracy clearly thinks Rum as important as Max Nicholson did. Is it?

I began by visiting Martin Curry, the Reserve Manager for SNH. Martin is a feral lawyer. He qualified as a solicitor in Cheshire, but soon discovered that the law was 'not my scene' and went into wildlife management. He worked in a variety of places in England before moving six years ago to Scotland and joining

---

5   *Rhum, the Natural History of an Island,* ed. T. M. Clutton-Brock and M. E. Ball, Edinburgh University Press, Edinburgh 1987, pp. viii–x. Dr Boyd wrote *Fraser Darling's Islands,* as quoted above, and co-wrote, with Fraser Darling, *The Highlands and Islands.* Until his retirement in 1985, he was Director of the Nature Conservancy Council in Scotland.

6   *Eighth Annual Report of the Nature Conservancy* HMSO, London 1957, p. 50, 51.

7   *Glasgow Herald* 5 April 1957.

8   *Ibid.,* 29 November 1957.

SNH. A tall, tousle-haired man, he was initially very guarded – 'Why do you want all this information?' Answer: 'You are a public body and in my view have a duty to disclose it to serious inquirers.' But he gradually opened up, finally permitting me the pleasure of a look at the small historical archive in his care, on which I have drawn for my account of the Bullough period. I asked two main questions: what has been achieved on the island after 40 years of serious scientific research, and how much has it all cost?

The broad answer to the first was increased knowledge of trees and deer. Starting with the trees, Martin said, 'All the research was aimed at the final end of restoring the productivity of the island in a way which would represent the more natural landscape the island once possessed.'

'What do you mean by "productivity"?'

'I mean ecological productivity. "Biodiversity" is the word these days. We know that Rum supported a greater variety of vertical structure – trees – than it does now. Up to 22 different species have been identified by pollen analysis. The ground is now becoming more productive again, because of chemical change in the soil under the new woodlands. There are also physical improvements in terms of ground-dwelling invertebrates, free-flying invertebrates, bird populations, floristic qualities. What happened when the trees had been removed was that, because there is so much rainfall here, any mineral content in the soil was just washed away.'

'Once you have demonstrated that you can improve the quality of the soil by the methods you have used here, in other words, once your experiment has worked,' I asked, 'is it the intention of SNH to use that as evidence to persuade other Highland landowners that they should make similar improvements?'

'No,' Martin said quite emphatically. 'I don't think we should be seen to be mounting a crusade to get the whole of the Highlands in a totally natural, pristine state. What we do say is that in a whole range of ways, of which the National Nature Reserve is only one, we are seeking wise and sustainable use of the land.'

'What does "sustainable" mean in a context like this?'

'Thou shalt not deplete the land and its quality.'

'But you make nothing out of it; you take nothing out of it; you're not farming the place.'

'It's a sustainable environment.'

Changing tack, I asked at what point in history the environment on Rum had been in the 'totally natural and pristine state' he referred to. Was it 15,000 years ago when the island was covered by ice? Was it the brief period between the retreat of the ice and the advance of people? Or was it 50 million years ago when the island was covered in molten lava when the volcano, which threw up the mountains we see today, was active? Which one of these was SNH trying to recreate?

'You can't put it in a point in time, 500 years ago, 10,000 years ago,' Martin said. 'We have to allow modern environmental factors to take a very large hand. Each ecosystem has a climax and it is a climax vegetation that we are looking for here on Rum. Everything which is capable of growing here and which is relevant to growing here and which would have been here in the inventory has the opportunity to find its niche again.

'Having said that,' he went on, 'my own view is that we will always want to temper that with a form of land management to *prevent* it happening because my own view is that conservation is largely defined by the sculpting of the land by humans. Here on Rum, for instance, we know that we have herb-rich grasslands and they are very largely the result of intensive cultivation. I would not want to see trees overgrowing those sorts of areas, and so we should manage those areas by herbivores to ensure that the trees don't grow.'

In fact, on most of Rum, trees don't stand a chance because of the 1500-odd red deer. They are the other great experimental project, mostly under the aegis of Dr Tim Clutton-Brock from Cambridge University.

'The purpose of the deer research is to contribute to knowledge about the best way of managing red deer in Scotland,' Curry told me.

'What has been achieved in this regard?' I asked.

'We have established culling regimes, the knowledge of the behaviour of individual species, the relationships, the movements, the vegetation demands – a whole range of pure research so that the red deer is one of the best studied large mammals in the world.'

'What's the use of that, given that the red deer is not a commercially significant resource? Your research presumably doesn't help the sporting interest?'

'It does,' Martin said. 'Everybody is driving towards a reduction of deer numbers. We want to show that numbers can be reduced without detriment to the perceptions of the landowners and the deer managers.'

'But surely that it is common knowledge to any half-decent stalker?'

'It needs proving in scientific terms.'

'Why?'

'It depends who you are trying to convince. If you're going to try to convince politicians, they are going to want something more formal.'

'So you see the main market for your research as politicians and bureaucrats?'

'Recently our research has been geared towards red deer management, to show that you can retain productivity with fewer numbers of animals, because that is not what people believe.'

'But that matters only to landowners,' I said.

Martin did not disagree. The amazing conclusion must be that SNH is spending public money on deer research in order to convince politicians to persuade sporting landowners, through the Red Deer Commission, to act in their own best interests – and it is doing so only because some lairds do not listen to their more experienced stalkers. Surely it should be private bodies, the Game Conservancy for example, rather than publicly-funded ones like SNH, that should be shouldering the burden of educating stubborn landowners in the best ways of enjoying themselves?

I asked Martin if there were any other significant research achievements on Rum. He mentioned geology, but I ignored that as it is not necessary to have all the bureaucratic paraphernalia of a National Nature Reserve to conduct geological research. The only other programme he could point to which was dependent on the SNH management of Rum was the reintroduction of the sea eagle to Scotland by the NCC and the RSPB. The birds were captured in Norway and released on Rum.

This has been a highly controversial project – it has stopped for the time being – which has infuriated farmers whose lambs the eagles take. Ironically, all the birds have left Rum, about the only place where they could do no commercial damage, and set up shop in places like Mull and Skye where they can do a lot. The project has also disturbed those bird-lovers who can appreciate what a horrible experience capture and exile to a strange environment must have been for the eagles themselves. One hundred and forty-two birds have been moved to Scotland; but only 11 pairs are currently nesting here. The main winner has been the RSPB which has made deft use of the publicity surrounding the programme. It evades responsibility for the suffering imposed on the birds themselves by saying it is not an animal welfare organisation and as such is not concerned with the fate of individual birds, only with species and populations.[9] Martin told me he thought the whole programme a jolly good thing. I asked him why.

'The sea eagle was made extinct by human beings within living memory,' he said. 'We have a habitat here which is still totally unchanged from the habitat they used to live in. You could say the decline of the sea eagle was the fault of humans, so what is wrong about accepting responsibility for extending its range and bringing it back?'

'By the same argument,' I countered, 'you could start ploughing up some of the newer suburbs of Birmingham to get back the Warwickshire corncrakes which Baldwin said were one of the characteristic sounds of summer in England.'

'Yes you could, but not on the criteria that I have just mentioned. It is not living memory, it is not the same habitat any more. Also you have to get your mind around the philosophy of conservation. Everybody has a different view. The philosophy of conservation is very much a personal thing.'

This seemed to undermine the case for conservation by bureaucracies like SNH, which must operate impersonally. Not only that, it was contradicted by his answer to my question about the place of the castle in the SNH vision of Rum.

'Rum has a lot of very rich natural heritage features,' Martin said, 'the Manx shearwater population, the geology, the flora, animal life and that is one reason why, when people come specifically to visit the castle, I virtually insist that they see the castle as part of a National Nature Reserve of international significance.

---

9 When asked about this by the *Herald,* the RSPB was unconcerned. 'David Minns, head of RSPB public affairs, reckons a loss of "collective knowledge" is partly to blame [for the deaths]. "Since the sea eagles have been absent from Scotland for most of this century, the newcomers are having to rediscover the place. This takes time, and meanwhile starvation and bad weather take their toll." ' (12 October 1996)

Without seeing the whole of Rum, the castle itself becomes a distraction to the importance of the island. People must be aware we are talking about an internationally important Reserve.'

'Conservationists always use this word, "important",' I said. 'It reminds me of a Sotheby's sale catalogue. If a painting is not very nice to look at they describe it as "important". It's an impersonal categorisation. If conservation is very personal, how can things be "important" in a general sense?'

'There are a series of criteria whereby you can measure the quality of a place,' Martin said. 'How many different species of x, how many individuals of a species of y are there in a particular place.'

'But that's a contradiction in terms. You can't quantify quality.'

Martin did not answer that point directly, saying only, 'We would still own and manage Rum even if the castle wasn't there. In fact many people in the organisation wish the castle wasn't there.'

In 40 years, then, Rum has given the nation some sea eagles and a statistical gloss to certain aspects of woodland and deer management. What have these rather modest achievements cost the British taxpayer?

'The problem with Rum from a budget point of view,' Martin said, 'is that it is operated on a host of different levels and bases. I only deal with the annual operational budget, buying new fencing materials, etc. I don't have anything to do with rates, salary costs or major infrastructure or capital works. Equally the income side of things isn't directly credited to Rum, it is recorded in the books as being generated by Rum, but it does not come back into Rum's pot. So I can't say, oh wonderful I've made lots and lots of money on the stag cull, I can spend it on a new Land Rover. It doesn't work like that.'

'But you must have *some* idea of the total cost of running this place?'

Martin thought for a moment then said, 'I would suggest that the nett cost at the moment is somewhere in the region of £250,000 including all salaries, rates, etc. and after all income, but excluding capital works or anything to do with the castle.'

I could accept that the castle should be treated separately. It is a completely different operation, more to do with *un*-natural than natural heritage. Indeed, Martin told me that SNH have tried to off-load it onto the National Trust for Scotland, but without success. Still, it was a shock to realise that there is, apparently, no such concept as a profit centre within SNH. How on earth can decisions be taken on priorities? It would be absurd to expect all nature reserves to make money, but equally it would be absurd to run a reserve system not knowing which, if any, do and which don't, and how much they lose.

I wanted to get an idea of sales revenue so that I could add it to Martin's guess at the overall loss, and try to arrive at a figure for reserve turnover. 'What would you say would be the total income from all your activities here, in very round terms?' I asked.

'Again, difficult to estimate,' he said. 'Take the venison, for example. The stags go off the island to the game dealer and he pays regional headquarters in Inverness. We are not involved.'

'Crikey!' I said, staggered. 'You must have *some* idea of your income, surely?'

For the second time, Martin turned away and looked out of the window for a long moment, pondering. Then he said, 'Income from venison, letting accommodation, sale of publications etc. might be in the region of £75k – *perhaps*.'

He had no idea what the extent of the 'capital works' budget might be, so I moved onto the estate agent's question. 'Does SNH put any value on the land?' I asked. 'Eigg is for sale at the moment and we are told it is worth £2 million. What is Rum worth?'

'Rum is a National Nature Reserve,' he said a little crossly. 'I've just been through a heap of things which constitute its value as a National Nature Reserve. If you then say, what else does it do, you are raising the question of whether National Nature Reserves are of any value.'

'Sure am,' I said.

'This island must have an estate agent's value. It is three times the size of Eigg, has a much bigger castle – '

'And no awkward crofters.'

'Absolutely. If it went on the market to an Arab sheik, would he pay £8 million for it? I don't know.'

'What I am really asking,' I said, 'is what is the amount of capital tied up here? On a historic cost basis, obviously there is very little, £23,000 but on either a replacement cost basis, or a break-up value basis, it must be very considerable.'

'These are philosophical questions,' Martin said, 'and they are also political questions. They are in a sense questions which perhaps SNH would be reluctant to answer. I am not sure I am the right person to get involved in an on-the-record discussion about that element of government policy.'

That, surely, is the problem with bureaucratic management of nature conservation? Questions of money are either 'philosophical' or 'political': one thing they are *not* is simply financial. Yet, in a crowded world, cost analysis is critical in land-use decisions. The state may choose to spend a certain amount of money in order to keep a particular mountainside empty, but it has a duty, surely, to the taxpayer to account for the national income foregone (if any). It is only private owners who are at liberty to adopt any concept of waste or value they like. That is the freedom which comes with vacant possession and a feudal superiority. That is also why lairdism, for all its many problems, at least gives Scotland a patchwork of management regimes. No two owners have identical views. In that respect lairdism, despite and possibly even because of its often bloody history, is closer to nature, in all its infinite variety, both ugly and beautiful, than any bureaucracy can ever be.

Pressing on with my figures, I decided to assume that Rum is worth very little more than Eigg, say, for ease of calculation, £2.5 million. In back-of-the-envelope terms that would mean a notional capital cost of about £250,000 a year which, added to Martin's annual operating loss, gave a round figure of half a million as the cost to the nation for the provision of Rum in the state it is, excluding capital works and anything to do with Kinloch Castle. That must be a conservative figure.

Rum has been publicly owned for just about 40 years. Some costs have risen in that time, while others have fallen, notably staff, whose numbers have almost halved. The rises and the falls probably more or less cancel each other out. It would therefore not be unreasonable to say that today's annual cost could be multiplied by 40 to get the total project cost to date, at 1996 prices, of the Rum National Nature Reserve. It has cost the nation £10 million in direct expenses, and about the same again in notional capital costs: a total of £20 million.

Who has benefited from the expenditure of this vast sum? All the people who have had free laboratory space for their out-door PhD research have obviously done so, as have the birdie folk who have been able to play eagle-eagle on the island. Since the tree work concerns entirely non-commercial woodlands – there is no market in birch, rowan, hazel and scrub oak – the only other possible beneficiaries might be the owners of ground with red deer on.

'Have many deer forest owners come to see what was being done here and to take advice?' I asked.

'Not one,' was Martin's astounding answer.

'So has the money been entirely wasted?' I asked, thinking that for all I had been told the founding fathers might just as well have drawn £10 million from the bank in white fivers and stuffed them up the stags' bottoms.

'Well, there are the visitors,' Martin said.

'How many do you get?' I asked.

'Something in the region of 7-8000 individual heads per annum. We prefer to translate that into visitor days, which comes out at around 15,000 visitor days. From that figure we subtract the number of day visitors, as distinct from visitors who stay overnight on the island.'

Since the day visitors come off the boat and have less then four hours on the island before it returns to the mainland, all they have time to see is the castle. Thus they are not, strictly speaking, users of the National Nature Reserve.

'How many of your 15,000 visitor days are day visitors?' I asked.

'I think it is about half and half now. The overnight visitors stay an average of three days each.'

The 7000 visitor days represented by non-day visitors, staying an average of three nights each, means that there must be close to 2500 people each year who visit Rum and get beyond the environs of Kinloch Castle. These are the people who have principally benefited from the vast expenditure of money on the nature reserve aspect of Rum. But the island was more or less closed under the Nature Conservancy, and only opened to the public in the mid 1970s. Demand was there, but, as the management plan for 1996–2006 notes, this was 'resisted on the ground that the research work required a lack of disturbance.' I calculated the total number of overnight visitors to Rum, throughout its history, at about 60,000. They have all had the free use of a resource which has cost the taxpayer at least £10 million to provide, thus benefiting to the tune of £167 each, or £334 if you include the notional capital cost.

What do these visitors do on the island? Which of the main foci of SNH's expensive work programme are they most interested in? The plants? The deer? The woodland? Do they come to look for the Rum mouse *(apodemus hebridensis hamiltoni)*, the only mammal peculiar to the island? The Hebridean vole and the pygmy shrew are also mentioned in the Declaration Statement for the National Nature Reserve as reasons for treating the island as special. Visitors presumably do not come to look at the main bird interest, the Manx shearwater *(puffinus puffinus puffinus)* since they return to Rum to roost only after dark, spending their days far out at sea where yachtsmen and others can marvel at their beautiful flight without costing the taxpayer a penny. So might it be the forked spleenwort that appeals, or the pyramidal bugle, both plants mentioned in the SSSI designation? Or could it be the slender green feather moss, which helped qualify the island as a Special Area of Conservation?

None of these, is the astonishing answer. 'The main visitor uses are hillwalking and rock climbing,' Martin told me. 'Though the bulk of them just come for a holiday, nothing specific.' This is confirmed by a full survey which SNH carried out in 1994–5. 'Nearly three quarters (72 per cent) of respondents pursued hill/mountain walking,' the survey concluded.

This, surely, shows two important things. First, free public access to important conservation areas is perfectly compatible with successful nature conservation, provided such locations are not too successfully marketed. Max Nicholson's idea that science necessitates closing islands to the public – as the RSPB have done with the two islands it owns in the Hebrides, Monk's Island and Isle Martin – is thoroughly disproved. True, on Rum certain areas are from time to time closed for research reasons or for deer culling, but that is quite a different thing and causes no problem either to visitors or to SNH staff. Each finds it can accommodate the other.

Secondly, all these facts and figures taken together show that SNH is really running two different enterprises: an excellent holiday island and a largely useless research station. Taking the latter first, it cannot be denied that hardly anybody takes advantage of the research done on the island, except the people who get jobs as a result of the degrees they have obtained after working there. By what logic does SNH rack up losses in order to provide facilities which should properly be financed by the Department of Education? Similarly, why should Cambridge University – not a poor institution – be given research facilities for their deer management programme at anything less than their full cost to SNH? Finally, if Highland deer forest owners or managers, whether sporting or commercial, want to benefit from work which has been done on Rum by SNH, why should they not be charged for what they are given? Any commercial laboratory would do so: techniques of balancing and improving a deer herd are as much intellectual property as knowledge of any other form of genetic engineering.

My sympathies lay with Martin Curry and his team who seemed to me to be having to take the consequences of a hopeless lack of clarity in headquarters thinking. Why should the reserve staff be squeezed when head office has not even begun to address the problem of the real purpose of the reserve? Economise for what? Surely SNH research should be confined to the small task of understanding how best to run a National Nature Reserve? Certainly that is implicit in Lady Bullough's deed of gift. She said nothing about a 'great outdoor laboratory'. What happened was that her generous bequest was hijacked by the wannabe Fraser Darlings who muscled in after the Nature Conservancy had drawn its unhealthy veil of secrecy round the island. In fact, the only users of Rum who are in harmony with Lady Bullough's ideas are the holiday-makers. And they, too, want a reserve, not a laboratory. The SNH visitor survey makes this point clearly. '97 per cent of respondents,' the report noted, 'were aware that Rum is a National Nature Reserve and over half felt that the fact that Rum is a National Nature Reserve was either very or fairly important in their decision to visit the island.'

Having said that the research station is largely useless, I should emphasise just how wonderful Rum is as a holiday destination. In part this is because, like the castle, the island has aspects of the museum about it, having been closed to ordinary life for so long. This first happened under Lord Salisbury who brought with him the English concept of amenity landownership insofar as it includes the idea, foreign to most Scots, landed and landless alike, that the owner has the right to *exclusive* enjoyment of open hill ground.

Though in public ownership, Rum was still the Forbidden Island, and the dark, acquisitive spirit which brought that about lent a dark, forbidding air to the island. Like domestic animals, there is no doubt that land absorbs the spirit of its owners to a certain extent. Gavin Maxwell caught the mood of those years better than most:

> Rum is a strange place, eerie and haunted if ever a Hebridean island was. It is all mountain – hills as dark and savage as the Cuillins themselves, and falling for the most part steeply into the sea. But they seem to have a different soul, something older and more brooding, almost evil. If there is a place where I could believe every Gaelic folk-tale and wild superstition it is in their shadow. I know a man who found himself in a high corrie of Askival with a dead stag after dusk. His coat was clutched and he felt himself being dragged uphill, while from right below his feet a voice screamed as if in an extremity of fear.[10]

My own impression, in 1996, could not have been more different. On the morning after I had talked to Martin Curry, I woke to a day of searing blue sky, so hot and still that at eight o'clock, when I poked my head out of the hatch, there was a haze on the surface of Loch Scresort. It largely obscured the foreshore and the terraces leading up to Kinloch Castle, but it left the turrets and castellations fresh and crisp in the brilliantly clear air. They seemed to float above the earth, like the scenery in a romantic ballet. Rum, for all its horrible reputation, struck me as actually a very beautiful island. The whole panorama of Kinlochscresort, with its Bullough-planted policy woodlands, particularly the vast pines, has a scale which is exactly appropriate to the larger vista. Visually, the man-made

---

10 *Harpoon at a Venture* Gavin Maxwell, NEL edition, London 1972, p. 37.

elements are robust enough to take their place in the grand setting they have been given, but they do not dominate it. You still feel nature is king here.

I slapped a shoal of sausages into the frying pan and went up on deck to drink my tea in the sun. The merest feather of a breeze ghosted across the water, soon dispersing the morning mist, but hardly rippling the surface of the sea. By the time I had eaten, coffeed and rowed ashore, it was so hot that dust hung in the air after vehicles passed along the roads. It reminded me of Africa, or southern Russia.

I had an appointment with Anne Taylor, SNH's Site Management and Interpretive Officer – a cumbersome title for an elegant girl – who had kindly agreed to show me round some of the more easily accessible parts of the island. We started with the nursery which in 1997 – the 40th anniversary of the bureaucratic coup – will produce its millionth tree for the island.

Then we lumbered up into the hills from Kinloch. SNH economists have calculated that it is cheaper to repair Land Rovers than the road, so the surface is in an appalling condition. It was not always so, Anne told me, as she pointed out the stone crusher which was used by the laird's private road gang. Sir George Bullough used to love racing cars around the island, indeed the rusting chassis of an Albion still lies on the foreshore.[11] It is eight miles from Harris, where the mausoleum is and where the Bulloughs had a hunting lodge, to the castle. Apparently Sir George could make the run in ten minutes! Considering the narrowness and twistiness of the road, as well as the fact that cars in the 1920s were not that nimble, to have averaged 48 mph must have been an extraordinary feat of daredevilry. For comparison, the 1929 Monaco Grand Prix was won in a Bugatti and on a much wider and better surfaced road, though possibly a twistier one, at an average speed of only 50.23 mph.

Anne also showed me Lord Salisbury's burst dam and the aqueduct which destroyed the salmon spawning grounds. In between times we discussed the more contemporary problem of the fact that her job is only temporary. This is because of the 13 per cent staff reduction, which is supposed to take the staff count down from 'seven and a half' to 'six and a half' permanent jobs. The job to be shed is her own: the Site Management and Interpretive Officer. But as such an officer is actually needed on Rum the solution has been to keep her on the Reserve but not on the 'permanent staff'. This feat of organisational legerdemain has been achieved by putting Anne on a temporary contract. The bean counters at head office are happy with their little self-deception but Anne, understandably, is not. Neither is Martin, who would like the situation regularised. He knows she is needed, and if the holiday-makers are the Reserve's *raison d'être* then he is surely right. Anne conducts herself with an attractive combination of informal

---

11 A more holistic conservation policy would give protection to this rare and valuable relic. It is undoubtedly a Machine of Special Scientific Interest. As it happens, my paternal grandmother spent much of her brief working life in charge of the stationery office at the Albion Motor Company's works at Scotstoun in Glasgow. Her main achievement, she used to say, was to have kept the consumption of pencils within sustainable limits by restricting the 'chewers' on the staff to one a week.

friendliness and informed professionalism – she is the best possible advertisement for SNH, yet she is the one person the bureaucracy pretends to itself it does not need.

The next day, Saturday, I set out on foot to have a closer look at the island. Under grey, but slowly lifting, skies I walked over to Harris and back. I went out by the 'servants' road'. This is a path which runs parallel to the road which George used to race on, but 200 yards or so away on the opposite side of the Kinloch burn. It was built so that the Bulloughs, in their comings and goings, did not have to see or be seen by their employees. Over at Harris, the hunting lodge has been laid out with the same aim in mind. Though the building is smaller than a modern, suburban house, the staff side is completely segregated from the Bulloughs' side.

This unfriendly spirit has not entirely left Rum. Climbing back up from Harris towards the saddle of the island, I noticed a stag on the skyline above me. By now it was late afternoon and the light was low. The dramatic silhouette would have made a striking photograph. I sat down on a rock beside the road to set up the camera and change lenses. Just at that moment, the only other person I met on the whole day's hike appeared from nowhere, carrying a fishing rod. Garishly dressed in a Matra-blue romper suit, he yomped up the slope from one of the lochs.

'Catch anything?' I said.

'Joost two,' he replied, without a glance in my direction. 'Turned out naaice,' he added quickly, before stonking off at a brisk pace, as if he had a 'bos' to catch. As his bustle had disturbed the stag, I packed the camera then set off down the road, perhaps three minutes behind him. He walked the six miles back to Kinloch in the gathering dusk without once looking round to see if I was there, much less stopping for a blether.

Back at Kinloch I discovered there was a sort of doorstep ceilidh going on outside the little Post Office-cum-shop – amazingly well stocked for so small a community – which is run by Martin Curry's wife Midge. Midge's is the 'half job' in the SNH head count, though not due to her diminutive stature, but rather because she works mornings only as Reserve secretary. Researchers and visitors, though not The Angler in Blue, were sitting and standing around chatting and drinking cans of beer in the last of the evening light. Tired after my 16-mile hike, I gratefully bought a couple of cans myself and sat down. I asked Midge about life on Rum. She liked it, she said, though she told me that when Martin retires they plan to go back to Yorkshire, where they already own a house.

'Do you regard yourselves as British people at home or English people abroad?' I asked.

'British people at home,' she replied, 'very much so. But then the old NCC was very British indeed, which is why you've got so many English people working in Scotland, even after the split. NCC moved people all over the place. SNH itself is very, very much British. There is no question of, oh you have to be Scottish to get a job in SNH, absolutely not. It is just the best man for the job. And they trawl through English Nature [SNH's equivalent in England as successor to the NCC] to make sure they get absolutely the best person for the job every time. There is none of this nationalism within the organisation. It is very much a British concern, still. The old NCC still lives, it is just in three bits. I know there is a lot of Scottish nationalism about, but in the six years I have been here nobody has ever hit me with it.'

'Have you enjoyed your time in Scotland?' I asked.

'I've made so many friends in Scotland it is unreal. Real friends, not fair weather friends. The Scots are all right.'

'Friendly people?'

'Tremendously.'

'More so than in England?'

'No. The Scots in England are welcomed with open arms. I wouldn't say the English are welcomed with open arms in Scotland on the grand scale. You've got the "Nat." business behind it all the time. But the people we've met, the Scots on the ground, are just terrific. We were only two years in Fife, and we made so many friends there it is silly. And they stay in contact; they come to see us. There's certainly no "Nat." in Scottish Natural Heritage at all.'

Midge closed her shop at eight o'clock, and the party quickly dispersed. Walking back to the pier under the great pines, I saw a human shape dawdling slowly through the deepening, olive-grey shadows. It was Anne, eating a bag of crisps.

'A lively Saturday night on Rum?' I ventured.

'Aye,' she said, smiling.

'Don't you get bored here?'

'No, not at all,' she said in an attractive Perthshire lilt.

'Not even occasionally?'

'It would be nice to go to the cinema sometimes.'

'And have a curry?'

'Aye,' she said, laughing, 'I could do with that right now. But at least I never, ever have to set foot inside a supermarket. And you meet very interesting people in my job, both tourists and researchers.'

We discussed what seemed to me to be most conspicuously missing on the island: people who have nothing to do with SNH. The atmosphere is a little claustrophobic, even precious. Anne said she would like to feel she could spend the rest of her life on the island.

'It'd be rather nice to have an SNH retirement home here,' she said. 'It's not as if there isn't plenty of space.'

'What about some crofters as well?' I asked. 'They could live their own lives, but also be available for seasonal work, like ghillieing, or working in the hostel in the castle.'

'Yeah, why not?'

'So far as I can see that would make the place more rather than less appealing as a holiday destination.'

'I quite agree,' she said.

We sauntered along as far as the house she shares with one of the deer researchers, Derek Thompson. Derek is an Aberdonian rough diamond who took a sociology degree but afterwards became a stalker up in Dundonnell, working for Paul Van Vliessingen, the Dutch owner of Letterewe and pioneer of hillwalking access agreements. Derek has worked for seven years on Rum assisting the deer research. Though he counts and shoots deer, his official job title is 'laboratory technician'.

Derek gave me another can of beer and we sat outside in the gloaming chatting about this and that, including SNH. Apparently morale is very low now that the organisation has, as Derek put it, become more cost-conscious and Thatcherite. *Cost conscious!* Parsimonious, maybe, but hardly cost-conscious.

Derek told me that an early-retirement scheme had been offered recently but the take-up had been so huge that it had had to be cancelled. He thought SNH was losing interest in Rum. He would not be surprised, he said, if the time came when it subcontracted the management to some other conservation body – the John Muir Trust perhaps.

Derek is one of those who would prefer that the castle were not there as it monopolises the attention of the visitors and distracts them from the wildlife interest. I said I could not disagree more; it had been the highlight of my visit. We batted this back and forth for a bit, neither of us getting anywhere with the other. Then Derek scored a winner.

'Do you like venison?' he asked.

'Sure do.'

'Would you be open to a little bit of, well –'

'Bribery and corruption?' I suggested.

'Aye.'

'Absolutely. What've you got?'

Without answering, Derek got up and went inside the house. He reappeared with a lump of something solid, about the size of a kettle, which he handed me.

'There's half a haunch of venison. That's for you on condition you don't write anything bad about Rum.'

'Thank you very much,' I said. 'No problem, sir.'

I devoted most of Sunday to repairs to the boat, finally weighing anchor in the late afternoon. Most importantly, I had to fit a new bracket to the tiller, connecting it with the rudder stock. I had broken the original aluminium bracket a year ago and had made up a wooden one, from oak and plywood, before departure. That had lasted only as far as Iona, and ever since I had been relying on a lash-up. This had finally given way in the approach to Rum, under stress of the sudden and violent down-draughts off the mountains. Scott, the SNH mechanic on Rum, had kindly welded up a replacement from mild steel, fitted it to my tiller and painted it a serious Hebridean black. It was just the job, far stronger than the original. It will last for years. Scott would not accept any payment, so I left some cans of lager in his shed. I was very grateful indeed.

Lolling on deck while, as it were, continuing my repair work, I picked up *Hansard*, which I had been reading for some days. Before departure I had photocopied some of the main wildlife and conservation debates over the last 15 years, both Lords and Commons, thinking I could beguile a few quiet hours in lonely anchorages with the cut and thrust of parliamentary debate. I had filed them in alphabetical order and by the time I reached Rum had got as far as the Natural Heritage (Scotland) Bill, the measure which provides the legislative framework for the SNH. That afternoon I came upon a highly relevant passage. On 11 February 1991, Sir Hector Monro, then Scottish Environment Minister and the Bill's sponsor in the Commons, called Rum 'the jewel in the crown of the Nature Conservancy Council'. Replying, Mrs Ray Michie, the Member for Argyll and Bute, said this:

> The Hon. Member for Dumfries talked about the island of Rum as the jewel in the Conservancy crown. Great – we saw the return of the sea eagle. Anybody who cares to go north sees miles and miles of empty land in the straths of Kildonan, where once there was laughter and, indeed, tears, but no one is creating the condition in which people can return. People used to live on the island of Rum. Now, as the Hon. Gentleman said, it is full of deer, and that is a tragedy. People, conservation beauty and the countryside are intimately entwined.
>
> Every inch of Scotland is worth caring about – every lovely part of it, with is history, its traditions, its culture and its potential. The people's affinity with the land is demonstrated so often in the language – be it Scots or Gaelic – in poetry, song and music. We cannot have the land without the people.[12]

The same thought was put more forcefully 60 years previously by Compton Mackenzie writing in *The Book of Barra*. Arguing that in the Hebrides the land should be managed for the benefit of the people who live on it – or ought to be living on it – Mackenzie wrote about the sporting use of Rum in terms which many would apply to the Darling-Nicholson 'outdoor laboratory' approach:

> The knowledge that there are still many who believe that it would serve the state to allow the Islands to become a wilderness for sportsmen like so much of the Highlands is always bitter with those of us who would rather see London a heap of ruins like Ur of the Chaldees than have one more abomination of desolation like Rum.[13]

Sailing out of Loch Scresort that afternoon, I thought about Rum and what it is that makes it such a wonderful island to visit. Certainly it could be improved by having some inhabitants who were not part of the whole SNH world, but that is a small point. Details aside, it is a very special place just as it is. Why? Part of the reason, obviously, is that it is not too heavily used. Martin told me that the SNH policy was not to promote the Reserve. That undoubtedly helps. But there

12 *Hansard*, Vol. 185, col. 663.
13 *The Book of Barra* (ed.) John Lorne Campbell, Routledge, London 1936, p. 30.

is more to the island's appeal than a mere lack of undue visitor pressure. What? Thinking hard about it, I came to the conclusion that it has something to do with the fact that SNH management has been, at least in terms of the aims declared by the pompous visionaries who created the present regime, an almost complete failure. A successful laboratory would be horrific, just as a successful holiday destination would. Like so many places in the Hebrides, Rum's charm derives from the fact that it is untouched by success. It struck me that the best way to preserve Rum as one of the greatest holiday destinations in the west of Scotland would actually be to keep the present arrangement going, whereby an underfunded Edinburgh bureaucracy flounders incompetently towards a half-remembered vision of something utterly ghastly, signally failing to get there. Anything more 'successful' would be the ruin of the place.

As afternoon slowly faded into evening, *Sylvia B* butted north into a short, steep sea. The wind was from the north-west, and the tide was flowing from the south-east. Wind against tide means choppy water, but there was enough wind to keep us bouncing along, close-hauled, with lumps of sea flopping onto the foredeck from time to time. We were making for the island whose recent past incorporates one of the most colourful stories of failure in the whole of the Hebrides: the Isle of Soay, on which Gavin Maxwell based his amazing shark hunting venture.

5

STRATHAIRD TO SOAY

THOUGH EN ROUTE TO SOAY, I made my first landfall in Loch Slapin on Skye. I had heard so much about Tex Geddes, the legendary Hebridean wildman who had been Maxwell's harpoon gunner and now owned and lived on Soay, that it seemed respectful to approach crab-wise, taking the rover's route from A to B, which is to go via C.

I cast anchor below the township of Torrin on the east shore of Loch Slapin at about eight o'clock. With the wind still in the north-west, *Slyvia B* lay with her bow facing Bhlàbheinn, or Blaven at it is pronounced and generally spelled. Breaking through dark but scattered clouds, the sun set spectacularly behind the mountain – one of the holy totems of Scottish alpinism. The whole area is now owned by an organisation called the John Muir Trust. A famous nineteenth century environmentalist, John Muir was one of the first to publicise what he called 'wildness'. Born in Dunbar, East Lothian, in 1838, Muir emigrated to the United States with his family when he was still a boy. He grew up on a farm in Wisconsin but ran away to escape the tyranny of a father who was personally despotic and spiritually dead, practising a Presbyterianism that was so rigid and rule-bound that it was almost talmudic. On his travels, Muir conceived a love of unpeopled nature and later on developed a great skill in writing about it. He was one of the first to say publicly that he was affronted by the incredible rate of ecological destruction which the expanding American state was inflicting on the lands newly subjected to unfettered capitalism. It was Muir's writings that eventually persuaded Congress to declare Yosemite a National Park. So far, so worthy. But Muir was also nuts.

He was an enthusiastic tree-hugger and general nature mystic. His writings are full of an almost unhinged adoration of insensate life, the more insensate the better, rocks and mountains apparently being his ideal since they were the farthest removed from human life. A modern writer has described his attitude as follows:

> Muir held nothing back when it came to attacking people who would destroy the wilderness. Nature was his church, the place where he perceived and worshipped God, and from that standpoint protection of nature became a holy war. Muir lashed out at the 'temple destroyers' who wanted to dam the Hetch Hetchy Valley [for water for San Francisco]. San Francisco became 'the Prince of the Powers of Darkness' and 'Satan and Co'. Muir's was a manichean world of black and white, good and evil, vying for the American environment. Compromise was difficult when ethics were involved. One's opponents were not merely in error but morally wrong.[1]

---

1   *The Rights of Nature: A History of Environmental Ethics* Roderick Nash, University of Wisconsin Press, 1989, p. 41.

Like Fraser Darling and Sir George Bullough, Muir had a disastrous relationship with his father. According to his modern biographer, Graham White, it progressed from a 'master-serf' level of contact in boyhood, to an 'undeclared battle' throughout adolescence. Thereafter, the relationship more or less ceased. Though he loved his own family and was a good and kind father, Muir was, at a more general level, deeply misanthropic. He once wrote that in a war between people and the bears, he would be on the side of the bears. Mankind, he said, was the only unclean animal, and the march of civilisation was co-extensive with the spread of 'filthiness'. By contrast, Muir wanted to maintain his own purity. He once recorded his own sense of anticipation on going up into the Yosemite: 'I will fuse in spirit skies. Hotels and human impurity will be far below.'

Muir was also a pacifist. During the American Civil War, he dodged the draft, considering himself to be 'above' the conflict. But he was a tough customer, both physically and intellectually. He was an original thinker who was always happy to abandon a view if he discovered it was false. He was also an extremely popular writer, who never allowed success to go to his head. Muir undoubtedly merits a small chapter in the long history of conservationology. But he is not quite big enough to fill the role given him by some of his more uncritical acolytes.

The John Muir Trust has taken for its slogan something the guru is supposed once to have said: 'Do something for wildness and make the mountains glad.' Though Blaven's reactions are unrecorded, it is attested fact that in 1994 the Trust paid £668,011 for the Strathaird Estate which surrounds the mighty peak. The vendor was Ian Anderson, the entrepreneur behind, and flautist and singer in front of, the 1960s band, Jethro Tull. Anderson started what is now a very large salmon farming business, to which he gave the name of his estate, and which has provided a good deal of work in the area. That business was not part of the sale. Neither was his house and its grounds, which were disposed of separately. The Trust bought 3000 acres of croft land, which comprise the township of Elgol at the southern end of the peninsula, and 12,000 acres of farm and mountain to the north of this. At its eastern end, this marches with the crofting township of Torrin, which the Trust had bought in 1991, giving a total area under Trust ownership of 20,000 acres. Of this, 40 per cent is tenanted croft land, while the remaining 60 per cent was bought with vacant possession.

The JMT plan to do absolutely nothing with the estate. I talked to one of the Trustees, Andrew Currie, who lives in Broadford and who used to be, before he retired six years ago, the NCC Area Officer for Skye and Lochalsh. Andrew took me on a long trip round the estate, describing the personalities and explaining the politics involved. The Trust's policy is simple: no advertising, no signposts, no paths, no car parks, no interpretation boards, no visitor centres, no exclusion zones, no research, no penetrometers, no local rules: nothing. Great! Total freedom to explore! What more could you ask?

In sharp contrast to the RSPB and SNH, the Trust is solicitous of local opinion about its management policies. It runs the two crofting townships through local committees which are elected at public meetings. The John Muir Trust gives the impression of having solved the great problem of how to combine conservation, community life and tourism without undue friction.

Later on, I discovered that things are not quite so simple. I talked to the Reserve Manager, Keith Miller, a keen young conservationist from Cheshire whose hobby is mountaineering. Keith was friendly, but somehow, I felt, cold in his militantly – I imagine he would say 'professionally' – unromantic feeling for the fascinating and beautiful area which he has been put in charge of. Over a cup of coffee in a local hotel, he talked of 'respecting the needs and aspirations of local communities' without any sense of belonging to these communities – which of course he does not, yet. He declared more than once that he was 'taking an all-embracing view'. Thinking of John Muir's behaviour towards trees, I asked him what the difference was between embracing things and hugging them. But my joke fell completely flat, so I composed my features into a 'caring' frown and returned to business.

'Would you describe the Trust's policy as altruistic?' I asked.

'Yes, oh yes, but all-embracing,' he said again, as if emphasising a Unique Selling Proposition. 'We are here to benefit everybody, not just birds, not just wildlife, but the whole community. I would argue that we benefit the majority of the population in that we are trying to integrate all these things. I would argue that it is in the interests of the public at large.'

'What if the public changes its view?' I asked. 'In 20 years' time the fashion might be for hang-gliding off Blaven, or the Japanese might be offering huge sums of money to crofters to permit chalet developments. What would happen if the whole of Elgol wanted to get involved in this but the Trust did not? Is there any mechanism for the community to get together and chuck you out?'

'We are totally and utterly responsible to members,' he replied.

'So you are not responsible to the crofters?'

'Oh yes, they are our members.'

'But there are 100 of them among 5000 other members. They could be outvoted.'

'They could be. But the whole of Torrin and the bottom 3000 acres of Elgol are all crofted land. They could all exercise their right to buy, including the common grazings, and simply depart from the JMT estate.'

'But until then you are lairds, benevolent lairds you will say, but lairds nonetheless?'

'Yes. At the end of the day, we own the land.'

Well, that was clear enough. I turned to the subject of population, conscious that the middle 12,000 acres of Strathaird is largely uninhabited, even though it contains the best ground for farming.

'Would you like to see more people living on the land here?' I asked.

'More people? Yes.'

'Do you have any concrete plans to bring more people in?'

'At the moment, no,' he said.

'If a crofter in Elgol came to you tomorrow and said, my son wants some land, I can't give him any, can you? – what would you say?'

'The current answer would be that we haven't got enough information together to have formulated our management plan. We don't have a policy on it. That's not prevarication, it's just fact. We just do not have enough information.'

'How long would you tell him to wait before you had gathered the information and had formulated your policy?' I asked.

'I'd have to pass that up to the Director of Land Management,' Keith said, 'as it has implications elsewhere. I don't have responsibility for that.'

I walked back to the boat in a flat, dull mood, wondering why it is that all these environmental managers, good and worthy people though they may be, so consistently ruin the beautiful mood of freedom, and dim the lightness of spirit, which otherwise pervades the Hebrides. I wished I had thought to ask Keith what reaction he had had from Blaven to his plans. Was the mountain pro-land reform, or anti?[2]

Back on board, I decided I would dispel the gloom by throwing a small party that evening on the beach at Torrin. I invited myself and the lump of venison which Derek Thompson had given me on Rum. It had thawed by now and would not keep indefinitely in the bilges. It was far too large to be cooked on the meths burner on board so I rowed ashore and collected driftwood and rocks and lit a fire. Sipping a dram, I slowly roasted the meat while the sun set, once again, over the mighty Blaven.

I ate an exquisite meal, though the midges, who never left me alone, unfortunately did the same. In that sense it was a relief to get back out to the boat, the one place where you can depend on freedom from these microscopic tourist-repellents. For a beautifully peaceful half hour I sat on deck in the gloaming, drinking a glass of cider and listening to the cavorting of the seals on the islands off the point.

The next day dawned clear, bright and hot. By the time I had breakfasted and rowed ashore, the beach below Torrin was full of happy noise. A large group of children was playing in the water while a farmer and his friend were enjoying

---

2   The most amusing example I have come across of the prosaic humourlessness of the conservation world involves a Mr Nicholson from Middlesex who wrote the RSPB a letter saying, 'Do you realise that birds do not have sex? All is done through the power of light.' Neil Barton, a wildlife advisor from head office at The Lodge in Sandy, Bedfordshire, replied at courteous length saying, 'Birds do have sexual intercourse [but] it is arguable that birds do not lust after one another in the way that humans do. As far as we know, birds do not perform the sexual act for fun.' Mr Nicholson replied to this by saying, 'I am afraid you do not have the light in you. Birds do not sink to human levels. If there is contact, it is through the eyes, like Adam and Eve before the Garden of Eden.' Barton replied curtly. 'I enclose a photograph of two birds copulating. I regret to say that as a conservation rather than a theological organisation we are not prepared to enter into any further correspondence on this matter.'

themselves with a four-wheeled bike which they were racing round on the sand, chased by a frantically barking collie. It was a real holiday scene. Blaven must have slept well as it looked very cheerful and craggy in the strong sunlight, quite different from the ominous darkness of the previous evening.

I walked up the dusty track from the beach and called on Mrs Catherine Mackenzie, the lady who was instrumental in bringing the John Muir Trust to Skye. A bright-eyed, grey-haired women, she had read about the organisation in the Women's Rural Institute magazine just about the time Torrin was put up for sale and thought a charity owner might be better than another under-capitalised laird.

I asked Mrs Mackenzie when the current fashion for all things croftish started. She said she didn't know; it had been going on as long as she could remember. Even as a child before the war – she grew up in Applecross, where her father was the Minister – she could recall earnest researchers coming with carefully worked-out questionnaires to ask about the 'way of life' of crofters. There was an interlude while the Second World War was fought, then the questioning resumed. It has not abated to this day, she told me. The only innovation has been that since Torrin has changed hands, students also come to research the activities, methods and 'philosophy' of the John Muir Trust. Last year the loop was closed, as it were, when a PhD student descended from the east coast with a questionnaire which was designed to explore the relationship between the Trust and crofting.

Had she read the resulting thesis, I asked? Yes, she answered, she had. Could she remember what conclusions it arrived at? No, she said, she could not. She gave an apologetic smile, then we laughed at the thought of the university libraries all silting up with this mass of unread material. None of it has made the slightest difference to life on Mrs Mackenzie's croft, nor, as far as she was aware, to that on any other.

She mentioned some of the difficulties which the Trust has encountered in Torrin, the main one resulting from a plan to plant trees on the common grazings. The proposal has aroused suspicions, particularly as the species in question – birch, rowan, hazel etc. – have little or no commercial value. The Trust told the crofters they could one day make wicker baskets and other such items from local materials. They were not impressed. Mrs Mackenzie pointed out that it is always the incomers, looking for a role in the community, who take up these largely decorative trades. I asked why the crofters did not do so. She said they used to use wicker baskets to get peats in, but now they burn coal and gas. They have no further use for 'creels'.

In calm, sunny weather I motored the ten miles round to Elgol, marvelling at the immense number of caves on the south-eastern end of the peninsula. One day, I shall come back and explore them from the sea. In Elgol I talked to Ian Mackinnon who is the Strathaird farm manager, responsible for the estate's large agricultural operation on the non-crofted land. He is also a crofter himself, and chairman of the Trust's Elgol management committee. In the neat sitting room of the comfortable, modern house on his croft, Ian gave me a bit of the background. Elgol is a younger community than Torrin, he said, and a busier one. What with a new pier at Elgol itself and the Strathaird salmon farm, there is more or less full employment. For both these reasons, Ian said, the community has a more open outlook than Torrin and has received the Trust very positively. 'This is the first time local people have ever had a say in what goes on,' he told me.

'What did people think of Anderson?' I asked.

'I don't think anybody was shedding any tears when he left,' Ian said, speaking in a soft lilt, 'but at the same time, nobody was saying, good riddance.'

Apparently Anderson had put a lot of money into improving the properties, but had ruined the effect by refusing even to consider a crofter buy-out, on the Assynt model, which had once been mooted. He wanted to keep control of everything. In the end, he lasted only 16 years before he went back south again.

'The thing about incomers,' Ian commented, 'is that they never seem to stay that long. Several years and the majority of them will go away. It's fine to turn up here on a beautiful summer's day when the sun's shining. It's lovely. There's no argument about that, none at all. But then they come and live here, when it's wet and bleak, and with the long drawn-out winters, and they realise how difficult it is to live in areas like this. Also the indigenous population thinks differently from the population on the outskirts of London – or anywhere in the world. The thinking is different.'

Ian said he was very happy with the way things were, seeing only one serious cloud on the horizon. 'People have their roots in the land here. If you look back in the records it is all the same names. That has been the role of crofting, keeping people on the land. I have said to the John Muir people that I'm not too happy that you have an organisation, whether it is the John Muir Trust or whatever, that will continue buying up land, so you'll end up with half of the Highlands owned by one owner. I don't think that's right at all. It's not like other landowners who come and go, or die. The John Muir Trust have told me that their constitution says they can never sell any land. If they turn out to be a bad landlord, then we've got a bad landlord forever.'

My last call was on Colonel Lachie Robertson, who had come back, at the close of a lifetime of soldiering, most of it in the Parachute Regiment, to the village where he grew up. The Colonel was one of the very few native Gaelic speakers in a senior position in the British Army. I walked up the hill in the gentle but still warm evening sunlight to find him hanging out mackerel to dry on the clothes line in his garden. He showed me into his garage, which was full of boating equipment. He offered me an upturned fish box and handed me a can of beer.

The Colonel is another member of the Trust's Elgol management committee and, in between telling me about some of the people he had known at 'the IRA' (the Inverness Royal Academy) and describing incredible dinners with George MacDonald Fraser, whom he had known 'out East', he told me why he preferred the new regime on Strathaird.

'You do feel part of the situation,' he said, 'instead of being bought and sold, as is happening on Eigg.'

The Colonel told me how he had tried to negotiate a lease for a few acres of land for a football pitch for the village youngsters from Anderson. 'He just sent me around in square circles,' he said. 'I ended up having an hour and a half's telephone conversation which didn't get anywhere.'

'Why was that, do you think?'

'He didn't want to give anything away. Now the Trust have given the club a 21-year lease, which makes a difference. They can apply for grants and so on.'

The Colonel had views on wildlife conservation on the estate as well. He regretted the decline of the birds under the influence of blanket protection.

'The hoodies here are killing off other birds, raiding eggs, as are the black-backs,' he said. 'The song-bird life, compared with when I was a child, when there was a certain amount of control – there were two keepers on the estate – is much less.'

He also told me fish stocks were suffering from the explosion in the seal population. 'When I was young,' he said, 'the seals were killed, not killed off, but killed for their fur. And otters were killed, but we never had a scarcity of otters up here. The propaganda about otters is nonsense. You could go along the shore here and see them everywhere.'

'Talking of otters,' I said, 'did you have any experience of Gavin Maxwell?'

'Oh yes, I knew Gavin well.'

'What was he like?'

'Very interesting character. I was coming home from India once and I met him on Euston station. We had a dram there, then another dram on the train, and then another dram. Finally we ended up at Inverness station, feeling very pissed, when Gavin realised he had left all his kit in Euston.' The Colonel took a long swig at his beer. 'But he was a mysterious character.'

'In what way?'

'Well, he had a dark side to him. He would get depressed, you know, sort of almost as if there was a fate awaiting him. He sometimes said he felt there was. But he was a great companion.'

From the hill on which the Colonel's house sits, above Elgol, you get spectacular views of Rum and Canna to the south-west as well as a very clear view of Soay, less than five miles due west, where the shark-hunting venture had been based. I asked the Colonel what he knew of the place. He told me that it was the only island in the Hebrides which was evacuated due to a lack of tobacco. As I gaped at this assertion, the Colonel said, 'Go and see Tex Geddes.'

'I'm going to,' I replied. 'I've heard so much about him.'

'Aye, you've got a storyteller ahead of you. You'll get all the facts from him, plus a few more bits and pieces.'

The problem about sailing to Soay (the island of sheep) is that the good anchorage, to the north of the island, has a shingle bar across the mouth which almost dries at low tide and which would give *Sylvia B* enough water to cross only up to about 10 p.m. that evening. As it was already close to nine o'clock by the time I was back on board, it was either an immediate start, or a fairly early one the next morning. I decided to go immediately,

The sun had already set and the whole aspect of the scene had changed. There was hardly any wind but much of the sky was obscured now by an ominous, dark and almost stationary layer of cloud. I motored out of Elgol up towards the rapidly darkening mass of the Cuillin, where they fall 3000 feet almost sheer into the sea.

As we rounded the headland on the north-east of Soay, and opened Soay Sound, the channel that leads down to the mouth of Loch Brittle, one of the most desolate parts of Skye, a kind of mist, half cloud half fog, floated past the Skye massif, well below the main cloud base and separate from it. The vast and darkening shapes conveyed an atmosphere of primal menace, of mocking tolerance at my presence in such a small and fragile boat.

Not a light was visible in any direction, at least not until I rounded the point leading into the anchorage on Soay, where a large, unwieldy 'caravan boat' was lying at anchor – the first yacht I had seen for nearly a week – with 12-volt neon strip lights blazing into the moonless night and loud music pouring from a speaker in the cockpit. There was a middle-aged man and a younger-looking woman aboard, and they were clearly having a party. I am not sure they realised I had slipped past them in the darkness. (To conserve my batteries, I had not been showing navigation lights.) They were certainly behaving in a way which suggested they thought they were alone.

Snug at anchor as far up the creek as *Sylvia B*'s shallow draft would allow me to get, I ate another delicious venison dinner in the warm glow of my paraffin lamps. Intending to be up early in the morning, I soon crawled into my sleeping bag where I tried to read until the party-goers astern of me turned up the volume even higher and put on 'Stand By Your Man'.

At first light I made the exciting discovery that I was anchored right below the ruins of Gavin Maxwell's shark oil extraction plant. I saw a partly roofless two-storey building, two evidently abandoned sheds and a rusting steam engine. They stood above the remains of the pier where sharks, some weighing as much as seven tons, were once hauled up for dismembering. Connoisseurs of commercial failures in the Highlands will know the full story of this extraordinary enterprise. Others might like to consult *Harpoon at a Venture* by Gavin Maxwell and, for indirect illumination, *Hebridean Sharker* by Tex Geddes. ('I wrote my book', Tex told me later that day, 'to take the mickey out of Gavin. I told him his factory was no fucking use, a waste of time.')

To recapitulate briefly: Maxwell was born into a semi-aristocratic family from Wigtownshire (he was the third son of the fifth daughter of the seventh Duke of Northumberland), educated at Stowe and at Oxford, where he read estate management, cheating in some of his exams by stealing the question papers in advance. His father was killed when he was four months old, at the start of the First World War, and he was brought up under the influence of a very strong mother, whose spell, some people think, he never fully cast off.

Maxwell spent his boyhood on the moors of Galloway to such effect that during the Second World War he was taken on by the Special Operations Executive (SOE) as an instructor in small arms craft and survival techniques at the commando training centre in Moidart. There he met Joseph 'Tex' Geddes, who was an expert in boat-handling, unarmed combat and knifemanship. Apparently Maxwell had an incredible eye. He could, Tex told me later, walk into the mess, lay his old-fashioned .45 revolver down on the billiard table, throw a ping-pong ball up in the air and be able to pick up his gun with the same hand and hit the ball before it landed.

'But,' Tex added, 'I could pin his sleeve to the deck with a knife before he got his hand out of his pocket.'

Maxwell ended the war a Major in the Scots Guards, determined that he would live as far away from the crowded world of modern cities as possible. In 1945 he bought the Isle of Soay from Dame Flora Macleod of Macleod, for £900 which he had borrowed from his mother. He called it 'my island Valley of Avalon'.

To begin with, Maxwell had no clear idea of how he would make Avalon pay. Then he remembered an incident that had made a considerable impression upon him a year before. One day, while cruising off Mallaig with a friend, during the latter days of his service in SOE, he had for the first time in his life encountered a basking shark, the second largest fish in the world. Today they are rarely seen in Hebridean waters – in all the years I have sailed off the west of Scotland I have never encountered one – though from the 1930s to the 1950s they were common and a nuisance to fishermen whose nets they regularly destroyed.

Very little is known about this immense animal, where it goes in the winter, or why its customary breeding grounds seem to change from time to time. Totally harmless, it cruises around with its vast mouth wide open sucking in plankton. It has a brain the size of a dog-fish's, so the huge organism operates almost entirely by subconscious instinct. Even after the brain is severed from the spinal column, the other organs carry on working for several hours. 'One Billingsgate firm to which we sent samples of the flesh,' Maxwell noted in *Harpoon at a Venture*, 'wrote jocularly to say they had asked for the sample to be fresh, not alive. The blocks of flesh, each no bigger than a large book, had been twitching in a disgusting way when the cases were opened in London, and had continued to do so for half a day afterwards.' A scientist who came to study Maxwell's carcasses, Professor Harrison Matthews, has written about his own experience of parts of the body continuing to function after the animal was brain-dead. 'When I first cut a male shark's clasper off – its sexual organ, which is a yard long and eight inches thick – the nerves were stimulated and the thing flew up and hit me in the face.'[3]

Maxwell knew nothing of any of this on that summer afternoon in 1944 when he saw his first basking shark. On the foredeck of the boat he then owned, the

3   Quoted by Douglas Botting in *Gavin Maxwell, A Life*, London 1993, p. 98.

Gannet, Maxwell had mounted a Breda light machine gun. His idea was that if he came upon a U-boat he would be able to knock out the periscope, capture the disabled craft and become an instant hero. It was a calm day when Maxwell suddenly noticed two immense fins sticking a yard out of the water. They were about 20 feet apart and moving in line astern. It was a few seconds before he realised, with a shock, that they belonged to the same vast animal.

In an instant, the future doyen of animal lovers had decided on his response to this strange creature: he would machine-gun it. Maxwell leapt to the foredeck, swivelled the barrel round and fired a 30-round burst at point-blank range into the shark's back, then stood off while it thrashed about in the sea beneath him. When the activity subsided Maxwell closed in for another burst, eventually repeating this performance six times until he thought – wrongly as it turned out – the animal dead.

His curiosity aroused by this encounter, Maxwell started to enquire about basking sharks. Few people seemed to know very much, though he did learn that the livers could be worth £20–£30 apiece (£400–£600 at 1996 prices) since they weighed anything up to a ton and contained valuable oil. Maxwell decided he would go into business, hunting the sharks on a commercial basis, and processing the carcasses on Soay. Avalon would become a fish factory.

Borrowing another £11,000 from his mother, Maxwell formed the Isle of Soay Shark Fisheries and took on Tex Geddes as mate and harpoon gunner. Geddes's family came from Peterhead, but he had grown up in Newfoundland, whither his father had fled after chucking a member of the Aberdeenshire Constabulary into the harbour. At the age of seven, Tex was orphaned when his father was killed in a logging accident. Brought up by a Frenchman, Tex was expelled from school at the age of 12 as 'unmanageable'. He became a lumberjack, and later went to sea, soon getting involved in rum-running to the United States. Since this was the era of Prohibition, it was not long before he had to emulate his father and escape the law by crossing the Atlantic.

Back in Scotland, Geddes joined the Army on a whim, enlisting in the Seaforth Highlanders in 1937. In 1940 he found himself at St Valéry in the chaotic weeks after Dunkirk with the rest of the doomed Highland Division, including Hugh Mackinnon of Coll. After the general order to surrender was given, Tex escaped, made his way back to Britain and joined the Commandos. He was badly injured during a raid on Norway and spent the rest of the war at the SOE training school near Arisaig, where he was known for his wild antics, including playing darts with his commando knives. There, in 1941, he met Maxwell.

Out hunting sharks, Tex was the man who either fired the harpoon gun or, if they got close enough, plunged the nickel-steel shaft straight into the back of the beast as it drifted under the gunwale of the boat. In his book, Maxwell described the killing of their first shark. This time he was on the gun:

> I fired and I felt quite certain that the harpoon was in him. [After the thrashing subsided] I could see the end of the harpoon sticking a foot or two out of his side and a dark plume of blood trailing from it in the water, like smoke from a chimney.

Tex saw it too, and gave his war-cry for the first time, a war-cry that I came to associate with every kill, and which in later seasons I remember hearing across half a mile of sea, following the boom of his gun in the summer dusk: 'He feels it! He feels it!'[4]

Keen to meet this extraordinary man, I rowed ashore and, after spending an hour or so poking through the buildings and ruined plant above the pier, I set off across the low-lying isthmus which connects the west loch with the east loch. Soon I was hopelessly entangled in head-high bracken. Eventually this gave way to ground so boggy that it frequently threatened to overwhelm my boots, and on two occasions did, once each boot. I escaped from that into a birchwood so dense that I could get through only by walking backwards at a protective crouch. In retrospect, my advice to other visitors to Soay who want to cross from west to east is: use the path. I would have done this myself if I had known there was one. But I knew nothing of the island, not where the houses were, how many, nor whether, as seemed likely, I was going to be met by a psychopath who would threaten to use me for knife-throwing practice.

I broke out of the jungle onto high ground above the east (more properly south-east) bay, Camus nan Gall (Bay of the Foreigners). Around it on the west side were scattered seven or eight houses, most looking as if they were inhabited. Despite the lowering cloud, and the occasional spit of rain, it was an entrancing scene, though I should perhaps say no more since, when I eventually caught up with Tex, he said to me, 'I don't want tourists on my island, nor do I want you to write books about Soay and say what a wonderful place it is.'

'OK,' I said.

'There is no public road on this island. When you came down the hill, you opened a gate and you walked through my garden to get here?'

'I suppose I must have.'

'You're a bloody nuisance,' he said. I thought I detected the ghost of a twinkle in his eye.

I had found Tex sitting in the house of a charming girl who had moved to Soay from Luton to paint. She offered us both a cup of tea. 'I'm sorry I can't give you anything to eat,' she said to me, evidently embarrassed.

'Don't give him anything!' thundered Tex. 'Don't encourage these buggers!'

Tex is lean, bearded, tallish and craggy, but with the look of a man in some sort of inner, non-physical pain. I learned later that his wife had died the previous year of motor neurone disease and that he himself had suffered a minor stroke. I confess I took to him immediately.

As he sat spraying used tobacco over our hostess's floor from the pipe he was trying to clean, he expostulated about tourists. Possibly because I said I had just come from Rum, he started by telling us about a party which had arrived some years earlier on a Norwegian cruise ship.

'They were birdwatchers from the Nature Conservancy,' Tex said, between sucks on the stem of his pipe, coughs and attempts to find the hole in the bowl

---

4 *Harpoon at a Venture* Gavin Maxwell, NEL edition, London 1972, p. 57.

where he should insert his pipe-cleaner. 'And about 50 or 60 of them walked in line abreast through my hay looking for ground-nesting birds. I gave them a bollocking. "Leave the little buggers alone," I said. "You say you are conservationists. *I* am a conservationist! You come back here again and I'll have a harpoon gun waiting for you and I'll put a couple of stone of gravel in it and I'll kill 40 or 50 of you in one bloody shot." That's what I think of the Nature Conservancy.'

Then he looked at me hard and said, 'You're not so bad: I'd only need one bullet for you.'

As the tea was being poured, Tex went on with hardly a pause. 'But wait a minute now, and I'll show you I'm on your side,' he said. 'Do you know south Uist? Well, the Duke of Edinburgh – why should they call that bugger the Duke of Edinburgh, what has he got to do with Edinburgh? – there's a place called Loch Druidibeg and I was on my way to St Kilda and had to put in there . . .' We got a long story about geese and crofters, as well as the arrogance of the Duke of Edinburgh and the stupidity of the wildlife protection people – or was it the stupidity of the Duke of Edinburgh and the arrogance of the wildlife protection people?

Eventually we agreed that I would call on Tex at his own house after he had eaten, and he would tell me about Gavin Maxwell. When I arrived, Tex sat me down in front of a warm fire, handed me a very large dram and kindly offered to give me a pair of dry socks. ('Take them; I've got thousands of pairs of socks.') Since he was from Peterhead, I mentioned by way of introduction that my mother and her family were all from up that way, from Aberdeen, the Buchan coast and also from Shetland.

'What were their names?' he asked, sucking at his pipe.

'Jappy and Flett,' I said.

He said he had known an Alec Jappy from Thurso, then, obviously relishing a memory, he settled slightly in his chair, took a sip of his dram and said slowly and almost theatrically, 'I'll tell you about a man I knew called John Flett from Flotta.' He pronounced the two 'F's with extreme emphasis, as if speaking about a hero, a man of mettle. 'You know Flotta in Orkney?'

'I've heard of it,' I said. It is one of the islands surrounding Scapa Flow. Today it has a large oil terminal on it.

'Well, I was in the army before the war. I wasn't a very good soldier: I was five times a sergeant. We had a fellow from Stornoway called Donald McLeod and he was only about 5' 3". When the Colonel saw him he nearly went mad, "I don't want anyone like that in my regiment!" This was the Seaforth Highlanders, at Fort George. But wee Donald was a wonderful piper, he became the world champion. He was still in the army when he was damn near 60; they kept him, teaching the pipes. Now, he had a chum called John Flett from Flotta and John was bloody nearly seven feet long, and broad as well. One was huge and the other minute.

'About wee Donald,' Tex went on. 'They were all sitting in the officers' mess at Fort George one beautiful summer's evening. And there's huge ramparts, with green grass growing on the top and a little wall, about five foot high on top. The Colonel was in the mess this night, and he heard someone up on the ramparts playing the 'Lament to the Children', which is a pibroch, classical – bloody awful thing it is, I'd rather have a tune myself – and he said to whoever was with him, "My goodness, the Pipe Major's playing beautifully tonight." At that moment the Pipe Major walked in the bloody door. The Colonel says, "Who the hell's up there?" "I don't know," he said, and the two of them listened. "My God, that lad can play. Who can it be? None of my men can play like that. Get him down here."

'Now the Colonel could see the drones of the bagpipes sticking above this wall, but he could not see the bloody man. So they brought the little man down. It was wee Donald. He should never have been allowed into the Seaforth Highlanders. They couldn't get a uniform small enough for him to send him to the Games. Eventually, they cut the pockets off a jacket and he went and won everything. He was only about 18, so they sent him to Edinburgh Castle to be taught by Willie Ross who was the Highland Brigade piping teacher in the Castle and Willie sent him back in a week and gave him a Pipe Major's certificate. He said, "I can't teach that boy anything. He's teaching me."

'Anyway, wee Donald and big John became pals, and a couple of years later, the two of them were going to the Inverness Games or some bloody thing like that and the two of them got drunk. And Willie Logan, the Pipe Major, got a hold of them and he put them out of the carriage. He sent them to the guards van. Do you remember the shitpaper you used to have in railway carriages?' Tex asked.

'Yes,' I said.

'Horrible bloody stuff.'

'It was like greaseproof paper.'

'Damn right,' he said. 'You're on it. While they were in the guards van, wee Donald wrote a tune and he called it Flett from Flotta.'

'Wrote it on the lavatory paper?'

'Aye, it was a famous tune, Flett from Flotta.'

As Tex settled himself further into his chair and took a long sip of his dram, I thought, what a charming way to say, 'you're welcome in my house'. We sat in silence for a moment while Tex fired his pipe. Through the window, I could see the last of the light seeping slowly into the grey expanse of the Bay of the Foreigners. The sticks crackled in the grate. I was about to reply to the toast, as it were, when Tex resumed his tale.

'I was the Scottish champion bayonet fencer,' he said. 'Do you know anything about bayonet fencing?'

'No.'

'Right, I'll quickly tell you. You've got a rifle and a bayonet at the end of it. A fencing bayonet was in the barrel on the end of a spring, a 5/8th bolt with a bobble on the end of it, and it weighs the same as a bayonet. You wear a visor and rhinoceros hide over the top of your head and over your left hand and a straightjacket tied up the back and a bollock pad. You can do what you like. Your duty is to kill the other fellow. There's no ropes in the arena; it's twice the size of a boxing ring. And you can do what you bloody well like, you can hit him over the head with the butt, anything. You understand?'

'Yes.'

'Now the Highlanders were unbeatable, traditionally. Nothing could touch the Highlanders at fencing. It was beautiful to watch. I was fighting at the Royal Tournament at Olympia in London. Now always at the Royal Tournament, there was massed bands. And wee Donald was the Sergeant Piper then. Big John was playing too – he was a bloody good piper as well. But he was a private soldier, so they shouldn't have been fraternising, but they always did. And it came out on orders that there was some reason we weren't going to have a practice that afternoon. So what did they do? They buggered off to the pub, and got pissed, the two of them. Both of them drank like fish. Pipers all do. They put a wee drop whisky in their bags and they get the fumes when they're blowing and sucking the bloody bag. Well, they came back pissed as bloody newts, and of course the orders had been changed, so they had "gone missing", a serious offence. Now I don't remember what I had done but I had done something too and been given six extra guards: no sleep for a week.

'They got ten days in the jail, but we couldn't put them in jail because we needed them to play. After we finished in London – it was 1938 – we had to go to the Empire Exhibition in Glasgow, to troop the Colour. When we'd finished with that, they still couldn't put them in jail, because we had to go to Ballater to be the King's guard at Balmoral. Then, at last, we went to Stobb's Camp at Hawick, in Roxburghshire, under canvas. "Right, into bloody jail!" But the jail was a bell tent. The guard room was a tent too. I had this six extra guards, so I was in charge of the buggers while they were in the jail.

'Now, the rest of the boys were going out for a piss up at night, off duty. And when they came back one of them would have a fish supper and the other would have a half bottle of whisky and all they had to do was lift up the flap of the tent and throw it in, as long as I didn't see them. Then at Last Post, ten o'clock at night, I said, "Right boys, we'll go and visit the jail birds." And there they were, they had fish suppers, bottles of beer, half bottles of whisky. What a fucking carry on we had getting them sobered up before the morning, so we could inspect them again! And I remember old Hamish, he's a friend of mine, he was a Captain at the time, ended up a Brigadier, and he said to me, "God Almighty, I don't know how these men can stand to attention." If John farted Donald would follow him and everyone knew they were pissed as newts, but no one said a bloody word.

'Now years later – six, seven years ago – I was in Flotta and I was driving along with a friend who was a guard at the oil terminal there. He wanted me to tell him how I would blow it up. They were frightened of the IRA. I was telling him about all this. I said, "I once knew a man called John Flett from Flotta." He says, "The piper?" "Yes," I said. "Well, you know, that man is here," he said. "He's going away tomorrow." Now I haven't seen that man since the summer of 1940. He was taken prisoner at St Valéry. This fellow I was with turned the car round and took me and showed me this portakabin, at the edge of a field, which John had hired for a couple of weeks. After the war he had gone to Australia, and married. He had come back to show his wife where he came from.

'John must be 80 and he saw me walking round the edge of the field. He came down the steps and he said straight away, "I know who you are. You don't need to hide behind that fungus." He introduced me to his wife. He had always told her that the best week he ever spent in the army was in the jail and that he had had this wild sergeant, who was wilder than any of us. And there I was. So the woman began to cry – you know how there is a very close correlation between tears and laughter. And they were going away the next day back to Australia. I spent the evening with them. But that's my story. That was John Flett from Flotta.'

Stunned at the warmth of this welcome, I suddenly felt embarrassed at having to rush my visit. But I had no option. I had to get on. So I asked Tex about Soay. 'Colonel Robertson in Elgol told me yesterday that this was the only island ever evacuated because of a lack of tobacco,' I said.

'That's true, in a way,' Tex replied. It turned out that, having come to live here after the failure of the shark hunting venture, he had been a witness to the events, which happened in the summer of 1953. 'You know that prior to 1886 there was no such thing as a crofter,' Tex said, 'Technically, legally, they were just serfs. If the landlord didn't like them he just told them to fuck off and burnt their houses down. They had no right to have a house anywhere. Only in 1886 did they get security of tenure. Well, the people who originally lived on Soay all went to North Carolina, in seventeen hundred and something.'

'They were all Macdonalds, presumably?'

'They were all Macleods' Tex said with emphasis. 'If there had been any Macdonalds about here they would have cut their cocks off. This island filled up with people chased away by Lord Macdonald, who was a real bastard. There were Campbells, MacDonalds, Stewarts, Lamonts, Ritchies from the east coast. They managed to plant some potatoes and get some seaweed up and they survived. In 1886 Macleod of Dunvegan's factor came here to find out how many people there were on Soay, and he nearly pissed himself: there were over 120 people. Now the best of the Highlanders went to Canada, to American and Nova Scotia, of their own free will, and there was a whole lot of duds who came here, you understand?'

'Yes.'

'I'm not belittling the people, I'm only telling the truth. From God knows where they came. Nobody knew and they kept quiet. They didn't bother getting married. They slept with their own sisters-in-law and they deteriorated. There was a hell of a lot of melancholia and a hell of a lot of imbecility. One family had a man with the brain of a child of two; another family had three illegitimate children, one was deaf and dumb, the other was as daft as a brush; and there was another family in which one fellow called himself Gray and the other Castle, because they had different fathers, and they were forever arguing about who they were and what they were.

'And they were all very, very, very religious, and yet they would steal the sugar out of your tea. They had no pride. And not a single indigenous man from Soay went to the war. When the census man came they all took to the hills and the mothers swore blind that they had no children, no men. Not one of them went.'

'This was the First or Second World War?'

'The Second War. *My* war. At that time they had two boats a week. We've got a boat once a month. And when Maxwell came here after the war, not one of them would take a job. Not one, because they were fishing lobsters; lobsters were straight cash. And they all had the public assistance, the whole bloody lot of them. They would pull down the telephone line, say it was the birds and get a tenner for fixing it. Half of them were daft, but some of them were clever. I remember this, I experienced it myself, they made a song and dance about being poor starving crofters, "We've no peats, we're all going to die of cold." And the church in Mallaig collected money and bought coal for them. The Minister rang them up and told them that the coal would be delivered by a fisherman, to save the freight on the steamer. The man arrived and left the coal on the beach. Only one man took it home. "We were told you would deliver it," they said.'

'You mean they wouldn't even take it up to their houses?'

'That was their excuse. In fact they couldn't give a monkeys for any coal. They didn't want coal. They had any Christ amount of peats. It was *money* they wanted, not coal. Only one man took the coal to his house. The rest sold it off the pier. I bought a couple of bags myself. I was on a herring boat, and I paid over the odds for it because they said the money was going to the church.'

'Bloody hell.'

'Aye, that's the sort of folk they were. Anyway, one day they ran out of tobacco. It was a day when no boat was calling. They kicked up all hell. They said if you don't give us three boats a week, you'll have to come and take us off. So somebody called for the papers, someone in authority, and asked, "What does it cost to have a steamer going there twice a week?" None of them paid any income tax, and every one of them was getting money from the government. The whole island was a massive parasite. The government decided it would be cheaper to move them. So the Department of Agriculture bought some land on Mull. They sent officers here and they went round the island saying, "Sign there, right there." It was all nicely typed. "I hereby renounce my holding." And they signed. They were no longer crofters. Then they realised the Department was serious and they tried to get it stopped, but the Department said, "No. That's you. You'll move and get a job." The evacuation was on a Friday. On Sunday morning they were back to carry on with their fishing, salmon and lobster as if nothing had changed. They had left their boats here. But it had. They were soon dealt with.'

Later I was amused to read, in *The Soay of our Forefathers* by Laurance Reed, that at the time of the evacuation, the Member of Parliament for the area telegraphed the departing islanders saying, 'I send you my heartfelt understanding [and hope] you may draw consolation from the knowledge that your experience will serve to call nationwide attention to the economic plight of the Highlands.'

Since Tex's time on Soay overlapped with Lady Monica Bullough's on Rum, I asked if he had known her. 'I didn't know her, I spoke to her,' he said. He did not seem to have liked her, though he did say he sympathised with her desire for privacy on Rum.

'She has friends who come for a week's deer stalking,' Tex said. 'Some damn fool hiker from London or Edinburgh or somewhere, comes along saying, "There's no law of trespass in Scotland." Her friends have been out all day on the hill. "Come and look at this beautiful deer," Joe Bloggs says to his mate, and the deer are gone. The man who has been up to his knees in muck all days asks, "Who the hell are you?" And they say, "It's a free country, we just want to climb the mountain. There's no law of trespass." But there is. So she fixed it that you could buy a ticket to Rum on the steamer, but you couldn't get ashore. She owned the boat that ran between the ferry and the jetty. Did you go to Rum?'

'Yes.'

'How did you get ashore?'

'In my dinghy.'

'You've got a dinghy?'

'Yes.'

'Bloody nuisance you are,' Tex said, getting up to pour us another dram. 'In her day, she would meet you and stop you and say, "Where are you going, sir?" "I want to go for a walk." "No you're not. There's men stalking today." And if you argued, they would chuck you into the sea.'

'Sir George had died before you came to Soay,' I said, 'But did you ever hear anything about him?'

'He was terribly interested in horses. And he was more of a philanthropist than she was. When he died she drew in the horns.'

'By doing what?'

'By not inviting the people of Soay to come to a piss up. He used to do that.'

'Really?'

'Oh yes.'

'He was quite a sociable guy?'

'Very. Some of the men from Soay were on his yacht, the *Rhouma,* as occasional crew, and he used to ring up Soay and say, "Right, come on, we'll have a piss up."'

'He was quite well liked, was he?'

'Oh, he was quite well liked. They would all arrive and he would wine and dine them, and they'd have a ghillies' ball. They liked that.'

'That's not the impression you are given by SNH. I was told that he was a nasty piece of work.'

'Well, that is not what I was told by the old men who lived here,' Tex said.

My remark provoked another story about the awfulness of the Nature Conservancy people.

'I used to go to St Kilda,' Tex said. 'You see, I have got a number of hobbies. One of them is parasitology. Fleas, flukes and cuckoos and beautiful blonde women: they are all parasites. Nematoditis was a problem on the sheep on St Kilda. The Nature Conservancy wanted to investigate it. But in order to find the worms, they had to kill the sheep. I was told to kill six of them. They were dying anyway. And one of the Nature Conservancy men *committed suicide*, went off his rocker, took to the hills in St Kilda and we had a hell of a job to find him, he wouldn't come back.'

'Why?'

'Because I was a ruthless, murdering bastard.' Tex mentioned his name; it meant nothing to me. 'He was a pretty famous man, but he was daft as a brush. Mustn't kill anything.'

'Except the worms.'

'Except the worms, and do you know how I killed the worms?'

'No.'

'I fed the sheep on fag ends. Nicotine. I sent the shit every week to Regent's Park Zoo so they could count the eggs. I cured them of all internal parasites without using any drugs at all. Then I brought two of them back here.'

Eventually, we got onto the subject of Gavin Maxwell.

'A nature nut, too,' I said. 'Was he also odd?'

'You say a nature nut,' Tex replied, 'but go back to *Ring of Bright Water*, and you will find, if you study it carefully, that he is very, very seldom there. It is somebody else that is with the otters. Lavinia, his wife, or Terry Nutkin, or whoever. Gavin doesn't stay very long.'

'Why was that, do you think?'

'Because he liked to talk about it all, but when it came to the blood and guts, he was not there.'

I asked about Maxwell's homosexuality.

'He always had young men with him. He seemed to be afraid of women. He didn't like women. One or two girls that I knew set their cap at him, but he would just have nothing to do with them.'

'What about his wife?'

'Lavinia Lascelles: a cousin of the Queen's. She only married him because he was being lionised after *Ring of Bright Water*. She was as daft as a brush. It didn't last.'

Tex's view of Maxwell was of an extremely loyal friend – 'though I think he was frightened of me' – as well as a generous companion. 'He used to say he was broke,' Tex said. 'I said I was broke, but his broke and my broke were two different things.'

'What was he like as a hunter?' I asked.

'The truth is,' Tex said, 'that Gavin couldn't catch his own penis.'

Eventually, and with great regret, I left Tex to his drams and his memories. I could have stayed for a week.

I walked back to the boat, on the path this time, in pitch darkness and in a soft, almost warm rain which brought the midges out in their billions. As I rowed out to *Sylvia B*, I was treated to the most fantastic display of phosphorescence I think I have ever seen. Even the drips from the oars shone like illuminated gems. It is said that this indicates particularly clean water.

I am a glutton for old men and their stories and I felt in the mood to celebrate. Unfortunately the party at Strathaird had cleaned out my drink locker. So I rowed astern and tapped on the side of the caravan boat, which was still there, though silent now. The man came to the rail and I asked if I could buy a few cans of beer off him. He disappeared below, and reappeared with what he said were his last three cans, plus a quarter-full bottle of whisky. I took them all gratefully and asked how much I owed him.

'Nothing at all,' he said smiling. 'No problem. Enjoy your dinner.'

Since venison was on the menu for the last time, I certainly did.

6

CANNA

By morning the rain had gone. I set sail for Canna under a beautiful blue sky, with a gentle breeze blowing from the north. So gentle was the breeze that it was slow going. I read for a while, steering with my foot; I looked about a bit; I fiddled with the rigging; I untied and retied the dinghy lashings. I managed to beguile five minutes or so by working out what day of the week it was. Having established that it had been a Sunday when I had left Rum, I was able, after a certain amount of thought, to calculate that today must be Friday. That job done, I thought I would heat up some soup. I ate it with cheese on water biscuits, topped with tomato relish and Tabasco sauce, while sitting in the sun in the cockpit and watching the huge mass of Rum, still forbidding even in the sunshine, loom up on the port bow. Canna, by contrast, was emerald green.

Gavin Maxwell wrote of this island: 'I have never mastered a temptation to stay forever on Canna. It is unlike any other island, and it is entirely beautiful . . . It is habitable and inhabited, warm and living.' Maxwell had been a friend of the then proprietor, John Lorne Campbell, who lived there until his death in 1992. Indeed it was he who first opened Maxwell's eyes to the possible economic value of basking shark livers. Campbell's widow, Mrs Margaret Fay Shaw Campbell, still holds court in Canna House, and it was one of my purposes to visit her and see the famous library which her husband had built up. Maxwell wrote of his friend that he was 'a scholar of all that is Gaelic in tradition, an explorer of every way in which his and like communities may be improved.'

Campbell had met his future wife when they were both researching Gaelic traditions and folksongs in the outer Hebrides in the 1930s. She was an American, tiny, vivacious and determined, while he was one of the Campbells of Inverneil in Knapdale – his family home is now an aromatherapy and Rolfing centre. He was a friend of Compton Mackenzie and other luminaries of the interwar phase of the eternally unconsummated Gaelic revival. In 1938 Campbell bought Canna with the primary intention of farming it. He had studied Rural Economy at Oxford, and after graduating worked on farms in England. But he had already published *Highland Songs of the '45*, which drew on his knowledge of Gaelic language and culture, and for the rest of his life, he was both a farmer and a scholar.

This combination of activities enabled him to write with first-hand authority about most aspects of Hebridean life, past and present. Campbell's most important work is a three-volume collection called *Hebridean Folksongs*. This complements a book by his wife, Dr Margaret Fay Shaw, as she calls herself in print, *Folksongs and Folklore of South Uist*.[2] Among Campbell's other major publications were *The Book of Barra* (1936) and *Canna: the Story of a Hebridean Island* (1981). The latter is still in print and well worth consulting by anyone seeking to understand the history of this part of the world. Campbell approaches his subject from a consciously Gaelocentric point of view.

> Scottish historians for the most part seem to be incapable of realising that the islanders had a point of view and a way of life to defend . . . The destruction of the archives of Iona and those of the Lordship of the Isles leaves the clan histories of the MacVurichs and of Hugh MacDonald as the only source where the islanders' point of view is stated, apart from what survives in contemporary Gaelic verse – and Scottish historians have never felt knowledge of Gaelic to be indispensable when writing about the Highlands and Islands. This leaves the official records of such bodies as the Scots parliaments and the Scots Privy Council as the main source of information, and their language is continually coloured with official prejudices and only states the official point of view – which may at times be no nearer the truth than what *Pravda* was likely to print about the East German Czech, Hungarian and Polish disturbances in 1953, 1956, 1968 and 1981–2.[1]

It now seems that this imbalance might one day be redressed by the foundation of a University of the Highlands and Islands, one of whose campuses will be on Canna, in John Lorne Campbell's library. This is a venture pregnant with possibilities since for the first time since 1560 the Hebrides will acquire a proper centre for intellectual and cultural life. The University's headquarters will be in Inverness, but the plan is that the campuses will be distributed all over the Highlands and Islands, from the North Atlantic Fisheries College in Shetland to a mooted Gaelic centre on Islay. Furthermore, the intention is that it will be an 'on-line' university so that, as one recent report put it, 'even in the smallest crofts, from Shetland to Kintyre, it should be possible to take part in a seminar or tutorial'. This will mean that the University will also have a world market open to it.

John Lorne Campbell's library incorporates the largest collection of Gaelic folksongs and tales ever made. There are 1500 of the former, and 350 of the latter, all recorded from native Gaelic speakers – many of them monoglot – in the Uists and Hebrides in the 1930s and 1940s. Some have been transcribed and about a tenth of the collection was published by Dr Campbell in his book *Hebridean Folksongs*. In addition, all the relevant scholarly journals are in the library in complete sets, as well as books in Irish Gaelic, Welsh, Manx Gaelic, Breton, Cornish and Faeroese, a language with which Dr Campbell was also familiar. There is also a large collection of documents, manuscripts, research papers and correspondence on Scottish, Celtic and Norse historical subjects, ranging from

---

1 *Canna: the Story of a Hebridean Island,* John Lorne Campbell, Canongate, Edinburgh 1994, p. 38.

2 Re-issued in 1999 by Birlinn, Edinburgh. It includes many of Dr Shaw's fascinating photographs.

local sources to the Vatican. Moreover Margaret Fay Shaw Campbell's archive of historical-cultural material, which focuses on music and photographs, might well be added to all this at a later date. Together they make a unique scholarly resource.

Right now all this material sits, or much of it does, round the walls of a room about 15 feet by 20, in the middle of which is the desk at which John Lorne Campbell used to work. It is piled high with books, journals, card-index boxes and tape reels. The still air, the age of the books, and the lovely, calming odour of indoor dust combine with the faintest hints of damp, old clothes and leather to give the room a wonderful, vintage 'nose'. The dimmish light, the orderly clutter and that sense of utter peace which exists only on remote islands are enough to bring out the scholar *manqué* in anyone. I felt that I could have spent a month there, just browsing, noting and generally refreshing my brain.

I saw all this when I went up to take tea with Mrs Campbell on the afternoon following my arrival. She is an intense, obviously highly-strung lady with a piercing gaze and dark edges to her eyes. I had been told that she has 'the sight', but she did not say anything about it and, deeply curious though I was, I felt it would have been disrespectful to ask. She did, however, say at one point that, though she had no idea who I was, 'when I begin to talk, I begin to sense something'. Whatever it was she sensed, it cannot have been too uncomplimentary as she proceeded to help me to both tea and cakes and to give me a very full account of the state of the island.

Later she gave me a demonstration of the huge, heavy camera which she used to lug all over the outer Hebrides before the war, up the cliffs of Mingulay, and across the bogs of South Uist, taking pictures for her book. Since she is five feet tall at the most, and slight with it, and since she also carried lenses that weighed a lot and a heavy, old-fashioned tripod, this was a considerable feat of physical endurance. It was also a great photographic achievement. Her camera had no exposure timer: she simply told her subjects to remain 'absolutely still while I count to six'. The resulting pictures, which she showed me, are wonderfully evocative of a lost world.

Canna House is an elegant, medium-sized, neo-Georgian structure, built in 1865. It stands amid lush policy woodlands, once again illustrating the potential fertility of these islands. With a long, old-fashioned conservatory stretching out to one side, the house has a comfortable, lived-in atmosphere. It still has the feel of being the 'big house' within a largely self-sufficient island community.

I was shown into the drawing room, where we were soon joined by a small court of resident and visiting ladies. One sat in the window seat, another opposite the grand piano, while Mrs Campbell perched on the edge of a chair ten sizes too large for her and held the ring. While tea was served we discussed life in the Uists in the 1930s and I asked about the mood of the people. Did she think they had been happy then, even in their poverty?

'I think they were happier,' she said, 'because they were much more philosophical. They had much truer values. People today haven't got any values; they get everything from television. Their whole attitude to life was different.

They were amused by little things and beautiful things. Today it's hard to amuse people.'

I asked if her husband, as a scholar, ever felt cut off from the world, living on an island as quiet as Canna.

'No, that was why he was able to get his work done,' she said, 'although it used to be rather irksome to some other scholars. One person said to him, "You are far from the world here." He replied: "I'm in the centre of my world." '

Mrs Campbell said she saw two main dangers to what her husband had achieved on Canna. The first was tourism and the second was agricultural change. In 1981 her husband gifted the island to the National Trust for Scotland. Two years later, after a bout of ill-health, he handed over the farm to the Trust as well. Mrs Campbell told me what she thought of the new operators, but said, 'Don't you dare write this up! If you do I'll shoot you.' Since I entirely believe her, I will confine myself to quoting the last sentence of her husband's book: 'It is to be hoped that difficulties which have arisen since 1986 owing to the Trust's natural lack of experience in dealing with Hebridean people and Hebridean farming problems will soon be solved.'[3] I inferred from what Mrs Campbell said that they still await solution.

Leaving Canna House, I went back out to the boat to eat. Afterwards I rowed ashore and walked up to the small Lodge which the National Trust maintains on the island for the use of its staff and other visitors. There I met Ian MacIntyre, the Trust's part-time factor for the island. He is a large, kindly man of about retirement age. I asked him about the farming problem and he told me the main difficulty was that staff numbers had to be reduced from five to three. The loss of two jobs on an island with a total population of 16, in six households, is obviously catastrophic, equivalent in national terms to closing down the whole manufacturing industry. But the Trust, as employer, has a genuine difficulty in that it has to make the island cover its costs. But the only point of having such a body own the island is to preserve something of the traditional Hebridean way of life. That Trust ownership is viable only after adaptation of the sole industry to modern methods should give food for thought to all proponents of the 'museumisation' of the Highlands.

Ian said that the only other feasible option under the current arrangements would be to increase the number of independent agricultural holdings, whether crofts or smallholdings of a different sort, and hope that these can be supplemented either by fishing, tourist-related work or 'telecommuting'. Once the University gets going, there will be a post for a librarian and work for people looking after the researchers who come to use the library.

Since the house was a Lodge for visitors, and the Trust is not a poor organisation, I was bold enough to ask if I might take a bath. No problem, Ian said. Afterwards he gave me a dram and beer and told me a few stories, including

---

3 *Ibid.*, p. 197.

some about Lillian Beckwith, the author of the well-known book about the Hebrides and its people, *The Hills is Lonely*. Though he now lives on the mainland, Ian had grown up in Elgol, where his mother was the school teacher. Beckwith – her real name was Comber – had arrived in the village from England with her husband, who was a fisherman, in the late 1940s. She was one of the first incomers to the district and was immediately taken into everybody's confidence. Her response was to exploit the situation.

'The book is supposed to be fiction,' Ian said, 'but the characters were obviously based on local people, whom she used for jokes and stories. They were too obvious: Mary became Morag and Peter became John and so on. The people thought she had let them down. They had welcomed her and made her one of them. Then when this book came out she was making fun of them. She fell out with a lot of people in Elgol.'

'What happened?' I asked.

'Oh nothing really,' Ian said, 'except they rather cold-shouldered her. But she did get into serious trouble later.'

'When was that?'

'When she moved to Soay and fell out with Tex Geddes. The police were forever up and down the road. It was the topic of the district.'

Apparently, there was one occasion when she tried to ambush Tex by waiting behind the wall of a house on Soay with a pitchfork in her hand. As an ex-champion bayonet fencer, he would not have been unduly perturbed by that. In the event he responded by throwing a pot of pepper in Comber's face and disarming her while she shrieked and pawed at her eyes. Soon afterwards, she left the area for good.

The next day dawned fine but windy. The forecast was for it to blow up. A couple of large, expensively equipped yachts wearing blue ensigns arrived in the bay, preferring to wait out the blow in shelter. The crews went ashore immediately, neither waiting to see what the holding was like, nor setting an anchor watch. In fact the holding is not that good nowadays. The number of visiting yachts has increased and most drop sewage into the bay. That is very good for the kelp, which has spread dramatically, but it is bad for the holding as kelp is a very slippery substance. Consequently one of these boats dragged its anchor, and nearly collided with another one lying behind it.

On shore, I was buttonholed by two other tourists: a couple from 'Oolswater, in Coombria'. The husband wanted me to know that he used to own a craft of the same make as *Sylvia B* but that he had replaced it with the larger vessel I could now see anchored in the bay which gave him what he called 'a wider passage-making envelope'.

As quickly as I decently could, I skedaddled, making for the Church of Scotland building which stands above the anchorage, and which, since John Lorne Campbell had been so ostentatiously Catholic, I was interested to see. Built in 1912, it is one of the most peculiar 'church' structures that I have visited. It has a spire shaped like a V-2 rocket, while the main body of the building resembles what I imagine a small Gothic warehouse might have been like, had the Goths wares to house.

Inside it is even stranger. The National Trust Management Plan for Canna describes it primly as featuring 'asymmetrical fenestration'. Centre-stage is a pulpit – there is no altar – which bears the legend, 'The Lord Endureth Forever', embossed in pseudo-Celtic, Killarney-gift-shop script. The seating accommodation is four enormous benches which are arranged fore-and-aft, rather than athwartships, so that the non-existent congregation – the island has always been almost entirely Catholic – sits facing each other, as in the House of Commons. The aisle is taken up with a huge table, though for what purpose, other than holding one's debating notes, or possibly a gin and tonic at Parish budget committee meetings, I could not think. Most remarkable of all, there was a collection plate near the door which contained something like a pint and a half of money. Much of it was £1 and 50p coins, so the total must have been huge. Since there are not *that* many visiting yachtsmen, nor foot-passengers coming off the ferry for a couple of hours, this plate could not be very regularly emptied. What sort of Presbyterian is it, I wondered, that leaves cash in such quantities lying about uninvested?

Canna is really two islands: Canna and, on the other side of the anchorage, Sanday. Sanday is wide and flat and shelters the harbour from the south. It features an even more extraordinary building than the island's Protestant church: the main Catholic one, the Chapel of St Edward the Confessor. The name is explained by the fact that the building was financed by the English wife of the then Marquess of Bute. Though the architect, William Frame, was also English, the style is ostentatiously Italian. There are echoes of Venice or the villages of Tuscany which are given a bizarre twist by its situation on a tiny Hebridean island, with neither trees nor houses in sight as you approach. According to the Trust, the building is constructed of 'dark grey, bull-faced sneck coursed rubble with contrasting tooled sandstone dressings'. That may well be true: either way, it is a striking edifice, though a visit reveals the sad fact that nobody confesses there any more.

The building is in a fair state of disrepair, having been abandoned in 1963.[4] After the war the population balance on the two islands shifted when so many crofters abandoned independent agriculture and went to work for large farmers, or left the land altogether. In 1890, when St Edward's was built, Sanday was more heavily crofted than Canna. It had a population of over 60 while that of its neighbour was closer to 40. Not only that, the main outside links, through both fishing boats and ferries, were with Barra, Eriskay and South Uist, all Catholic islands. St Edward's would have been well used at the time. Today there are only four crofting tenants left in both islands, Donald John MacKinnon, Nora

---

4   Since my visit it has been announced that the National Heritage Lottery Fund has gifted £580,700 to the Trust for work on St Edward's to convert it into a visitor centre for use by people consulting John Lorne Campbell's library.

MacKinnon, Angus MacKinnon and Winnie MacKinnon. Mass is celebrated in
the old Post Office on Canna, now consecrated as St Columba's, which abuts the
machinery shed belonging to Patrick MacKinnon, and which stands between
the house of the Trust's farm manager, Ian MacKinnon, and the new, smaller
Post Office, which is run by Geraldine MacKinnon.

Walking back from St Edward's, I crossed to Canna by the footbridge, at the
Sanday side of which is an icon of the Virgin Mary in stained glass built into a
five-foot high wall-like cairn. It is angled – I don't know whether deliberately –
so that the evening sunlight in summer shines through, giving a warm glow to
the image. Seeing such reminders of matters spiritual simply plonked down amidst
the landscape is a reminder of how different the Catholic outlook is from the
Presbyterian tradition (in which I was brought up). John Lorne Campbell's book,
Canna, illuminates the history of the island by giving the religious dimension
equal weight to the political.

Canna was part of the endowment of the Monastery of Iona after the
Benedictines took it over in about 1200. The island was, through Iona, subject to
the Archdiocese of Trondheim. Today it is governed from Oban, by the Archbishop
of Argyll and the Isles.[5] The official Scottish version of Hebridean history tells
the story of a successful struggle for control of important territory against rebellious
subjects. This is not the only view. Campbell emphasises that 'the Islesmen
considered their rights derived from Norway, not from Scotland, and their customs
and traditions from Ireland, and that they owed the Scottish Crown little in the
way of allegiance.' Thus the story of how the Scottish kings brought about the
downfall of the Lordship of the Isles and extended their power throughout the
Hebrides could be told as a tale of imperial expansion rather than the conventional
one of the legitimate exercise of pre-established regal authority.

What few historians would dispute is that the consequences of the Scottish
invasion were disastrous. The clan warfare which destroyed the relative peace of
life in the west Highlands for three centuries was a result of the fact that Edinburgh
could not offer an effective substitute authority to that previously exercised by
the Lords of the Isles. As Moscow did in post-war eastern Europe, Edinburgh
created disorder in the Highlands, playing one clan off against another, to give it
an excuse to intervene. The period of what might be called 'clanarchy' – roughly
1450 to 1750 – saw a long campaign of extirpation against the Gaelic way of life.
Its epitome was the Glencoe massacre and its most uninhibited epoch the years
of murder, destruction and repression after Culloden.

Later echoes were heard in two campaigns mounted by the Edinburgh

---

5   When I arrived on Canna, that personage was the Very Reverend Roddy Wright, but
     by the time I left, two days later, the Bishopric was vacant, the Bishop having fled his
     post and gone into hiding after confessing that he was involved in a long-term liaison
     with one of his parishioners and that he had had a child many years previously by
     another. Most people I spoke to took the view of one islesman who said to me, 'I
     think you are a man before you are a priest.'

'establishment' in the nineteenth century, one in favour of the clearances and the other against the Crofters Act.

Gaelocentric history tells a very different story, which occasionally has more than a purely Hebridean, or even Scottish, significance. Campbell draws attention to the fact that the 1688 Revolution in England, from which Glencoe flowed immediately and Culloden and the Clearances in due course, was not, as is popularly supposed, a blow struck for toleration. It was exactly the opposite. The immediate cause of the *coup d'état* that put the Protestant King William on the throne 'of Scotland, England, France and Ireland' was the edict issued by the Catholic James VII – James II in England – in London on 12 February 1687 proclaiming religious *liberty* for all his subjects, except extremists who advocated violence, most of whom were in fact Protestants. Campbell comments:

> One man's terrorist is another man's freedom fighter; James VII's attempt to secure freedom of conscience in Scotland failed, so he has been vilified and the Covenanting fanatics have been canonized, metaphorically speaking. James might as well have been the late Shah of Iran urging moderation and tolerance on the followers of Ayatollah Khomeini. His attempt was generations before its time, not realised until the foundation of the American Constitution, with its clause forbidding the establishment of any particular form of Christianity, in 1787; and the repeal of the Penal Laws on Britain in 1829.[6]

The issues at stake have not gone away, even if they now manifest themselves in arguments about economic rather than religious liberty. Campbell is surely worth listening to when he comments about the long war of the east against the west: 'Many will regret that the Lordship of the Isles did not survive under Norwegian protection in a form that could have led to the Hebrides now possessing the present liberties of the Isle of Man, associated with the Scottish Isles in Norse times.'

My final call on Canna was on a man whom I had met quite by chance when chatting to Ian MacIntyre in the National Trust bothy. He was Sean Morris, the RSPB summer representative on the island. The Society has no reserve on Canna but the National Trust had invited it to send someone to advise on policies relevant to that old warhorse of Hebridean conservation, the corncrake. Morris was the answer to that request. The other aspect of his job is conducting wildlife tours on the island and explaining to the visiting public about the corncrake, eagle and other species found here.

It turned out to be such an odd interview that a little bit of background is necessary to understand it. As I told Lord Strathcona on Colonsay, I had written to all the conservation bodies who own reserves in the Hebrides to ask for sight of their managment plans before setting out. To my surprise the replies were far from uniform. The Woodland Trust told me that their plans were not public documents (though they have subsequently changed that view and let me see the one I asked for). The John Muir Trust said they had no management plans drawn

---

6 *Ibid.*, p. 87. The Penal Laws were those denying full civil rights to Roman Catholics.

up at all, which I did not believe at the time but now accept to have been the truth. The Scottish Wildlife Trust gave me precisely what I asked for, while the National Trust for Scotland provided me with six comprehensive and beautifully presented booklets. Nothing was omitted. The management plan for Canna is 150 pages long and, apart from giving a full history and description of the island, reproduces in facsimile the Deed of Gift of the islands, the SNH Management Agreement, the full estate inventory, the annual accounts going back five years and much, much more. 'We are a charity', Julie Duff, head of countryside management plans explained. 'As far as we are concerned, once the plan has been agreed, it is public knowledge.'

The RSPB reacted quite differently. David Minns, the glum Yorkshireman who is head of public relations in Scotland, refused my request and questioned my motives for making it. What is so secret about the way the RSPB spends its members' money, I wondered? I had also asked for copies of the species action plans for a couple of the birds I might expect to see and/or discuss on my trip. One of them was the corncrake. Minns did not even refuse this request; he ignored it completely.

Before I left Islay, I had written a feature for the *Guardian* telling this story, and describing the different responses from the various bodies. I made the point that the compassion business is as much a market as any other sector of the economy and suggested that prudent potential donors might like to shop around before signing any direct debit forms.

I was under no illusion that the RSPB would like this since it clearly hates public scrutiny, but I was not prepared for the childish way in which the Society actually responded. My visits to James How and Clive Mackay had taken place before the article was published, on 31 July. Sean Morris was the first staff member I was to see after that.

Arriving for my appointment at the National Trust bothy, I immediately noticed a different atmosphere. Ian MacIntyre had left for Oban and there were no more beers in the cupboard. Morris was the only resident now and it was either teabags or instant coffee. The fire was out and the kitchen-cum-sitting room was cold and uninviting. Alone on the island, Morris struck me as a lonely and rather sad figure. He is a young agriculture graduate of Nottingham University, desperate to get into conservation as a profession, but unable to find a permanent job.

He received me coldly. This is clearly going to be a sticky conversation, I thought, so pleasantries will be pointless. I decided I should get down to the corncrake straight away. Morris told me that this bird was the main reason he was here. I asked him how many were on the island this year.

'None,' he said.

'What! None at all?'

'No. There used to be 15 pairs.'

'When was that?'

'1930s. The last one was here in 1994. So I'm just trying to improve the habitat, increase early cover, mainly. If there is a corncrake here next year, it will have been a success.'

'What does "improving the habitat" mean?'

'Planting cow parsley and nettles in corncrake corners.'

'Sort of corncrake gardens?'

'Uh huh.'

'How do corncrakes know to come back here if they weren't here in the first place? How do they know what you've done for them? You've no means of communicating with them, have you?'

'They're migratory birds. They'll land here on passage, and if the habitat is suitable, they will stop.'

'But then the Uists will be short one corncrake, will they not?'

'Maybe.'

'What about the theory, offered by some of the people I talked to on Coll, that the best way to encourage corncrakes is simply to plough up the land and use it? Has that been investigated at all?'

'I don't know. I think the guy you need to speak to is David Minns. He does all the publicity for that sort of thing.'

'This is really a technical question,' I said.

Silence.

'I take it you are some kind of corncrake expert,' I went on.

'I know about the birds,' he said.

'Are you aware of those theories?'

'Um hm. The best thing for corncrakes is hay.'

'What about corn?'

'I don't know about that.'

There followed a long pause, after which he said, 'I am in a difficult position. I've been told not to say very much.'

'About what?' I asked.

'David Minns is the guy you need to speak to.'

'Why? Is the corncrake a secret thing?'

'No. They're not secret.'

'Are theories about whether they live in corn something you are forbidden from discussing?'

'No, I'm sure they would use corn.'

'Why is all this so difficult?'

'I don't know. It's coming from much higher up than me.'

'What, saying don't speak to the public about the corncrake?'

'No. Not that. I can speak to the public.'

'Well, I'm a member of the public.'

There was another long silence.

'It's really awkward,' Morris said, twisting round in his chair and swinging his gaze from a pile of rucksacks under the stairs to the window and back to the rucksacks again.

'Why is it awkward?' I asked.

This time he didn't reply at all. I must say I felt rather sorry for him, but then I remembered that I was not talking to Sean Morris, Esquire, but to the public face of a public charity, a man who gives talks to visitors and shows them round the island.

'I'm curious to know why you cannot discuss the corncrake,' I said. 'I would hate it to be thought that the RSPB is a secretive organisation.'

'They are not.'

'Well perhaps we can resume the conversation about the corncrakes then?'

'Well, the corncrakes like the hay but they will use other vegetation, like cow parsley and nettles, and iris, and they'll maybe use oats. They are omnivorous birds.'

I changed the subject and asked some more general questions.

Morris told me that he would be unemployed come the end of August. He said he had done a greenshank survey for the RSPB last summer, then been unemployed until he started this contract earlier in the year. I asked if he had ever thought of going to work as a temporary gamekeeper or as a beater at grouse or pheasant shoots during the winter, before the conservation season comes round again and he is rehired.

'No,' he said, 'I have not thought of doing that.'

'Would you consider it?'

He shook his head.

'Why not?'

'It's just something I have never thought about.'

'You don't think you might learn something about birds from gamekeepers?'

'Not really.'

We discussed other birds on Canna, including the seabirds. 'Birds are my passion,' he said. 'I could watch them all day.'

'But do they, *in toto*, need conserving?'

'Things like the corncrakes do.'

'Not globally, only in this country,' I said.

'How do you mean?' he asked.

'There are hundreds of thousands of corncrakes in the world, possibly millions. The main threat is surely their being killed by Nile valley quail netters, isn't it?'

'I don't know,' he said.

'There is no evidence that the corncrake is about to go extinct, it is just that there are very few of them left in Britain.'

'It would be a real shame to lose them.'

'Why?'

'Because we would miss them.'

Well, that was a point, if an entirely personal one, so I moved on to the cost of providing this amenity for British birdwatchers. I went over the corncrake costs I have mentioned in connection with Tiree. 'Would it not be better to give all that money to the Egyptian quail netters so they don't have to live on corncrake pie?' I asked.

No answer.

'The corncrake would be far better off,' I continued. 'And you could go and be a grants officer in the souks of Alexandria and play backgammon all day long.'

There was silence for a minute or more. Through the widow, I could see Mr and Mrs Oolswater rowing about the bay in their dinghy.

'Do you have any views on that?' I asked at length when it was clear that no answer was likely to be forthcoming.

'I don't know that it would work,' Morris said. 'It may do; it may not.'

Another long pause.

'Well, there we are,' I said. 'If I may say so, as a form of public interpretation of your policies, this isn't what I would describe as terribly informative.'

'Um hm.'

'Are you personally interested in the corncrake?'

'Yeah.'

'Does it embarrass you to be asked to talk about them?'

'No.'

'So why won't you answer the questions?'

There was another long pause. then Morris said, 'It would be great to have the corncrakes back here, don't you think?'

'OK, that's the corncrake,' I said, feeling that I had had my answer about the RSPB. I changed tack. 'Tell me why you think you have been ordered to say nothing.'

'I've been told that publicity matters should be dealt with by David Minns.'

'But I'm not asking about publicity matters, I am asking technical questions about corncrakes.'

'I speak to the general public.'

'That's me. I'm not a member of the Society or anything like that. Why am I not a member of the general public?'

'It depends in what capacity you are here.'

'What do you mean by that?'

There was another long pause.

'I can see I am digging myself into a hole,' he said. 'I knew that would happen. I am a quiet, quite shy person. I'm not a public relations person.'

'OK, just tell me, where does this directive come from?'

'Maybe you should speak to Alison.' Morris was referring to the local area officer of the Society, Dr Alison Maclennan, who is based in Broadford on Skye. I made an immediate note to do just that.

'So your instructions came from her?'

'Um hm.'

There was another pause.

'This is really embarrassing,' he said. 'She didn't say don't speak to you.'

'But just not to tell me anything,' I suggested.

'No, not that either.'

'What did she say, then?'

'It seems to me I am getting deeper and deeper all the time.' There was another pause, a very long one this time. 'I don't know what to say.'

'Did she say you are not allowed to discuss the corncrake with me?'

'No.'

'In that case why are you so reticent about the subject?'

'It depends what you know already. I'm not going to divulge information about confidential birds that are possibly going to be disturbed by people coming here and collecting their eggs.'

'But there are no birds here, you've just told me that. There are no eggs to collect. In any case, I am a writer. I am not an ornithologist, and I am certainly not a criminal. The last thing I would want to do is to encourage egg thieves, if that is what you are implying. I am all in favour of having more wildlife all over the place. What I am interested in is how the RSPB tries to achieve this.'

'I know. I think it is bloody awkward. I'm going to make an idiot of myself,' he said.

'Are you beginning to think you hate working for the RSPB?'

'No. I love working for the RSPB. I love my job.'

'What do you think personally about this policy? Do you think it is going to work? Do you think I will live the rest of my life in ignorance of the truth about the corncrake?'

'No.'

'Do you think all this gives a good impression of the RSPB?'

'No.'

'Assuming you were running the organisation,' I asked finally, 'how would you deal with this sort of situation?'

'I wouldn't put people like me in this situation.'

I decided to leave it at that.

Lounging on deck after dinner that evening, I saw a single light gleaming in the uncurtained window of the NTS lodge. I pictured the dedicated researcher at home alone, counting nettle seeds and greasing his penetrometer.

Poking my head out of the hatch next morning, I saw that the wind had moderated slightly. But it was still coming south-west and blustery and clouds were scudding by overhead. Outside the anchorage, the sea was flecked with white. It must have been blowing a good 5 or 6. Occasional rain squalls passed through. My next port of call was Loch Boisdale on South Uist across the Minch. The forecast was for the wind to veer and drop further during the day. It always does that once an isolated depression has gone through. I decided I would sail. I was keen to have a good breeze for this leg of the journey, which is quite long, as I was low on petrol. I had not found any since Coll, a fortnight before, and I did not want to be stuck out in the middle of the Minch with no wind, no fuel and no larboard watch to relieve me as night came on. Caution dictated a day like this. Heavy weather, within reason, is not a problem: *Sylvia B* is a brave little boat. Like Joshua Slocum's father she is 'not afraid of a capful of wind'. She sails quite comfortably well reefed down in a solid blow, provided, of course, that the sea state is tolerable and you are not too close-hauled.

After eating breakfast and making coffee, soup and sandwiches for the voyage, I hoisted the working jib and a single-reefed main. The anchor came out of the sand with a huge lump of kelp attached. I picked it out of the flukes, leaped aft to the cockpit, took hold of the tiller and winched in the sheets. We raced across the smooth water of the harbour and out beyond Rubha Carrinnis. After reaching at high speed up past Compass Hill – so called because of a magnetic anomaly – we turned west, hardening up into the wind and laying a course for Loch Boisdale.

Incredible gusts were sweeping down off the huge cliffs on this side of the island. These would be followed by short periods of almost complete calm. Then the wind would blast down savagely again, on one occasion almost laying *Sylvia B* over on her beam ends before I was able to let the mainsheet fly. There was nothing to do but hang on, head offshore and wait for the wind to settle. In due course it did, but there was a lumpy, confused sea running and, worse, a slowly thickening mist. Nonetheless we soon stared to make good progress and it was not much more than an hour after weighing anchor that the darkening bulk of the Celtic history campus of the future University of the Highlands and Islands slid into the windswept greyness astern and was lost to view.

7

SOUTH UIST

ALL DAY *Sylvia B* plunged and bobbed, lolled and yawed through a confused sea, which did not really moderate until late in the afternoon. To a slowly declining swell from the south-west was added a slowly building one from the south. The wind backed a few points, but then, after dying slightly, started to get a little more lively, bringing drizzly rain with it. No boat likes these sort of conditions, small boats less than most. To add to the discomfort, the visibility did not improve either. At one stage, I was suddenly confronted with the vast bulk of a grey-painted merchant ship looming out of the murk on the starboard bow, less than a mile off.

By about five in the afternoon, I calculated that I should be approaching the coast of South Uist. But still there was nothing to be seen ahead but a choppy sea under a curtain of mist. Possibly another half hour went by until, in quick succession, the rain stopped, the mist began to lift and I saw cliffs rising out of the sea a mile and a half ahead. Not being familiar with this coast, I could not be sure whether I was to the north or the south of the entrance to Loch Boisdale (which is more than a mile wide). No lights, buoys or other identifying marks were visible. As it turned out, I was about two miles south of the entrance. On leaving Canna, I had calculated that the set of the tide (north to south) would more or less cancel my leeway (south to north). Either the tide had flowed more strongly than I had allowed for, or I had not held to my course. So I had to turn either south or north and explore the coast until I found the entrance to Loch Boisdale. But which way to turn? In the end I turned south, reasoning that the coast to the north was largely featureless and I could have sailed for hours before realising that I had gone wrong, whereas it was not far south to the sound of Eriskay so that the first major inlet I would come to would either be that or Loch Boisdale.

Within half an hour or so, I could see the land starting to recede on the starboard side. But it was still not clear which of the two entrances I had found. In the end, I sailed for another couple of miles before I was sure that this was the sound of Eriskay, then gibed the boat and headed north again, conscious that I must now have at least another hour's sailing still to do to get right up to the pier at Loch Boisdale. Though the mist had largely disappeared by now, the light was beginning to fade. By the time I finally dropped anchor among the yachts and

The mighty Blaven: sunset over Skye from Loch Slapin
on the evening I roasted the Rum venison on the beach.

The Forbidden Island:
Rum from the north, on passage from Loch Slapin to Elgol.

Sunset over the Black Cuillin on Skye, from Elgol.
I had just emerged from Col. Robertson's garage-cum-bar.

The road out of Loch Maddy, North Uist.
'I started walking west, in blazing sunshine, making slow progress out towards the township of Solas.'

Clouds piling up over Lingerbay on Harris.
Directly ahead is Runeval, the hill which is threatened with conversion to roadstone.

On passage to the Shiant Isles:
sails set, helm lashed and a cold sun setting over the great mountains of Harris.

At anchor on the Shiants:
as Nigel Nicolson said, 'How lovely were the lovely moments, how bloody the bloody.'

Anchored off Gruinard (anthrax island):
The wind was blowing north-east and clear so the next stop was
Eilean á Chlerich on the top right of the picture – see front cover.

Little Loch Broom from Scoraig: another hot day in the making.
In the Foreground is the *Dewey Rose*, to the left is Topher Dawson's trimaran and in the path
of the sunlight is *Sylvia B*. The ferry can be seen chuntering over to 'civilisation'.

Topher Dawson's house on Scoraig: the designer and builder of this
beautiful dwelling saved the trip by repairing *Sylvia B*'s motor between an early lunch and late tea
after the united resources of industrial Britain had failed to do so in a week.

A stiff blow outside: *Sylvia B* riding at anchor in the roadstead off the Isle of Pabay,
north of Broadford on Skye.

Scoraig: the party approaches. The A-frames for the shelter are being erected and the first of the instruments are being arranged on the stage.

Eigg: the flit boat has docked after arriving from Arisaig with the weekly shopping.

Home at last: an October sunset over the Lagavulin distillery.

fishing boats, ten hours after leaving Canna, it was nearly dark, blowing hard from the south-east and raining. I snugged everything down, ate a quick snack and got ready to go ashore. I packed a towel and dry clothes in one bag and my dirty washing into another, then set off in a downpour to make a laundry delivery and to have a beer and a bath. Bliss!

After my bath, I finished my drink in the non-residents' lounge, reading *Hello!* and *The Shooting Times* which was the only reading matter available. A restful hour was marred only by a middle-aged holiday-maker from another country who rudely insisted on turning the television on, without even asking the other occupants of the room. Worse still, he did this solely for the benefit of his badly behaved ten-year-old son. I managed to scupper the plan by covertly withdrawing the aerial cable from its socket when their unattractive backs were turned. After fiddling in vain with the controls for a few minutes and getting steadily more irate, Holiday-Maker Senior stumped off, cursing the Hebrides because 'noothing werks properly in this place'.

By morning, the rain had stopped, but the sky was still overcast. This was the first time since leaving Tiree nearly two weeks before that I was in range of a supermarket and therefore able to revictual the boat properly. Since Loch Boisdale is the only port and the largest township on South Uist, I assumed that the supermarket would be there. Not a bit of it! Like Tiree, the Uists are largely crofted land, and so everything is scattered about: the Co-op was actually three miles up the road, near the crossroads at Daliburgh. Likewise I was disappointed in my hope of buying some more meths for the galley in Loch Boisdale. It was suggested to me that I might try the garage, which was half a mile away. I walked up there with my containers, only to be told that they did not sell meths, which I should find at the Co-op. Thinking this unlikely, I asked the young girl at the till if there might be an alternative. 'My friend works at the Co. I'll phone and ask her,' she said brightly. I was intrigued to notice that as soon as she had her friend on the line, she spoke Gaelic: the first time I had heard young people using it as their lingua franca. On Islay some of the older folk do, but seldom the youngsters. English was clearly this girl's second language.

The story of Gaelic, and its ruthless suppression by Edinburgh and its allies in London, is too well known to bear repetition here. For nearly two centuries an Anglophone ruling class waged war on the independent culture of a Gaelophone peasantry, with increasing success until the Crofters Act of 1886 imposed the armistice which holds to this day. The result is that vast sporting estates co-exist with Gaelic-speaking garage girls on terms of at least outward amity. Almost all of South Uist, Benbecula and Eriskay (92,000 acres in all) is owned by a company called South Uist Estates Ltd., but their rights are largely confined to shooting and fishing, while the land is worked by 900 crofters, all of whom have complete security of tenure. But after a century of relative peace, a new element has entered the equation, threatening to destabilise the situation once again.

As on Canna (and Oronsay, Tiree, Coll and Rum too), the conservationists have arrived, uninvited, on South Uist with the aim of rearranging the relationship between the land and the people, both lairds and crofters. On South Uist, this incursion started in a small way in 1958, the year after Lady Bullough gave Rum to the nation, when the Nature Conservancy declared Loch Druidibeg – which lies towards the northern end of the island – as a Site of Special Scientific Interest and a National Nature Reserve. The aim was to create a protected breeding site for the greylag goose whose numbers had been dropping alarmingly. The NCC's first management plan put this species at the head of the Reserve's list of priorities, increased numbers being urgently called for.

Since then, goose numbers on the Reserve have continued to drop steadily. From about 150 breeding pairs in 1958, numbers slumped to 65–70 pairs in the 1970s, then to 38 pairs in 1981 and finally to a mere 13 pairs in 1994. Outside the Reserve, where the greylags had no bureaucratic protection, and where they continued to be shot both for sport and the pot, numbers have soared from next to nothing in 1958 to a current population of about 2500 birds. In the commercial world – one is tempted to say 'in the real world' – an enterprise like Loch Druidibeg which has so comprehensively failed in its original purpose, a purpose which in any case is no longer needed since goose numbers are rising strongly worldwide, would be quietly put to sleep. The assets would be sold and the staff laid off. But that is not the way of the nature bureaucracy, and it is in that fact that the danger to places like the Uists lies. There are two reasons for this. The first reflects the general bureaucratic tendency to worship size before usefulness – in commercial terms, measuring performance by turnover rather than profit, British Leyland-style. The second reason is more interesting, and it derives from the particular character of the British nature conservation world, a character which to a remarkable extent derives from the personality of two men: Fraser Darling and Max Nicholson. Darling's background and outlook I have already described: Nicholson's needs now to be briefly sketched in.

Edward Max Nicholson, born in 1904 and educated at Sedbergh and Oxford, was head of the Nature Conservancy from 1952–1966. He, more than anyone else, set the tone of the organisation in its formative years. He was a formidable bureaucrat, who had previously served as Head of the Allocation of Tonnage Division of the Ministry of War Transport during the Second World War. Nicholson was arguably the most distinguished conservationist of this century, and certainly he held more important jobs than anyone else. Apart from being Director General of the Nature Conservancy for 14 years, he also served as President of the RSPB and Vice-President of the Wildfowl and Wetlands Trust for many years. He sat on the boards of the Trust for Urban Ecology, Earthwatch Europe, the International Institute for Environment and Development, the World Wildlife Fund, the International Commission on National Parks, the UK Advisory Council on Scientific Policy, the UK Standing Committee for World Conservation Strategy, the International Union for the Conservation of Nature and the American Ornithologists Union; he was also Secretary to the Duke of Edinburgh's Study Conference on the Countryside – to name just the main positions he has occupied. He is the author of several influential books on birds and editor of the nine-volume bible of European ornithology, *The Birds of the Western Palaearctic*.

In 1970, Nicholson published his seminal work *The Environmental Revolution*. Subtitled *A Guide for the New Masters of the World*, it describes how the relationship between humanity and nature was going to be rearranged by people such as himself, the new masters referred to in the subtitle. The first page sets the tone. 'Our degenerate and self-disgusted, materialist, power-drunk and sex-crazed civilisation,' Nicholson asserts, needs to be cured by a 'return in some form to the wilderness'.

Nicholson's early interest in birds was stimulated by having seen, at the age of four, a sparrowhawk making off with his favourite yellow chicken.[1] Nicholson's interests later expanded to include 'the earth's surviving wildernesses' which, he felt, 'held secrets which could add to the dimensions of the spirit and of the mind. The power of a great waterfall or the silence and vastness of a desert commanded surrender [in me] and gave serene ecstasy.'

Nicholson wrote of the founders of the NCC that 'we desired a paradise to care for'. But 'drastic change [was] needed'. That change required that people be forced to recognise their own good. Nicholson describes common humanity as evolutionarily useless:

> The vast majority have originated nothing. They go along, dragging their feet, wherever they are led. All that they have contributed would have left mankind still in the Stone Age. They change their fashions of dress, they learn to operate machines and to apply techniques which are handed out to them and they preen themselves on a spurious sophistication and an unearned affluence to which they are only superficially attuned . . .
>
> Man [is] a major and menacing delinquent element in nature [who needs] to purge himself of the alarming tendencies to destructive violence which threaten his environment. This perennially upwelling barbarism [presents a problem] of fundamentally adapting primitive psychology inherited from the distant past to the totally changed requirements of sophisticated living . . . An intensive spell of ecological repentance is called for.[2]

Nicholson not only condemns people but their faith, in particular the Catholic Church. The Old Testament contains 'chronic and uninhibited incitement towards aggressive, exploitative and reproductively irresponsible behaviour in the human species'. The New Testament is informed by an equally destructive spirit, though Nicholson expresses surprise about this since Christ once spent 40 days 'in the wilderness'.

Nicholson attacks the education system, which he describes as 'the other great organised source of neglect, of misdirection and of obstruction in relation to the

---

1   Nicholson is not alone in getting a thrill from such attacks. A prominent pro-bird campaigner from Glasgow, Bernard Zonfrillo, wrote recently in the *Herald*, 'I attract small birds and pigeons to my garden table, as do many conservationists and birdwatchers, in the hope that sparrowhawks will come and make a kill. Such sights are interesting to witness.' (18 July 1997)

2   *The Environmental Revolution* Max Nicholson, Penguin edition, London 1972, pp. 300–1.

attainment of the needed harmony between man and nature.' The remedy lies with the mass media which, 'if rightly used, can powerfully assist in re-educating adults as well as juveniles'. But this education will not be like the first-hand experience he enjoyed, once the nature bureaucracy has closed off 'wilderness' to those whom it does not think merit permission to experience it. 'Modern man,' he says, 'cannot hope without some serious preparation and training to be anything other than a misfit and a blot on the wilderness scene.' Instead non-conservationists should be prepared to limit their experiences to watching films or visiting 'some substitute wilderness near to home'.

In his conclusion, Nicholson draws his threads together in one, overriding statement about the importance of people like himself:

> Man's obstinate stupidities, his character defects due to badly adjusted aggression, possessiveness and greed, and his passion for embracing myths strongly at variance both with objective circumstances and with manifest human needs, far from diminishing along the line from brutish savagery to ostensible civilisation, have actually gone on increasing, right up to our present day . . . The kind of aspirations and attitudes of the conservation movement largely correspond to the feelings of those who are most keenly critical of various dominant tendencies in modern materialist civilisation.[3]

My first thought on South Uist was that, after reading such confidently expressed righteousness, from such an authoritative and presumably expert source, it came as a shock to realise that the New Masters of the World have been unable to cater even for the breeding preferences of the greylag goose.

I filled six plastic bags at the Co-op with the products of our self-disgusted, power-drunk civilisation, and left them in the charge of the attractive and evolutionarily rather useful-looking lady at the till for collection a few hours later. I then set off up the road to Askernish to see Bill Neill, the local representative of the Scottish Wildlife Trust – Robin Tapplcy's counterpart in the Uists.

Undei a steadily lightening sky, I walked between lochan-filled bogs on one side and machair land on the other, with peat drying in small stacks everywhere around. The poor quality of the land is immediately striking, but the whole scene has a strange, dark beauty to it. This comes, I think, partly from the colours, and partly from the incredibly wide sweep of the horizon. It is low in the west, where the machair slips gently into the sea, but it rises up to the highish but very barren-looking hills on the east coast. This was the first time I had ever walked in the interior of these islands, and the impression given by innumerable travel

---

3   *Ibid.*, pp. 322,3. Nicholson is not alone in his quasi-religious – some would say pagan – approach to nature conservation. The opening passage of the centenary history of the RSPB makes a similar point. 'Man is a species born in sin, and conservationists are the high priests of a religion whose solitary premise is guilt. That guilt is the beating heart of the RSPB. Its more sanctimonious members should try never to forget that the mantle of responsibility they have assumed is reversible: they are among the saved, yes, but they are also the enemy, the devil incarnate, man the destroyer.' (*For Love of Birds*, Tony Samstag, RSPB, Sandy 1989, p. 7)

books of a bleak environment struck me as only half true. In fact, within a limited tonal range, it is a richly-hued scene. It is easy to see why people who grew up in this landscape love it and so often express that love in music and words. The feeling of endlessness, as if the land over the next rise would be much the same as the land this side of it, gives a powerful sense of freedom, almost like being at sea.

Bill Neill, a sandy-haired, bright-eyed man in his late 40s, was born and brought up in Cheshire, although his parents were Scottish. He came to South Uist when his wife got a job as health visitor at the island hospital. Bill is a wildlife artist and we spoke in the small gallery he runs in the front part of his house.

Bill started by telling me how he had run into problems with South Uist estate after reporting the shooting of a swan to the police. The police went up to the lodge where they found the guest involved, an accountant from Buckinghamshire, unloading the swan from a Land Rover. He was convicted of the offence on his own admission. From then on, Bill said, he had lived between the estate, the police and the local people (some of whom are still active 'one for the pot' shooters) in what he called a 'a state of armed neutrality'. I asked him why he was so much against shooting.

'For a start, it's against the law,' he said.

'But it's against the law to drive at 32 mph in a built up area,' I said, 'and don't tell me you never do that!'

Bill abandoned that argument with good grace, so we got onto the more reasonable one of which species actually need protection, and eventually agreed that this should be very much a matter for local decision. The interventions of bureaucracy are unhelpful in direct proportion to their remoteness from the location concerned. The South Uist bird-lovers committee, supposing such a thing existed, would be better placed to take intelligent decisions than SNH in Edinburgh, he said, which would in turn be better placed than the RSPB in Bedfordshire. 'That is why the NCC was split up and we now have SNH.'

'Do you think that has improved matters?' I asked.

'On the whole, yes,' he said.

'Do you think it would be better if the RSPB were "downsized" in the same way?'

'I'm sure it would,' he replied.

After a long chat Bill showed me round his gallery, gave me a cup of tea, then kindly offered to give me a lift back to the boat, collecting my shopping at the Co-op on the way. Back at Loch Boisdale, I reciprocated with the offer of a drink, and we went into the hotel for what turned out to be a very enjoyable couple of hours. He told me about the decline in religious feeling on the islands, saying that he thought it was not so much going away as changing into something different but related, which he could best describe by calling it 'cultural, perhaps'. As in much of the rest of Scotland, there was slow but consistent growth of interest in new cultural forms which had their roots in the past but were not constrained by it. This showed itself in the resurgence of Gaelic. Intriguingly,

Bill went on to say that the Catholics seemed much more at ease with this trend than the Protestants, which, in these islands, meant the Free Church. They harboured, Bill thought, a certain jealousy of the Catholics with their rich heritage of music and dance. None of it was specifically Catholic, nor even Christian, it was just that their Church had never banned such activities, with the result that today the older, festive customs were much more alive in the Catholic than the Protestant parts of the islands.

Bill also said that he sensed a kind of desperation about the Free Church since declining numbers of worshippers threatened its existence. Even if all religious observance stopped on these islands, the Catholics would still have a vast, worldwide organisation behind them, from which a future revival could always spring. But once the Free Church, a tiny sect now largely confined to the Hebrides, died out here, they were gone forever.

I asked Bill if he missed life in Cheshire. Certainly not, he said. Most of the hedges had been ripped up and the ponds filled in. This was in sharp contrast to France, where he had also lived for a few years. Interestingly, Bill said it was his time in France that had led him to understand the persistent feeling of outrage about the clearances. (They were particularly brutally executed in the Catholic parts of the Uists.) Not until he had lived outside England did he appreciate the strength of feeling that communities can have towards their own environment. We agreed that people who treated land purely as a conservation resource had much the same, ultimately detached, relationship to it as those who treated it only as a commercial asset. It is people like the crofters, who share neither attitude, that are caught in the crossfire.

With the boat once again full of food, fuel and clean laundry – though not meths for the galley which I had failed to find – I set out the next morning to sail the 15 miles north to Loch Skiport, where I had an appointment to meet the Conservation Officer of the Ministry of Defence Rocket Range on Benbecula, Major Robert ('Call me Bob') Cockburn. It was a lovely clear day, with patches of cloud over the highest of the hills which, in contrast to the bright land round about and lower down, loomed dark and chilly-looking in the shadows.

There was a fair lick of wind, but unfortunately coming due north, with a short, steep sea, against which a light boat like *Sylvia B* struggles to make much headway. As a result I was chronically late arriving in Loch Skiport, and the Major, who had kindly waited over an hour for me, gave up and went home. But he was quite unperturbed when I telephoned him at about five o'clock from the phone box near Loch Skiport and he immediately hopped into his Volvo and came to collect me.

A robust-looking, mustachioed man from the Borders, the Major is responsible for conservation on what is correctly termed the Royal Artillery Range Hebrides. He had previously written to me, in a letter marked 'Unclassified', saying, 'In accordance with MoD policy we take our stewardship very seriously and strive to maintain and where possible improve the habitat for wildlife.' With 3200 separate sites across the UK, the Ministry of Defence owns 600,000 acres of land – more than all the conservation charities put together. This huge estate has grown up since the time of the Napoleonic Wars, when a suddenly increased need for military training exposed a growing shortage of open land to train on because of the enclosure of the commons and heaths.

It is a paradox of conservation that the one British organisation which is dedicated to disturbance, destruction and domination of the landscape should be the one that has had the best record in actually preserving wild flora and fauna. This is partly because so much MoD land is left alone for so much of the time, and partly because a few explosions actually do nothing but good to an undisturbed ecosystem. Indeed, the Scottish Wildlife Trust has taken to dynamiting beech trees at its Falls of Clyde reserve near New Lanark 'to recreate the damage which would be created by a storm, thus aiding natural regeneration of the woodland'. Since so many of the conservation bodies use 'human disturbance of fragile ecosystems' as an excuse to exclude the public from land they own, I wanted to ask Major Cockburn about the effect on the rare and delicate environment of the Hebridean machair of intensive military activity.

We set off, not up to Benbecula as I had imagined we would, where the main base is, but down to Ardivachar on South Uist where the 'rangehead' and ammunition store overlooks the sea. This is where the rockets are launched. In the back of his car the Major had several bags labelled Uist Machair Seed – I had no idea you could buy 'wild' flora in this way – which he was going to plant in a 'rabbit exclusion zone'. On the way we passed the huge statue of the Virgin Mary which looks down at the treeless machair from equally treeless hills to the east. I was reminded of Max Nicholson's angry comment in *The Environmental Revolution:* 'In South America giant crucifixes stand proudly on summits overlooking deforested hillsides.'

In the 1995 edition of the Ministry of Defence conservation magazine, *Sanctuary,* Major Cockburn wrote an article about his work here which he started as follows: 'There are benefits to the NIMBY syndrome. I am glad that nobody wants an ammunition depot or a live firing range in their backyard. It means that people like me spend their service lives in and around some of the finest nature reserves.' On the 3000 acres of this site, most of which is an SSSI, an Environmentally Sensitive Area, a Special Protection Area for birds and a Ramsar site (i.e. an 'internationally important wetland site') they have 122 species of bird, including sea eagles, corncrakes, Montague's harrier, dunlin, oystercatcher, ringed plover, lapwing, snipe and redshank. They fire 1200 missiles per year out in the direction of St Kilda, and have been doing so for the last 35 years. In addition, they launch numerous jet drones for the missiles to 'hunt', which make even more noise than the rockets.

'Does this disturb the birds?' I asked.

'Not at all,' was the Major's reply. 'See that post over there?' he said, pointing to something about the size of a telegraph pole which was situated perhaps 200 yards from the office building where he works. 'That is where we launch the drones from. Between there and my office we have oystercatchers nesting.'

There is no disturbance to farming activity either. Apart from the dunes, the crofters' cattle and sheep still graze the ground, and oats and barley are planted on part of it. The only restriction is that when the flags go up and barriers go down, nobody is allowed into the launching area. But all these times are notified well in advance to the clerk of the crofters' grazings committee, so nobody need be inconvenienced.

As regards the human impact of the base, it is worth observing that, in complete contrast to conventional nature reserves, the Royal Artillery Range is a substantial employer. Though the 50 or so servicemen come in from outside the area, a couple of hundred jobs – Major Cockburn's estimate – have been created at the range and the base. The Ministry of Defence is by far the largest employer in the Uists. That, if nothing else, ensures its popularity. In addition, all building, repair and maintenance work is undertaken by local contractors and, unlike the RSPB who would not even give the Coll telecottage its photocopying work, the MoD puts out any 'white collar' work which can usefully be done locally.

I asked if all this was likely to be a victim of the 'peace dividend'. Quite the reverse, Major Cockburn assured me. In fact, with increasing restrictions on activities like missile testing in other countries, the range is starting to get work from foreign armed forces. Much of the Eurofighter's armaments testing programme had been done here, and a contract for the Swiss airforce had recently been undertaken. The base could well become a solid export-earner.

Both the missile range and the Loch Druidibeg reserve were started in the late 1950s, but the extraordinary fact is that it is the military base which has been the more successful at nature conservation. Certainly, if greylag goose numbers are any criterion, then the rocket range, where the geese are still shot, has proved a more eco-friendly environment than the National Nature Reserve, where they are just looked at, studied, counted, discussed and written about.

Major Cockburn very kindly drove me all the way down to my next appointment, with David 'Digger' Jackson, a freelance researcher temporarily employed by the RSPB. Jackson, a serious-looking, 30-ish bachelor, had been recommended to me by Bill Neill as an expert on the birds of South Uist. I wanted to ask him to confirm or contradict the Major's claim that a guided-missile range can provide an excellent habitat for birds.

Jackson's qualifications are impressive. He has both a BSc and a PhD in ecology, he told me, the doctorate having been obtained on the strength of a study of the breeding waders of South Uist. Since then he has worked for many years on a contract basis for the RSPB researching herring gulls and other 'fish-eating' birds. Dressed in 'Oxfam' clothes and boots, Jackson offered me two cubic inches of fruit cake and a cup of rather Oxfam-ish tea. Though the cottage was his family's holiday home – Jackson comes from Middlewich in Cheshire – it was at least as uncomfortable and unhomely as the National Trust bothy on Canna after Ian

MacIntyre had left. Was this an outward and visible sign of 'ecological repentance', I wondered?

Jackson said straight away that he was not prepared to discuss anything other than his work here for the RSPB. Frankly, in view of the Canna comedy, I was surprised that he was even prepared to discuss that: I put it down to the fact that he was not properly 'staff' and had not been sent the latest memos by Minns or Maclennan. I started by asking him to give me some idea of the level of bird interest on South Uist. There are six species of wader which breed on this island, he told me, which are of 'European significance': dunlin, ringed plover, redshank, lapwing, oystercatcher and snipe. The first two breed here in higher densities than anywhere else in the world. Whereas dunlin, for example, nest in the Flow Country at a density of 'a handful of pairs per square kilometre', on South Uist the corresponding figure is more like 300 pairs. 'Here we have very, very nationally important numbers of these species,' Jackson said.

The reason why there were so many birds was largely due to the way the crofters farm. Were this landscape to revert to wilderness, the numbers would almost certainly decline drastically as much of their food supply would be choked out. Conversely, if it were to be farmed intensively, the necessary drainage would destroy the wet ground that is particularly attractive to the dunlin and snipe. 'So the challenge if you like is for crofting to develop into the next century and at the same time to retain the bird populations,' he said. 'The birds without the crofting would not survive, at least not in such numbers.'

The particular focus of Jackson's interest was the dunlin and the ringed plover. Though, South Uist he said, 'is very much paradise island' for these birds at the moment, 'all is not well with them'. When he conducted his doctoral research here in the mid-1980s, the two species' populations were each about 2500 pairs. Since then, numbers have halved. His current work here involves finding out why. There are several possible hypotheses. They might be facing persecution in their wintering grounds; the crofters might be changing their way of managing the land; they may just be suffering from a couple of bad breeding seasons due to weather or some other temporary factor; or there may be more predation here. The last was Jackson's favoured hypothesis. 'The big finding,' he said, 'is that predation has changed markedly due to the introduction of hedgehogs. Over 50 per cent of the dunlin, redshank and snipe decline is due to hedgehog predation. It's bad news really.'

The cause of this was a schoolteacher who arrived from England with a couple of pet hedgehogs – the animal did not previously exist on the island – that escaped and started breeding furiously (as, incidentally, has happened on Islay).

'It's going to be an interesting one,' Jackson said. 'The estate aren't too pleased as it's affecting the birds they shoot. It's debatable what should be done. We don't know the biology. All we have is a snapshot. Will the birds decline to half as many in another ten years, and so on until they go extinct, or will they reach a new equilibrium at a lower population level which is sustainable? We need to know.'

'Why should birds be protected from hedgehogs?' I asked.

'The hedgehog is not native here.'

'But nothing's native anywhere,' I said. 'Pretty well everything's arrived where it is from somewhere else.'

'The hedgehog was introduced by man so it is not a natural part of the community.'

'But man is an introduced species.'

'Man introduced himself,' Jackson replied. 'You could enter a long philosophical debate about these things. But if it is considered by the general public or the government that these bird populations are of such international importance that they are worth conserving, then the only way to conserve them is to understand the biology of the system.'

'What do you mean when you say "international importance"?'

'European conservation legislation is based on whether a site meets the criteria for the usual significances: 1 per cent of the international population would be internationally important and 1 per cent of the national population would be nationally important.'

'So if they continue to decline, the time will come when they are no longer "important", and all the work you have done trying to save them will retrospectively be rendered irrelevant?'

I hardly expected a reasoned answer to that provocative question, but to my surprise I got one. Dunlin populations, Jackson said without a hint of a smile, are declining elsewhere so the proportional relationship remains similar. That sounded glib: I made a note to check it later.

Moving on to the subject of the rocket range, I asked about its significance in all this. Jackson said it is the most important nesting site in the world for dunlin, hosting about 300 breeding pairs.

'So the humble hedgehog does more damage than 1200 missiles a year?' I asked.

'The missiles do no damage at all,' he replied. 'The missiles are probably a positive thing as the danger area excludes disturbance by humans: crofters and birdwatchers. Also there are fewer fences. The birds don't mind explosions.'

That was clearly a 'confirmed kill' for the Major. I thought I would end with a broader question. 'You are a Doctor of Philosophy,' I said. 'You won't mind, I hope, if I put to you a "philosophical" question.' Jackson looked at me silently. 'What is the point of all this? You say you like dunlins but you don't like hedgehogs. Is it not just a matter of personal preference?'

'There are several points. One is that there is an international obligation to safeguard these populations.'

'So you're an agent of the European bureaucracy?'

'No, I'm not,' he said, beginning to look a little uncomfortable. 'I'm merely saying that that is the world we live in. The government of the day is obliged to safeguard its nature and the only way it can do that is by understanding it.'

'Hedgehogs are nature too, aren't they?'

'They are, obviously, nature,' he said. 'But they would be considered in this case as something that is upsetting natural communities.'

'But they're not upsetting nature even a trivial fraction of the amount that the cereal farmers of East Anglia, for example, are upsetting things. So why doesn't the government do something about them?'

'There's millions of different initiatives going forward on different fronts. They are doing that at the same time. You only need to have three or four places like this and these birds go extinct.'

'Who does that matter to?'

'It matters to lots of people. There are those who believe that man has a duty not to be a destroyer of nature.'

'Who imposed that duty?'

'They feel it's a personal, a moral thing.'

'What does that mean?' I asked.

'I'd rather restrict the conversation to the work I do here for the RSPB,' he said brusquely.

Back aboard ship, I looked out my *New Atlas of Breeding Birds* and my *Red Data Birds in Britain* and turned up dunlin. While potatoes boiled merrily on the unrefuelled meths burner and my equally merry cider glass emptied, was refilled and emptied again, I investigated the claim that the dunlin was a bird likely to go extinct if unduly persecuted in 'three or four' places like South Uist. 'The dunlins breeding in Britain comprise more than 90 per cent of the EC population, thereby meriting special protection under EC legislation,' the *New Atlas* noted. British numbers were about 9000 breeding pairs, so within that total, the South Uist population was of obvious significance. But what about the global picture? The *Red Data* book says that there are seven 'races' of this bird, only one of which breeds in Britain. The dunlin is, in the ornithological argot, 'holarctic', which is to say that it occurs all round the higher latitudes of the northern hemisphere. The *schinzii* race (of the species *calidris alpina*) is the one which breeds in Britain, but the 9000 pairs can hardly be *that* significant when, as the *Red Data* book notes, 300,000 pairs of that race occur in Iceland alone. Two of the other six races are also seen in Britain as migrants, up to 150,000 birds being reported in this country in one year. The British winter population of the *alpina* race was estimated in the early 1980s as 430,000 birds, though this huge figure represents only 38 per cent of its total population.

Quite contrary to the impression Jackson had given me, the dunlin is not a rare bird. There are millions of them in the world, quite literally. The 'international importance' claim for the British population is based only on the way in which that term is defined statistically and that, in turn, depends wholly on the political geography of the European Community. Were the EC to include Iceland, then the British population of the *schinzii* race would no longer be 9000 out of an EC total of 10,000 but 9000 out of an EC total of 310,000. Thus without the gain or loss of a single bird, globally speaking, the dunlin's status in Europe would be drastically altered. That is how irrelevant these statistical criteria are to real conservation.[4]

Loch Skiport is a lovely place. It reminded me of the north coast of County Mayo, on Donegal Bay, where I sailed once a few years ago. It is a landscape of heather and bracken, though dotted with ruined buildings. Whereas north Mayo is poor but inhabited, this part of South Uist is poor but deserted, or should I say cleared? The anchorage is in a narrow neck of the loch, and quite sheltered. By the time my dinner was ready, the wind had got up and turned cold, blowing out of the west where a breathtaking sunset of amber and metallic blue glowed above the black mass of the deserted, uncosy hillsides.

Next morning I had an appointment at Loch Druidibeg with Gail Churchill, one of the three SNH Area Officers employed on the Reserve. The senior Area Officer, John Love, did not have time to meet.[5] The Reserve used to have wardens in charge, but not now. The staff are no longer primarily custodians of nature. Instead their job is to project power, bureaucratically speaking, in remote communities. It is an essentially imperial operation. In the days of the real Empire, such people were sent out to the South Pacific with the title of District Officer. Now *mutatis mutandis* they are 'out-posted' to places like South Uist and called Area Officers. The titles are similar; the administrative reality identical.

Gail comes from Birmingham, and she did not, to my eyes at any rate, look at home in South Uist.[6] She seemed bored with the place, though when I saw the office, I could quite see why. The whole atmosphere was arid, over-heated and claustrophobic, like a bank. Every flat surface was cluttered with files or academic papers for use in the war against local knowledge and custom.

---

4 Something like this actually happened when Sweden and Finland joined the EC in 1992. The bird in question was the dotterel, a few hundred of which breed in the Cairngorms. Being a bird of the snowy north, the Cairngorms were host to almost the only population group within the EC prior to the accession of the new Scandinavian members. But Sweden has over 7000 pairs of dotterel and Finland about 9000. One of the reasons why activist bodies like the RSPB have long tried to prevent further tourist development in the Cairngorms was to preserve the habitat of birds like the dotterel, on the ground of its rarity as defined on an EC-percentage basis. Before Sweden and Finland joined, Britain's share of the EC population was 95 per cent and therefore very 'important'. On the accession of the new members, it dropped to 5 per cent. The conservationists are only lucky that Norway voted 'No' to EC membership since its dotterel population, about 28,000 pairs, would have totally shattered the whole bogus argument.

5 Neither, incidentally, did the official RSPB representative on the island, Gwen Evans. I must have telephoned six or seven times, but on each occasion she was 'in a meeting'. I drew the inference that she, unlike Jackson, had been memoed by Minns and/or Maclennan

6 Postscript: She moved soon afterwards. One of the inherent problems with the bureaucratic approach is that most officers do not stay long enough in one place to understand the environment in a real, hands-on way. This is a permanent source of friction with the people who do.

Gail had no experience of agriculture, having trained as an engineer. She had been on South Uist just three years, yet it was her job to tell the crofters how they should look after their ground. The biggest part of the work of all three Area Officers, she told me, was dealing with the site designations. She estimated that between the three of them they will have to make 600 visits to individual land users in connection with the latest round of designations, each of those probably lasting a couple of hours.

Gail gave me an example of the kind of difficulties they encounter. In the Environmentally Sensitive Areas (ESA) scheme an 'eyesore' clause aims to force crofters and farmers to produce what the bureaucrats see as a 'tidy' landscape – in particular there should be fewer wrecked cars lying about. But the crofters pointed out to the SNH officers who had the job of enforcing this legislation that many of these are holding up the sand dunes at the beach. Sure enough, the dune system, which is at risk from erosion, was being kept stable by a large number of vehicles which had been abandoned on the beach where the wind slowly buried them. This was actually an environmentally beneficial way of disposing of dead machinery, which eventually rusts away to nothing. But it was hardly what the office wallahs in Edinburgh and London had in mind when they framed the 'eyesore' clause.

'That is an example of how we are learning all the time,' Gail said, blithely unconscious that it is hardly a matter for congratulation that advice on key policies is taken from local crofters *after*, rather than before, they are formulated officially.

Our discussion was interrupted by a crofter called Murdo who looked into Gail's office and, in the midst of a certain amount of administrative banter, told us an amusing story about an American who had preached in the island church two Sundays before.

'He was a typical lecturer type,' Murdo said in a sing-song voice. 'We got 23 acknowledged quotations, anything from Woody Allen to Beethoven. The sermon was only about 25 minutes long and you got one every minute, it was like a machine gun. He was a real, typical academic bighead.'

I thought I detected a meaningful pause. But Gail was 'liaising with the local community', and smiled courageously. The story ended with a quiet but effective put-down of the American by the organist in Murdo's church. The point was that the American clearly never realised he was being mocked. 'Oh! Beauty!' said Murdo, laughing loudly. 'Now that to me is how to deal with these people: how to shoot somebody down in flames and he does not even realise his parachute's on fire.'

Gail made a splendid show of enjoying the joke. It seemed clear to me, from the twinkle in his eye, that Murdo intended an Aesopian undercurrent to his tale. From the extraordinary force of Gail's laughter, I suspect she was thinking the same thing, and had a horrible suspicion about who the target was.

Gail drove me back down to the boat. On the way we discussed the problems that all these designations cause farmers and crofters. An SSSI, for example, the oldest, most general and least specific designation lists 28 activities which any landuser may not carry out without notifying SNH. They start with (1) 'cultivation, including ploughing, harrowing and reseeding', and go on through (11) 'the destruction, displacement, removal or cutting of any plant or plant remains, including tree, reed, sedge, shrub, herb, turf, dead or decaying wood, moss, lichen, fungus' and (21) 'construction, removal or destruction of roads, tracks, walls, fences, hardstands, banks, ditches or other earthworks' to (28) 'changes in game or waterfowl management and changes in hunting practices'. Crofters have automatic permission to manage the land in the way they were doing so at the time their croft is designated, but any changes which come within the 28 Potentially Damaging Operations as they are called – and they effectively include everything – are illegal if not notified to SNH. The fact that SNH agree to proposed changes much more often than they disagree, does not alter the fact that it is the conservation bureaucrats who are, in Nicholson's phrase, the new masters of this world. They have a massive, heavy book which they can throw at anyone who displeases them. Without a Conservation Ombudsman, they are judge and jury in their own court.

What is the justification for this, I asked Gail, given that it is the crofters themselves who have created the environment they are now being forced to 'protect'? 'People are beginning to realise,' she said, 'that unless we start doing something, we are going to damage our environment.'

She accepted the point that the crofters of South Uist, far from damaging their environment, had created something of unique ecological value, which was recognised in the fact that so much of it is so heavily designated. She also accepted that there was a certain injustice in the fact that farmers in the ecological desert which is so much of southern England do not have to put up with these designations, having got rich while destroying the ancient beauty of their own countryside. In essence, I suggested, the crofters' reward for sensitive stewardship of their land has been to have control of it taken out of their hands and given to the enemies of the East Anglian cereal barons.

'That's one way of looking at it,' she said. 'But you've got to practise what you preach. We've got to at least try to get our own country in order, as far as conservation is concerned, so that we can say to countries like Brazil, "We've turned around and we're doing something about the environment, so you should do something about it as well."'

'You mean to stop them cutting down the rainforest?'

'Yes.'

'But why should Britain expect Brazil to listen when Britain has already cut down most of its forests in order to get rich?'

'It is a problem, I agree, but we have to do what we can.'

'So are you saying that the job of SNH is really just to help Britain tell foreigners not to behave as we ourselves have behaved in the past?'

'We've got to get our own country in order,' she said again, 'before we start telling everybody else how they should behave, and SNH is one of the organisations in this country that is trying to do that. Unfortunately some of it requires legislation.'

As I rowed out to the boat, it occurred to me that this was simply another case of Highlanders being asked to make sacrifices in support of British foreign policy. The Tiree war memorial recorded one sort of sacrifice: the bulging files of the SNH offices throughout the Highlands record another sort of sacrifice.

Under a grey and lowering sky, I raised the anchor and motor-sailed down the loch on the last of the ebb tide, hoping to catch the flood in an hour or two's time which would help carry me up to Loch Maddy in North Uist. The sea was almost flat calm and what little wind there was steadily dropped. After an hour or so, I took the sail down and set the autohelm. Visibility was quite good, despite a warm, summery drizzle which came on and sent me down below.

Trying to banish thoughts of Nicholson, tree-worshippers and the imperialistic pharisees of the SNH from my mind, I turned on the radio and made a large, late lunch of smoked fish, boiled potatoes and spring onions in mayonnaise. By the time I was halfway up the coast of North Uist, with Loch Maddy about five miles distant, my spirits were quite restored. I popped my head out of the hatch for another quick look-about, and was almost enjoying the rain and the close, slightly muggy feel of the still air, when, without warning and for the first time in the 15 years I have owned *Sylvia B*, the engine stopped dead.

8

NORTH UIST

IT MUST BE FUEL, but it can't be, was my first, sinking thought when the engine cut out. I am not much of a mechanic, and the repair of two-stroke engines is quite beyond me. *Sylvia B* slowly lost all way, and was soon drifting helplessly. Fuel starvation does not produce a sudden cut-out, but I refilled the tank from my spares just in case, and pulled the starting cord, more in hope than expectation. To my amazement, the engine fired immediately. Well, that's a relief, I thought, getting everything tidy on deck again, resetting the autohelm and going below to get out of the rain. I half-removed my waterproofs, and settled down with a book. Less than ten minutes passed before the same thing happened again. This really is trouble, I thought.

For the second time, I was able to restart the engine at almost the first pull of the cord. The sea around was deserted. I had seen one other yacht and one fishing boat all afternoon. Could the problem be a dirty plug? Until the engine stopped completely I thought I would carry on. Soon a faint breath of wind came up and at the same time, the rain let up. By the time I turned into Loch Maddy, there was enough wind to sail the boat, albeit slowly. The problem now was that it was dark. For most of the way in, the Loch is so wide that it is not possible to navigate accurately with reference to the shore, at least not at night. After passing the Ruigh Liath light, about half a mile from the pier, I had to stand on the foredeck to keep a lookout as the chart showed a very tight anchorage. I tried the engine once again. It started and ran for a couple of minutes, then died. I restarted it and carried on like this, dashing between the foredeck and the stern every couple of minutes, sometimes also leaping down below to consult the chart. Soon I was sweating like a pig.

Finally, at about 9.30 p.m. I cast anchor just off the pier but inside both the ferry and the Highland Board moorings in about 20 feet of water. Once again, it seemed like time for a drink and a bath in the hotel. But the facilities were better patrolled here than in Loch Boisdale, and so I ended up having a drink only, and taking a shower next morning in the youth hostel.

After my shower, I took a look at the motor, as well as the dinghy, which had sprung a leak. By then the weather had turned absolutely gorgeous. Though chilly, it was bright and clear, with an enticing hint of autumn in the breeze. The sea was rippled and sparkling. *Sylvia B* sat lightly on the water, her red burgee snapping smartly in the crisp, Hebridean air. Like Moley in *The Wind in the Willows* when the imperious call of spring got the better of him and the routine of domestic spring-cleaning, I said to myself, 'Hang dinghies! Hang motors! I'm going for a wander.' I packed camera, note-pad and lunch, then rowed ashore and set off to explore the interior.

There is really only one road on North Uist and it circles the island, following the coast except that it misses out the extreme north and the peninsula to the south-east. I decided for no particular reason to go anti-clockwise, or widdershins, and walked out through the couple of dozen houses which comprise the township of Loch Maddy and into a lovely green landscape. I was very quickly offered a lift by a man who, it turned out, came from Berneray, the small island immediately off the north coast of North Uist. He introduced himself as Angus McCuish and said he had just come back from a Council meeting where they had been discussing the local structure plan. He told me about the problems of getting it agreed by all the new influences on the islands. The RSPB, he said, were trying to ban windsurfing from one of the lochs and SNH wanted the Council to discuss a proposal to channel visitors into particular areas around Loch Skiport.

'We've had a belly-full of them,' he said. 'That meeting was a total waste of time. We wanted to discuss other things we thought were more important. The estates up here, and the crofters, have always been pretty conservation-minded anyway. There's been no excessive peat cutting; they respect the wildlife. I'd like to kill a few geese right enough! But there was a lot of comments that really got up our noses. Gwen Evans [of the RSPB] was doing her job, I suppose. She has to put forward the company policy. But it's a load of total and utter rubbish.'

'Do they make themselves quite unpopular by doing that sort of thing?' I asked.

'Not really, no,' Angus said. 'We're all good friends. But they want to protect this and designate that, and it was going into a document for legislation, and we didn't want it.'

Angus left me at the Berneray road end, and I started walking west in blazing sunshine. The wind had dropped almost completely and it was positively hot. Apart from a few puffy clouds, the sky was the intense blue which you only get in maritime areas. I wandered this way and that, taking a photograph here, and inspecting an old ruin there, but all the time making slow progress out towards the township of Solas, where I thought I would turn south and cross the island by what is known as the Committee Road, since it was built as a make-work scheme. It is the only other road of any length on the island, and it crosses from north to south. But a truck driver offered me a lift, and as he was going west, I went with him. He pointed out the island of Vallay, a large tract of low-lying green land, possibly three miles long, situated a mile or so off-shore, across a vast expanse of golden sand and very shallow-looking water. It used to be crofted by three families, he told me, as it was excellent for barley. But in recent years goose numbers have risen dramatically, with the result that the barley became impossible to farm. The families left and the island is now uninhabited. Without farming activity, the grazing has deteriorated, so the geese have also left, moving onto North Uist, where farming still continues.

I was dropped off at the Balranald road end, and since the RSPB run a Reserve on estate-owned croft land there, I thought I would wander in and have a look. In fact there was little to be seen except a small, deserted cottage inside which was a tatty and not very informative visual display and a pile of equally uninformative leaflets. I was, however, interested to see the graveyard which stands 100 yards or so away from the cottage, as it had recently attracted a certain amount of controversy when the RSPB had outraged local opinion by proposing to lead visitors through it to a new hide overlooking Loch nam Felthean. This was the most 'logical' route, the North of Scotland Reserves Manager, Dr Peter Mayhew, had been quoted in the press as saying, since for visitors to walk through the graveyard rather than round it would 'minimise the possibility of disturbing birds on the loch.' The local Councillor, Donald Maclean, was quoted in the opposite sense: 'We have never heard of such unbridled arrogance,' he said. 'Not disturbing birds is more important than respect for the dead!'

Apart from the graveyard, there was little on Balranald which could not be seen elsewhere, except sweet little Nature Trail signs. So after a bit of a prowl around, I set off south-east, intending to pay a call on Mrs Ena McNeil, a crofter and District Councillor – Donald Maclean's counterpart on the southern side of the island. Before knocking on Ena's door, I spent an hour or so on the beach at Bayhead, near where she lives, taking photographs and eating my lunch (while plagued by flies). The sand was almost white and glared powerfully in the early afternoon sunlight. Mile upon mile of it stretched, flat and deserted as far as the eye could see. Across about half a mile of water, there were more sandy beaches on the island of Kirkibost, which I was very tempted to explore. It was an almost tropical scene. The land round about was much more fertile-looking than the South Uist machair, and inland it looked richer too, more Galway than north Mayo. It was also more folded and varied. As on most of the other places I had visited, I felt as if I could happily have stayed a month rather than just a few days.

I found Ena raking hay on what turned out to be her son's croft. She has the handsome, weathered look of a person who has lived a long life in the fresh air. After a few cautious preliminaries, she invited me indoors and offered me a cup of tea and a cheese sandwich. Having just lunched, I declined the sandwich, but happily took the tea. Sitting with her dog and her three-legged cat (which she talked to in Gaelic) in her cosy but pleasantly unmodernised sitting room, we discussed the omnipresent greylag geese. She started by telling me how rare these birds had been in former times.

'I was born here,' she said, 'and my father was probably *the* best hunter on the island. He's dead 20 years ago, but when we were children there was no money so we lived off birds and rabbits and sheep and whatever we could find, and poached salmon. I can't remember eating a goose as a child because they were so scarce. When we used to go to school – there was no fences in those days – we would go across the fields. The geese would get up and head for Kirkibost island so my father would walk along the beach and try and get one, hiding in the dunes. See nowadays, we could have a goose every day if we wanted to, they're so plentiful.'

'Is that a problem for you as a crofter?' I asked.

'Well we've got to watch them coming into the corn,' she said. 'Once the corn is getting ripe, they're really desperate for the seed. If there's people about, your crop is all right. But if your crop is isolated, you've not much of a chance. My son, Angus, is full-time on the croft. We would like to make more dry corn with the old-fashioned binder, and we do a lot with that but we would like to do some more but no way can we risk it because sure as fate we will lose the seed anyway. The geese really love the oats and the rye seed. We would like to harvest more oats and rye in a dry state, instead of putting into silage, for feeding the cattle. We've got 150 head of cattle, Highlanders. We keep the young ones indoors in the winter, and the sheaf of corn is the best feeding you can give them. But the geese are really making a mess. They love anything green, the reseeds particularly. We rent 40 acres just off the Committee Road, in an area where there is no danger for the cattle, no bogs and there's two lochs in it and the Highlanders love it. A month ago we took stock off it, because we want to graze them there come October, yet every day I go up that Committee Road there's about 70–80 geese there. I walk through it and I see their shit all over the place. It makes me ill.'

'Could you not shoot some of the geese?' I asked, since they are a legal quarry species from September to January.

'When Angus goes shooting it's just to get something for the dinner. Otherwise he doesn't have the time. It's not that easy to shoot a goose, you know.'

'Do they eat well?'

'Oh, they're delicious. We eat quite a few of them. And they're just as nice in February as they are in January, provided nobody catches you. It seems to taste better when you're not supposed to kill them.' She laughed and said, 'Put that in your book too.'

'But you don't shoot to scare them off the corn?' I asked.

She told me that Angus had applied for an out-of-season licence for August, which is when the migrating birds arrive nowadays – much earlier than 20 years ago. He was given a permit for just seven geese. 'Luckily he isn't very good at mathematics,' Ena added with a smile.

I asked for an example of the damage the geese do. 'This spring,' she replied, 'they were even eating the silage. We had one group of 23 heifers in a field. See, Highlanders are not greedy. My son would spread out a bale of corn silage and they would come and eat, but there was too much there for one day and that would do them for two days. After eating their bellies full they would go a wee bit away and lie down and sleep for a bit and chew the cud. Once they moved away from the silage the geese came in. So when the cattle went back the next day, they weren't enjoying it because the geese had been shitting all over it. Otherwise that silage would have been fine for the next day.'

Ena's main worry was that, with all the bureaucracy and form-filling, 'one day it's going to be all geese and no crofters. We don't want to fall out with SNH, but we don't want them to control us too much either. I was hoping to move cattle around this week. I said to Angus, "I'll put these couple of beasts in that field." "Can't put them there till 1 October," he said. "Well I'll put them in that bit across the river." "That's taboo too till 1 October." I said, "Why?" "I don't know," he said, "that's what's in the plan, something to do with the seed of the flowers or whatnot." So I asked John Love, the SNH man, about it. I said, "Tell me, what are we preserving?" "Well," he says, "you'll have better foliage there next year because you are letting the seed go back into the ground." I says, "John, there's flowers and everything that's there now as been there since I was born and we've had cattle there every year, and you know yourself, by October the grass is going to be up to their knees. There's no goodness in it at that stage." I cannot understand it. What's the purpose of it, and who makes that rule?'

I asked Ena if she knew Gail Churchill.

'Oh, I could just grab her by the back of the neck,' she said. 'We had a field down on the machair, with cattle in. I wanted it to grow again so that the cattle could go back again in, say, a month's time. But you couldn't feed a sheep there because the geese were there. I took her there and showed her. She said she would tell them in the office about it. I never heard another thing, nothing at all. That was an eight-acre field and it was covered with goose droppings. If the grass had grown, I could have put 50 cattle there, whereas I couldn't put any in there: there was nothing for them. And you couldn't scare them away. It didn't matter how often you went down there, as soon as you were back home, the geese were back in the field. That's the way it is all the time. We're fighting them all the time.'

'Do you think she doesn't understand the local problems?'

'She understands, but she doesn't want to help. I would just love to grab her and stick her nose in it. That's how I feel about it. And what's going to happen in the future? Crofting's dying anyway. I'm 56 and all the other crofters that are full-time are round about my own age group. The five best ones are all bachelors, so there's nobody coming after them. My own son's the youngest full-time crofter. Who's going to take over? With having to fight like this all the time, how can you do it?'

' Do you think all these designations and regulations are helping to undermine crofting?' I asked.

'It's putting a lot of people off. People are fed up of rules and regulations. See, when I think back, we never did cut hay in the summer time, and maybe that's why the corncrakes survived so well. We just did corn and the hay was just the natural grass that grew in places which hadn't been ploughed and where the cattle hadn't been all summer. It was usually cut in September. In the olden days, the barley always ripened about the third week in August. So that was the first cut of the season. Then in the 1950s or 60s the government introduced a cropping grant. The rule was a crofter got so much for every acre that he ploughed, but the

condition was that he put three hundredweight of artificial fertiliser on each acre
he ploughed. That was when people stopped putting on seaweed and dung, and
that is when the change started. You were allowed to plough the land three years
in succession, and on the third year as well as planting the corn seed, you had to
plant bought-in hay seed. So in the fourth year you were cutting hay instead of
corn, from the beginning of July onwards.'

'Why not harvest corn now?'

'We do.'

'Is that where the corncrakes are?'

'I think there's far more in the corn fields, which we don't cut till September
anyway. But we don't use much artificial fertiliser. Some years, we don't use any
at all. I remember my cousin next door to us, he was putting an awful lot of
artificial fertiliser on his fields and he was spraying it, and we weren't, and we
were using seaweed and you could actually see the corncrakes in our fields, and
an awful lot of wildflowers, but in my cousin's field next door it was so thick
because it was so forced that none of the corncrakes were in there. I'm sure the
crofters would be happy enough to do more corn and cut down on the hay, if
they got help to do it because making dry corn is very labour intensive. So people
do just one stack, for the seed.'

'Why do they bother doing even that?'

'You can't get seed out of silage. We can't buy seed from the mainland because
it won't grow here. There's no manganese in the ground, so we have to save our
own seed. That's where the goose problem is because you're watching your corn
grow and you say, that field is really looking good, it's strong ground that was
fallow for quite a few years so that's the best seed to keep. But it's so risky: you're
terrified the geese are going to get in there. All the time you've got the goose on
your mind, and that didn't happen in the olden days. How can you work in that
kind of atmosphere?'

Ena offered me a lift up to the round-the-island road. I would happily have
walked, but I was so interested to listen to her I accepted. In the end she drove
me all the way to the main inter-island road eight miles away, on which there
was quite a lot of traffic. As we drove, she told me she was thinking of writing
children's stories about her life on the croft. I encouraged her to do so, but I got
the impression, very sadly, that she considered that an impossible dream, and
that in reality she would be turning over hay for the rest of her life.

Though it was by now late afternoon, it was still hot as I hitched back up to
Loch Maddy. I got a lift easily, so thought I would stop in the hotel for a quick
pint before going back down to the boat. As speed was my goal – I had a later
appointment – it was a mistake to have gone into the public bar, which I did
because I heard loud music coming from there. I found an attractive red-haired
girl sitting drinking vodka, while her boyfriend poured money in immense
quantities into the jukebox. He particularly favoured the more operatic Elvis
tracks, which came over at thunderous volume – 'You're Always on my Mind'
sticks in my memory.

Tired after all my walking and talking, I was happy to sit and listen, then to have a second pint, and listen some more. After a while, we got talking. The girl was from Benbecula (The Dark Isle), and he was an English squaddy posted up here at the rocket range. He disliked the army and was trying to leave it. But for some reason that I never discovered his dislike of *orn*ithologists (he stressed the first syllable luridly) was even stronger. He gave us a hilarious impersonation of Derek and Clive (Peter Cook and Dudley Moore) 'getting the "orn" ' – only in this case the stimulating sight was not pornography, but birds or 'being goosed'. 'And corncrakes,' he said in a splendidly unforced imitation of a Dagenham accent, 'Vey really give me the orn.'

The result of all this was that I was late for my assignation in the lounge bar, and rather drunk by the time I went through. The further result was that I was incapable of making any notes of what I seem to remember was quite an interesting conversation about the SNH plan to declare no less than 20,000 acres of the crofters' common grazings an SSSI, on the ground that it is 'an internationally important breeding area for both red and black-throated divers'. I was clear that the whole island was bitterly opposed to this further bureaucratic intrusion into their lives, but beyond that, I would not care to be too definite.

Still chuckling at my army friend – 'Red-throated divers! Now vey *really* give me the orn' – I punished myself for neglect of duty by ordering a deliciously expensive dinner in the hotel dining-room.

Up on the pier in the morning, my first telephone call was to Donald Maclean, the Councillor involved in the RSPB graveyard protest. For the only time on this trip, I met with open rudeness from an islander. Angrily he asked me what right I thought I had to interrupt his important business? Did I not know he was in a meeting? I was later told that his claim to islander status is not totally solid. Though he grew up on North Uist and still keeps a croft on the island, he spent his adult life as a policeman in Glasgow, where he still lives. No business resulted.

Next I phoned Abbie Patterson, the RSPB warden at Balranald. I encountered the expected reluctance to meet, though for the first (and last) time it was politely expressed. He had no time, he said, because he had 'end of season reports to write', though I could join him on one of his guided walks round the Reserve if I wanted to. That was the last thing I wanted to do. After a great deal of cajoling, he agreed to meet me down at the pier later in the day

Finally, I telephoned the factor of North Uist Estates, George MacDonald, and asked if we could meet. Come up right away, he said. I did.

It was another glorious morning, and I stepped out in high spirits, even though I was beginning to worry about my mechanical repairs. Also, having failed to find meths in South Uist, I was desperate to buy some here. But the shop situation was even worse. I mentioned this to the secretary when I arrived at the estate office. No problem, she said, she would find some. And she did. She not only located a five-litre bottle at about half the normal price for 500 ml quantities, she also arranged for a friend to collect it for me since it was stocked at the only substantial shop on the island, which is at Clachan, nearly ten miles away. I had no money on me at that moment, but that was no problem either. Her friend would put it on the estate account, and I could drop the money in to the office later that afternoon.

George MacDonald was a tall, well-built, open-faced man in his 40s. He had been on the island for just a year, having previously worked on his native Lewis. He explained the problem of activist conservationism as seen from the point of view of the manager of two large estates (he also factors North Harris). Apart from some land owned by the Department of Agriculture, all of which is crofted, North Uist is almost entirely owned by North Uist Estates (62,000 acres). The laird is Lord Granville, a cousin of the Queen's and a man who, though English and not always resident on the island, was well-spoken of by most of the people I talked to.

'The fear is,' George said, 'that these new bodies like RSPB and SNH which are coming in now represent a new tier of authority above everybody else, both landlords and their tenants, the crofters. In fact we get on very well with the local officers of SNH, but the problem stems from the fact that they are constantly looking over their shoulder to Edinburgh, and a lot of things are referred back to Edinburgh. Our worry is that people from Edinburgh are influencing the way things are done here.'

'And how is that a problem?'

'To give you a small illustration,' George said, 'this year we had an otter which was killing hens and ducks. The crofters made a list of all the kills that were known to have been made by the otter, about 60 birds. We asked the Agriculture Ministry for a licence to get rid of it, and they went to SNH who took the advice of the otter specialists, the Vincent Wildlife Trust in London. I was quite prepared to trap the otter, and if he was an old beast, maybe having difficulty getting its natural feeding to get a vet to put it down. At the end of the day SNH came back to the Ministry and said they were not happy giving a licence but would recommend that a licence be granted to trap the otter provided we relocate it *in North Uist!* From my point of view, that is absolutely ridiculous. All I would be doing is transferring my problems to somebody up in Solas or wherever. That highlights the problem that the local person has because the Vincent Trust is probably doing a sterling job reintroducing otters to areas in England where there are no otters, but otters are two a penny here, and the population of otters would not suffer any particular detriment from having that particular animal taken out. So what's going to happen at the end of the day? I'm certainly not going to pay £300 for a trap, simply to relocate the animal, only for somebody down the road to shoot the blessed thing, or put a gin trap out.'

The Vincent Wildlife Trust is a charitable Trust with no members and consequently no obligation to explain itself to the public. (Most of my letters requesting information have been unanswered.) It was founded in 1975 by someone called Vincent Weir who, as the secretary told me, 'has had a keen interest in conservation for over 50 years'. The Trust operates out of offices in the

City of London and dipped into otter ecology during the late 1980s and early 1990s when the species was in fashion in England as a charismatic charity object. Their only substantive achievement was to conduct a national survey, which showed numbers increasing strongly in Scotland, and no possible cause for conservation concern. In the Highland Region, 99 per cent of sites surveyed were occupied by otters. Numbers generally were up by 15 per cent over the previous 12-year period. The Trust has now transferred its attention to bats.[1]

There is something horribly contemptuous about SNH giving more weight to the opinions of a shadowy body from the City of London than to those of the natives of North Uist on a matter that concerns nobody outside Loch Maddy. But as Commander Tappley pointed out, if you want to be taken seriously in the conservation industry in Scotland, it helps to be English.

I asked George about all the designations SNH were imposing on the island. Were they as much of an inhibition on estate activity as Ena McNeil said they were on crofting? Not surprisingly, George came at the problem from a completely different angle: finance.

'The other thing we feel about SNH,' he said, 'is that they've been given a tremendous amount of power but not very much money. They seem to be grossly underfunded for grant-aiding specific projects. A lot of money has been poured into them to build up their own structure, staffing and so on. It's one of the few growth industries in the islands. I remember in Stornoway 20 years ago the NCC had an office, one officer and a secretary. Now I can think of five officers, and probably as many administrative staff again.[2] They are growing as an organisation and their powerbase is frightening. We are quite prepared to work in harmony with SNH to alter our working practices to accommodate the things they are concerned about, but we are actually in a non-negotiating position, because all the power is taken from us.'

George illustrated the futility of disagreeing with SNH decisions by quoting the example of the Estate's application for permission to site a fish farm in Loch Obisary. It would have created a good deal of local employment and the local

---

1   Though the correct Gaelic for otter is *dobhran,* the colloquial term is *beist dubh,* or the black beast. The pejorative implication is obvious. They are considered sleekit, destructive creatures, like foxes, which can all too readily acquire a taste for domestic fowls. They are under threat in England because farmers poisoned the rivers they live in with pesticides in the 1960s and 1970s. This has not happened to any appreciable extent in the Highlands, yet Scottish fowl owners are deprived of the liberty of protecting their stock because the British state makes no legislative distinction between the two countries in wildlife matters.

2   The 1995 SNH Income and Expenditure Account, in the *Annual Report 1994–5* (the latest then to hand) showed that total expenditure for 'Management Agreements' (i.e. payments to landusers, for SSSI-related 'profits foregone') was £4.3 million (p. 86) and 'Grants: Assisting Land Managers' was £2.4 million (p. 62), making a total of £6.7 million. However 'Board Members and Staff Costs' was £11.2 million (p. 86), or nearly double the total spent on land stewardship.

Council was happy to grant planning permission. But SNH in Edinburgh was not. The estate tried to fight the decision and ended up spending 'well in excess of £20,000' doing so without any result except soured relations.[3]

We discussed Loch Scadavay, the 20,000-acre proposed SSSI, all of which is on estate ground.

'Is there a need to designate the place in the first instance?' George asked. He pointed out that the Loch itself contains no more than 15 pairs of red-throated divers and only two pairs of black-throats. 'I am not against the divers receiving proper protection, or the bog plants, but what we're saying is the actual form of designation is not the right one. An SSSI may be appropriate adjacent to an urban centre where there is a threat of development affecting the particular site, or where there is a need to restore an existing site, but not here on North Uist. We've been using this ground for certain activities for a very long time and that has preserved it in a state which is, as far as the wildlife goes, second to none.'

'Do you think this is an example of SNH having to enforce legislation that was formulated for English conditions?' I asked.

'Yes,' he said with emphasis. 'Yes. It should work by negotiation and agreement, rather than by imposing blanket rules. That way the community preserve their rights to the land. We have as much right as anyone to develop the ground in our own area, particularly compared with someone who has not worked the ground or paid for it, who has just had it handed to them on a plate by the government. The existing users have preserved the ground in its present state and there is no threat to it.'

By the time we had finished, my bottle of meths had arrived from Clachan as promised. On my way out, we briefly discussed the geese, and George mentioned that there was to be one of the two annual counts in the morning. Since I had never been on a goose-count before, I asked him if there would be any possibility of my being allowed to go along with one of the counters as an observer. This is a request I have made perhaps half a dozen times to SNH on Islay, where the counts are made monthly through the winter, but I have never had any response. By contrast, George simply picked up the phone and organised it. I would have to be at the shop at Clachan by nine o'clock the following morning, which would be no problem because I could get there from Loch Maddy on the Post Bus.

---

3 In the eight years of SNH's existence there have been many such challenges, both to existing and proposed SSSIs, but only one has ever been upheld by the independent scientific adjudicating committee (appointed by the Secretary of State). This was the proposal, made in June 1998, for a seal sanctuary off the south-coast of Islay in a place where seals are so numerous they have become a serious threat both to the migrating salmon and the livelihoods of the local fishermen, particularly the lobster-potters. The basic objection was that it was contrary to the principle of biodiversity to protect a large and expanding population of a predatory species at the expense of a small and declining population of a prey species, particularly so when they have equal international conservation status. The adjudicating committee criticised SNH's science as inadequate and its administrative methods as inequitable and underhand.

Walking down to the pier to meet Abbie Patterson, I reflected on the fantastic amounts of money which bodies like SNH put into Public Relations.[4] Yet all that results is a kind of semi-accommodating stand-off with the local people that in many respects actually operates against the interests of wildlife and nature conservation. By contrast, North Uist Estates had knocked the bureaucracy into a cocked hat, without any PR budget, just a little genuine helpfulness and frankness.

Abbie Patterson turned out to be a short, taciturn though not unfriendly Aberdonian, who was clearly inhibited in what he could say by his role as an RSPB employee. Like Morris, he had a summer-only job, though unlike Morris, I detected a human being trying to get out from behind the façade of a New Master of the World. I was curious to know the Society's view of the goose problem on North Uist.

'I honestly don't see greylags as being a big problem here,' Abbie said. 'But I've never looked into the geese here and how the numbers have built up. I really don't know much about it.'

'Really?'

'No, I don't.'

'A staggering admission from the RSPB.'

'Well, there you go,' he said in a quizzical tone of voice which I took to be a hint that he had been ordered not to discuss that subject beyond denying the premiss of my predictable question. 'I've never been here at a time of the season when I have had time to go and look at any goose damage. Areas where I have worked a little bit with geese are at Strathbeg, near Peterhead, where they are quite a big problem. Here it's nothing by comparison. When I was at Strathbeg, seven years ago, you were talking about something like 36,000 geese in a night. The geese would roost on the Loch, which the RSPB owned, and then in the day would move out onto the farms and cause havoc, real havoc.'

One thing Abbie was prepared to concede was that the RSPB were wrong to employ so many people from outside the areas they want to influence. He said there had been one or two spectacular failures, one of which had happened here on North Uist, and still affected the way people like himself were received by the locals. I asked for details and he referred me to a book called *A Curlew in the Foreground,* by Philip Coxon.

---

4 *Ibid.* In 1995 SNH spent £384,900 on 'publicity and education' and just over £1.1 million on 'publicity, information and training', making a total of about £1.5 million on overall public relations. Earlier in the year when preparing for this trip, I interviewed Jean Balfour, ex-Chair of the Countryside Commission for Scotland. She had served on almost every major conservation body in this country over the last 30 years, and she told me that in the 1960s and 1970s these organisations used to compete among themselves by offering visiting delegations from other bodies ever more extravagant lunches. Then in the 1980s, long lunches went out of fashion. Today competitive bureaucratic virility assertion takes the form of absurdly elaborate publishing programmes, which is why public relations budgets are so large.

Coxon was one of the first RSPB wardens at Balranald and has left an account of his time there – he has subsequently died – which is the only book I know of which describes the life of an RSPB warden in Scotland. What comes across very powerfully is the contempt, amounting in some cases to loathing, of the people of North Uist who do not share the author's 'visionary enthusiasm' for birds (even though, as he admits, their knowledge of them was greatly superior to his). For example, Coxon's immediate neighbour was a Mr Cameron. Cameron had once owned the house which was to become the RSPB visitor centre and on his third day on the island, Coxon made his way over the machair to his neighbour's 'unattractive croft-house'. Cameron opened the door 'and, windy though it was, I could smell the interior of the house: a strongly lavatorial air with traces of decaying foodstuff, stale sweat and paraffin.' Cameron himself was 'a monument to decrepitude and self-neglect.' His face was 'a strange yellow in colour, darkened by dirt and unshaven beard, deeply lined and unspeakably senile. His mouth hung open and his loose lips dribbled frothy spit. He wore a grey cheap suit, trousers and jacket both caked with grease and sweat, and down the trouser front was a wide stain of urine.'[5] Coxon's response was to wonder if all the other crofters were like this, since 'someone in the south' had warned him that they were. 'If so, what earthly chance was there of making a success of the "Public relations" aspect of my job?'

All Coxon had wanted from Cameron on this, his introductory meeting, was to know his first name so that he could fill it in on a form. Coxon offered neither a formal greeting, nor an informal exchange of new-neighbourly courtesies. Despite this mannerless approach, when he called the next day, Cameron gave him a dram, 'a golden, generous measure', and a bowlful of eggs. Now, Coxon says, 'I almost liked Cameron's hairy, filthy old visage.'

And Coxon was mean with it. Next to the cottage the RSPB was taking over, was an old shed which Coxon demolished. Cameron asked for some of the wood, but Coxon refused. 'I was anxious to get on with Cameron,' he writes, 'but not sufficiently to allow him to sell his foul old barn to the RSPB, then receive the wood at my hands.' So he offered Cameron 'the occasional box of firewood' and kept the rest for himself, though he accused Cameron of having subsequently stolen some of it. Despite all this, Cameron helped Coxon with his work on the barn and told him the history of both the cottage and the township. More than this, Cameron helped him with his birdwatching since he had, Coxon was forced to admit, 'an acute, almost extra-sensory perception of geese'. Despite this, Coxon writes contemptuously that 'Cameron could hardly be expected to be moved by geese or any natural phenomenon.'

More generally, Coxon found the townships of North Uist 'peculiarly unattractive', being 'bleak and devoid of any evidence of aesthetic sensibility'. Those on Benbecula and South Uist were worse. They were 'uncompromisingly

5 *A Curlew in the Foreground* Philip Coxon, David & Charles, Newton Abbott 1988, pp. 32–4, *et passim.*

squalid' and 'oppressively dreary'. South Uist was 'Britain's junkyard'. At one point Coxon looked at the moorland and expressed surprise that this was part of the same country as 'the Britain of cider orchards and hedgerows'.

Coxon felt that, in a non-legal sense, he owned the ground he was employed to warden. Within a month of arriving – he had never set foot in the Outer Hebrides before – Coxon was worried that 'a crofter could work all day, earning a living from the land, and his claim to proprietorship would be as valid as mine'. In order to set things to what he saw as rights, Coxon 'sought some special experience which would make the area uniquely mine, justify my possessive love for it.' He found it in counting the birds. 'My experience during the censusing period gave me more than a cognisance of numbers and species. At the end of six extraordinarily intense weeks the Reserve was incontestably mine.'

The practical result of this is that Coxon now felt free to indulge in acts of what he calls 'unlawfully assumed authority'. He erected a notice telling visitors where they should and should not walk, even though he knew they were (and are) in law perfectly free to walk anywhere.[6]

But Coxon was foiled in the end. In the closing pages of the book he mentions his 'rage' at the way the crofters, representatives of 'the most notoriously intractable people in Britain', reacted to an RSPB attempt to prevent them clearing out some of the choked drains on the marsh at Balranald. The RSPB wanted to take over management of the marsh. Three townships were involved and the crofters deliberated at their own pace. Finally, they decided that they would proceed with their ditching as planned and that they did not need the RSPB's managerial intervention. The reason they gave the visionary enthusiast could stand for all such conflicts in the Hebrides: 'Why should they pass lands which have been grazed by their animals for generations into the hands of a comparative stranger, working for a remote authority, all to a purpose which conflicted with traditional ideas of how land should be used?'

The day of the goose-count dawned, once again, fine and clear. By the time I was down at Clachan, it was positively hot. A crowd was gathered over the road from the shop among a gaggle of vehicles. A friendly-looking man with thinning, sandy hair and a chin-beard, looking not unlike a smiling Solzhenitsyn, introduced himself to me as Paul Boyer, my contact. (I subsequently learned that John Love was there, but he forbore to say hello.) Paul was with his teenage son who was dressed in a bright red soccer jersey. He said he hoped to go to Liverpool University, a choice he had made because the campus is close to the Liverpool football ground. What a sensible idea! I said I wished I had thought of that way of choosing a

---

6   The habit of arrogating rights is common with the RSPB. On Islay, for example, the Society's public leaflet for visitors to their Reserve on the island tells visitors that they should not get out of their vehicles on the public road that runs through the Reserve, lest they disturb the birds. Of course, pedestrian traffic is perfectly legal at all times on all rural roads except motorways.

university myself: I might have ended up at Maranello, round the corner from the Ferrari factory.

Paul is a serious amateur birdwatcher, who has done quite a bit of volunteer Reserve wardening in his native Lincolnshire. He is an official ringer for the British Trust for Ornithology, making lapwings his speciality on North Uist. He had lived on the island for 13 years, having come to take a job as an architect with what is now the Western Isles Council. I asked him if, as an architect, he did not find the wrecked cars and general junk lying around the place an eyesore.

'Not at all,' he said. 'It's part of the charm. If everywhere were tidy, they'd start tidying up sheep carcases and we wouldn't have so many golden eagles.'

Paul told me that there are two sea eagle sites on the Uists and, taking all the islands down to Barra Head, no fewer than 22 golden eagle home ranges. This is the maximum possible due to the area and type of ground. They are all occupied, though not all by breeding pairs. In the time he has been here, numbers have been either constant or increasing very slightly.[7]

I asked about persecution. Paul said there was still a bit by crofters, but it made no difference to the population.

'So they are not under any threat at all?' I asked.

'Not really, except possibly from egg-collectors.'

'Where do they come from?'

'There's an awful lot of Geordies,' Paul said. 'An awful lot of them seem to come from the Newcastle, Sunderland area. The national tip-off system says they've been seen coming through Argyll and we are expecting them to come your way; keep an eye open for them.'

I asked Paul what he thought of all the often ludicrous secrecy surrounding the location of bird nests.

'I don't agree with it,' he said. I've got this theory that the more people you tell about nest sites the better it is because then it isn't a secret. In a way, the more locals know about these things the better. If something happens there is more

---

7   A general impression has been created by the conservationist community that golden eagles are under threat. This is not true. Roy Dennis, who was employed for 20 years by the RSPB to study eagles in the Highlands, produced figures in 1983 which showed that the theoretical maximum number of golden eagles in Scotland should be about 600 pairs, given the areas available for them to hunt over and the size of territory each pair needs to feed itself and its young. (See Dennis *et al*, 'The Status of the Golden Eagle in Britain' *British Birds* 1984, Vol. 77, pp. 592–607). At the time, the eagle population was said to be something over 423 pairs, and since then eagle numbers have certainly not fallen. (See R.E. Green 'The Status of the Golden Eagle in Britain in 1992' *Bird Study* 1996, Vol. 43, pp. 20–27) Yet the 'Dennis number' has fallen since he deduced it, due to the expansion of forestry, the reintroduction of the sea eagle which tends to displace golden eagles and the improvements in agricultural practice which leave less carrion per square mile of hill as food for the birds, thus necessitating an expansion of the area each pair needs to scavenge over. So eagle numbers, which were nearly 80 per cent of their theoretical maximum in 1981, are probably closer to 90 per cent of it now. So far from being under threat as the RSPB would have the public believe, this bird is close to saturation point.

chance someone will see them and report them. Secrecy doesn't work, apart from anything else because the collectors know where the nests are.'

'How do they know?'

'Grapevines. Information technology. They're just like modern birders, with telescopes and phonelines and bleepers, except that the egg-collectors take things. And they have to have everything. It's not enough to have a red kite egg in your collection, you have to have a clutch of red kite eggs taken in Wales, a clutch of red kite eggs taken in England, if you can find them, a clutch of red kite eggs taken in Scotland; and one taken in 1986, one in 1987 and so on. They go back to the same sites year after year. Because these people are so keen on documentation, when the police raid them, they know exactly where all these eggs have come from.'

'People like that need psychiatric help,' I said.

'Yes, I think so. But they must be really good birders all the same. I spend a fair amount of time looking for nests for different purposes and I think, how on earth do these people find these things, like firecrests' nests? I've never, ever found one.'

We pottered about, on a pre-planned route, with Paul and his son counting geese through their own telescopes and me trying and failing to take the odd photograph of a bird. The conclusion was that goose numbers were up, very slightly, on 1995. With that, everyone went home. There was no convivial flask of tea or can of lager by the roadside with all the other counters, much less a pint in the pub. Weird lot these birders, I thought, not for the first time.

Back aboard ship, it was time to go. I changed the plug on the engine, tested it three times and found it worked perfectly. I repaired the dinghy, which did not take long, ate a large lunch, filled a flask with coffee and raised the anchor. There was not much wind in the loch, so I motored out beyond the Ruigh Liath light and then hoisted the mainsail. The further we got out to sea, the more wind there was, coming almost due east. Right outside, it was blowing a weakish three, so I raised the headsail and doused the motor.

I settled down for a drowsy afternoon helming, or rather watching the lashed helm, in the warm sunshine. Light, fluffy clouds were piling up over the mountains of Harris. All around the sea glowed an almost luminous blue. It was a glorious afternoon for a sail. It is less than 15 miles from Loch Maddy to Rodel on the south-east tip of Harris, so it looked as if we would be there in time for a late tea – at least it did until the wind started to die.

9

HARRIS AND THE SHIANTS

BY THE TIME WE HAD THE SOUND OF HARRIS ABEAM, the flood tide was flowing strongly up the Minch and out through the Sound, one of the most treacherous waterways off the west of Scotland. The only navigable channel is very narrow. Many of the rocks are slightly submerged and therefore invisible. Not only do the tides flow strongly but they do so in a completely unpredictable way. For some reason, at neaps the tides set from east to west during the day and the reverse at night, though why this should be, I have no idea. Nonetheless, it is a beautiful stretch of water on a sunny day and I passed by wishing I had had time to attempt a passage and then explore the west coast of Harris, reputedly one of the most beautiful parts of the Hebrides. Instead I sailed slowly north, with the wind dying, until I dropped the genoa and motor-sailed into the tight but perfectly sheltered natural harbour at Rodel.

Rodel is distinguished by having what must surely be the most – how shall I put this? – unpretentious pub in the whole of the west Highlands. The main part of the structure was built as a mansion for Macleod of Harris in the eighteenth century out of a fortune plundered in India. It was turned into a hotel which the grandfather of the present owner bought in 1935. For many years it was a thriving concern, not least because Rodel was then the ferry port for Harris. But the water alongside the pier is too shallow to allow big boats to tie up, so passengers went ashore in lighters, or 'flit boats' as they are known. Since then a deep-water berth has been constructed at Tarbert, where the modern, roll-on roll-off ferries go alongside. Today Rodel is deserted, apart from a few visiting yachts, and the hotel presents a picture of easy-going decay.

The building is in three parts. Looking from the sea, the left-hand wing houses today's pub; the handsome, three-storey central part is the mansion house, deserted but not derelict; and the right-hand wing looks, quite literally, as if a bomb had hit it. It used to be a lounge bar area, until the owner pulled it down to reduce his rates bill. But he has not cleared the site in any way, so the inquiring visitor can enjoy a few moments exploring another fascinating Highland ruin. I found all sorts of interesting artefacts, like crate upon crate of unopened but very old bottles of Newcastle Brown Ale and an incomparably 1950s painting of the paddle-steamer, the *Waverley* going 'doon the watter for the fair'. The vessel is just casting off from the Broomielaw. You can almost see 'Bob and Mary on the Govan Ferry/Wishing jet propulsion could be there'.

In what was now slightly hazy sunshine, I walked the three miles up from Rodel over the hill into Leverburgh as I had arranged to visit Alison Johnson and her husband Andrew who live at Strond, a small settlement which looks south over the Sound of Harris, halfway back from Leverburgh towards Rodel. Both husband and wife are committed conservationists. Alison is from the east coast and represents the SWT in Harris – Bill Neill's equivalent. On an island as economically derelict as Harris – possibly the poorest area in the Highlands and Islands – the question of conservation versus commercial exploitation rears its head with even greater force than it does on the Uists. If the basic problem posed internationally by activist conservationism is the extent to which economic expansion should be curtailed in the interests of the conservation of wildlife and natural resources, the basic question posed by island life, at least in the Hebrides, is: to what extent economic expansion should be encouraged in the interests of the conservation of people?

Alison is an attractive, dark-haired but awfully serious-looking woman. She gave me a cup of tea and a slice of cake then sat down and waited coolly for me to start. Thinking, rather stupidly as it turned out, that in the circumstances it might be best to kick off with a joke, I tried to quote – since I thought it rather funny – a passage I had read in *Hansard* some days before. It was spoken by the Earl of Onslow in the House of Lords during the committee stage of the Environmental Protection Bill in 1990. The noble earl had opened his remarks as follows:

> I have just returned from a treat. This morning I woke up and looked over the Grand Canal in Venice. As I was preparing my papers for today's debate one or two thoughts crossed my mind with a certain amount of irony. Had Attila the Hun attended the Ramsar Convention, it is probable that Venice would still be a heavily protected wetlands site. Had Theodoric had a regional fund, there is not the slightest doubt that he would not have invested it in Venice hoping that it would become the centre of the spice trade between the eastern Mediterranean and the Western world. Had the blind doge Danolo been subject to building regulations, there would have been no buildings.[1]

I got to the third sentence (which was the only one I could remember verbatim): 'Had Attila the Hun attended the Ramsar Convention, it is probable that Venice would still be a heavily protected wetlands site', and Alison interrupted saying, without the ghost of a smile, 'And much better it would be, too.'

Oh dear, I thought. Nervously, I turned my attention to Andrew who runs a small company in Cambridge, publishing a journal called *Environmental Values*. He commutes weekly from Harris, which must be a fearful drain of the world's non-renewable resources. Andrew is a tall, softly spoken, academic-looking Englishman who lacks the abrasiveness of his crisply Scottish wife. He gave me a copy of the current edition of his magazine, from which I should like to quote a short passage since, like Lord Onslow's speech, I found it rather funny. It is the abstract (quoted here *in toto*) of a paper entitled 'Ecology: Scientific, Deep and Feminist' by two Texans, Markus J. Peterson and Tarla Rai Peterson.

---

1   *Hansard* (Lords), Vol. 520, col. 2103, 4 July 1990.

The application of hierarchy theory to ecological systems presents those who seek a radical change in human perspectives towards nature with a unique window of opportunity. Because hierarchy theory has enabled scientific ecologists to discover the window through which one chooses to observe a system influences its reality, they may be more amenable to including the perspectives of deep, feminist and scientific ecology into their self-definition. A synergy between deep, feminist and scientific ecology could improve environmental policy by encouraging more ecofeminists to encompass the marginalisation of non-human life-forms within the ethic of care, more deep ecologists to encompass the issues of overconsumption and militarisation within the anthropocentric-biocentric polarity, and more scientific ecologists to scrutinise the politics behind their investigations.[2]

Beyond the laughs, the Petersons' prose style surely illustrates one important point: the difficulty people like Ena McNeil must have in arguing with ecologists. If she were to address the Petersons in Gaelic, she would presumably make as little sense to them as their gobbledygook makes to me and, I would imagine, to her. Since people's lives and liberties are affected by the international environmental debate, it is high time that a common language be enforced for this sort of discussion. I suggest plain English: it is readily comprehensible to Ena, and might also be understood by the Petersons.

Andrew's contributions to his magazine were mercifully lucid. They concerned the issue which is probably the starkest illustration of the choice between environmental protection and exploitation which has ever faced the Hebrides: the Lingerbay 'superquarry' which is planned for this part of Harris.

The 'spiritual' background to the conflict was concisely described by the two Johnstons in a jointly-written editorial: 'We count ourselves as deep environmentalists, and marginally or not at all religious. Most of the people in Harris are deeply religious, and marginally or not at all "environmental".'

The political background takes a little longer to explain. In 1991 an English quarrying company, Redland Aggregates, applied to the Western Isles Council for planning permission to excavate what could become one of the largest quarries in Europe at Lingerbay, just two miles north of Rodel.[3] An entire hill was to be removed for roadstone, at a rate of ten million tons per annum for 60 years, and shipped out in bulk carriers from a specially constructed pier. This would, of course, be by far the largest industrial undertaking ever to have come to the western isles, and would completely overshadow the economy of Harris. The Western Isles Council was in favour of the proposal, looking for economic growth and job creation in Harris, where unemployment is among the highest in the outer Hebrides. It was also hoping for a massive cash injection from business rates, which would help cover the losses made by their unwise investment in the crashed Pakistani bank, BCCI, in the 1980s. But objections were lodged, initially by incomers who feared that the quarry would destroy the peace and 'quality of life' that they had come here to enjoy, and latterly by SNH who took up the issue of the visual impact of such a massive operation on what is an outstandingly beautiful area. The result was the longest planning inquiry in Scottish history.

2 *Environmental Values* Vol 5. (1996), p.124.
3 Redland was later bought by a French company. The applicant is now Lafarge Redland.

The cost so far to the Scottish Office has been over £2 million, and it has not, as of this writing (early 1999), yet reported.

The reason for the proposal was not that Scotland is short of aggregates for road-building but that England is, though that shortage is artificial rather than natural. England has plenty of suitable stone, it is just that few people are prepared to tolerate large quarries in their backyards – the NIMBY question again. Consequently, it has become politically necessary to inflict the noise and dust on people who are less likely to complain. In his article, Andrew quoted the Council for the Preservation of Rural England as saying that establishing the quarry at Lingerbay 'will simply shift our environmental problems to someone else's backyard'.

The people of Harris were initially in favour of the development since they imagined that there would be lots of jobs created as a result. Then opinion began to shift. First, it was realised that most of the jobs would go to specialist quarrymen, none of whom lived on the island, and, secondly, that the pollution might affect the fishing in the Minch as the bulk carriers would arrive in ballast and deposit that ballast, most probably a filthy, oleaginous sludge, on the sea-bed in the middle of the local fishing grounds. This would damage the fisheries, and might even introduce aggressively colonial life forms – marine versions of rhododendrons or rabbits – from wherever it is in the world that the ballast is pumped in. People began to realise that the quarry might actually *destroy* local jobs rather than create them.

Redland's combination of arrogance and meanness did not help its cause either. Without any undue impact on its balance sheet, the company could have offered the local people some real benefits in cash or community facilities from the projected revenue of £600 million (at £10 a ton) to compensate for the inconvenience and environmental damage. But they made such a derisory offer that it looked contemptuous.

Unfortunately for the people of Harris, the body which should have been their champion, the Western Isles Council, displayed an attitude almost as contemptuous as Redland's. In particular, they were determined that any money the company paid would not go directly to Harris, but be filtered through the Council, who would then distribute it as they saw fit, presumably on the pork-barrel system so disgracefully common in Scottish local government.

More than this, the Council made it as hard as they could for Harris people to participate in the Inquiry. Normally these hearings are held in the nearest convenient hall to the subject of the application, but the Council ordered that the Inquiry sit in Stornoway, which meant that neighbours of the future quarry had to make a 120-mile round trip every day they wanted to attend the almost interminable hearing. Finally, some truly underhand tactics by the Council were revealed. One of the Council officials was caught trying to smear one of the objectors personally, alleging that he had been on a sex holiday in Thailand on the grounds that 'the handwriting appears to be that of a very tired man'.

The result of all this was that whereas before the Inquiry opened local opinion on Harris was solidly in favour of the development, by the time it closed it was solidly against.[4] But that may prove to be irrelevant. Andrew attended most of the sittings and he told me how struck he was by the way the QCs Redland's had brought in from Edinburgh completely ignored all the points made by the Harris people, while they replied seriously and at length to every point raised by the QCs SNH had brought in, also from Edinburgh. He was left in no doubt about the essential *locus operandi of* the Scottish environmental decision-making process. Harris be hanged!

On the opposite side, that of the islanders in favour of the development, the most committed individual is undoubtedly the man on whose land the quarry will be sited and who stands to gain an estimated £1.5 million per annum from Redland if it does. He is Mr Donald ('Donnie Rodel') Macdonald, the proprietor of, and barman in, the Rodel Hotel. Despite the wreckage of his lounge bar, Donnie still serves drinks in the other wing of his hotel at lunchtime and in the evenings, Monday to Saturday (all pubs are closed on Sundays in Harris). He is a friendly, rubicund man in his 50s who was born and brought up in Stornoway.

When I dropped into the bar, Donnie was alone except for a couple of young holiday-making bikers from Edinburgh. Donnie was telling them at exhaustingly courteous length about the history of the MacLeods of Harris and their relationship with the MacLeods of Dunvegan. The male biker interrupted, speaking in a surprisingly 'Morningsaide' accent for one dressed up in Kawasaki leathers. 'Could you tell me,' he said, 'what is the state of the herring fisheries on the ailand at the moment? Ai was here in 1984 and the boats in Stornoway were landing maickerel. Ai didn't see any herring at oll.'

Ever the gentlemen, Donnie responded by describing the recent history of the herring catch in the Minch and the current balance of the outer Hebridean fishing fleet. This seemed to satisfy Mr Kawasaki who took his girlfriend and their drinks over to the corner where they settled down to watch an American football match on satellite television from 'Chicaggo'.

I asked Donnie about the quarry.

'If it doesn't happen, then we won't have a community left on Harris,' he said gravely. 'It'll cease to exist because the cost of living here is prohibitive. There's no employment. The fishing fleet won't sustain the community. There is only one Harris Tweed weaver left on south Harris.'

'Will the quarry create much local employment?' I asked.

'If there are local people here who are capable of being employed, then the quarry will be available for them.'

'Yes, but will most of the jobs not be for specialists who will come from outside?'

'We already have a lot of people who have left here, for specialist jobs in other quarries,' Donnie said. 'One is Glensanda, in Morvern. There's quite a few who

4   In 1993 the Harris people voted for the quarry by 62%–38% on a 61% poll. In 1995, immediately after the Inquiry closed, they voted against it by 68%–32%, on an 83% poll. Both were postal ballots conducted jointly by the Harris Council for Social Services and the Electoral Reform Society.

have left here to go down and work at Glensanda in the quarry there and have already been trained and would give their right hand to be given the opportunity to come back and work in their own area.'

Somehow the idea that Harris' unique human export in recent years has been quarry engineers sounded a little far-fetched, but I thought it would be rude to press him on this. 'Would you like to live next to a quarry?' I asked instead. 'It would surely not be very pleasant here in a northerly breeze?'

'We don't get a northerly breeze all that often,' Donnie said. 'The prevailing wind is from the south-west.'

'If the quarry is built, will you get rich and buy yourself an island in the Bahamas?' I asked.

'I'm already rich,' Donnie said. 'I don't have to go somewhere else. I'm quite happy here. I don't need a quarry to get rich. I'm a millionaire, because I live here.'

'You mean you are a millionaire in scenic amenity?'

'Yes.'

'Would that not be degraded by the quarry?'

'I don't think so. Don't get me wrong. I enjoy my environment. I enjoy hillwalking and I enjoy my landscape. But at the end of the day, you have to ask yourself, do you want a landscape without people or a landscape with people? It's fine for somebody to come from London, or New York, and say 'beautiful', and take a couple of photos. But I want to see a community here. Whatever happens here will be the template for the development of the north-west of Scotland for the next 50 or 100 years.'

'In the meantime, you enjoy the quiet life here, then?'

'I won't call it quiet. It's interesting. There's a sense of hubbub about life that does go on, but to the outsider it looks very sleepy and backward.' He gave me a dram and said with a wink, 'Spread the word.'

Back down on the pier, I talked to an old man out walking his dog who remarked acidly that if it was local employment which Donnie wanted, he would do better to renovate his hotel and open it properly for business.

'But he probably needs the money from the quarry to pay for the renovations,' I ventured.

'Aye, well whose fault is that?' the man said gruffly, before stumping off up the hill.

Next morning I toyed with the idea of going to have a look at the best known historical monument in Rodel, St Clement's Church. The Highlands and Islands volume of the Buildings of Scotland series, by John Gifford, calls the church 'the grandest medieval building in the Western Isles'. It is another structure which was abandoned after the Reformation, and restored only in modern times. Today it is, in Gifford's words, 'a piously pointed Ancient Monument'. I didn't like the sound of that, so I decided to give it a miss, preferring to remember Harris by the fascinating wreckage of the Donnie's lounge bar and the ingeniously non-pecuniary reasons he gave for supporting the Lingerbay quarry.

With a chilly wind coming almost due north – Donnie's nightmare – I spent a few hours aboard breakfasting at length and reading. I dipped into Nigel Nicolson's account of the creation of Leverburgh by Lord Leverhulme in the 1920s.[5] This was an even bigger project than the quarry. In fact it was the largest scheme of social engineering ever undertaken in the Highlands of Scotland, possibly anywhere in the British Isles. It was financed by the almost limitless capital of one of the richest, most determined and in many ways the best intentioned men who ever tried to interfere with the relationship between the Hebridean and his native sod. Yet the project ended, in less than seven years, in complete and ignominious failure. Nicolson's book is an attempt to answer the question, why?

Lord Leverhulme started life in 1851 as William Lever, the heir to a substantial wholesale grocery business in Bolton, Lancashire. By dint of brains, effort and luck, he built the business up into the giant Lever Brothers group (now Unilever, one of the largest corporations in the world). His headquarters were in Port Sunlight, a mock-Tudor company town which he had had built to his own design across the Mersey from Liverpool. It was named after Sunlight soap, the company's first and most lucrative brand, and was part of his attempt to improve the lives of his employees by a policy of what he called 'prosperity sharing, not profit sharing'. In other words, Leverhulme kept the money, but handed out perks – on his terms. A secretary said of him, 'The ruling passion of his life was not money or even power, but the desire to increase human well-being by substituting the profitable for the valueless.'

Leverhulme fell in love with Lewis during a six-hour visit to Stornoway in 1884 on what Nicolson calls 'an August afternoon of exceptional brilliance'. In 1918 he bought the island from Lieutenant-Colonel Duncan Matheson, and the following year he acquired Harris. In doing so he took control of 530,000 acres and 34,000 people. Leverhulme thought the land valueless and the people unnecessarily poor due to their excessive dependence on it. Nicolson describes his purpose as being 'to raise people's standard of living by a rapid transformation of the island economy from one based on crofting and small-scale fishing to a new economy based on large-scale developments in the tweed and fishing industries'. In other words, the people were to leave the land and work in factories. But many of his islanders – the Lewismen more than those on Harris – wanted not to reduce their contact with the land, but to *increase* it. This was the root of the conflict which brought all Leverhulme's schemes crashing down.

It was Lewis which went first. There is no doubt that many of the islanders liked Leverhulme personally, but business is business for Lewismen as much as it is for Lancastrians, and those of them who wanted land rather than wages were never deflected from their main aim, which was to translate what they saw as their moral right into what the world would acknowledge as a legal right. The claim to moral right derived partly from customary occupation from which they argued they had been displaced by violence during the Clearances, and partly

---

5 *The Lord of the Isles* Nigel Nicolson, Weidenfeld & Nicolson, London, 1960.

from the ancient idea that defending their country gave them a right to occupation of a portion of it.

Lewismen had not stinted their blood in defence of Great Britain. In 1914 and 1915, just three years before Leverhulme arrived 6000 Lewismen out of a total population of 30,000, had volunteered for the armed forces. By 1916, when conscription was introduced, there was almost no one left on the island to conscript. Lewis was much publicised at the time as having a higher percentage of volunteers per head of the population than any other place in the whole of the British Empire. If that percentage of recruitment had been achieved throughout the United Kingdom by the end of 1916, total enlistment would have been just over 9,000,000 men, instead of the actual figure of 3,400,000.[6] Most of the Lewismen went into the local regiment, the Seaforth Highlanders (Tex Geddes's regiment; the earls of Seaforth had been the island's rulers for many centuries) which fought in France, Flanders, Macedonia, Palestine and Mesopotamia. When the survivors came back home, they wanted land. 'Who would grudge [these men],' asked one Lewisman in public in 1917, 'the soil which they so bravely defended from the savage and brutal Huns?'

In making this claim, the Lewismen had the backing of the government which wanted the Highland land question settled once and for all. Nicolson quotes the Lord Advocate, speaking in Inverness in 1917 on behalf of the government in London, who said, 'Everyone is agreed that the people of the Highlands must be placed in possession of the soil.'

That undertaking was made under the stress of war. Predictably, when that stress was removed by the Armistice of 1918, the undertaking was reneged upon. Lord Leverhulme had made millions in the meantime from contracts with the Ministry of Munitions. He wanted to spend some of this money bringing prosperity to the islands. The price was that the islanders give up their claims to the land. This they would not do. It was a war-time profiteer versus several thousand ex-servicemen. It would have been an unequal contest except that Leverhulme had the law on his side, while the Lewismen had only the promises of a government which had been desperately anxious to keep them fighting in the dark days of 1917. Peace exposed the political duplicity. Agitation, litigation and finally violence ensued during what were called 'land raids'. Raiders would occupy uncultivated ground and start to till it, attempting to establish *de facto* rights of occupancy. The government would not go so far as to back Leverhulme in using violence to evict ex-servicemen. An extraordinary stand-off resulted, until, in 1921, the great magnate admitted defeat and abandoned all his schemes on Lewis.

Leverhulme then transferred his benevolence to Harris (where the only land raids had been at Rodel and Lingerbay), and started construction of the port which he called Leverburgh, previously Obbe. This was to be the centre of his projected fishing fleet. He had already established MacFisheries, a chain of

---

6   See *The Politics of Manpower 1914–18* Keith Grieves, Manchester University Press, Manchester 1988.

fishmongers throughout Britain, to act as outlets. Though the shops were a very successful enterprise over the next half century, the fishing on Harris was a total failure. Despite warnings from the Scottish Fisheries Board, the skippers of the ferries that serviced Harris, the Northern Lighthouse Commissioners and many local sailors – described to Leverhulme by an expert as 'the most fearless I ever knew' – to the effect that the rocks in the Sound of Harris made it too dangerous for navigation in all but perfect weather conditions, Leverhulme went ahead and built a port with jetty space for 50 boats to lie alongside and huge port-side facilities including fish-curing sheds with barrack-house accommodation for the curers, a packing station, a kippering house, a net store, a refrigeration plant, a water-tower and parking for 20 cars – the latter a bizarre novelty on what was still a semi-roadless island. In all, Leverhulme envisaged that the population of his new town would eventually top 10,000, nearly three times the highest-ever population for the whole of Harris. 'Determined not to be thwarted by a mere accident of geography,' Nicolson says, 'Leverhulme blasted away some of the rocks and put gas-beacons on others . . . He was always complaining that [the experts] were incapable of thinking big.'

The final outcome was almost pathetic. Leverhulme landed only one summer's catch, in 1924, and that only because he bought an English fishing fleet in Great Yarmouth and ordered it up to Harris and then imported hundreds of girls from the mainland to cure the fish. Hardly a single local job was created. Leverhulme died the next year, and his successor as chairman of Lever Brothers, an accountant called Francis D'Arcy Cooper, immediately ordered the total cessation of all expenditure in the Hebrides. Enraged by the obduracy of the Hebrideans, D'Arcy Cooper said to a native of Lewis, 'The best thing you can do with your islands is to sink them in the Atlantic for four hours, and then pull them up again.'

The islands were put up for sale. Whereas Leverhulme had paid £210,000 for the two of them, and spent another £1.3 million on his 'improvement' schemes, the total realised for all the assets was a mere £55,000. This represented about two shillings per acre, if you exclude all the built assets: Lews Castle, Amhuinnsuidh Castle, Borve Lodge, thousands of cottages, a whaling station, a modern but almost totally unused spinning-mill and two half-improved harbours.[7]

Is there any way for economic development schemes to work in places like the Hebrides? The short answer is, yes, provided they are locally organised. A good example from recent times was the Integrated Development Program (IDP), a broadly-based economic upgrading project for the Western Isles which ran through the mid-1980s on European money, though it was almost derailed by a different form of 'benevolent' interference from outside. Central to the IDP was agricultural improvement – fencing, drainage and so on – which aroused the wrath of the environmentalists, principally the RSPB. Whereas Leverhulme had

---

7 The whaling station, another complete failure, provides a good illustration of Leverhulme's paternalism. He intended to use the oil from the whales at Port Sunlight and to sell the meat to 'African natives' in the form of tinned sausages. 'Whale meat is rather tough,' Leverhulme once minuted, '[but] the native is not an epicure.'

tried to sell optimism to the people on the islands, the RSPB tried to sell pessimism to people off the islands. 'We are in no doubt that the programme devised for the Western Isles could cause great harm to birds and other wildlife,' wrote Ian Presst, then Director. 'The RSPB views the scheme with alarm: it could become one of the greatest single threats to bird conservation in recent years.'[8]

David Minns pitched in with a long article calling the IDP the 'Imminent Destruction Plan'. He was worried about the dunlin and the ringed plover, and his reasons were interesting, particularly in the light of David Jackson's conclusions about the dunlins on South Uist. 'Our breeding populations [of these two species] are rather small and declining rapidly due to the continuing loss of wetland habitats.'[9] Since almost all of those wetland losses are in England, the reality behind his words was that Hebridean development should be curtailed in order to compensate for the English refusal to curtail development. The islanders should be content with non-material riches. 'The beauty and wildlife of the Western Isles should be viewed as amongst their best assets,' Minns wrote patronisingly.

All this absurd alarmism is still remembered in the islands, 15 years later. Bill Lawson of Northton on Harris, who was on the Western Isles Council in those days, subsequently told me that he used to be phoned from the south of England by anxious callers wanting to known how many miles of hedgerow were going to be grubbed up. *Hedgerows* in the *Hebrides!* 'Well-intentioned but ignorant' was how Bill viewed most of these people, though the RSPB he found unpleasantly aggressive.

'They kept telling us that corncrakes were going to fly into the new fences and be killed,' he said. 'Then they reckoned we were going to create barley prairies. Of course, they'd never been to see it.'

'So you were being criticised for creating field boundaries and for destroying field boundaries?' I asked.

'That's right.'

'Seems odd.'

'Different departments writing the letters, I suppose.'

Bill remembered the arrival of Lord Melchett, a prominent environmental campaigner, at the time connected with the RSPB and subsequently, chairman of Greenpeace. 'He was annoyed to be given tea out of plastic cups,' Bill told me, 'though the office was still being set up. "Since this is all public money, I want china," he said to the secretaries.'

In the event, the IDP went ahead and was a great success mainly, in Bill's

---

8 *Birds* Autumn 1982, p. 5.

9 *Ibid.*, Winter 1982, pp. 23-5

10 The whole scheme was one of three pilots for a larger Europe-wide project, which was never implemented. Ironically in view of criticisms of the character-failings of the Hebrideans, the Western Isles scheme was the only one which worked. The French one collapsed halfway through due to bureaucratic squabbles, and the third one, in Belgium, never got of the ground at all as the intended beneficiaries could not agree about which language should be used, Flemish or French.

view, because it was all done on a small scale, croft by croft basis.[10] The wader populations were unaffected, though it is possible that corncrake numbers were reduced by a few breeding pairs. But against that should be set the vast increase in goose numbers. Nett nett, the avian life of the western isles has undoubtedly benefited from what Mr Presst called 'the greatest single threat to bird conservation in recent years'. In short, the whole RSPB campaign was either a false alarm raised out of shameful ornithological ignorance (if you think the Society fundamentally honest) or a cynical marketing ploy based on the widely used conservationist strategy of foretelling imminent disaster in order to recruit new members (if you do not).

Bill's view was simpler: 'People in the deep south tend to think that nobody is interested in bird life but themselves.'

So engrossed was I in my books that by the time I poked my head out of the hatch to see what the weather was doing, it was early afternoon. The wind was still blowing quite strongly, but the sun had come out. A blue sky was dotted with fluffy, rainless clouds, though over Runeval, the hill which is to be converted to roadstone, the clouds had a greyish cast. My next stop was the Shiant Isles, about 25 miles away, east-north-east, out in the north Minch. With the wind coming north and steady, it seemed like the moment to leave.

In these conditions and with a favourable tide, I calculated that six hours should be adequate to get me there. If conditions changed I could always turn west into east Loch Tarbert – for shelter if it blew up, or to save fuel if the wind died away completely. There are no off-lying dangers around the Shiants, so a landfall at dusk is not unduly risky. A final consideration was that settled northerlies afforded the best conditions for getting right across the Minch to the Summer Isles, which are almost due east of the Shiants. There was a good chance, looking at the weather chart, that these conditions would hold for the next 36 hours. Taking all this into consideration, I decided to sail immediately.

Outside, the wind was, for some strange reason, lighter than in Rodel harbour, so it was slowish going up the east coast of Harris. At about four o'clock I lashed the tiller and went below for some lunch. To the sound of water rushing past the hull and a good 'thrum' from the rigging, I enjoyed a leisurely sardine roll and a cup of coffee – in a plastic mug; no china aboard – while studying the chart and the *Clyde Cruising Club Sailing Directions*. Well heeled over, *Sylvia B* surged over the long swells, occasionally flicking a breaking wave up onto the coachroof. The conditions were ideal for a windward passage. I read a bit, listened to the radio a bit, looked around me a bit, then shortly after copying down the 5.50 p.m. shipping forecast, I took a photograph of the westering sun, half clothed in pale pink clouds, as it threw shafts of cold, evening light onto the massive, dark hills of Harris.

By this time, the Shiants were visible ahead, though further away than I would have liked. The tide had begun to turn, or at least lose its northerly movement, and progress seemed to slow slightly. But the sky was clear, a full moon was due

to rise soon, and the wind was holding reasonably steady, so I took the decision
not to turn for Harris but to go for the islands.

By the time it was completely dark, I was still six or seven miles off, though
sailing under a very bright moon. The dark lump of Eilean an Tighe (the island
of the house, the most southerly of the four that comprise the group), loomed
high above the sea, but I seemed to be making slow progress, presumably because
the tide was now flowing strongly north-to-south. The *Sailing Directions* had
warned of the strength of the tides round the Shiants, so I decided to tack inshore.
But the wind was dropping and it was becoming clear it was going to take a long
time to get round the top of Eilean an Tighe and into the anchorage off the
shingle spit between it and Garbh Eilean. So, possibly a mile off the island, I
dropped the genoa and started to motor-sail. Progress was still slow but at least it
was directly towards my goal. It was nearly ten o'clock and I was keen to come to
anchor. Apart from anything else, I was looking forward to having something to
eat.

After perhaps quarter of an hour's motoring, as I was approaching the
southerlymost tip of Eilean an Tighe, the engine stopped dead. I leapt aft and
tried to fire it up, but it would not go. I tried, and tried, and tried again. But not
a cough. The only thing for it was to raise the headsail. By the time I had done
that and gathered everything together, I found I had drifted back almost to the
point where I had started to motor. The only difference was that I could not now
make my way directly up the side of the island, but had to tack far out to sea.

Due to the strength of the tide and the relative lack of wind, it was another
two hours before I was finally able to weather the shoulder of the island and head
into the anchorage. By now clouds had obscured the moon. There was just enough
brightness in the sky to be able to distinguish between sea and the island, but it
was a dark and ominous scene. The vast cliffs rose sheer at least a couple of
hundred feet. The anchorage was exposed from north-east round to east and
there was a gap between the islands to the north, through which the swell was
running. All around I could hear the subdued rumble of the surf on the rocks
outside.

I buoyed the anchor and made it ready to drop, then started, very gingerly,
sailing round the bay looking for the best place to come to. In the near total
darkness the shore would seem a hundred yards away one moment, then ten
yards away the next. That was clearly too close, so I would go about and sail for
a minute then seem far too far off-shore. Distances can be very hard to judge at
sea at night. The chart showed the bottom shelving very steeply, so I started
probing the depths with my lead line. This is difficult to do unless the boat is
almost completely stopped, so I had to tack up to where I thought it would be
right to take a sounding, luff up, drop the lead, and then simultaneously take the
reading while all the time keeping enough way on to be able to pull the helm up
and be able to bear away before getting 'in irons'. On the fourth or fifth go, I
fumbled the line and dropped it overboard. Luckily by then I was clear where I
wanted to be, and soon let the anchor go.

I got the sails down, then inflated the dinghy. I rowed about briefly looking for the wooden batten at the top end of the lead line, which would be floating, but failed to find it. The shore was less than 30 yards away, and downwind. It was imperative that the anchor not drag in the night. As the bottom is shingle, and very steeply shelving, I thought the prudent thing to do would be to put out my spare anchor. So for the first, and as it turned out last, time on this voyage, I heaved this into the dinghy and rowed off-shore as far as the chain would stretch then dropped that anchor too. By now I felt we were fairly secure, so long as the wind did not go round to the east, which was unlikely. I secured the dinghy, took off my waterproofs and went below. It was now one o'clock in the morning, and I had not had so much as a cup of coffee since about 4 p.m., nine hours earlier. But I was too tired to eat. I drank a glass of lemonade and climbed into my sleeping bag. I set the alarm for 5.30 a.m. so that I could listen to the shipping forecast for the morrow, as I still hoped to make it across the Minch to the Summer Isles while the weather held.

It was almost impossible to sleep as the anchor chain was making the most fantastic noise I have ever heard in 15 years of cruising on *Sylvia B*. It would grind and scrape for 30 seconds or so, the sounds being carried up from the sea-bed like vibrations on a child's string-and-tin telephone, then it would give an incredible bang, so loud that at first I wondered if something had broken. In fact it was just the bow rearing up on the swells and the anchor, clearly well dug in, snapping the chain taught with a report inside the hull that sounded like a muffled shotgun blast. All the while, I could hear the sea pounding on the cliffs outside. It was not a comfortable night.

The early morning forecast was for much of the same weather, which was what I wanted. I took a quick look outside, saw everything was reasonably settled and went back to sleep. I woke at eight, feeling refreshed but ravenous. The sea had gone down and the wind dropped, though it was still coming north. The sky was largely covered with a strange, thin, corrugated-looking layer of cloud, through which a weak sun would sometimes shine. The prudent sailor, bearing in mind that it is 35 miles to Badentarbert Bay, off Achiltibuie, or eight hours sailing with a fair wind, would have weighed anchor immediately and set sail. The curious traveller, however, would not have passed by such an unusual place as the Shiant Isles without investigating them, particularly as it looked like a very nice day for a walk on shore. Being a traveller first and a sailor second, or possibly being more curious than prudent, I settled to a huge breakfast and then hopped into the dinghy.

First of all, I looked for the lead line which, in the daylight, took just a minute to find, though it was alarming to see just how close inshore I had been when I dropped it. Contrary to the feeling the night before, the Shiants (the name in Gaelic means 'enchanted') struck me immediately as having a very friendly atmosphere. They have a long history of habitation. In the days before roads, when everything and everybody in the Hebrides travelled by sea, they would

have been a less remote spot than, say, Morvern, Dundonnell or almost anywhere
north of Loch Broom. On Eilean an Tighe, there are the buried remains of a
Chapel of the Virgin Mary. The islands are very fertile and in the eighteenth
century they were inhabited by about six families. More recent records tell of
boats laden with hay – 'floating haystacks' – being rowed over to the island of
Scalpay at the mouth of Loch Seaforth. All over the three main islands today you
can see the lazy-beds.

The Shiants were finally abandoned to the sheep, the birds, the black rats and
the seals in 1911. The only evidence of former habitation is a small bothy on
Eilean an Tighe. As an insular pendicle of Lewis, the islands were acquired by
Lord Leverhulme in 1918. At one time he wanted to farm silver foxes there; at
another to breed goats. Neither happened and when he died in 1925 the islands
were sold to Compton Mackenzie. In 1937, they were bought by Nigel Nicolson,
the author of Lord of the Isles. Nicolson was then an unhappy and socially diffident
undergraduate at Oxford, but he had just inherited a sum equivalent to about
eight times the price then being asked for the islands. 'I would be different from
other undergraduates,' says Nicolson in his autobiography. 'I would be the man
who owned uninhabited islands and marooned himself there. Looking back, I
recognise an element of arrogance in my island mania.'[11] Nicolson paid £1400
for the whole 600 acres – Compton Mackenzie had paid £500 – and he values
them today at about £100,000. After his second visit there, in 1937, when he
spent a month in a tent studying Greek philosophers for his Oxford exams,
Nicolson wrote to his brother about the islands in terms which echoed my own,
much briefer, experience, 'How lovely were the lovely moments; how bloody the
bloody.'

I walked up to the top of the table-like hill which dominates Eilean an Tighe
and took some photographs of the distant mass of the Trotternish peninsula 15
miles away to the south on Skye. For five minutes or so, I worked hard on the
plot of a spontaneously projected post-Kailyard romance, The Bogs of Trotternish.
I was snapped out of my reverie by looking east and seeing that, even from 300
feet above sea-level, my destination that day was invisible over the horizon. I
decided to curtail my visit. I wished I had had time to explore the other three
islands, but all I could manage was a keek in the windows of the two-room bothy
to which the current owner, Adam Nicolson, takes his family for a couple of
weeks every three years or so. Apart from bunk-beds and chairs all was empty
except for the sitting-room window-sill, on which were arranged three objects
which struck me as neatly conveying the plot of a tiny domestic drama. From
left to right, they were: a can-opener, a tin of Andrews Liver Salts and a partly
used roll of lavatory paper. 'How lovely were the lovely moments; how bloody
the bloody.'

---

11 Long Life Nigel Nicolson, Widenfeld & Nicolson, London, 1997, pp. 235–6.

Back aboard ship, I hoisted the sails and raised the anchors. To my shock and surprise, I realised that the auxiliary one, a folding grapnel, had not opened. In the dark, I had failed to remove the ring which holds the flukes to the stock when it is packed away, I was annoyed at my own sloppy seamanship, but doubly pleased that the main anchor, a CQR, had held on its own. Moreover, it had done so with only a short length of chain on the bottom: the last ten feet came up gleaming as if it had been shot-blasted, so heavy had been the friction on the shingle the night before.

The wind was very light now. We drifted out from under the huge cliffs, which glowed a shamrock green from all the moss in the crevices. The large genoa was too heavy to fill properly. While ghosting along, I cleaned the engine's spark plug, the only remedy I could think of for the previous night's problem. I tested the motor and it started. My thought was that I would just get across the water today then, when in easy contact by road with Ullapool, look for an outboard mechanic at my leisure.

After an hour or so, the wind freshened a little and we started making reasonable progress. I ate some lunch and settled down on the port side of the cockpit, with my face in the sunshine and a copy of Alasdair Alpin MacGregor's *The Western Isles* on my lap. This is one of the forgotten classics of Scottish travel writing, forgotten I presume because it is totally different from the normal formula, a formula which was satirised so effectively by Compton Mackenzie, and which was so well exemplified by none other than MacGregor himself in all his books about Scotland written before *The Western Isles.* Mackenzie, an English convert to Roman Catholicism and Scottish nationalism, was an acute observer of the west Highland scene in the 1930s and 1940s and the author of many books, the most famous of which is *Whisky Galore.* After selling the Shiants, he moved to Barra where met John Lorne Campbell and contributed the chapter on Catholicism to Campbell's *Book of Barra* from which I quoted in connection with Rum. During the war, Mackenzie repented of his nationalism and started writing the series of gently mocking novels about the Highlands which made his name and gained him a British knighthood.

Alasdair Alpin MacGregor makes an appearance in several of these books. He is thinly disguised as Hamish Hugh Mackay, the author of such rose-tinted 'classics' as *Happy Days among the Heather* and *Faerie Lands Forlorn,* which contain passages of absurdly purple prose about the Hebridean people and their past. It was years before MacGregor realised the joke was on him, but when he did he took revenge, not on Mackenzie, but on the people he had previously treated as objects of sentimental adoration. He did so in *The Western Isles,* published in 1949 as part of an otherwise unremarkable series on the counties of Britain. MacGregor expresses perfectly the attitude of sniggering superiority which 'respectable' Scottish society adopted in those days towards 'teuchter' life (some would say it still does).

MacGregor starts with the music of the Gaels. Singers 'bellow like the biblical bull of Bashan . . . They bawl and bellow with every atom of their being, the better to eject, as if under high pressure, the noisy matter pent up within them. This primitive screeching and caterwauling may be all right round the peat fire of a winter's evening; but one must surely take exception to its being transferred, remuneratively, to the cities, there to be accorded professional status.' Worse than the music is the habit of drinking on these occasions, often before the final curtain because 'the temporary sobriety enforced by his attendance at a concert, while the pubs are open, is often more than the Gael can bear.'

MacGregor has more serious criticisms of the inhabitants of the outer isles. There is an incredible amount of promiscuity, so that in Benbecula, for example, it is often difficult to know who was born in wedlock and who was not. 'A Protestant clergyman in the Outer Hebrides, with whom I discussed this problem recently,' MacGregor writes, 'assured me that it is wellnigh impossible to enter a house in the Roman Catholic islands where there is not at least one bastard.'

The local people are a 'peasant population without either hobbies or interests'. They congregate 'in furtive groups chatting, chaffing, smoking, spitting, swearing, blaspheming, and not infrequently giving off alcoholic fumes.' Many other vices are described, with sanctimonious relish, from poaching and cruelty to laziness and vandalism. All are attributable to drink, a vice to which MacGregor devotes more than 30 pages, starting with a description of the measures taken by the Scottish Privy Council to counter the evil under King James VI. He lists with censorious amazement the purchases for the wake of the Laird of Ardnamurchan in 1651 and notes that when Flora MacDonald, the saviour of Bonnie Prince Charlie, was buried on Skye in 1790 the funeral procession, on its 16-mile journey to the graveyard, consumed no less than 300 gallons of whisky.

The attack culminates in a long description of the events surrounding the wreck of the SS *Politician* in the Sound of Eriskay in 1941, the story on which Compton Mackenzie based his *Whisky Galore*. When the knowledge that there were 243,000 bottles of over-proof whisky aboard a stranded vessel got around the islands, suddenly the whole male population desired personal 'verification' of this astounding fact. That took the form of nocturnal visits to the sands below 'the *Polly*' as she was by then affectionately known, armed with long ladders and ropes. 'The unlawful removal of the intoxicating cargo went unceasingly,' MacGregor writes. 'In the dead of night, as many as 50 men, black beyond recognition with oil, might be seen in the hold with their bright Tilly lamps, standing up to their thighs in oil and sea water, probing, tugging, hauling and slinging cases of whisky to the upper decks.' The result was that the islanders 'enjoyed the most convivial spell on record'. This was not only because of the enjoyment of consumption of the loot. 'You couldn't visit the *Polly* without meeting someone you knew,' a participant subsequently told MacGregor. 'You would meet people there from the other islands that you hadn't seen for years.'

But even MacGregor cannot fail to find a few good qualities of the people of the western isles: they are surprisingly healthy; they are hospitable to strangers; they are capable of great kindness; and they are physically very brave and warlike. At the end of his coruscating chapter MacGregor softens a little. He had served with them in the Seaforth Highlanders in the First World War on the Western

Front, and he says gallantly, 'Shall I ever forget the heroism of my platoon, composed almost exclusively of men from Lewis? Never was there such dash, such nonchalance, in the midst of death. Before the war ended, while I myself lay in hospital, they were killed to a man.'

By the time I had finished reading, the Shiants had dropped below the horizon, and I had left the Western Isles behind. Low on the horizon, fine on the starboard bow, was Rubha Reidh, the point where the mainland coast, coming north from Loch Gairloch, turns east for Loch Ewe and Loch Broom. A brief squall brought a fresher breeze, which continued to pick up, until we were scudding along as fast as *Sylvia B* would travel. A considerable swell was rolling in from the north, suggesting more wind to come. I felt confident that we could get as far as the Summer Isles before nightfall.

10

THE SUMMER ISLES

FOR SEVERAL HOURS *Sylvia B* barrelled along on a beam reach in a cold but dry wind, her skipper sitting down below, looking out every few minutes but otherwise inactive. Greenstone point, between Loch Ewe and Loch Gruinard, came up to starboard, possibly three miles off, then dropped astern as Monk's Island (Eilean á Chlerich), the first of the Summer Isles, grew slowly larger. This was one of Fraser Darling's islands, but I had no time to stop now. As Tannera Mor, another of Darling's islands, loomed up on the port bow, the wind began to moderate. The swell started to go down as we entered the mouth of Loch Broom. We had to get round behind Tannera Mor and into the broad anchorage off Achiltibuie. It quickly became a race against the gathering darkness, a race which the darkness won. We were almost into September now and the sun set well before nine o'clock. But soon after that the moon rose and we sailed on smooth water almost up to the beach below the Summer Isles Hotel, brightly-lit in the autumn night, then tacked off-shore and dropped anchor in 20 feet of water. After snugging the boat down, it was a glass of cider, dinner, book and bed.

Unlike most of the other ports of call on this voyage, I had never visited this part of the coast before. I had a mental picture of the place simply from knowing the name the Summer Isles and remembering that Lucy Irvine wrote *Castaway* here. But this was contradicted first thing next morning when I looked out of the main hatch to see a landscape of extreme bleakness. Not a coconut palm in sight, nor a single limpid, opalescent lagoon either, just a grey sky and sea and an almost grey-brown landscape. If I had expected to see naked girls, with knives clasped between their teeth, wading into a sparkling sea in search of breakfast, I would have been disappointed. Hardly a tree could be seen in any direction and hardly a green field either. For the first and last time on this voyage, I confess I went ashore reluctantly. The thought that this was the mainland did not help either: islands are so much themselves, insular, individual and interesting, whereas places on the mainland are, so to speak, all on the same island. But there was a contrary consideration: I had tried the engine that morning and it had once again totally refused to fire up. I was now only 30 miles by road from Ullapool, or about ten by sea. Here, if anywhere on this trip, I could hope to find someone who might repair the engine.

Achiltibuie is the main village on the Benmore Coigach estate, now run by the Scottish Wildlife Trust. The whole area is heavily crofted because, in the middle of the last century, it was one of the few parts of Scotland where a laird attempting a clearance was defeated by the tenants. Tiree was a comparable case, except that, because that revolt took place in 1885, resistance was strengthened by the knowledge that Whitehall was already considering legislation which would soon give the crofters the security they sought. At the time the people of Coigach won their victory, in 1853, the Crofters Act was still quarter of a century away. Their resistance was much bolder. Alexander Mackenzie has described how they cleverly managed to avoid potentially ruinous conflict:

> [In Coigach] the people made a stout resistance, the women disarming about twenty policemen and sheriff officers, burning the summonses in a heap, throwing their batons into the sea, and ducking the representatives of the law in a neighbouring pool. The men formed a second line of defence, in case the women should receive any ill-treatment. They, however, never put a finger on the officers of the law, all of whom returned home without serving a single summons or evicting a single crofter.[1]

Thereupon, the lady laird, the Countess of Cromartie, decided to abandon the attempt. The consequence has been that the descendants of those crofters still occupy the land of Coigach.

In 1959, after 350 years of overlordship, the Cromartie Estate sold Coigach. The next owner sold it to a prominent English conservationist, Christopher Cadbury, who, in 1975, gifted it to the Royal Society for Nature Conservation (RSNC).

Cadbury was a socialist and pacifist who was independently wealthy from the family chocolate firm. He had worked in industry until, at the age 50, he cashed his chips and turned to 'good works' – like many a mid-century conservationist, he was a Quaker. He was involved with both the World Wildlife Fund and the RSPB but he had his desk and secretary at the RSNC, of which he was president for 26 years. His main interests were birds and antique dolls. His collection of the latter, called the Playthings Past Museum, is today housed by the English National Trust at Sudbury Hall in Derbyshire. In 1990 Cadbury endowed the Christopher Cadbury Medal which the RSNC was to award annually 'for services to the advancement of Nature Conservation in the British Islands'. Four years later his organisation awarded the medal to himself. The *Guardian* commented sarcastically, 'Lest this sound incestuous, it should be made clear that [Cadbury] is a lovely, selfless man who has been one of the key figures in the post-war conservation movement.'[2]

According to his obituary in *The Times,* Cadbury's 'special skill' was 'in saving areas of special conservation interest.'[3] Benmore Coigach was, apparently, one of those areas. The RSNC is the parent body of what in England are called the County wildlife trusts. Their counterpart in Scotland is the Scottish Wildlife Trust, which covers the whole country. In 1988 the SWT was given a 21-year

---

1   *History of the Highland Clearances* Alexander Mackenzie, 1883, reprinted by The Mercat Press, Edinburgh 1991, p. 308.
2   21 September 1994.
3   30 June 1995.

lease on Benmore Coigach by the RSNC. In 1991, the SWT persuaded the
Highland Regional Council, the Highlands and Islands Enterprise and the Nature
Conservancy Council (shortly to become SNH) to pay for a study into what
might be done with the 14,600 acres of Coigach. The report was written by
Andrew Currie, the John Muir Trust representative I had talked to on Skye, and
Angus Macleod, a native of this area who had done a college dissertation on how
the locals in Achiltibuie preserved their identity against the flood of incomers –
of the 180 homes in the area, 40 per cent are holiday accommodation of one sort
or another. ('My paper showed,' he told me, 'how the locals have their boundaries
and people cannot cross them.')

Angus is a young, capable-looking man with a growing family, who drives the
school bus because, as he said, 'jobs around here are few and far between.' But he
comes of a crofting family and would like to find some land for a croft of his own
where he can run the ten sheep he already owns and 'have a few potatoes and
turnips'. At the moment that is almost impossible. In that fact, lies the root of
the problem of Coigach: land hunger.

The crofters, having won control of their land after so many struggles, were
determined that no landlord would dispossess them of even the smallest right or
liberty. It mattered nothing to them that the estate had been bought by the
apparently unthreatening figure of a pacifist orniphile who spent his spare time
collecting dolls. The crofters were not going to surrender the right to graze their
sheep on the common grazings, which form 97 per cent of the estate's total area,
without either good reason or acceptable compensation. The SWT wanted to
plant trees to restore what it called 'the biological productivity' of the ground.
But the trees needed to be fenced from sheep (and from deer), and land from
which the sheep are excluded no longer has any economic value to crofters.
Deadlock. 'The people are not averse to change,' Angus told me. 'What they are
against is outside agencies imposing change.' Without permission from the
grazings committee of the various townships which fall within the estate, no
action could be taken by the SWT. With some dismay, the Trust's management
in Edinburgh realised that the owner's rights are limited to the collection of rents
from crofters, the sale of stalking tenancies and the sale of fishing rights. Everything
else has to be done by agreement with the crofting tenant.

I asked Angus if the benevolent image of the SWT made co-operation any
easier.

'I think the crofters saw the SWT as just another landlord,' Angus replied.
'It's the same with anyone new who comes in and says he's going to make a lot of
changes: everybody gets a bit worried. None of the crofters are against
conservation. I think they'd all like to see improvements being done, but who is
going to pay? Doing the Report I was told, not in so many words, that if the
people on the estate did accept the proposal to fence some ground for tree-
planting it would mean a lot of money straight away, for fencing or whatever,
and from pony-trekking and other suchlike things later on. The Highland Region,
the SWT and so on would put in money. But I kept asking, "How *much* money?"

I mean, everybody's got to be fed. But all they said was, "Wait and see." So I said, "Why should we accept it, without knowing what we're getting?" '

Once the Currie–Macleod Report was completed, the SWT called a meeting in the village hall to discuss it. They bussed in all the top brass of the bodies who had funded the study and some others besides. The top table had 18 people sitting at it. John Smith, the SWT's current representative in the area was there. I saw him the next day and asked him how many local people came. Eight, was the astounding answer. 'And four of those were father-and-son combinations,' he said. I asked him how many people would have been eligible to come. 'Between 50 and 100,' John replied.

'Why so few, then?'

'Not interested.'

'Not interested in conservation?'

'Not really, no. Just not interested in the SWT and its plans.'

John is a joiner from Aberdeenshire who sports a thick head of the straw-like hair that children's books always give Vikings. Having grown up on a well-managed farm, it grieves him to see the land of Coigach in such bad heart. But, he said, the younger generation of crofters are different and much more flexible in their outlook than the older. The wounds of the past are healing. The memories of the powerful, aggressive lairds, who demanded deference and pursued vendettas if they did not get it, are slowly fading – at least they are in those places where such men are not still in charge.

Somehow the distant prospect of change was not enough to make the brown desert of Coigach any more attractive-looking. I went into the Summer Isles Hotel and spent an enjoyable afternoon in the public bar discussing everything under the sun but conservation while waiting for a bag of laundry to go through the washing machine (not the dryer). The pleasant mood was shattered when I was handed the bill: £5.50.

Next morning I went round to the office to see the owners of the hotel, Mark and Geraldine Irvine. Mark is the brother of Lucy 'Castaway' Irvine and has the fit but unweathered look of a man who takes a lot of urban-style exercise, by which I mean he runs and 'works out' rather than gets sweaty and dirty up the hill, in a shed or out on a boat. Mark's father moved up here from London in 1969. In those days Coigach was still a sporting estate, and a certain amount of stalking plus a great deal of fishing provided the main attractions for visitors. Since the decline in the salmon and sea-trout fisheries, the hotel has converted to a 'good food' operation, which the brochure describes as 'an oasis of civilisation'.

I started by asking Mark how he viewed the 'desert' round his oasis. 'It's desperately overgrazed,' he said. 'No tree can get an inch above the ground before it is eaten. I think a lot of people are slightly shocked by that, and by the fact that the sheep wander round the village and everybody has to fence their own property to keep them out rather than the farmer fencing his sheep in. I think if it was better run, more people would be interested.'

'How do you think it might be better managed?' I asked.

'I think for a start the sheep should have areas which are fenced. Other areas should be kept sheep-free, for heather and trees and what-not. I think it would be really quite straightforward to do that. It saddens me that it does not happen, because of the crofters' negative attitudes.'

'What do you think is behind those attitudes?'

'I think generations of "It's our right to do with it what we want." I understand their point in a way; it's all they've got. They have a terror that any form of management, however gentle, is going to take their sheep away from them, and their subsidies. But it is in a terrible state. One or two of them burn the heather, totally indiscriminately, and it gets out of control and they have to call the fire-brigade out. We have farmers from the south of England who come up here, and they can't believe what they see. They feel that sheep should be kept in fields or in areas at least, and not just be allowed to vaguely roam.'

Mark went on to tell me that Neil Willcox, the SWT Reserves Manager, uses him as an 'ear on the ground', so I asked about the famous 1992 meeting to discuss the tree-planting plan.

'The SWT wanted to come in and make friends and they thought by doing that they would get the crofters on their side. Neil Willcox was aware of the situation here, and he wanted to "educate" the crofters – that was the word he used. He had that thing down at the hall and they thought he was a complete idiot.'

'How does the rest of the village see things?' I asked.

'There's quite a build-up of local people now who are really quite annoyed by the attitude of the crofters,' he continued.

'When you say local people as opposed to crofters, do you mean incomers?'

'Yes,' Mark said.

'Is there any counter-criticism?' I asked. 'Do the crofters say the incomers should dig their gardens differently or not build ugly houses?'

'Not really,' he said. 'The feeling, which is really quite strong now, is that somebody should properly take a grip.'

'But nothing's going to happen, is it?'

'That's right, unless the SWT get a little bit tougher. You have to go in like a ton of bricks around here to get anyone to understand anything.'

At this point the phone rang. While Mark accepted a booking, Geraldine spoke. 'I remember the meeting with the crofters,' she said. 'The SWT tried to show them the fact that the state of the land was such that it was the worst piece of land in Scotland, sheep grazing everywhere, no natural regeneration, and the crofters said, "We think it's absolutely great." They just were not prepared to be educated. There's not going to be any coming together. It's just going to have to be, right this is the estate, we're going to close off this bit for two years, then this bit.'

'So you think their rights should just be expropriated?'

'I don't know what their rights are,' Geraldine replied.

'Do you see the crofters' attitude as different from any other group of people who want to defend the rights they have won in the past?' I asked.

Booking taken, Mark replied to that question. 'I know all these guys well,' he said. 'They come in the pub. They're good blokes, they really are. But there seems to be something, which has been handed down through the generations, that as soon as you talk about sheep and rights, they get very blinkered. I was brought up in London, and went to school in Sussex. I just come up here and read the situation for what it is, which is that land is being abused.'

' It's no more abused than the land in Sussex,' I ventured. 'Think of all that ghastly green desert, stuffed with chemicals.'

'I know, I realise that,' Mark said. 'But for what this area is, it could be substantially regenerated, and I'm quite convinced with the crofters having their sheep on there as well. There's a cultural gap, but there is also a certain amount of pride at stake.

'But what right do you think outsiders have to say, with the expectation of remedial action, that the crofters' land is in a bad way? The crofters might say that England is in a bad way, but you don't really expect the English to jump to the crofters' tune, do you?'

'Well, quite,' Mark said. 'I agree. That is a complete argument.'

'At least,' I continued, 'not without compensation. How important do the crofters' critics regard the tree-planting scheme? If asked to pay into a fund to buy the crofters out of their rights to part of the hill, do you think they would contribute?'

'I doubt if many would be prepared to pay compensation because what are they actually going to gain financially from it?'

'So they just want other people to behave in a way that would suit themselves, only without having to buy their co-operation. Is that not fair?'

'Yes,' Mark said, 'I guess you are probably right. Though I think it is a slightly more genuine thing than that. It is such a fantastic area, one of the last unbelievably beautiful parts of Britain. Wouldn't it just be nice if it was managed a little more? That's not just the view of people living here, it's the view of people who visit and who understand about nature.'

Mark's reference to the SWT wanting to make friends in the area was interesting since one of the points John Smith had impressed upon me was that the Trust's effort to do so in the mid-1980s had been a disaster, one which still had repercussions in the wariness of the crofters towards the Trust. That disaster, it seemed, had come up from Romney Marsh in female form and had moved into a caravan on the estate in 1986 to work, initially, as a summer warden. Over the next three years 'she stirred up a lot of ill-feeling,' John told me.

'How did she do that?' I asked.

'Through her devotion to the job,' John said. 'As a warden of a wildlife reserve you could not fault her. But unfortunately, there's people on this Reserve. She thought those secondary to the Wildlife Trust's interests and really walked over a lot of folk. For example, she would criticise people, to their faces, for taking "rare seaweed" from the beach to fertilise their gardens. She went about her job totally the wrong way. She'd been with the RSPB and had worked for the NCC on Rum.'

An hour after leaving Mark Irvine's office, I knocked on the door of the ex-warden, Anne Barnes. She now lives with a local fisherman in the council housing scheme at the southern end of Achiltibuie, where it merges with the township of Polglass. Anne was very happy to talk and offered me a cup of coffee in her comfortably lived-in sitting room. She is a large, strong-looking woman with an 'early Bowie' hairstyle and a manner reminiscent of those forceful Victorian women who imposed English morality on so much of the British Empire. Talking to her it was obvious that she is a kind, well-meaning person, but equally obvious that she is one of the multitude of modern British conservationists to whom nature is something external to, and separate from, their lives and imaginations. They are *on* the land rather than *of* the land. They understand more about bureaucracy and plans than beasts and people. When I asked her how she would ideally like to see the Coigach estate, Anne's answer was completely impersonal. 'It could be a perfect example of a coastal Highland habitat,' she said.

Anne is well aware of the difficulties of her time as warden. I asked why she thought it had been so problematical.

'I'd dealt with farmers before, in Anglesey,' she said, 'but I wasn't aware of quite how sensitive crofting issues were, and I didn't realise how strong the anti-English thing was. I wasn't aware how nutty the situation up here can get. I was here to show the visitors round and to show the crofters that the SWT were interested.'

'You say you did not expect the situation that you found,' I said. 'Can you describe the situation that you did find?'

'Schizophrenic alcoholics, basically,' Anne said. 'It was a discussion about making part of the ground into an SSSI that made the SWT realise they might not be able to deal with the people here. Their reaction was just totally unbalanced.'

'But SSSIs are controversial everywhere; why should this be different?'

'It was just the sort of way they . . . ' Anne tailed off, searching for words. 'They just didn't understand, they had absolutely no . . . it was just totally unreasonable. That was the first time that the chap over me at SWT, Kenny Taylor, had really sat down and talked to a crofter, and I think at that point he realised how hard it was going to be.'

'He's not a crofter himself, then?

'No, he came in as an expert.'

We moved on to discuss her own background in conservation and Anne told me about her work for the RSPB and the NCC. She made the fascinating point that she found both organisations very sexist. This chimed with my own observation that birdwatching attracts an odd sort of individual. I was first alerted to the emotional dimension of orniphilia by a press profile of a man called Lee Evans. Evans is a so-called 'twitcher', and 'twitching' is the *ne plus ultra* of birdwatching. Bird sightings are collected like stamps or railway engine numbers. The bird itself has lost all meaning. Competitions are held to see who can spot the largest number of species in a given time. Since the locations of the birds are public knowledge, through phone services like Birdline, which Evans himself started, this is essentially a driving competition – a sort of permanent, production-car rally on public roads. From his home in Buckinghamshire, Evans covers 90,000 miles a year, many of them at extremely high speed, in search of 'ticks': so called because once a species has been ticked off a list it is of no further interest. Evans lost his wife to his obsession. The passage which caught my attention was this one:

> Carmel, 38, his present partner, has a theory about his obsession. 'She thinks it was because there was no love in my family,' Evans says. 'That's why I escape to birds and am not interested in people. But I'm normal compared to other twitchers. Most are weird misfits. They run away at the sight of a woman.'[4]

The entries in *Who's Who in Ornithology*[5] are interesting in this regard. At a rough count there are 30 men to every woman, whereas in the real *Who's Who*, hardly a feministic catalogue, the ratio is about ten to one.[6] In the ornithology directory the most commonly listed 'other interest or recreation' is drinking, and in particular drinking 'real ale'.

Anne has support from the Gay Birders Club. It is a tiny organisation, based in Berwickshire, which publishes a magazine called *Out Birding*. This features a 'Page Three Pin-Up' (Arctic Redpoll: 'a Siberian blond beauty') and carries articles on such subjects as 'Lesbian Gulls in California'. A recent editorial entitled 'Out Birding with a Proud Club' discussed the sexism and homophobia which is so common in conventional birdwatching circles.

> Let's face it: in some corners of the birding world, the appearance of a Gay Birders Club must have raised some eyebrows so far that they almost left the scalp. The birding world is not acknowledged for being the most liberal of spheres and lengthy debates on issues such as women birdwatchers (or the lack of them) have appeared on the pages of highbrow journals such as *British Birds*.[7]

Paradoxically, Anne said, the chauvinists tended to be rather wimpish men. 'When I came here conservation was a very dirty word,' she explained. 'The crofters were just pushed around. It was meddling southerners. I can now see it from the local perspective. You see conservationists on television, but they're always fairly weedy-looking individuals, officey types. That's what they look like to somebody in Achiltibuie, and after ten years here I see it with the same eyes now. Those people just don't understand what it means to chuck a sheep around, or to dip 400 sheep at one go. They've got education but no physical or practical experience. In that respect it's worse now than it used to be. In my time it was a

---

4 *Independent* 27 January 1993.

5 Ed. John Pemberton, Buckingham Press, 1997.

6 Birdwatching is also an overwhelmingly 'white' activity. An article in the RSPB's *Birds* magazine (Autumn 1993) noted how few members of any ethnic minority 'find their way into birdwatching, botany or bug hunting . . . Environmental organisations in the UK are predominantly white and middle class.' One Reserve warden was quoted as saying 'I have only ever seen one black birdwatcher here.'

7 *Out Birding* November 1996, p. 9.

bit hands-on, but now they're just out of ecology courses and into on-the-ground jobs without ever having put a fence-post in. I think that's the main thing. The crofters here feel that the people who are coming to talk to them don't have any understanding.'

Anne told me she felt she was much more use to conservation generally, now that she no longer worked for SWT. People feel free to come and ask her about this bird or that plan without feeling that they are truckling to the enemy. As on Rum, the practical success is in direct proportion to the official failure.

As I was leaving, Anne said something which has turned out to be very prescient. 'In the last few years, I have started to think it might have been about the right time to come to the crofters and go for a community woodland. You see, what they would object to is the SWT saying, "We want woodland." But if it was the crofters' woodland, and would help tourism in the area, then that might work.'

Two years later, just as this book was being completed, it was announced that 3500 acres of Benmore Coigach are to be fenced and planted for trees. Though there was opposition from recreational walkers, access groups and retired SNH officials, 'the crofters believe the plan will rejuvenate the local economy and environment.'[8] Shortly after that it was announced that the project had won the UK Forestry Accord Award for the most imaginative woodland scheme in Britain in 1998.

I weighed anchor and spent a day sailing round some of the islands, visiting Isle Ristol, a small (just under a square mile) and rather pointless-looking 'reserve' owned by the SWT. I also set foot on Tannera Mor, the island where Fraser Darling had his croft during the Second World War. I met the family of Wiltshire farmers who had recently bought it. Over a cup of tea, they told me of their plans for an ornamental garden. They said they thought that would attract different birds, though they were concerned that I should understand that they were not the type of suburban gardener who is sentimentally attracted to blue tits, robins and the like. They said they saw birds as 'wild and free'. They were nonplussed when I pointed out that that is exactly how the suburbanites who constitute the RSPB's principle target market see birds – which is why the Society offers feeding tables and nut dispensers as its main recruitment incentives.[9]

In the early afternoon I anchored off Polbain, west along the coast from Achiltibuie a mile or two, and walked up the hill to visit a person who views the

---

8 *Scotland on Sunday* 9 September 1998.

9 Author interview with Paul Easton, RSPB Brands Manager, Sandy, Bedfordshire, 20 February 1996. Easton, a cheerful New Zealander with no interest in birds, has been hired from Saatchi and Saatchi to raise money from 'new products'. These will represent a departure from the 'fluffy bird' image which was previously sold to 'middle-class people by middle-of-the-road methods', as he put it. Easton told me his hope for success was based on the fact that 50 per cent of the adult population of Britain feed birds in their gardens, giving the Society a theoretical maximum membership of 12 million. The Department chasing this goldmine employs a total of 40 people.

Highlands from a different perspective. Reiner Luyken is a German who moved to the area in the 1970s with the idea of plying his trade as a harpsichord maker and organ builder. Neither instrument is in tremendous demand in Wester Ross, so he soon found himself working as a salmon netsman. Later he discovered he had a talent for journalism. In the meantime he had married a local girl and settled down in Polbain with pigs, geese and a vegetable garden. He now has a large family and an even larger collection of horses. He works as a full-time feature writer for the liberal Hamburg heavyweight, *Die Zeit*.

I was greeted at the door of a tastefully modernised house by a tallish, dark-haired man with a firm handshake and steady eye. Reiner (pronounced *Rye*ner) took me into his kitchen and gave me a delicious cup of Swiss coffee. He could spare an hour, he said, but not more since he was busy finalising a big story on Greenpeace that he had to dispatch to Frankfurt the next day. He gave me his views on crofting ('a dead world and a pointless activity') and the crofters ('strong characters with original thoughts: they are remote from mainstream life and they think for themselves; not like the Germans who drive up and down the motorways with anti-pollution stickers on the backs of their cars, just above the exhaust pipe'). Reiner compared the locals with another group of people, whom he had met while researching the Greenpeace story, the fishermen of the Lofoten Islands in north Norway: 'They use their heads and think about things,' he said. 'They do not simply watch television.'

Reiner expanded on this in the piece as finally published:

> Fishermen are of necessity inventive people. There has never been any security for them and dramatic changes in fortune are a natural characteristic of the sea. This is what fishermen get their living from. If their circumstances change in one way, they have got to help themselves in another way, and they always take on board any idea. And they also feel that when something is apparently useless, it can also have another use. On the harbour wall, they can sort out torn nets, rusted anchors, stolen ropes, plastic barrels and half ruined winches, as well as braggart Harbour Masters who spend their lives administering threats and punishments in a futile attempt to maintain order.[10]

The story Reiner was working on concerned the controversy over the disposal of the Brent Spar oil storage platform. As is now well known, Greenpeace got its statistics wrong, but Reiner's piece argued that 'the mistake was not a mistake'. Very briefly: in order to find out what was in the tanks, the leader of the activists occupying the platform ('*der Führer des Besatzungstrupps*'), was asked to find out about the oil in the platform. He gave the job to an accountant who happened to be on the rig, who lowered a peanut-butter jar, weighted with bolts, down the ventilation pipes which led up from the storage tanks. The results were sent to the Greenpeace laboratory at Exeter University which then announced that the Brent Spar had 5500 tons of oil on board. But this was a gross misuse of the evidence. Reiner reported the accountant as saying, 'We only wanted to see what was there, not how much.' Since the peanut-butter jar never plumbed the tanks

---

10 *Die Zeit* 6 September 1996. Translated by Janice Whitelaw.

(the pipes did not run straight into them), this result was based on paper computations of tank capacity, not on an actual investigation of the contents. But Shell was in the dock and defensive. Ironically it took the German Campaign Director for Greenpeace, Herr Jürgens, to ask the obvious question: why would Shell want to sink a platform containing $1 million-worth of saleable oil?

It was then that the story came out. In fact there was barely a tenth of that amount of oil in the tanks. But was the mistake pure accident? Greenpeace will not release the calculations by which they arrived at their erroneous conclusions. Paul Johnstone, the chief of the Exeter laboratory, said they could not be made public as they are in an 'internal document' – the phrase used so often by the RSPB. But the result of the Brent Spar campaign, together with the Murorawa nuclear-testing protest in the same year, was that Greenpeace took an additional $6 million in donations in 1995. The Exeter laboratory, which had been scheduled to close due to lack of money, stayed open.

My interest in all this was in the misuse of science. One Greenpeace officer was quoted as saying that science was, for him, an instrument with which to conduct a campaign. Reiner commented that, 'People in Greenpeace have absolutely no idea of the old-fashioned concept that science means knowledge.'

Reiner also told me that Greenpeace denies access to information to journalists whose point of view they do not approve of. But their dissemination of misleading information has had important consequences for the press itself, as Reiner noted in his article. 'Greenpeace has a problem, but so do the journalists who reported their original, false claims as fact. In Britain the BBC and Channel 4 brought in new guidelines for more detached reporting, as did *Die Zeit.*'

Glad to be on the move again, I ghosted in very light airs south-east up Loch Broom. The engine was completely dead now. The weather forecast was that the large high pressure system, already static over England and southern Scotland, would expand to cover the whole of the British Isles. Even lighter winds were in prospect. The breeze, such as it was, lasted until I was just off Isle Martin, where it died completely. This is the point at which Loch Broom narrows, and also where the main road from Loch Inver drops down to the shore. I could leave the boat safely in the anchorage between Isle Martin and the mainland and hitch the five miles into Ullapool if I needed to collect any engine parts.

But it was a struggle just getting that far. When winds die, they do so in a variety of subtly different ways. There is one sort of dying which means not only that the wind vanishes completely but also that there is no prospect of it coming back for a long while. It was this sort of death which I experienced just off Creag nam Fiadh, a cliff on the mainland about a mile and a half from the anchorage. There was nothing for it but to inflate the dinghy, lead a warp over the bowhead and row. This I did for nearly an hour until the midges got the better of me. By then I was halfway across and close under the north east point of Isle Martin, where I anchored.

Early next morning, there was just a breath and I was able to sail over to the pier by the campsite at Loch Kanaird before the calm descended again. After breakfast, I went in search of a phone. The first thing I encountered was an outboard servicing centre just above the pier. The speciality was Johnsons, and mine was a Yamaha, but I thought the mechanic might at least be able to diagnose the problem so that I could order a part by phone and effect the repair. The only solution he could suggest was that I order an entire electrical system, the coil, the 'power pack' (whatever that is) and the points. That would come to an estimated £200 and still there would be no guarantee that it would work. The further problem was that it might take up to a fortnight to get the parts.

The Yamaha agent in Inverness, Caley Marine, could not tell me if they had the parts I might need in stock because their computer was 'down', and Stoddards, the Yamaha agent in Oban, replied to my asking if they could post parts to Ullapool by saying, 'Where's Ullapool?' The only solution the Yamaha head office could offer was that I take the motor to Aberdeen to have it tested. The only other solution was to finish the cruise under sail alone. To do so would make some serious demands on my reserves of both seamanship and patience. But what else could I do? I decided to look on the bright side and trust to luck.

Next day the weather defied the forecast and was both wet and windy. I should have taken the opportunity and sailed. But by then I had already arranged for a guide to come out from Inverness to show me round Isle Martin, which was of interest because it is an RSPB-owned bird reserve on which, according to the last warden, the crofting/conservationist problem has been addressed. In the Currie–Macleod Report on Benmore Coigach, the authors had noted, 'Bernard Planterose [the ex-warden of the island] has pointed out that on Isle Martin plantings for the Royal Society for the Protection of Birds are continuing as an experiment in the integration of crofting and woodland management.' That was five years ago, so it would be interesting to see what had come of the experiment.

In telling the story of Isle Martin I am handicapped by the fact that Planterose would not talk to me, though he lived close by and easily could have done. Whether this was a further example of the Minns–Greenpeace style of left-handed news management, I cannot say. My guide round the island was John Martin, an ex-Green Party activist from Inverness who had been a close friend of one of the RSPB's tenants on the island and who had himself spent quite a lot of time trying to find a solution to the problems. John kindly drove the 60 miles over from Inverness on a foul day, bringing three of his children and a female friend, Elizabeth, who helped look after them while he and I walked and talked.

Isle Martin was bought in 1965 by Mrs Monica Goldsmith and gifted by her to the RSPB in 1981. The RSPB's plan, right from the start, was to plant trees in order to improve the habitat for birds. But it also planned to rent out the four houses which Mrs Goldsmith had recently renovated. 'The island is feasible as a Reserve,' the Society stated at the time, 'because its houses can be let to provide an income to counteract some of the costs.'[11] John's criticism of this idea was

---

11 *Birds* Spring 1981, p. 39.

that the island would be turned into a 'company town' because the tenants would not be given the security which real crofters enjoy. Relations with the tenants deteriorated and the RSPB got bored. Though it had originally claimed Isle Martin was an important sanctuary for herons, terns, red-breasted mergansers, eiders, oystercatchers and ringed plovers, it now announced the island was not a place of 'outstanding ornithological significance' and made moves to divest itself of its burden, but without actually selling anything. The solution was to hand over management of the island to a Trust administered by Planterose, the unpopular warden, who would turn it into a crofting museum – real crofting would have involved giving long-term tenants real rights.

The announcement of the handover rang warning bells with the existing tenants: they were clearly on the way out. But had not the RSPB told them some years previously that Mrs Goldsmith had imposed conditions on the gift, one of which was that the houses be kept inhabited? Had not the RSPB itself noted 15 years previously that 'to comply with Mrs Goldsmith's wishes we have agreed to negotiate a covenant with the National Trust for Scotland should we need to sell the island in future?[12] The tenants asked for sight of the Deed of Gift (something which the NTS routinely publishes as an Appendix to its Reserve Management Plans). This was refused on the ground that it was an 'internal document'. With Mrs Goldsmith dead, there was now no way to ascertain whether the Society's new plans for Isle Martin accorded with the donor's wishes. Consequently the evictions went ahead and the island is now deserted. The Scottish Crofters' Union commented acidly: 'Don't say we didn't warn you. The New Lairds are already amongst us and they don't act very differently from the old ones, do they?'[13]

Over a cup of coffee in the camp-site restaurant, John showed me a lot of the correspondence between the tenant and the RSPB officer in this area, a Dr Peter Mayhew. Mayhew's aggressive tone on paper made a revealing contrast with the cringing, hand-wringingly humble, 'more-in-sorrow-than-in-anger' manner which RSPB spokesmen are trained to adopt in public. I agreed with John when he said, 'There's a kind of smugness about it: "I am a scientist, you're a peasant." Mayhew had this attitude that through his job he had some kind of superior earthly status. "How dare you question our right to manage this island?" '

The most notable feature of the correspondence was the number of letters from the tenant which the RSPB had simply ignored. The claim that Isle Martin illustrated anything about the successful integration of crofting and forestry was as empty as the island itself.

After a good deal of coming and going – I had to make three trips in the dinghy to convey everybody out to *Sylvia B*, and then another three to land everyone on the island – we went ashore beneath a sign which said: 'RSPB No Landing'. In the adjacent shed we found two other signs, 'No Landing' and

---

12 *Birds* Spring 1981, p.39. Managed acreage totals are one of the key virility indicators in the conservation industry, which is why straightforward disposals are almost unheard of.
13 *Scottish Crofters' Union News*, June 1996, p. 6.

'RSPB Breeding Birds No Landing'. I asked John whether he thought that these signs implied that if the RSPB owned the whole of the Highlands they would close it off to the public entirely between March and August? 'No,' he replied. 'They just mean, "This is *ma* fitba' and you're no' havin' a shot wi' it." '

The island contains ten ruined houses as well as the four restored ones. These latter were quite obviously habitable: they even had telephones. Like Tannera Mor, Isle Martin has a large walled garden where thousands of tons of rich Irish soil were dumped after having been brought over as ballast in ships loading up in Loch Broom with herring: nineteenth century klondykers. In short, the island looked as if it had a great deal of potential for quiet habitation. Certainly the trees Planterose had planted were growing well: all the place needed was people.

As we all tramped through the wet bracken and half-grown 'native hardwoods', I asked Elizabeth if she had any experience of the owners of this small island. Not much, she said, except that for many years she had been a paid-up member.

'But no longer?' I asked.

'No, I resigned when I heard the RSPB were involved in killing the ruddy duck.'

The ruddy duck is a recently controversial species. It was introduced to England from North America in the 1940s by Sir Peter Scott, the founder of the Wildfowl and Wetlands Trust, who brought over three pairs as pets. Though the policy was to pinion all birds, some nests went undiscovered until the young, unpinioned birds had escaped from the Trust's reserve at Slimbridge in Gloucestershire. They bred well in Britain and the population expanded into Europe, eventually reaching southern Spain where, to the anguished cries of conservationists, they started interbreeding with the white-headed ducks there. The RSPB told its members that 'male ruddy ducks force copulation with female white headed ducks [with the result that the racially pure white-headed duck] may be wiped out by the amorous intentions of a foreign escapee.'[14]

The solution promoted by the RSPB was to shoot the ruddy ducks. This caused howls of outrage from bird-lovers. The Director of Animal Aid, Andrew Tyler, said, 'If ruddy and white-headed ducks wish to procreate, they should be free to do so without interference from human "experts".' Others called the RSPB racists and one expert said the ruddy duck cull was 'the Brent Spar of conservation'.

Decisions were taken in secret and journalists denied sight of relevant material, like research into whether the two types of duck are sufficiently different genetically to make them two separate species. The RSPB's excuse for secrecy is that they are working with English Nature; English Nature's excuse for secrecy is that they are providing confidential advice to Ministers. Finally, there was the small matter of money. It is estimated that the cull will cost £800,000 and, on the 'polluter pays' principle, many argue that the Wildfowl and Wetlands Trust should foot the bill. Naturally, the Trust would prefer the taxpayer to do so. In this they have the

---

14 *Birds* Spring 1993, p. 40.

RSPB's support. In the light of this mess, it was probably predictable that the RSPB would ignore Elizabeth's letters of protest.

'What would your reaction be,' I asked her, 'if you were to learn that the RSPB sits on the committee which is organising the shooting of the greylag geese on Tiree?'

'That is just the sort of thing,' she said, 'that really made me think about charities and about conservation. What are we conserving? They're not conserving indigenous species and they're not conserving the culture. They're not looking at it holistically. Especially since hearing about Isle Martin. People have been turfed off. It all seems so absurd. Then I started wondering exactly what all the charities did. I think they should be in the hands of local people.'

After another three dinghy trips out to *Sylvia B*, a rough sail across in a damp, gusty wind, and then a further three dinghy trips to get ashore, I was tired, cold and wet. John gave me a lift into Ullapool and I took a bath in a B&B which was owned by a charming old lady who said that though her family had been running the place as a guest house since the 1920s, she had never heard of anyone wanting just a bath. She refused to make a charge, so I left £1 for the immerser and £1 for the hassle and went round to the pub for a pint, feeling deliciously clean, dry and warm. I followed that with a fish supper on the pier, and then hitched back to the boat in the dark – not an easy task.

The following morning I ate breakfast on deck in a warm, though hazy, sunshine: high pressure was definitely building. In flicking through my *Sailing Directions: Ardnamurchan to Cape Wrath* I happened to notice that Scoraig, the peninsula between Loch Broom and Little Loch Broom, was listed as having a boatbuilder. Though I had not intended to visit the place – my itinerary was supposed to be confined to islands – I thought a change of plan in order. Maybe, just maybe, I could get the engine repaired there. After all, if corporate capitalism had failed to provide me with the service I needed, proper free enterprise, which the well-known 'hippy' community on Scoraig lives by, might be able to do the job.

I raised the anchor at eleven o'clock and sailed out of the bay at less than a knot. It is about ten miles round to the Scoraig pier in Little Loch Broom. By five o'clock I had covered about three of those miles, threading my way between the Russian klondykers anchored in the roadstead. I was going so slowly that at one point I was able to have a brief chat, in my halting Russian, with two *rabochniki* who were standing on a raft painting the waterline of the Murmansk-registered *Sevriba* ('severnaya riba' is Russian for 'northern fish'). I would love to have gone aboard for a look around and a sociable vodka. But with no motor, I felt I had to drift on.

Eventually, the wind died completely, and it was back into the dinghy again to tow the boat. I was less than a mile off the north shore of the peninsula and I rowed for nearly an hour. I dropped the anchor 50 yards from one of the most bizarre houses I have ever seen. It stood above a large grassy field with horses and cattle in so I went ashore for a wander. Immediately I was met by a woman who asked, 'Are you all right?' Working with the horses, she had seen me rowing and had presumed I was in some sort of trouble. What a nice gesture, I thought.

Next thing she invited me up to the house for a cup of tea, which soon turned into a delicious dinner of crab salad and raspberry pie, prepared by her grinning, heavily dreadlocked husband. The contrast with the drearily commercial atmosphere of Achiltibuie was total. I liked Scoraig from the moment I set foot on the place.

11

SCORAIG AND POINTS SOUTH

In fact I had visited Scoraig once before in the mid-1980s, when I came up with a group of friends to the annual music festival (now discontinued because of the excessive crowds). On that occasion I did not meet any of the inhabitants. For three days we had lazed about in the sunshine, eating, drinking and so on, and listening to music which got steadily worse as the weekend wore on. Everything else got better, including, I was told, the magic mushroom soup which was ladled out from a huge cast-iron pot that must have held at least 50 gallons. I remember peering into the depths after it had been emptied and seeing the bottom covered with a six-inch layer of hallucinogenic sludge. Up on the hill among the visitors' tents after dark I also remember a man in a very plummy accent shouting: 'Hash for cash! Roll up! Roll up! Hash for cash!' On the last night, there was the most magnificent aurora I have ever seen. For perhaps an hour, the whole sky seemed to shimmer with waves and curtains of light, all a pale, fairy green: like luminescent primrose leaves.

Scoraig was a crofting township which, like so many others, lost its way after the Second World War when Britain introduced large-scale agricultural support and tried to discourage low-intensity farming. As there is no road to it, it is for all practical purposes an island. The smaller the island, the more vulnerable the community, and Scoraig was a very small 'island' having only a handful of crofts. In the 1950s two social refugees from industrial England took over the tenancies of some of the crofts. Soon others moved up, from all over Britain, and a new community came into being. Once all the crofts were taken, they were officially subdivided. Today, I am told, there are ten registered crofts, but there are 13 other permanently established households whose status, technically, is that of 'cottars'. These people have no legal security of tenure, only the sort of security which used to be common in many country areas where landlords did not consider it part of their normally exercisable rights to evict tenants who paid the rent and did not disturb the peace. Since every new arrival on Scoraig can only be housed at the pleasure of someone already there, this amounts to an informal vetting procedure. The community has become a sort of club, with the freedoms and limitations that club life inevitably involves. This may be good; it may be bad. What is unarguable is that it is different from the purely commercial basis of most communities in Britain where anybody, however unwanted, can buy his or her way in. To that extent, Scoraig is a healthy development, at least if you believe in social diversity.

My hosts at dinner were Anna and Chris. They told me they had lived on Scoraig for 16 years. They had five acres, which included a herb garden and a small and rather ragged-looking spruce plantation – ideal for fuel. Timber-clad, and sporting an extravagantly-sized first-floor balcony, their house looked from the outside like a cross between a free-standing sauna and a miniature Berghof. Inside, it was quite different: more like a theatre set on the theme of Macbeth meets Magnus Barelegs. The core of the structure is a traditional crofting cottage which Chris has clad with waney-edged sitka spruce off-cuts. At the eastern end he has added another floor containing the master bedroom, in front of which he has constructed the balcony. This looks north-east over the sea towards Benmore Coigach and Stac Pollaidh. In summer it must get all the morning sun. The wood cladding makes the house very warm, while the stone core gives the walls great strength. The split-level layout within – the upper level being the sitting area – gives it a theatrical feel, which the hanging rugs and the strong but indirect lighting augment.

'How on earth did you get planning permission for anything so interesting as this?' I asked, looking about me.

'We didn't,' Chris said, grinning. 'Same all over Scoraig. The planners can't be bothered with us.'

'Why?'

'Because we are not on a road.'

By this Chris did not mean that the planning department could not be fagged to sail and walk the distance required to come and check up on them. Indeed, he told me that when the building controller came to inspect the school – with children involved, the planners felt they had to make a serious check – he walked up from the pier and asked jokingly for a blindfold, so varied and unconventional were the houses. He made no report about what he saw. That, we agreed, was the mark of a grown-up approach to the problem of rural housing in Scotland. That problem is a combination of scarcity and bureaucratically enforced conformity. The blame lies with the British planning system which was conceived in the late 1940s to deal with ribbon development in the English home counties. The system of green belts and the presumption against isolated rural developments have little relevance in the Highlands.

What Chris really meant about the lack of a road was that Scoraig was free from the homogenising pressure of popular tourism. Since most tourists stay within sight of their car or coach, they never get to Scoraig. That explains the architectural freedom. There are no complaints from 'local businesses' trying to sell a fake 'Brigadoon' image to visitors. Life can evolve naturally.

Apparently the Highland Region once offered to build a road into Scoraig from Badralloch, though it would have cost a great deal since the north shore of Little Loch Broom is at one point an almost sheer cliff rising 700 or 800 feet out of the sea. But the residents protested: they were well aware of the damage a road would do to their community. To its credit the Region did not press the offer and today Scoraig presents a wonderful contrast to the cultural and, I would venture, spiritual emptiness of places like Achiltibuie.

I asked Chris if the Scoraig community had any plans to plant trees on the hillsides, which are almost as bare as those on Coigach. Yes, he said, they had well-developed plans for the parts of the common grazings which are not used for sheep and cattle. As on Coigach, these plans were conceived in the context of the Crofter Forestry Act (1991), which brought crofters into the normal planting grant regime for the first time. However the Scottish Office inserted a clause into the Bill making planting conditional on the landowner's approval. So the Dundonnell estate, which owns Scoraig and which had no objection to trees as such, demanded half the grant money for the planting and half the revenue from the woods. Scoraig residents objected that this amounted to blackmail. The estate pointed to the law and said: no payment, no signature. Since Scoraig could only afford the planting if they had the benefit of the full grant, that was the end of the scheme.

Crofting legislation is complicated and the Scoraig community seems to have found a way through the legal thicket. By apportioning the common grazings to individual crofters they are able to proceed piecemeal without the landlord's permission. One crofter's ground will be planted by everybody one year, then the next crofter's the next, and so on until the whole original scheme has been carried out. This otherwise complicated arrangement will have the collateral benefit that the trees will not all be planted at the same time so the age of the resulting woodland will vary somewhat.

Chris told me he did not blame the landowner so much as the factor. I said I disagreed; he was being too kind. Lairds, like government ministers, skippers of boats and criminal masterminds, should take responsibility for the actions of the people they employ.[1] I asked how the laird was viewed locally.

'They're OK,' Chris replied.

'They?'

'Yes, there's two of them.'

Once there had been three: the colourful Rogers brothers. They were the sons of Sir Alexander Roger, an entrepreneur from Aberdeenshire who made a vast fortune in railways and telecommunications, and was latterly chairman of the Midland Bank. None of the three boys, Alan, Alexander ('Sandy') and Neil ('Bunny'), married and none took any interest in their father's business. Bunny was the most unconventional of the three, being throughout his life an ostentatious and unapologetic 'queer', as such people were known in the 1920s. Though born in England, he was educated at Loretto, which he hated. He then went to Balliol College, Oxford, but was prematurely sent down, apparently for buggering too many of the dons. He proved a very courageous soldier in the Second World

---

1   Postscript: soon after my visit the factor was sacked and the original scheme given the go-ahead. Scoraig residents decided they would retain the staggered planting scheme. They have established their own tree nursery and are now afforesting 90 hectares (rather less than half a square mile) at the comfortable rate of about 15 hectares per year.

War, fighting with great distinction in the Rifle Brigade both in the Western Desert and in Italy. He came back from the war saying, 'Now I've shot so many Nazis, Daddy will *have* to buy me a mink coat.'

In the 1950s the three brothers cashed in a nearly forgotten block of telephone shares and bought the 33,000 acre Dundonnell estate from Lord Tarbat, Fraser Darling's Masonic contact. They proclaimed themselves Scottish, though Bunny went further and called himself a Highlander. He affected to despise all Lowlanders while actually spending most of his time in Mayfair, lunching every day at the Spanish Bar in Fortnum and Mason's. He was in business for many years as a designer with Sir Hardy Amies, the royal dressmaker. He had at least one unconventional success. In the late 1950s, he was credited with lowering the male coat line, raising the trouser cuffs and inspiring the 'Teddy Boy' look.

While Sandy worked quietly in the City, Alan – who, like Bunny, had a distinguished war record, having risen to the rank of Colonel in the Indian Army – moved properly to Dundonnell. He cultivated roses and bonsai trees, becoming an expert on oriental art and a director of the National Galleries of Scotland. Unlike Bunny, Alan was not one for the bright lights. His preferred evening entertainment was to go to Ullapool to hear the Scottish Chamber Orchestra at the Ceilidh Place. In later life, he took a paternal interest in the community at Scoraig, whose independence of spirit he admired. In 1988 he helped them set up the secondary school in the village in the disused church so that they could withdraw their children from the state educational system.

In 1980 Sandy died, then shortly after I visited Scoraig, within the space of three months, both Alan and Bunny did so too. Dundonnell House was left to one of Alan's Chinese manservants, and the estate sold to the millionaire librettist, Sir Tim Rice. Bunny's effects were disposed of at a huge sale at Sotheby's about which the *Sunday Telegraph* remarked, 'Never has so much tulle or chiffon come under the auctioneer's hammer in the name of a man.'

Next morning there was a bit of wind and so I raised the anchor straight away and set off to round Scoraig point and get into Little Loch Broom where the boatbuilder was. We made fine progress for an hour or so, then the wind began to die. By the time we were into the mouth of the loch, there was hardly a breath. With painful slowness, *Sylvia B* inched her way round the shingle spit behind which the Scoraig anchorage lies. At about eleven o'clock, I tied up alongside the pier, having covered seven miles in about four hours.

Just above the high-water mark, there was a modern wooden shed, possibly 60 feet long, which looked as if it might be the boatyard the *Sailing Directions* had mentioned – certainly there wasn't much else around of an 'industrial' nature. I walked up and hallooed in through the open doors, to be greeted by a thick-set, balding man in his mid-40s who announced himself as 'Topher' (short for Christopher) Dawson. There was no doubt I had come to the right place since half the shed was occupied by the newly completed hull of a large (possibly 25-foot) clinker-built vessel. It was beautifully made, copper fastened and coated externally with grey lead paint. Topher was just starting on the interior layout and there were laminated beams being lofted and glued up on the spare floor space. Outside, there was a pile of timber 'in stick' and a generator which, I later learned, ran the saw-bench and planer-thicknesser. Scoraig has electricity from self-generated wind power, but this does not have the voltage to run woodworking machinery. I also saw the half-controlled heap of clutter and off-cuts which, though anathema to the modern factory manager, is the mark of the real craftsman: everything will have a use one day and, conversely, anything you need you will find *somewhere* within your shed – a crucial point when working far from suppliers.

Thinking this might be a 'wood only' operation, I nervously asked Topher if there was any chance that he might be able to do something with my outboard. He would certainly try, he said. When? I asked. Right now, he said. I humped the dead metal up from the boat and Topher set to work. First he changed the ignition coil and then he tried the points. Neither had any effect. He told me that it must be something called the 'high-tension coil' which needed changing. Apparently the plastic coating can degrade after many years (my engine was 17 years old). But he did not have one of those on hand. But Topher said he thought that somebody called 'Spanner' might have a part-share in a motor off which such a component might be taken if I were to agree to replace it once I got back to Islay. This I did, upon which Topher announced he was going home for lunch and did I want to come?

Under a gloriously hot sun, of which it would almost be true to say that it was beating down, we walked a few hundred yards towards what looked like a mound of earth decorated with painted plaster toadstools. Next to the mound, there rose up a shingle-clad circular structure with windows looking out across the mouth of the loch and westward towards Eilean á Chlerich. But that was just the master bedroom. As we descended into an exuberantly planted flower- and fruit-garden I saw that the mound of earth had windows round about its base. Through a set of French doors I noticed a lady busying herself with salads, while an older one sorted through a huge pile of washing. Topher introduced the younger lady as his wife, Jan, and the older as his mother-in-law, who was up from the Borders for what my grandmother would have called 'a wee bit holidi'. With the hint of a breeze wafting through the large, circular room, Topher and I drank a can of beer while we all ate a delicious lunch of pizza and green salad. Bliss!

After lunch Topher found a wheelbarrow and we set off to look for Spanner and his motor. We caught up with him as he was taking a tea-break at the only building site on the peninsula. Spanner explained that, though he was quite happy to lend me the part I needed, there were two other joint owners of the engine in question and they really ought to be consulted too. Topher ascertained who they were, and where Spanner thought the motor was. It was hot work sweating the wheelbarrow over walls and bogs and through fences and unbrashed woodland. We would call on one house without result then be directed to another one. It was a slow business, mainly because every house had someone inside to whom Topher gave a patient explanation of our predicament. Quite often there was other business to be attended to which his arrival at the door had brought, as it were, to the top of the in-tray. It was a sociable round and I was reminded of Hugh Mackinnon's comment on the Coll of his youth: 'Every house was lived in and you got a laugh at every door.'

Eventually, we got permission to take the part needed – though it was my impression that we did not actually meet the owners, just people who thought the arrangement would be 'cool' and who agreed to relay its terms to the person(s) concerned. The next job was to locate the engine itself. This involved a couple more calls until we were pointed to a wheel-less Daf van which was rusting peacefully in a clearing in the woods. Inside I could see a heap of outboard engines nearly four foot high. My recollection is that we never actually found Spanner's motor, but another one, a Mariner, which is just a rebadged version of the Yamaha and which would therefore do fine. Over this one, I gathered, Topher had individual power of attorney. I readied the wheelbarrow for loading while Topher levered the desired machine from the pile. I needn't have bothered, since Topher slipped into the house nearby, borrowed some tools and proceeded to remove the part we wanted. We then set off back to the shed, walking the empty wheelbarrow once again through the bogs and woods in the still-intensifying heat.

Within half an hour of getting back to his shed, Topher had my motor running as sweet as it has always done. By about five o'clock we had it back on board to test *in situ*. It fired second pull, as it has done consistently for 17 years – never first pull, always second. For a minute, I was so relieved at the thought of no more rowing and drifting that I could do nothing but stand and stare at it, listening to the familiar happy gurgle as it idled steadily.

By the time we were back ashore, Topher's two boys, Matthew and Peter (aged about eight and ten), had returned from school. The heat was still solid in the boat shed, so Topher and I decided that we should celebrate his success with a cooling swim. The boys were keen to join us so we all stripped off and plunged from the pier into the icy, and I mean *icy*, waters of Loch Broom – those which the guidebooks say are so happily warmed by the Gulf Stream. I swam about 50 yards out and back, by which time I had a headache, the water was so cold. As I was towelling myself down, the boys clambered back up onto the pier and told me, through chattering teeth, how warm they thought the sea was today. And they meant it, because they then proceeded to fetch some goggles and flippers from the boat-shed and, together with some friends who had by this time appeared from nowhere, plunge back in and swim about exploring for the next ten minutes or so.

I motored *Sylvia B* quietly out into the roadstead thinking that free enterprise had proved more flexible, friendly and quality-conscious than anything that corporate Britain could organise. Instead of two weeks, a bill of over £200 and no guarantee of success, Topher had done the job in an afternoon at a cost of £30 labour plus whatever the part cost when I got back (£27). From that day to this, the engine has never missed a beat. On top of all that, Jan offered to put a load of my washing in her machine and said that if I brought it over to the house at about eight o'clock, I would get dinner too. I was embarrassed by this hospitality as I had nothing on board with which to reciprocate.

Over dinner, Topher told me that there was going to be a grand party on Saturday night for one of the younger ones (children of the original settlers). Since this was Wednesday, I thought I could justify staying on as I wanted to make a couple of side visits in this area anyway. Discussing this, I said that one of the places I wanted to see was Gruinard, the famous anthrax island, which I gathered had now been cleaned up. Jan knew something about this as she had helped with the operation.

Topher told me an interesting story about why the island was finally detoxified. For years the Ministry of Defence refused to tackle the job, though the method they eventually used was so simple that it is hard to believe that the delay was purely technical. (They soaked the six contaminated acres, out of 484, with a solution of formaldehyde and sea water.) The background is important. Contrary to popular belief, anthrax was not developed originally as an anti-personnel agent, but an anti-bovine one. The British wartime plan was to parachute infected lumps of cattle-cake into Germany to kill the Reich's livestock. At Christmas 1942 a soap-maker in Old Bond Street was given a contract to produce 250,000 linseed meal cakes a week. These were taken to Porton Down where they were infected, sealed and stored. Soon a stockpile of 5 million lethal cakes was ready for a mission gloatingly codenamed Operation Vegetarian.[2]

Gruinard was in fact taken over by the British armed forces only after the initial stockpile had been assembled and when a new and improved way of delivering this poison to Germany had been developed. The island was not used to test anthrax as such, only weapons containing it. Cluster bombs, containing hundreds of small capsules, could release the toxin into the air, which would kill enormous numbers of people directly. It was a case of cutting out the middle-beast. Gruinard was used to test the bomblets which went to make up the larger weapon which, in the event, was never manufactured. Nonetheless the land on the island around the testing site was infected with *bacillus anthracis* and the principles of atmospheric dissemination of the poison were established.

After years of MoD stonewalling about the clean-up, Topher told me, an eco-terrorist organisation called Dark Harvest decided they would get radical. In

---

2   For further details see *Porton Down: 75 Years of Chemical and Biological Reseach* G.B. Carter, HMSO, London 1992. The Germans had equally odd schemes, possibly the oddest of which was the Battle of the Potato. (See *Biologists under Hitler* Ute Deichmann, Harvard, USA 1996.) After Hitler banned the Wehrmacht from using biological weapons, in early 1942, the German Army instructed the Cultivated Plant Institute in Vienna to experiment with dropping potato beetles from aircraft, with the idea that they would eat their way through Britain's staple source of starch. The Agriculture Section of the Wehrmacht Science Division deemed 40 million beetles necessary for the attack and they started assembling this huge, unconventional 'infantry' force. The plan failed only because it turned out that the Reich did not have enough potatoes to feed all the beetles as they awaited front-line deployment.

1985, at the time of the Conservative Party conference, they telephoned the hotel where Mrs Thatcher and the other bigwigs were staying and said that they had put anthrax spores, collected from Gruinard Island, in the air-conditioning system. In fact they had not done so, and a thorough security search soon revealed that fact to Mrs Thatcher. But the warning had the desired effect. Within months, the Ministry of Defence announced a clean-up. The work was carried out the following year, and the island has been safe ever since.

We also discussed boats. Though from Edinburgh himself, Topher has an engineering degree from Cambridge (where he rowed for his College) and he takes his family on holiday in a large trimaran. Topher told me, in tones of almost physical agony, about the tragically wasteful policy towards the redundant elements of the Scottish fishing fleet. I had noticed the hulk of a 40-foot boat called *Dewey Rose* drawn up on the beach not far from the pier. The hull planking had been chainsawed through vertically, below the waterline, just aft of the stem in about five places, to a depth of perhaps three feet. Such damage is impossible to repair, except at exorbitant cost. Otherwise it was a sound looking and very elegant hull. But Topher had been paid £100 by one or other of the government agencies to dispose of it. He told me why.

When the first decommissioning scheme for fishing boats came in, owners were paid to take their boats out of service and render them unfit for sea by removing engine and wheelhouse. But, Topher said, these boats were bought for next to nothing by foreign owners, many of them Irish, and were patched up and sent back to sea. The bureaucracy could see no other way forward than to compel the complete destruction of the vessels, and so a revised decommissioning scheme was introduced whereby the hull had to be sawn up in the way the *Dewey Rose's* had been. Thus craft which could have been used for houseboats, yachts, tourist boats and whatever, were reduced to scrap simply because the EC could not control its self-generated paperwork.

Thursday dawned just as bright as Wednesday had, but with a gutsier breeze, blowing from slightly north of east. After a leisurely breakfast, I weighed anchor and sailed out of the loch and down to the west coast of Gruinard Island. By now it was blowing a solid 4 and *Sylvia B* raced along under a single-reefed main and the working jib, the bow-wave creaming past under the gunwhale. The sky was cloudless and the crumpled surface of the Minch sparkled cheerfully in every direction: a perfect day for a sail.

We came to anchor in a shallow bay which was strewn with skerries and submerged rocks. The green of the shallower water showed lighter where, all around, rocks rose above the marine undergrowth. I buoyed the anchor in case it fouled a concealed rock, and rowed ashore. The island itself is featureless, rising smoothly to a low summit, and being completely devoid of trees or shrubs – at least on the western side. There was no evidence of British military presence, and so, after a brief photo recce, I counter-marched to the beach and evacuated my expeditionary party, consisting of self and Pentax.

By now it was early afternoon, and after substituting the small genoa for the working jib, I raised the anchor and laid a course for Eilean á Chlerich, five miles away to the north-west. This was the island where, in 1936, Fraser Darling watched birds in a blaze of self-generated publicity. With more canvas, on a very broad reach, *Sylvia B* sailed even faster. In less than an hour, we were underneath the south coast of the island. In a freshening wind, we were buffeted by ferocious squalls which swept down from the steep cliffs. There are very open anchorages on both the west and the east coasts, and with the wind in the east, the west coast was the one for today. Coming to anchor under sail was a dicey business as I was tacking into the squalls. Some were so strong I wondered if it would be wise to leave the boat at anchor at all. Or should I run a warp to the shore? In the event I dropped the anchor then sat on deck for half an hour, eating a sandwich and drinking a cup of tea, while I watched the position of the boat very carefully. Convinced that the anchor was holding, I rowed ashore, lashed the dinghy to a rock and set off to inspect this famous location in the life of the bastard messiah.

Fraser Darling wrote in *Island Years* that Eilean á Chlerich was 'heaven on earth', but my own impression was that it was just another Hebridean island, both beautiful and bleak in its own particular way, no more or less so than hundreds of others. I mooched around the ruins of the stone hut in the middle, where Darling had camped, then wandered over to the eastern side where the RSPB, who now own the island, have erected a prefabricated wooden hut. This overlooks a small fenced enclosure which presumably hosts birds which would not otherwise use the island: a half-acre bird table.

One thing that the reader of *Island Years* surely comes away with is the terrible *hardship* which Darling endured in pursuit of scientific knowledge. He says, 'Living on uninhabited islands is no lark but a responsible task . . . The type of simplicity I seek – hard living by mountain and sea – is not everybody's choice.' Throughout, Darling is at pains to describe just how difficult it was living on Eilean á Chlerich when the nearest shop was at Scoraig.[3] Contrary to the impression he gives, a half-competent sailor could have commuted between the island and the shop quite easily. It is only six miles to Scoraig, and no more than 13 to the fleshpots of Ullapool. Most of the time Darling spent on the island, it was summer; he preferred to winter on the mainland. But even in winter, there are many gentle, clear days on the west coast of Scotland for those with the patience to wait for them. In fact the whole image of the intrepid naturalist, travelling to the remotest outcrops of the British archipelago, careless of hardship or discomfort, in selfless pursuit of scientific knowledge, was a complete fiction. The only reason Darling experienced hardship was because he chose to live on

---

3 Darling describes the shop in terms which might be described as 'interwar camp': 'This is a man's shop. You can buy butter and sugar there, and crockery and stuffs, buckets and girdles and rope and tackle. It is such a shop as a man lingers in unashamed to discuss the affairs of the world. I verily believe I could buy drapery there without embarrassment.' (p. 12)

islands while being, by his own admission, hopeless with boats. The hardship was entirely self-inflicted. It was pure self-promotion.

That night, over supper, Topher told me about a very different sort of character who once spent a season on Eilean á Chlerich. 'You call us hippies,' Topher said, smiling. 'I'll tell you about someone who was a *real* hippy.'

The tale concerned a man called Jilal who had decided that he ought to cut life down to the barest minimum. He arrived barefoot at Scoraig and asked to be conveyed to Eilean á Chlerich together with all he had brought for year-round living: a barrel of salt herring, a sack of oatmeal, and a coffee-grinder to process the meal. Once on the island, he intended to collect shellfish, berries and mushrooms. 'We couldn't believe it,' Topher said. 'He said he was going to live in a cave, indefinitely.' That was real hard living by mountain and sea.

It was agreed that Jilal would be taken out to his new home, but that if an emergency developed he would summon help by lighting a heather fire on the rocks to make a smoke signal. The prospective hermit was duly conveyed to his cave and left to meditate. Nothing was heard for months, until one day a huge column of smoke was seen rising above the island. This was more than a simple signal, Scoraig folk thought. What was happening? A boat put to sea immediately.

The crew found Jilal up in his cave, doubled over in terrible agony, hardly able to speak from the pain. Very alarmed, the rescue party tried to extract from him the reasons for his agony. But all he was capable of saying was that the coffee grinder had broken. As a reaction to a trivial mechanical failure, this seemed a trifle over-done, until someone noticed the oatmeal sack, hardly touched. The penny dropped: Jilal had been left without any way of rendering his staple palatable, and so had been thrown back on the herring, which he had eaten exclusively until he developed the most terrible case of constipation. Rendered practically immobile, he could not oven get down to the rocks to light his rescue fire. In agony he had crawled out of the cave and set the hillside ablaze.

'You call us hippies,' Topher concluded. 'That guy made us look like a bunch of stockbrokers.'

On Friday I motored over to the south shore of Little Loch Broom and made my way up to the road. The other place I was keen to visit in this area was the National Trust for Scotland's estate at Poolewe, where Osgood Mackenzie's famous gardens attract even more visitors than poor Iona. It did not take long to get lifts and I was soon sitting in the office of Keith Gordon, the resident administrator for the Trust, listening while he briefly rehearsed the history of the estate.

Osgood Mackenzie was the son of the second wife of Sir Francis Mackenzie, the twelfth Laird of Gairloch. Since Osgood's half-brothers were to inherit their father's estate, Osgood's mother, Mary Hanbury of Essex, bought him the adjoining estates of Kernsary and Inverewe in 1862 when he was 20 years old. The whole area was largely roadless and, except for the islands in the middle of the lochs, treeless. Mackenzie spent two years deciding where on these 12,000 acres he might build himself a house – no problems of ribbon development in those days. The house Mackenzie built was burned down in 1914, but his daughter, Mairi Sawyer, replaced it on the same site in 1935. Designed by her South African husband, it is a wonderful example of *haute bourgeois* interwar Scottish domestic architecture. Though externally unremarkable, internally it suggests the domestic wing of a castle with a hint of Charles Rennie Mackintosh's revolutionary Hill House at Helensburgh, and more than a hint of opulent personal comfort. Today it is Keith Gordon's home and, as such, not open to the public. I saw only the entrance hall and the sitting and dining rooms.

Before his death in 1922, Osgood Mackenzie published *A Hundred Years in the Highlands*, one of the most evocative accounts extant of Highland life as it was before improved communications destroyed the self-sufficient, usually Gaelic-speaking, communities whose ruined houses and byres are everywhere to be seen in the hills. Mackenzie wrote with unsophisticated insouciance about his own and his keepers' adventures on the hill. For example, he admires the skill of the estate's first 'vermin-killer':

> By daybreak, Watson was on the top of Bathais Bheinn with swan shot in one barrel and a bullet in the other, peering over the rock. Away sailed one of the eagles, but the swan shot dropped him on the heather below the rock. Another eagle from the nest on the other side of the hill came to the same end. Then Watson hid himself among the rocks near where a wounded eagle was flapping his wing, and a third eagle, coming to see what this meant, was invited by a cartridge to remain, making one and a half brace of eagles before breakfast.[4]

The Inverewe garden overlooks the south-eastern end of Loch Ewe, standing amid the remaining 2500 acres of the estate. Mairi was just as keen a gardener as her father, so when she handed the whole property over to the National Trust for Scotland in 1952, they acquired a horticultural treasure that had taken nearly a century to mature. Today it is one of the Trust's 'big three' gardens, along with Brodick Castle on Arran and Crathes Castle in Aberdeenshire. It attracts 130,000 visitors per year and is one of the most profitable of all the NTS properties. It is also the largest employer in this part of Wester Ross. There are 17 full-time staff and up to 30 seasonal workers.

It comes as a shock to realise that something so harmless as an ornamental garden can be under threat from what might be called 'conservation correctness'. But it can, and Inverewe is one such case. The basic bone of contention, Keith told me, was the issue of 'native' versus 'non-native' species of tree. Osgood Mackenzie found the Corsican pine to be the best species for colonising treeless hillsides, deriding the Scots pine as being 'a dreadfully delicate tree when exposed to Atlantic gales'. The Forestry Commission controls part of the woodland at Inverewe where a long row of Corsican pines stands out magnificently on the skyline. But this is to be cut down to make way for a nondescript mixture of birches, rowans and scrub oak.

---

4   *A Hundred Years in the Highlands* Osgood Mackenzie, Geoffrey Bles, London 1949, p. 124.

'Personally I get a little bit tired of the tunnel-vision, one-issue organisations,' Keith said. 'They can become very cut off. But you have to be careful. I've even heard it said by one person within the Trust who is very anti-agriculture that all land that the Trust owns should be cleared, probably including people! It's not really what it's all about. There is an integration which works very well. These people don't realise that it is by and large the estate owners, the agriculturalists, the foresters and all the rest who have made these areas what they are, just as Osgood Mackenzie made this garden. There's room for everybody.'

Keith introduced me to the Head Gardener, an elfin Londoner with a sunny manner and a wry sense of humour, called Clive Murray. Clive was equally scornful of the attempt to homogenise nature by the imposition of politically-correct planting policies.

'The whole reason we are so popular here,' he said to me as we set out to tour the garden, 'is because we are so incongruous within the surroundings. We are an oasis.'

Clive told me that the attractive thing about the garden is not the plants themselves, so much as these plants in this setting. 'These South African and New Zealand plants give the illusion of being tropical,' he said, 'but in fact they would probably grow anywhere on the west coast of Scotland. It's very much an illusion, but it's an illusion that Osgood created. This is very much in keeping with what he did.'

'Is what we are seeing, then, much as Osgood Mackenzie left it?' I asked.

'No, not really. We have added to the garden,' Clive said. 'It is much more diverse than it would have been even in Mairi Sawyer's day: perhaps we have taken a bit of the charm away.'

'In what sense?'

'In the sense that we have created these wide paths. It was much more intimate before.'

The paths became necessary when visitor numbers started exceeding the 3000 per annum which the Trust projected when taking over the garden. Within two years the figure was over 200 per cent higher. The totals kept rising. In 1968 over 100,000 people visited the garden. In recent years the total has stabilised at about 130,000. Wider paths are the consequence.

Continuing the theme of the garden's former intimacy, Clive continued, 'I think Mairi Sawyer was more of a garden-lover than Osgood Mackenzie.'

'So what was Osgood?' I asked.

'I think he was very much a man of the heyday of plant hunters going to the Himalayas and China,' Clive said.

'Are you saying there was an acquisitive element to it?'

'In a way,' Clive replied. 'When you think that the first rhododendron was only introduced into Britain in 1826, it was a very, very fashionable plant, and every landowner wanted some. I think the acquisitive part was at the beginning. In later life Osgood started talking about the beauty of what he was growing, and making catalogues of what was coming out in flower. But I think that Mairi Sawyer was the born gardener.'

'I know you are a man and a head gardener,' I said, 'but do you think that women in general are more natural gardeners than men?'

'Certainly they have a different way of looking at gardens,' Clive said. 'Women are more particular. There's more intricate plantings with women. You can tell the difference between a woman and a man gardener.'

'If women are more intricate as gardeners, how would you characterise men?' I asked. 'Bold sweep? More general?'

'I would say so, yeah,' Clive replied.

'The grand vision?'

'Yeah.'

'Folie de grandeur?'

'Yeah, a bit of that.' He laughed.

'Is that what your wife says about your garden at home?'

'It's not my garden, it's my wife's garden,' said Clive with a twinkle in his eye.

We stopped while he asked a group of middle-aged German ladies not to walk in among the flower beds to take photographs. 'We have areas of the garden that we just cannot plant because people continually stand on them,' he said.

Since a large proportion of the visitors are foreign, I asked Clive what his experience of the various nationalities was.

'I do find the Germans rather aggressive,' he said. 'The French people to me are like artists, they always say the meaningful things.'

'Like what?'

'I remember a really miserable day; the midges were dreadful; it was dull; it was drizzling; and everybody was walking around looking thoroughly unhappy. Then this little old French lady – she looked quite stern – came tottering up and I thought, here we go again, another moaner. She put her hand on my arm and said very softly, "What a delight!" then just walked off.'

'And Americans?' I asked.

'Americans are a mixed bunch actually. The American horticulturalists are great: they are really enthusiastic. But the others tend to be, "Seen it all; done it all. Take me to the next viewpoint." '

Walking though a stand of huge eucalyptus-like trees, I noticed some strange-looking structures ahead. They turned out to be the garden's cat-houses.

'We first got these cats when we had a plague of mice,' Clive told me. 'It was similar to having a plague of rabbits in the garden. They would eat everything.'

'I didn't know mice ate plants,' I said.

'Oh yeah. You'd go out to a bit of the garden where you'd planted herbaceous plants and before you'd arrive you'd hear this crunching noise. Then you'd see them like timber, falling over. You'd investigate it after, and what they must have been doing was building nests because they'd munch a whole herbaceous plant, about two feet high, and they'd chop it up into little bits an inch long, heaped up in a pyramid. It was incredible what they were doing. And they were so tame.

You'd be working on the rock garden and you'd have a mouse sitting next to you eating the plants. You couldn't really turn round and hit it with a spade because there'd be people walking past going, "Oh look, a mouse! Isn't that sweet!"'

By late morning the sun had come out. The gardens which, in 1862, had contained nothing but grass, heather, willow and crowberry, sparkled in the early autumn sunshine. It was easy to see the attractions of life as a gardener – in such weather. I asked Clive how he had got into the business. He said he had been working in a tax office in Wandsworth and got fed up. Soon he was washing dishes in a hotel in the Scilly Isles. Towards the end of the season, the manager told him there were not enough dishes to wash, so he should go out to the garden and sweep up the leaves. Next thing, Clive was a gardener.

'If I was applying for a job here now,' he said, 'I would never get it. I wouldn't even be given an interview. Some of the people applying for ordinary gardener's jobs have got a BA in horticulture. I don't quite know how I feel about that because when I'm looking at application forms, I'm looking for qualifications too, though I really don't see that that makes anyone a better gardener – which is what counts, after all.'

I left Clive as he walked home for lunch in the now brilliant sunshine. There were fishermen dangling lines into the River Ewe and all the world looked at peace. I ambled the half mile into Poolewe and treated myself to lunch in the hotel. Afterwards I walked back to the main road and started looking for a good place to hitch. Before I had found one, a car had stopped.

'I'm going up Scoraig way,' I said, poking my head in through the passenger window of a very elderly-looking Japanese saloon.

'So am I,' replied the driver. 'I live there. Hop in.'

In a curious accent which sounded half-Scottish and half-Geordie, the driver told me his name was Damian and that he was now at sea, making a lot of money on a Portrush fishing boat. He was home for a break and the party. It turned out that he was from the other end of the peninsula to Scoraig, at Rirevach. His mother lives there with his stepfather who had been an engineer in Whitby, Yorkshire, until, at the age of 50, he decided he wanted to start enjoying life. 'He had worked really hard for years,' Damian said, 'had no children, and then wanted to do his own thing, get out of the rat race, and just be happy. That was ten years ago, so now I've got a little ten-year-old sister. "Tree" she is called.'

'Tree?'

'Aye,' he said laughing. 'She's a topper. They built a house, and have a few cows, and some sheep, and live a really self-sufficient lifestyle. It's funny, they don't have the sort of outlook on life that Scoraig people do, which is evident in the fact that they have a £10,000 Volvo estate in a garage on this side of the Loch. Although it's isolated and cut off, they do like to have their luxuries of life. My stepfather loves motor cars.'

'He must be one of the few there who do,' I said.

'Yes,' Damian said. 'But the two ends of the peninsula are quite different – an east–west divide. At Scoraig it's such and such is broken, can I borrow yours? No problem. At Rirevach, everyone's got their own things and they don't ask, and if it's broken they fix it. Though saying that, there is an element of sharing but it is nowhere near as strong. My stepfather built his house and in two years they were living in it but, at Scoraig, in 20 years they're not finished. You've just got to think what your priorities are. In Scoraig they are not so keen on their houses, whereas at the other end it's something you can pride yourself on.'

We stopped at the shop at Badcaul where I thought I would buy a bottle of whisky, partly for the party and partly because with the motor repaired and the trip more than halfway through, I suddenly got an excited sense of being homeward bound and thought I would celebrate. Possibly sensing the mood, Damian reached into the chaos of fishing stuff in the car and gave me two beautiful-looking mackerel.

Next morning I simmered the mackerel slowly in milk and mushrooms, while I scrubbed the deck in the sunshine. The air was a clear as a bell and the hills had the russet look they have when the nights are getting close to being frosty. I felt in such a good mood that if I had had a full set of flags aboard, I think I would have dressed the boat for the benefit of the guests arriving for the celebrations: 'Scotland expects that every guest will enjoy the party.'

After breakfast, Jan came out to the boat for a cup of tea and to deliver my laundry. I asked her what the best and worst features of living on Scoraig were, as she saw them. The best, she said, was the environment for children. They can be left to their own devices, exploring without any danger and yet with much more to learn than can ever be got from toys and computers and Saturday morning oboe lessons. The worst feature as Jan saw it was that, as a woman, there was almost nothing in the way of work available. She agreed with me that in a peasant society women would spend most of the day washing and cooking, but in a peasant society with washing machines and electric cookers, such as exists on Scoraig, women's role is simultaneously ameliorated and devalued. 'Time for art,' I said brightly. Jan smiled wistfully but said nothing.

I spent the rest of the morning cleaning down below, tidying up, stowing my clean clothes and getting water on board. In the early afternoon, I wandered up to the field above the anchorage where the party was to be held with the thought that I might give a hand erecting the stage. Fourteen trees had been felled, brashed, cut to length and hauled down to the field by an ancient but healthy-sounding Ferguson tractor. Nine of the logs were tied together to make up three 'A' frames, to which the remaining five, perhaps 20 feet long, were lashed horizontally: one at the ridge and the other four part way down the sides below where the cross of the 'As' joined the legs. Diagonal ropes were slung and hauled tight between the front of the ridge and the base of the rear 'A', and vice versa, on both sides. Then a huge tarpaulin was draped over the whole, making a very simple, strong and commodious shelter. Next, the Scoraig Ferguson chuntered back up into the woods and reappeared with the stage floor on a flat-bed trailer. Finally it disappeared and returned with a huge heap of gorse which, I was told, was to make smoke later on to keep the midges at bay.

Then the workers sat down and made immediate smoke. After a while somebody noticed a heavily overloaded boat crossing the loch. This was the band. We all went down to meet them. Amplifiers, instrument cases, a drum kit and five casually dressed musicians were unloaded onto the pier. Then the Fordson arrived and trailered the luggage up to the stage. After what might tactfully be described as a woodland wash and brush-up, the band, Salsa Celtica, from Edinburgh, emerged from the trees and started assembling the sound system. I asked what sort of music they play. 'Runrig goes to Rio,' someone said.

From that point on the afternoon began to mellow and develop. I ate some of the first sausages to come off the barbecue, drank a beer or two and took some pictures of the folk, the stage and the band. As darkness fell, I walked down to the boat to put the camera on board. On the way, I photographed the striking sight of the sun setting over the wide arc of the Minch, above a single bright light which glowed from Topher Dawson's windows down among the gathering shadows of the foreground. This was the hour when the spirits walk.

The rest of the evening passed in a magical haze. The music was excellent, even though the band was under-strength. For hours, the whole of the tarpaulinned area was full of dancers, leaping and shaking with red-faced, smoke-saturated abandon – your correspondent not infrequently among them. Outside there sat a ring of listeners, the nearest ones within the semi-circle of light, the others melting out into the darkness. Beyond that, more people came and went, like ghosts.

It was a clear but moonless night, and the path up through the trees to the house where many of the guests were staying was pitch dark. At one point very late on, I remember escorting a girl from Edinburgh through the spruce wood because she was too frightened to walk alone. She was someone who spent a lot of time in many of the less reputable dance-halls of the capital, places where I would feel extremely uneasy yet where she was quite at home. At first I thought she was trying simply to lead me up to the houses for her own wicked purposes. I could not believe that somebody unafraid of the city by night could be frightened of the dark in a place like Scoraig. But she recoiled in genuine fear as we walked through the conifers. I almost had to drag her along. It was only 30 yards to the clearing where the house she was to spend the night stood, yet she was shaking with terror by the time the lights of the cottage came into view, at which point she relaxed completely.

An hour or so later, the demons of the dance dispersed, I walked back down to the pier in the bright, hard starlight that threw into stark relief the hills beyond Rirevach and, further away to the south, the great mountains of Dundonnell. It was a cold, impressive scene, a reminder that autumn was upon us and that if I was to get home before the winter storms, I could not afford to tarry.

12

SKYE

THIRTY-SIX HOURS AFTER SAILING out of Little Loch Broom, I cast anchor in the busy roadstead of Portree, on the isle of Skye. I had spent the intervening night on the island of Rona, just north of Raasay, which very effectively smashed the beautiful mood that lingered from Scoraig. Rona is owned by a Danish lady who visits a couple of times a year but otherwise, apart from a caretaker, keeps the island completely empty. Her purpose, the caretaker told me, is to conserve the wild flora and fauna – Isle Martin revisited. Further reminiscent of Isle Martin, Rona is slowly being covered with politically correct 'native hardwoods', the difference in this case being that Highland cattle have been introduced as 'grazing tools'.

I explored the island briefly the following morning, a difficult job since it is very overgrown. The sad fact is that until comparatively recently Rona was heavily populated. Houses and a solid school building still stand just above what is known as the Dry Harbour. But the whole island is dead now: a conservationist's paradise.

That evening, it was a great relief to round the immense bluff (possibly 500 feet high) which conceals Portree from vessels approaching from the north, and I came suddenly upon the sight of brightly lit streets, pubs, shops and restaurants. By the time I did so, it was already dark, and turning cold. From the wilderness of a choppy, unfriendly sea, the sense of life and warmth in the town was palpable. I had a merry pint of Guinness in a pleasantly crowded pub and then – joy of joys! – indulged myself with the first curry I had eaten since I was in Glasgow buying equipment for the boat nearly three months earlier.

Next afternoon, I took tea in a respectable hotel with Dr James Hunter, the once youthful land-reformer who bought a tie and became chairman of Highlands and Islands Enterprise. We discussed his latest book, *On the Other Side of Sorrow*,[1] in which he describes the Celtic attitude to nature. Hunter contrasts its gentle, involved quality with the aggressive, fearful approach of the Saxons. Since bureaucratic control and personal freedom are mutually exclusive, it should be obvious that 'administering' nature in the manner beloved by SNH, the RSPB *et al*, can have only two possible long-term outcomes in the Highlands. Either it

---

1   *On the Other Side of Sorrow, Nature and People in the Scottish Highlands* James Hunter, Mainstream, Edinburgh 1995. For my money, this is the first book anyone should read who seeks to understand why the Highlands and the Hebrides are as they are, and why their inhabitants so resent the facile tutoring of outside conservation 'experts'.

will fail or, if it succeeds, it will destroy the traditional, confiding relationship between people and nature which created the paradise the interlopers seek to systematise.

An English friend of mine who is very senior in the Forestry Commission in Scotland recently put the same point to me from the opposite standpoint. 'There is a conflict,' he said, 'between the "Celtic" and the "Roman" view of trees, and therefore of forestry policy. The Romans disliked woods and cut them down because they were supposed to be dark and mysterious and the haunt of brigands. The Celts worshipped trees and loved the woods – probably because they tended to be the brigands.'

Hunter told me about the sad decline of the Crofters' Union, which he had founded in the 1980s. In particular, Hunter was concerned by the way in which the RSPB appeared to be slowly neutralising it as an independent voice by offering the tantalising, but chimerical, prospect of 'influence'. Whatever the office politics may be, such an arrangement does not reflect the character of the crofters themselves. 'I can see what the RSPB gets out of the arrangement,' Hunter said, 'an aura of "success", but I do not see what the crofters get out of it, except interference.'

It being my birthday that evening, I went 'out on the town' in search of entertainment. In a place the size of Portree, the visitor from smaller islands feels spoilt for choice. There was the Peat Bog Fairies in one pub, the Loch Carron Plonkers in another and a lecture on The Conservation of Burnett Moths in the town hall. After a fierce struggle for my patronage the moths defeated both the Fairies and the Plonkers. At 7.30 I sat down next to an attractive, youthfully middle-aged American artist who introduced herself as Sherry Palmer. Sherry said she was living on the Sleat peninsula, where she had her studio. She showed me some cards which she sold through gift shops on the island, then offered me a pack, which I gladly accepted. The originals were painted in oils on linen, but even the printed cards conveyed a vivid sense of the dramatic light which is the glory of the Hebridean landscape. I still have 'Road through the field, Lower Breaknish, Isle of Skye' next to my desk as I write.

Our conversation was interrupted by the arrival of the lecturer, a long, bearded Englishman from Aberdeen called Dr Mark Young. He started by telling us how important it was to conserve butterflies. 'They are important indicators of what is happening to the habitat,' he said. 'They are our canaries in the mine.' Oh dear, I thought. For a start, the RSPB tell us that we must conserve birds because they are our 'mine canaries', and a hundred other single-issue conservation groups make similar claims for whatever it is they are trying to sell to the sceptical public. Apart from that, it is absurd to take measures to conserve your indicator species, since if you create an artificially favourable environment, they cannot do the job you are claiming they are needed for.

Dr Young described the situation of the Slender Scotch Burnett Moth. 'It is now found only at about five or six places on the island of Mull and only in one of those places do you still get the moth in abundance. Why is this? What is going wrong? Bracken is invading the site; the grass is getting long; it's rather ungrazed; it's getting too lush and too overgrown to be a very successful site. We've studied it and discovered that it needs bare soil areas, birdsfoot trefoil, unstable soils, shallow vegetation, lots of cattle grazing. So we urgently need to manage the habitat of the Slender Scotch Burnett now before it is too late!'

Dr Young rather ruined the effect of this by adding shortly afterwards that, though the Mull population is the only one in Britain, there are plenty of these moths in Europe.

By way of peroration, Dr Young asked, why should we protect this moth? 'Ninety per cent of you people – I won't say 100 per cent because there are a few Burnett experts here – but 90 per cent of you will never see this moth,' he said. 'We don't need it in the sense of it being necessary for human existence. But we need it for some reasons: we need it to show that we can succeed in conservation, that we can actually do something about the environment, and succeed in doing that. If we fail with this moth, we'll fail with others. Why should we care about that silly little moth? Most of you won't see it, there's only five or six left. If we say we don't care, what ones are we going to say we do care about? The Slender Scotch Burnett? It's only on Mull; there are other Burnetts on the same site. Do we care about that one? Where do we draw the line? I think it is very important that we do care about conserving butterflies and moths, partly for their sake, partly for our sake, for what it shows we are capable of doing, what we care about.'

So the purpose of moth preservation is to facilitate professional self-justification by lepidopterists and sanctimonious preening by society at large. One thing it does not involve, apparently, is any sense of personal affection for the objects of scientists' cold scrutiny.

Next morning I breakfasted on deck in bright September sunshine. There was hardly a breath of wind in the sheltered roadstead, and fishermen came and went between the harbour wall and their boats in a lazy, almost Riviera-like atmosphere. The forecast was north-east 4–5, at first. Certainly clouds were scudding by overhead, but with the wind in this direction, the bay was so calm the steam rose almost vertically from my coffee mug.

An hour later, outside the huge bluff and heading south, *Sylvia B* was bent forward under the press of wind on canvas. With the water creaming richly under the bow, we spanked down the Sound of Raasay towards Scalpay. It was a gorgeous day for a sail, and Raasay glowed a deep, inviting, emerald green. Out of curiosity, I kept close inshore, so close that in places I could practically read the instructions on the fertiliser bags which were flapping on the fences.

As we turned east to pass between the south end of Raasay and the north of Scalpay the wind freshened and I shortened sail. Even so, we were over-canvassed as we shot out into the Inner Sound. But soon I was able to bear away to the south-east and head for Pabay, the little island off Broadford, which I thought might be interesting to inspect since it was for sale.

The asking price for Pabay was £400,000 for 326 acres and a single, small house. In the sixteenth century, Dean Munro described the island as thickly wooded and 'a shelter for thieves and cut-throats'. Today the few trees offer no shelter for anyone except for top-rate income tax payers. One recent owner took a fortune in grants to 'improve' it for sheep, and another took a further fortune in grants to reverse all that and 'improve' it for forestry. The Savills brochure says, 'The current owner planted about 50 per cent of the island under the Woodland Grant Scheme in 1991 with native trees to recreate its past ambience.' I walked through the planting, which actually covers no more than a quarter of the island, and a more horribly regimented, unhistorical ambience could not be imagined.

After a calm dinner moored alongside the harbour wall in Broadford, I wandered into the village for a pint. I had a pleasant chat with a heavily ear-ringed 22-year old from Elgol after he leant over to me while I was giving the barmaid my order and said, 'Smell the perfume! It's like food when you're hungry.'

He told me how much money he was making at the fishing: between £600–£800 per week, he reckoned. 'We're fishing for prawns,' he said, 'but everything comes up, even small fish. If they're not dead when we throw them back, they're so knackered that the seagulls get them. We're destroying our own future. But see in the summer, in the last fleet of the day, we put down a can of beer in each of the last six creels and they come up a cold as ice, man. Then we crack 'em: *beautiful!*'

I asked him what he spent all the money on. He said he was building a croft house for himself, but apart from that it went mainly on girls. 'They're lining the dockside when you come in on a Friday. They know how much the fishing boys earn.'

'So they're just after you for your cash?' I asked.

'Who cares about the price of a couple of gin-and-tonics when you're going to empty your sump?'

The following morning I popped into the offices of the Scottish Crofters' Union at the Old Mill in Broadford. I tried to find something to talk about with the assistant director, a pleasant, chatty girl called Fiona Mandeville, other than complaints about SSSI designations or the corncrake scheme. Promisingly, she started to tell me about a trip she was soon to make on behalf of the Union to South Africa where she would participate in a series of visits and seminars with a view to finding out how, as she put it, 'the people there have reclaimed control over their own lives'. The idea was to apply those lessons to the crofting community in Scotland.

'In other words, you want to know how the servants took over the mansion?' I asked.

'Well, there's more to it than that, but I suppose that's the essence of it,' she said.

'Having lived myself in Johannesburg for 14 years, I can tell you in a single word. No need to go there.'

'How?'

'Violence.'

There was a short, uncomfortable pause. So I added, for couthiness, 'Just as in Ireland.' The silence extended itself somewhat. 'Sadly,' I continued, 'if you want real change in that sort of situation, you need Semtex, not seminars.' But Fiona did not want to know. She looked at me as if I had been making a recommendation, not an observation. The conversation tailed off and it was not long before I was ambling back out into the beautiful autumn sunshine.

There was one last call I wanted to pay in this part of Skye. I was still mindful of the strange conversation I had had on Canna with Sean Morris of the RSPB, and since the person he said had given him the direct order not to speak to me, Alison Maclennan, operated from just outside Broadford, I decided I should potter down the road and see if she was at home.

Being very much a crofting-type settlement, Broadford is dispersed. Rather as in Loch Boisdale, but in contrast with Portree, there is no 'downtown'. Consequently before I was through the village, I was not surprised to come upon a wildlife centre. For sheer badness, I decided to go in. The focus of interest was a tatty shed in somebody's garden which announced itself as the International Otter Survival Fund, part of the Born Free Foundation. With Gavin Maxwell's old home round the corner in the Sound of Sleat, I was not surprised to see they were funded by The Bright Water Appeal.

Inside the shed, I picked up a copy of the Born Free Foundation's *Campaign News* (Summer 1996) which carried the claim that the otter's 'habitat around the Highlands and Islands of Scotland are (*sic*) under threat, largely due to road building and quarrying.' In fact, as I mentioned in connection with Loch Maddy, otters in Scotland exist in huge and often damaging numbers, numbers which are increasing everywhere. Considering all the parts of the Highlands with which I am familiar, I cannot think of a single new public road of any length which had been built in the last 20 years. I know of many improvement schemes, but not *one* new road. Similarly with quarries. But these sort of claims are standard in the wildlife conservation industry, which now has a total turnover, UK-wide, in excess of £100 million per annum. Many of the more profitable warnings are completely bogus. They have to be, since in a reasonably well-managed country like Britain there are simply not enough disasters to go round.[2]

It is to protect this cosy racket that so many of these bodies fight shy of open disclosure of information, whether it is about science, money or the corncrake. Five minutes after leaving the otter shed, I knocked on Alison Maclennan's front

2 A related point is that far from all of the money raised goes to direct conservation action. For example, the RSPB's 1996–7 accounts show that from a total turnover of £37 million conservation expenditure amounted to just £21 million. Thus 46p in every £1 taken goes on things other than bird protection. So while £ 1.87 million was spent on buying land, over £3 million was spent on membership recruitment. The RSPB is not untypical of the industry generally in spending more money acquiring members than nature reserves.

door. I was surprised to see her come to the door dressed in a plum-coloured T-shirt, tight black jeans and fluffy slippers. It was immediately clear that she knew who I was before I told her my name.

'I wondered if you had a couple of minutes to talk about RSPB matters,' I asked. 'I gather you are the local representative.'

'That's right,' she said. 'Yes. But I am afraid I am terribly busy at the moment. I'm starting a meeting with someone just now.'

'When would be a suitable time to call?'

'Ummm, I'm not going to manage today or tomorrow. I have to go away tomorrow: I've got meetings in Inverness. How long are you on Skye for?'

'I don't know, a few days anyway.'

'Right. Well, I'm afraid it's not going to be possible in the next few days.'

'How about after your Inverness meeting?'

'On Friday I've got meetings over in the west. And then I have to go somewhere else.'

'And after that?' A long pause. 'After that? I'm not sure,' she tailed off. 'Can I just have a look at my diary?'

'Sure.'

She went inside for a moment. 'We're talking about early October now?' she asked. This was mid-September.

'Yes.'

'Looking into October now, I'm on leave for two weeks in October. Best thing is if you could contact me nearer the time and we could fix something up.'

'You can't make an appointment now of any sort?'

'I have some meetings floating at the moment which I have assured people I can do that week, so I just can't say for sure.'

'Can't I get a floating meeting as well?'

'Well, it would have to be the end of October.'

'I don't mind, can we make a time?'

Hesitantly she said, 'Um, right. Ummmm, what is it that you actually want to discuss about the RSPB?'

'I just want to find out what's happening on Skye,' I said.

'We don't actually have any Reserves or anything.'

'I know that. What do you do on Skye?'

'I just have a wide remit, which includes all sorts of things with which the RSPB has involvement.'

'What sort of things are they?'

'It's just general issues about birds, actually. Anything about birds.'

'That's what I am interested to talk about,' I said brightly.

'OK, do you have a number I could contact you at?'

'I can certainly give you a number, but can we not make a time now?'

'If I can take a number?'

I gave my home telephone number on Islay, then said, 'Can I also ask you: you've got a representative on Canna?'

'Aha. Sean Morris.'

'He told me that you had forbidden him to talk to me about the corncrake. Is that true?'

'Well that – uh, no, that's not true. I mean, ah, I mean I'm quite happy for him to tell you anything about the actual corncrake itself, there's no problem with that. All I said to him was that I did not think it was appropriate that you went into any of the financial matters that we were involved in. That is the same for everybody, it is an agreement between RSPB and the National Trust.'

'That is not what he said to me. He said that he could not talk about anything. I think he found it a rather embarrassing meeting. I asked him where this policy originated, and he said Alison Maclennan. Are you responsible for it?'

'Ah, only in that policy issues are supposed to be dealt with by David Minns. I think he's actually said that to you already, and if you wish to discuss policy issues, you would have to deal with him, but as far as Sean is concerned, he is a contract worker, he has just worked a short time. He can't be expected to know all the ins and outs.'

'Of course,' I said. 'I asked him questions like why he did not try planting corn in order to encourage the corncrakes to drop in and he said he wasn't allowed to talk about anything like that because Alison Maclennan had forbidden him to.'

'That was a misunderstanding because we've no problem with actually discussing why we are doing conservation work and what we are doing. It was really on the financial side.'

'That was not at all what he said to me.'

'He has misunderstood that then,' she said. 'The whole idea about planting is that it will provide early cover and I did say to Sean that any issues like that were all right.'

'Were you warned by David Minns then?'

'Um, David Minns just said that you may be visiting and that if there were policy issues that you wished to discuss at all that you should discuss them with himself.'[3]

'But he refused to discuss them with me.'

'Well perhaps you should go back to David then.'

'No, I want to discuss them with you. All I am trying to find out is what the RSPB does. If what you do is you don't talk to folk, that's fine. I just want to establish that. I've had my answer from Minns, by letter before I left Islay. I am not going to go back to him. What I am asking *you* is whether your directive to Sean Morris was on your initiative or Minns's because he, Morris, said it was on your initiative.'

---

3   I was not the only one. Ian MacIntyre, the National Trust for Scotland factor on Canna, told me that he had asked both Maclennan and Morris for details of the corncrake research they were doing, both on the island and elsewhere, and they would not tell him. 'I just haven't been able to get a straight answer on what research they are doing,' he said to me when I talked to him at the NTS office in Oban ten days later.

'Um, the directive to Sean was from me and from David Minns. That was the instruction he was given. Policy issues should be dealt with by our headquarters. That's what I am saying to you now. David Minns does not want all the individuals discussing policy with you. Not all of us deal with all the issues. Some policies refer much more to some areas than others.'

'I quite understand that you cannot talk about everything,' I said, 'but you can presumably talk about what you know about, or are you not free to do that?'

'Um, conservation issues, yes. I can tell you anything about conservation issues.'

'What is an RSPB policy issue that is not a conservation issue?'

'The actual work that is going on on the ground.'

'That's not conservation?'

She took a moment to consider that. 'Yes it is,' she said. 'I think you are being a bit, um, I am afraid I do not have time to talk at the moment, because I do have a meeting that is just about to start. I am sorry but I am going to have to go. If you want to discuss things in more detail you could always contact my boss in Inverness.'

'No, I am not interested in talking to Inverness, or Edinburgh. I am interested in talking to you. I had about an hour and a half with Sean and got nowhere. And it was all due to you, according to him. So therefore I thought, before I put that down on paper, I'd better come and find out your side of the story.'

'Yes, well, as I say, there has been a slight misunderstanding. There is no problem discussing issues relating to the actual corncrake and the conservation work we are doing on the ground. But from what I understood from Sean, you were asking all sorts of other things.'

'Yes, I was asking everything. I am interested in all aspects of your work. But we got no further than the corncrake. That was the point. Does the RSPB consider these matters secret? You are a charity after all.'

'The financial matters are. When you draw up an agreement with somebody –'

'I understand. I am not inquiring about your pecuniary arrangements with crofters or the National Trust. My question about corncrakes and money is how much do these corncrakes cost? It is a general question: it is not intruding on your privacy of contract.'

'But that's the sort of thing you'll have to talk to senior staff about.'

'Why? Is money a particularly sensitive subject?'

'No, the only financial arrangements that Sean was aware of was the one peculiar to Canna which, like I say, we couldn't discuss. He is not aware of the full implications of all the financial involvement in all the corncrake work.'

'I understand. I wasn't asking him to speak beyond his experience. I was just asking what his experience was.'

'Well, that's what I am saying. That's what he wasn't to divulge. Anyhow, I'm afraid I'll have to go just now. If you could contact me later in October, then we can work something out then.'

'OK. But right now, tell me one thing aside from all this. Are you not slightly embarrassed by all the secrecy surrounding the RSPB? Do you think it's right?'

'There is no secrecy about matters which shouldn't be kept confidential from the general public.'

'So the Habitat and Species Action Plans which I asked Minns for should be kept from the general public?' I said.

'There is a lot of sensitive information in a lot of these action plans, confidential bird information.'

'What would you say was sensitive within the Corncrake Species Action Plan.'

'You'd have to ask Dave Minns exactly why he doesn't want to divulge anything. That's his decision. I can't go back on that.'

'I'm asking a personal question. Do *you* actually think this is a right way for a charity to carry on? There is nothing about financial arrangements with crofters in the Corncrake Species Action Plan. I have a copy on board the boat. I've read it several times.'

'We are operating in the best interests of the birds, and a lot of the information that we have, it is not in the best interests of the birds to make it public knowledge.'

'But it might be in the best interests of the people round about the birds?'

'The people round about the birds we have a lot of contact with and there is a lot of information divulged there.'

'But they are not allowed to see the Species Action Plans, are they?'

'I don't think any of them have actually requested it.'

'I have.'

'I think you'll have to go back to David Minns on that. I am sorry, I really am going to have to go. I am really pushed for time at the moment. I have got meetings, OK?'

'OK, that's fine. I wouldn't want you to feel I haven't given you the opportunity to make your own reply.'

'Well, that is my reply. Conservation is what we are all about.'

'Birds come first?'

'It is a bird charity,' she said, with a wintry smile, 'a bird conservation charity.'

Well, I could not complain I had not got a clear answer. I made my way through her garden and headed for open country. I felt a curious sense of relief, as if the last vestiges of a debilitating illusion had been shattered. I stood for a moment by the side of the road, contemplating this liberating thought in the gorgeous sunshine. As I did so, a solitary Indian traveller stopped a rather battered Japanese car on the gravel verge opposite me and started studying a map. After a minute or so, he got out and came over to me. It was so nice to see a normal human being again, after the 20-minute bath of bilge I had just been through, that I could almost have hugged him. In a real 'any poppadoms?' accent, he said, 'Is it far to the Bridge?'

'Five or six miles,' I said.

'Oh well! I've time to go up north then.'

There was a split second's hesitation then he gestured round about at the hills and said, almost as an afterthought, 'Is it all like this?'

'More or less,' I replied.

'Oh well, I go straight back then,' he said with a laugh. Without further ado, he hopped over to his car, made a rapid U-turn, gave me a cheery wave and motored off in the direction of Kyleakin. I waved back almost until he had disappeared from sight, absurdly moved to have re-established contact with the human race.

Twenty-four hours later I dropped anchor in the little bay on Eilean Ban, the island on which the north leg of the Skye Bridge stands. It used to be the site of a lighthouse and it was in the two conjoined lighthouse keepers' cottages that Gavin Maxwell had his last residence. Unfortunately, by the time I visited, the island was under threat of purchase by the Born Free Foundation who planned, I had learned from their *Campaign News*, to make it a sanctuary for otters and to link it to Kyleakin with closed-circuit television so that bored tourists could spend a few minutes of their holiday prying into the otters' world.

I was curious about Maxwell, who seems to me a very interesting character. When I got up to the house by the interior, which had clearly been laid out by somebody with a sense of style. The main sitting room runs the length of both cottages and is dramatically proportioned to emphasise the entrance of anyone arriving from outside. The master bathroom was also intriguing, having a huge, nine-foot long mirror running behind the bath. But the main fact that becomes obvious from a visit is that the island would have been, in the days before the Bridge was built and the vegetation went wild, something of a stage. Most of the inhabitants of Kyleakin, many in Kyle, and the crew of any boat passing by, would have had a clear view of the outdoor activities of the occupants. 'I see Mr Gavin's back in residence'; 'The Maxwell party appears to be taking breakfast on the terrace this morning.' It is just distant enough that Maxwell could pretend to be unconscious of his audience, but not so distant that he would be in any danger of being forgotten.

On a pearly, blue-grey afternoon, I weighed anchor and motored slowly east towards Loch Alsh, having timed my passage carefully on account of the very strong streams running through Kyle Rhea at the north end of the Sound of Sleat. By the time I was ready to turn south, a bit of wind had sprung up and I rounded Rubha na Caillich under sail as well as power. To my surprise, I found myself suddenly elated at the very distant sight, really little more than a smudge on the horizon, of the great rock wall of Ardnamurchan: a hint of home.

After being buffeted by the tidal race at Kyle Rhea, we dawdled down past Glenelg, finally dropping the sails and motoring, in an absolutely flat calm sea, into the open anchorage at Camusfearna, the site of the house where Maxwell wrote *Ring of Bright Water*. By then the sun was getting low and the sea beginning to turn a rich blend of 'cocktail hour' hues, from liquid peach, through mottled amber to a sort of luminous ochre.

After anchoring, I slept for an hour, then went ashore to explore. Maxwell's house was burnt to the ground in 1968, and now all that remains is a slight hump in the ground where it once stood and a large stone of remembrance, beneath which Maxwell's ashes are buried. I was amazed to see that the memorial plaque was strewn with shells and stones, obviously placed there by pilgrims who had made the long trek down the unmarked forestry road against the wishes of the unsociably proprietorial landowner, Lord Dulverton. Some of the larger stones carried inscriptions roughly etched by hand. One which was typical said, 'To Gavin Maxwell: we miss you.' Close by, next to the stream that runs into the bay, stands another memorial, this time to Edal, the otter killed in the house fire. 'Whatever joy she gave to you, give back to nature,' the plaque says – wording of course by Maxwell himself. That too was strewn with shells and stones. I had no idea that this place was a shrine.

That night two families camped by the shore. Next morning, to my amazement, I counted no less than 20 visitors between the time I first poked my head through the hatch, at about nine, and the time I raised anchor, at about noon. Many of those were walking dogs – one couple had three lashed together like a troika. Maxwell himself wrote that he destroyed his idyll by writing about it and thereby attracting far too many tourists. I wondered what the place must be like in high summer.

That afternoon, I sailed over to Isle Oronsay, the sheltered bay opposite on Skye. In doing so, I understand from Douglas Botting's biography, I would have passed the spot where Maxwell machine-gunned his basking shark. My purpose was to visit a man whose interest is in the opposite of tourism, which depends on the outside world for its prosperity. Sir Iain Noble, Bt., of Ardkinglas and Eilean Iarmain, is the founder of the increasingly well-known Gaelic College on Skye, Sabhal Mor Ostaig. He is a businessman himself and his intention is to expand the Gaelic community in the Highlands and to teach it how to do business in its native language.

Sir Iain is unusual in a number of respects. For one thing, his must be one of the only entries in *Who's Who* that lists recreations in Gaelic: 'Comhradh, beul-aithris is ceol le deagh chompanaich' – no translation is given. For another, few people can have been as involved in the establishment of so many important financial operations in Scotland in recent years. He started in the late 1960s with the merchant bank, Noble, Grossart, then went on to Seaforth Maritime, Lennox Oil, the Independent Insurance Group, Noble & Co and now Adam & Co, the private bankers. In 1972 he bought the 22,000 acre Eilean Iarmain estate, which extends from Isle Oronsay to Broadford. After that he turned his attention to the economic problems of the west Highlands. His solution to poverty has been unconventional: to promote a language.

While he munched a scallop shell full of grilled cheese on crab, and we both drank some of his own, widely-marketed 'Gaelic' whisky, Sir Iain told me the reasoning behind this approach. 'You can rationalise it,' he said between forkfuls, 'but the best evidence is empirical. Wherever in the world there is a dying language, there is always a dying culture. I don't know of any exceptions. And equally where the language is thriving, you get prosperity.'

'Is it not the other way round?' I asked. 'When you get prosperity, the language thrives?'

'Not necessarily. The one that caught my attention was the Faroe Islands. There the language was almost underground, and that was turned around completely, and it was accompanied by an incredible surge in prosperity, and also an increase in population. In the eighteenth century, the population of Skye was 24,000 and the Faroes was 7000. By 1900 the population of Skye had dropped and that of the Faroes doubled. By 1970, the population of Skye had sunk to 7000 and that of the Faroes risen to more than 40,000. They have a very high standard of living, in a very unpromising landscape, yet they speak nothing but Faroese.'

Sabhal Mor Ostaig's brochure makes the linkage which Sir Iain told me about: 'Promoting Enterprise, Enhancing Identity, Strengthening Community'. The essential aim is to put the community in a position where it can take control of its own destiny. Apart from the language courses, students at the College study business administration, information technology, rural development, television technology and the like, but *all in Gaelic.* From a shaky start, the College now has a solid 60 full-time students, and is about to expand dramatically when it becomes a key campus in the dispersed University of the Highlands and Islands.

Before leaving Skye, and seeing the weather was still so balmy, I decided I would hike the five miles or so down to Sabhal Mor Ostaig. It is a very pleasant journey down the east coast of Sleat as it is well populated and comparatively heavily wooded. The road winds up away from the sea for a bit, then drops down to where the College stands amongst old oak-woods. It consists of some large restored farm buildings, to which have been added some modern structures. It is an attractively laid out and obviously well-equipped place.

I was early for my appointment with the Director, Norman Gillies, so I retired to the library to wait in comfort. While reading a book in a window seat, I noticed through the corner of my eye a tall American with a Kaiser Bill moustache – he turned out to be from Tennessee – chatting to the librarian in slightly halting Gaelic. The librarian was clearly not getting whatever point it was the American was making and she regularly butted in with suggested phrases which he would then repeat. But he was doing quite well and I was full of admiration since I don't imagine there is much colloquial Gaelic spoken around Memphis and Nashville. Then he stumbled. There was something which he clearly did not have the ghost of an idea of how to express, probably because it is not the sort of thought that is commonly expressed in Gaelic, and the conversation ended in shared laughter as he blurted out exasperatedly in English, 'I *have* to have it *tamaarrow.*'

Norman Gillies looked like a businessman, but he was immediately friendly and, after giving me practical details about the College, was happy to answer my main question which was, why? What is the use of the Gaelic language for business people?

'I think it's quite simple,' he said. 'My upbringing was a Gaelic one, and yet I wanted to go into business. I do not want to have to divorce myself from my roots in order to do that. Gaelic is a very important part of what I am, who my father was, and who my grandfather was. What's the use of it? What's the use of me? It informs my world. Part of the reason why Gaelic is dying out is that it was always the fact that you went away to get educated, and most people just didn't come back. There were few economically active young people. So what we were trying to do here in the first instance, with business studies, was to make it possible for such people to stay within the community and benefit the community.'

It was a shock to be told how recent the Gaelic revival is. It was only in 1985 that schools were permitted to use Gaelic as a teaching medium and only in 1990 that the Broadcasting Act formally permitted the establishment of properly funded Gaelic programming.

'What sort of people do you get as students?' I asked.

'I think when we first opened up,' Norman said, 'it was the native Gaelic speakers who would come. Now we have people from all over Scotland, half of them with little or no Gaelic. Many want to work in Gaelic television.'

'Any people from abroad?' I asked, thinking about the man from Tennessee.

'There is an interest in Gaelic from America and Canada,' he said. 'And elsewhere in the world, too. Surprisingly, the Germans seem very interested in Gaelic. We've even had a student from Alloa.'

I got a lift back up to the boat with a member of the College staff. The evening was clear and cold. The forecast talked of a high pressure system over the Norwegian sea and a low off the south of England. That explained the cloudless easterlies, though not the daytime warmth. It was good weather to move, and in the morning, after lugging my camera and tripod up to the Isle Oronsay light to take pictures of the sun rising in a dramatic flush of orange over Loch Hourn, I ate, stowed, raised the anchor and sailed out, bound for Eigg. I was very curious to see at first hand that very different example of an island community trying to take control of its own destiny.

13

HOMEWARD BOUND: EIGG, MULL, MORVERN AND LORNE

THE BALMY WEATHER HELD AS I sailed slowly down the Sound of Sleat at a gentle three knots or so, with Eigg directly on the bow. The wind stayed in the east, though slowly dying. Soon the boat was rolling and yawing, the sails slatting and the autohelm working too hard. For a while I read in the sunshine, then simply sat and dozed, with my trousers rolled up and my shoes off. By the time I had Mallaig on the beam, even though it was three miles off, the sea was so still that I could hear the tannoy on the ferry which was leaving the harbour as the recorded safety announcement was replayed.

As that finished, I was startled to hear, in the far distance, a steam whistle, then: CHUFF-chuff-chuff-chuff, CHUFF-chuff-chuff-chuff, CHUFF-chuff-chuff-chuff. Through the glasses I could just make out the west Highland express, drawing half a dozen antique Pullman coaches as it pounded up the line above the white sands of Morar.

At seven o'clock that evening I anchored in 12 feet of water off the Eigg pier. The sky was still completely clear but a chilly clip of wind had sprung up. The anchorage was deserted and not a soul moved on the island. The castellated roof-line of the tea shop – or should I say 'Tea Shoppe', since the effect is consciously 'Olde England'? – stood out crisply against the cold colours of the gloaming, which changed from a light, electric blue on the horizon to a dark gunmetal overhead. Towering above the Tea Shoppe was the proud profile of the Sgurr of Eigg. The huge firs and pines of the policy woodlands swayed powerfully in the wind. The occasional fierce gust would thrash suddenly through the rhododendrons like a cat fight.

Next morning I got up early with the idea of walking up to the plateau behind the big house and taking a photograph of the first blush of dawn light on the Sgurr. This I did, and my picture came out suffused with a lovely warm glow. In the morning calm I wandered down through the woods to have a look at the owner's residence. It was built in 1927 by the Runciman family who were millionaire shipowners from Tyneside. It is an imitation Tuscan villa: a striking structure, being painted a very light, yeasty yellow with white detailing. Because of its raised situation above the lawns and trees to the east, it gets all the morning sunlight.

At the time of my visit, the island was owned by the eccentric German artist, Marlin Eckhart Maruma, and since he was unlikely to put in a sudden appearance, I thought the coast would probably be clear for an internal inspection. I found an unlocked window, hopped over the sill and was soon wandering round the largely empty rooms. The house was filled with a golden glow, the colour of buttered toast, and I wondered how the previous owner, Keith Schellenberg, could have sold such a property voluntarily. Though it was obvious that there was wet rot, dry rot, rising damp and all the other ills an unlived-in house is heir to, particularly if it has a flat roof, I could not help thinking it one of the loveliest homes I have been in. It being by now about eight o'clock, I thought I would move in temporarily – to the lavatory. I found a copy of *Churchill by His Contemporaries* on a shelf in a bedroom and settled down for a peaceful half hour with the old war-hero in the silent, evacuated mansion.

On my way back down to the boat for breakfast, I happened to meet the gardener, Neil Robertson, who told me about the planned buy-out of the island by the residents. Neil said that an application for funding was going in to the National Heritage Memorial Fund next week. Well, actually it was tomorrow, he said. 'No it's today. It's Friday today, isn't it?' I was no surer than he was. He told me that he had shown round the two potential buyers whom Farhad Vladi, the international island broker who was handling the sale, had managed to rustle up. Both were from England and the first took no further interest after Neil explained the politics of the island to him. The second was not put off by the politics so Neil described in detail the condition of the big house, adding that the islanders had already an estimate of over £100,000 to repair it, an estimate which would be considerably exceeded if contractors from the mainland were to be employed.

The politics of the island of Eigg have become notorious in the Highlands.[1] The one sight I really wanted to see was the charred remains of Keith Schellenberg's 1927 Rolls Royce Phantom I which had been burnt out in mysterious circumstances one windy, winter night two years earlier. Since it appeared that

---

[1] Two books have been written about the island in recent years, and they attack the problem from completely different angles. *Eigg* by Judy Urquhart, Canongate, Edinburgh 1987, is an attractively presented book which tells the story of the island from an essentially lairdish point of view. Ms Urquhart was related to Schellenberg by marriage and, like most lairdophiles, is more interested in ancient lore than modern politics. The book is excellent on the pre-twentieth century history, but very sketchy on anything remotely contemporary. *Eigg, the Story of an Island* by Camille Dressler, Polygon, Edinburgh 1998, is good on all aspects of the history of the island but outstanding on recent times. The last quarter of the book is devoted to the post-Second World War period. Ms Dressler is a Frenchwoman, who has been resident on the island since the early 1980s, and her book is well furnished with footnotes, references and bibliography. As between the two books, I would say only that somehow the Frenchwoman's conveys a warmth of feeling for the island which is absent from the Scotswoman's, for all her politeness. Also it is more authoritative. Its flaw is that the author is a lairdophobe. She tells the story of the controversial last 15 years solely from the residents' point of view.

Schellenberg's will to continue owning the island had been broken by that act of what everybody seems to take as arson, the wreckage could be classed as an important historical monument. There was irony about it, too, as Judy Urquhart notes in her book. In 1975 Schellenberg nearly bought the island of Gigha, instead of Eigg. But he plumped for Eigg because, as he said, 'It was more savage.'[2] He now lives on Kintyre right opposite Gigha.

Unfortunately, by September 1996, the wreck had been moved, and there was nothing left but char marks on the concrete next to the Tea Shoppe. So instead of pursuing historical research, I helped the men of the island unload the flit boat, the *Ulva*, which had just docked with the weekly supplies from Arisaig. Everything was tractored up to the shop in the middle of the island. We all followed in a selection of the more or less – usually less – roadworthy vehicles which are the joy of any island where road tax is not levied. Everyone helped the two girls who run the shop unload the trailer and stack the produce.

By way of encouragement to our labours the girls gave us each a can of Export, which we quaffed while we worked. Then, having finished, we were given another couple of cans each, which we took out onto the gravel lot between the shop and the road. We found milk crates and dustbins and sat down in the sunshine for an impromptu roadside ceilidh, which I almost ruined by asking if I might take a photograph – I forgot that it was likely that several of the participants would want to be careful that no record should survive of their being there, doing what they were doing, at this particular moment in the week. But my indiscretion was taken in good part, and the party broke up an hour or so later in a high good humour.

For myself I wandered over to Cleadale, the crofting area on the north-west of the island, where Maggie Fyffe, the moving spirit behind the island buy-out project lives in what many people would think of as paradise. The slopes above Cleadale were bathed in warm, early afternoon sunshine. The mountainous ridge Beinne Bhuidhe rears up from sea-level to nearly 1400 feet behind the township, sheltering the croft-lands which run down to the Bay of Laig and the 'singing' sands of Camus Sgiotaig. Rum is less than five miles away to the west and the Skye Cuillin hover, jagged and dramatic, in the distance to the north.

The road winds down through heather and bracken to fertile-looking fields. Maggie's house stands high above them, halfway down the descent, in a litter of logs, trees, agricultural implements and the homely detritus of a residence in which no one feels the need to keep up appearances. Inside the cosily renovated croft house, we sat at a huge table while her daughter worked at a computer in an adjoining room, logging donations to the buy-out appeal which had been launched a month before. Maggie is a large, jolly lady from Lancashire who has a rasping, staccato laugh. She gave me a mug of coffee and asked with a smile what I wanted to know about the appeal.

'Just two things,' I said. 'The first one is this: there are approximately 20 families living on this very beautiful island, and you are asking the National

---

2 *Eigg* Urquhart, p. 153

Heritage Memorial Fund – in other words the public purse – for £1 million to support your buy-out of the island from Maruma. Can you tell me how you justify this raid on public funds?'

'First off, Scottish Wildlife Trust, who are leading the buy-out having had a Reserve established here for over ten years now, think it's worth preserving from an ecological point of view,' Maggie said. 'Then the people who live here obviously think they could do something with the island, and of the thousands of people who visit the place every year, lots of them think it's worth supporting.'

Maggie told me the appeal had already taken £20,000, which was quite a sum, but insignificant in terms of the final goal. Maruma was advertising the island for £2 million, though the islanders felt sure he would not get that much for it.

'By my calculation,' I said, 'you are asking for £50,000 per household. Why should you be given that money rather than, say, the homeless people in Glasgow?'

'It's important,' Maggie said.

'What do you mean when you say it is "important"?'

'It's not just from the point of view of people who live here, although that's obviously important also. Most people normally have the right to live where they like.'

'How is the change of ownership going to threaten your habitation here?' I asked.

'People do not have security of tenure because they have not paid any rent, at Maruma's request.' Maggie did not say that she and her husband actually own their home, as many others do.

'Is the battle primarily about security of tenure?' I asked.

'That's one issue,' she said. 'You've got to have security before you can put money into the place.'

'So, you are asking for £50,000 per family in order that your leases can be made more secure, and you can then raise more money from elsewhere. What would you say to somebody living in cardboard city who says that that is inequitable, and that all you are really doing is having a public appeal, under charitable auspices, on the back of public sentimentality about the Highlands and Islands, in order to secure your own present high standard of living?'

'I wouldn't call it a high standard of living,' Maggie said.

'In terms of amenity,' I said, 'I would call it very high – a better view here than the Broomielaw.'

'I know, I know, but everyone here's living practically on the breadline.'

'But you chose to live here, and now you're wanting well-disposed people to give you money because you would like to continue living in the location of your choice, a location which would probably be their choice too.'

'Possibly, and a lot of them would like to have access to it as a holiday destination,' she said.

'So is your pitch to these people that you could secure Eigg as a holiday refuge, while a new laird might withdraw it from the holiday market?'

'It might be ruined.'

'How?'

'Overdeveloped, and that fits in with the environmental project. From an environmental point of view, there's a lot here.'

'What is here?'

'There are conservation issues, land issues, whatever; birds, fishes, and so on,' she said.

'But there's all that on Rum, just over the water,' I said, pointing out of the window. 'If Eigg sank beneath the waves it would not alter the ecological balance of Scotland one bit.'

'No obviously it wouldn't. But obviously the SWT thinks it is a place worth managing.'

'Maybe it is, but that's not really the point. Forgive me for being so persistent, but many people feel that what happens on Eigg will be a model for what will happen elsewhere. The Labour Party has already hinted that it might support residents' buy-outs of Highland estates if it comes to power again. You might end up as some sort of national model for land redistribution. Eigg is important. That is why I ask, why should you people here be given £50,000 per household by the general public in order to secure your incredibly desirable – certainly on a day like this – standard of living?'

'I still don't regard it as being just us being given some money,' Maggie said.

'But that's what it will boil down to, will it not?'

'Well it will, but that's why I keep hammering on about all these other points of view. It's not just every household here saying, "We want £50,000 to keep living here." I just don't see it like that.'

'No, I'm sure you don't. But I do. Tell me why I am wrong.'

'Well, I think I've explained that already.'

'You've said that there is wildlife here; you've said that the place might be developed, in other words that your lifestyle might be ruined; and that one of the 150,000 tourist destinations in Scotland might be withdrawn from the tourist map. None of that sounds to me like a million quid's worth of reasons why you should be given all this dough.'

'OK, so we're asking for public money, but what we're saying is we can either sit here, shut up, and make do with whatever another private owner does with the island, or we can fight the system.'

'But you're using the system to fight it. In a sense, the system is fighting itself. There's a sort of civil war going on within the system. A system divided against itself cannot stand, so it gives money to Eigg.'

Maggie laughed, 'I suppose you're right, yeah.' She got up to make us both another mug of coffee.

Once she had sat down again and rolled herself another cigarette, I put to her my second question. 'Assuming your plan works, what are you going to do with the island? What are your plans for the future?'

'Well,' she said slowly, 'a variety of things. The Highland Forum talk of having workshops here –'

'Sorry to interrupt,' I said, 'but what is a "workshop"? I know what a *workshop* is – I worked in one for years – but what is a "workshop" in your terms?'

'As opposed to having one of these great, big, public meetings, the idea is to create smaller meetings, where everybody can say what their ideal wish-list is, what they see as the most important. We've had loads of them already, which was lucky because when the Highland Regional Council gave us a big map of Eigg and invited people to put on it what they wanted to see on the island, we'd actually done all the preparation for that. So what we'd done in our workshops actually ties in with what we're trying to link in with, and what the Council are actually able to help with. What came out of the workshops and what went into the general plan for the island is all very small-scale stuff. For example, there's no WCs for visitors, or a hall for the residents to use, or facilities for groups of people to stay the night.'

'You mean there's no hotel?'

'Yeah.'

'Can't your visitors camp?' I asked.

'They can,' Maggie said, 'but not everyone wants to. It won't be anything grand. And we want to do something about the farming.'

'What's the point in farming in a world of surpluses and intervention stores? Why bother, why not turn the island into a nature reserve, or a nudist colony?'

'You've come to the wrong person to ask that,' she said, laughing heartily.

'So your aims are – have I got this right? – to have a lavatory, a hostel, a community hall and a resuscitated farm. Anything else?'

'To market Eigg as a whole, as opposed to –'

'*Market* it? How do you mean?'

'Well, it would make a lot more sense to advertise Eigg as a complete entity.'

'So you want more visitors?'

'Slightly increase it, not millions of people.'

I harrumphed sceptically. 'So that all the tourists without initiative would come here, rather than just the adventurous people.'

'Ummmmm, no, that's certainly not what we are trying to do.'

'I'm sure it's not, but in reality that is the effect of making tourism easy. You'll get the day trippers, the island baggers, the crisp-packet leavers – all of whom, by the way, spend very little money.'

'We get that anyway.'

'All right, so the tea-room will do a little better. So let's look at it again: *tourism*, lavatory, hostel, community hall and farm. Anything else? You haven't got any grand plan? There's no big project?'

'No. We want to be able to keep the people on the island, and possibly bring back some of the folk who have left over the years.'

'If you do get hold of the island, would you make any of the 7500 acres available to new settlers?'

'That's on the list, but it's quite a long way down, because you have to get everybody to agree.'[3]

'So what are you going to export? You've got an island here, lots of things come in, from the telephone service bringing appeal donations, to the tobacco you're smoking and the coffee I've been happily drinking. What are you going to export to pay for all this? What's the big income earner? Or are you going to be a permanently dependent community?'

'The farmer's going to run more sheep, and cattle.'

'Nobody's doing boatbuilding, or remote computing, or anything like that? There's no industry?'

'No, there isn't.'

'So am I right in saying that your request for a million pounds from the public wealth of Great Britain cannot be justified on the ground that it will act as capital for productive economic activity?' Maggie looked at me darkly. 'I am not suggesting that you are acting fraudulently. I am just trying to find out how you get round the objection that in the end all you are asking for is a donation to your own personal lifestyle?'

'I suppose if you put it like that,' she said, 'then that is the way it is. But my reason for getting involved is that I would fight any injustice that I saw.'

'What injustice do you see?'

'That people are being messed about by one person who chooses to buy an island as a toy.'

'Why shouldn't he do that?'

'Because I think it is immoral.'

'Why?'

'It just is.'

'What do you mean by "immoral"?'

'In that the coffee you are drinking, rightly or wrongly, I buy from Café Direct. I try very hard not to buy any Nestlé's products because I think they exploit people. You just fight injustice in whatever way you can.'

'Yes, I understand,' I said, not really understanding, but this seemed to be getting off the subject. 'You want money not because of what you plan to make of the island, but simply because Eigg is special *per se* and it would be unjust to treat it as any other piece of real estate?'

---

3 Postscript: Now that the Isle of Eigg Heritage Trust (control: residents 50 per cent, SWT 25 per cent, Highland Region 25 per cent) owns the island, they have complete power over who may and may not live there. On 24 August 1998 the *Herald* reported that they had ejected a potential settler who had travelled from England, even though Maggie Fyffe was quoted as saying, 'There are several old houses on the island that need doing up.' This made a mockery of her claim in the interview that 'most people normally have the right to live where they like.' However, the islanders did make room for a Trust-employed Project Officer (salary £18,000 per annum) who would live on Eigg and 'co-ordinate funding applications'. More than 30 applications to live on the island have been turned down since the buy-out went ahead. The result of the Trust's policy has been that whereas under Schellenberg the island's population doubled, under the residents' control it has continued to stagnate.

'Yes.'

'So what is it that is so special about Eigg?' I asked.

Maggie described how nice a place it is to live in.

'So because you have got a high standard of environmental amenity,' I said, 'and a consequent lack of employment opportunity, you want the public to preserve the amenity for your benefit and cushion you from the effects of the employment problem?'

Maggie laughed, exasperated by my intractability. 'It's linking it to people who live here and linking it to all the people who visit here,' she said. 'Everybody loves it in the summer when all these people come and visit here because it is such a special place. That opportunity should be open to everybody.'

'To come and visit?'

'Yes. '

'But Schellenberg didn't put anybody off, nor does Maruma.'

'But it has become less and less pleasant to stay in.'

'But you don't know the pre-Schellenberg regime do you?'

'No.'

'By the way, who set fire to his Rolls-Royce? I don't want a name. I am just curious: was it an islander, a mainlander with a grudge, or an accident?'

Suddenly the chatty mood evaporated. 'That will remain Eigg's best-kept secret,' Maggie said. 'Nobody'll ever find out.'

To skip ahead a few days: while I was anchored off the mainland, I decided to take a day trip down to see Schellenberg at his new estate at Killean, near Tayinloan, just over the water from the island of Gigha. I wanted to get his side of this extraordinary story. Schellenberg is an ebullient, fit-looking Yorkshireman in his late 60s. He holds himself out as a lad of mettle: once a serious sportsman and always an entertaining gentleman. But for some reason I could not put my finger on, there was a hint of anxiety in his manner.

'My question to Maggie Fyffe,' I said, 'was why should the public stump up £50,000 per household to give them security of tenure?'

'But who hasn't got security of tenure?' Schellenberg asked.

'That's what they all say, not one of them has.'

'*This is the thing!*' he said, clasping his forehead like an exasperated schoolmaster. 'This is the thing! Who hasn't got it? All the people you've talked to have got their own land and their own houses, in many cases provided by 90 per cent improvement grants. This is a wonderful image, the poor old people living on the shore. It is complete and utter rubbish.'

I spent a most enjoyable afternoon down at Killean, during the course of which I saw the charred chassis of the Rolls Royce, which Schellenberg keeps close to his new front door. We discussed the people on Eigg, why the police had, as he saw it, done so little to find the alleged automotive arsonist(s) and what the motives might be for the Highland Regional Council's very public involvement in the proposed residents' buy-out.

'I think the Highland Region is an embryonic totalitarian state,' Schellenberg said. 'I think Argyll and the southern isles may not get the disease. There's far more basis for civilisation down here. The reason the Campbells used to be against the MacDonalds was to me the same sort of reason: they wanted the islands run by somebody who actually believed in a form of civilisation.'

Maggie had told me that to begin with she and most of the people on Eigg had found 'Schelly', as they called him, both charming and at a conceptual level sympathetic. 'His ideas didn't clash with people here,' she had said. 'He was into setting up small-scale stuff and that.' Among many other acts of personal kindness, he paid the school fees for the elder son of the island's farmer, Colin Carr, for four years at Aberlour and Gordonstoun. Schellenberg was far from being the archetypal swinish laird. It was just that nobody on the island could work with him over the long haul because they felt he had no understanding of their practical problems. My observation was that he had no understanding of his own practical problems either. By the time afternoon was melting into evening, we were still sitting in the elegant circular study of Killean House chatting away, but without having got any closer to a clear view of the politics of Eigg. He offered me a dram, then another dram, and then dinner and finally he gave me a very comfortable bed for the night.

Next morning, I said to my host over breakfast that I thought the best thing from his point of view would be if I were to take down a brief statement of his position – and I stressed the word 'brief' – which I could use in this book to balance the residents' view.

'My problem is that I simply do not have the time,' Schellenberg said, looking at his watch. 'It's nine o'clock now, and I have to get a boat up from the shore; I have to write to the Scottish Office about forestry; and apart from that I have an estate to run. When you are trying to make an estate pay, without taking a penny in grants from the government, you simply do not have the time for anything else.'

'It'll only take five minutes, literally,' I said. 'Then I'll be down the road.'

'But you have no idea what it means to run an estate like this,' he said, helping himself to another slice of toast. 'I have to do everything myself. You say it will only take five minutes. But I simply do not have time to spare for this sort of thing.'

Schellenberg then launched into an extended description of his organisational plight. It was after eleven o'clock before we rose from the breakfast table, he still explaining why he could not find five minutes to make a statement. Then he took me to see some of his other antique vehicles which I was fascinated to see. It was nearly noon before I finally said that if I did not break off now I would not have time to get down to catch the bus back to the boat. 'Don't worry, I'll run you into Tayinloan,' he said. I was quite happy to walk, but nothing I could say would prevent him from getting his car out and driving me down to the bus stop, which I reached at 12.30, three and a half hours after we started discussing why he could not find five minutes to make a statement on the situation in Eigg.

It was clear why the people on the island had found their landlord impossible to work with, for all his generosity and his real, though curiously boyish, charm. Thinking about all this on the way back to the boat, it occurred to me not just that Schellenberg was something of an egotist, which was obvious, but also that he was really quite lonely. Could it have been that he filled Eigg with people partly because he wanted more friends about?

I sailed from Eigg on another clear autumnal day, with a healthy breeze coming from the north. By now I was tired of travelling and very keen to get back home. The exceptional weather was a help, but it did not remove the feeling that I had been away too long. I spent a cheery evening in the Mishnish in Tobermory, then pushed on down the Sound of Mull to Loch Aline, where I had an appointment with the warden of Rahoy Hills, a Scottish Wildlife Trust Reserve on the edge of the Ardtornish Estate.

Donald Kennedy is an interesting, friendly man, who comes from the Oban area but has chosen to sequester himself in the wilderness of Morvern. After a quick drive round, we retired to the pub where Donald put to me an interesting paradox about wildlife reserves.

Apparently the Rahoy Hills Reserve was originally declared because of the unusually rich assemblage of Arctic-Alpine plants which live on the cliffs and scree close to the summits. They are very delicate organisms and do not take kindly to being trampled on. Before the Reserve was declared hardly anybody visited this particular piece of ground. Though Morvern has always attracted quite a lot of walkers, they dispersed throughout the vast area of the hinterland and did no significant damage to any particular spot. But now that everyone is aware, from SWT advertising, that the plant communities on the Reserve are of 'national importance' most people visiting this part of the world want, not unnaturally, to take a look at them. As a result, the Reserve is visited by about 600 walkers per annum. This is not a large number, but the plant communities are fragile. Even light visitor pressure is enough to damage them. So, if the species the Reserve exists to protect are not to be wholly destroyed, there are only two options: first, restrict access to Rahoy Hills, which would be deeply unpopular with ramblers and hillwalkers, arguably illegal and would do immense harm to the SWT's public image, or abolish the Reserve and hope it is not too long before everyone has forgotten that it ever existed.

The next day I crossed over to Fishnish to keep my last appointment, with a Mull farmer called Bert Leitch, who had recently made something of a name for himself by threatening, on BBC television, to shoot any sea eagles he saw taking his lambs unless action was taken to curb the nuisance. As I mentioned in connection with Rum, sea eagles were reintroduced to Scotland by the NCC in 1975. While the birds stayed on or near Rum, where they were released, nobody minded. But now the birds have colonised places like Skye and Mull, where they take lambs, the project has become highly controversial.

The sea eagle reintroduction is retrospectively justified by SNH, who inherited the programme from the NCC, and the RSPB, who now manage it for SNH, on the grounds of 'scientific' conservation. In fact, the decision was taken in 1975 for public relations reasons. The man who masterminded the project was Dr John Morton Boyd, the biographer of Fraser Darling and Director for Scotland of the Nature Conservancy Council from 1970 to 1985. It was he who persuaded both the Secretary of State for Scotland and the governing council of the NCC of the merits of the idea. His reasoning was clear:

> 'I felt that nature conservation needed a kind of convincing demonstration of the technology of wildlife management . . . [We wanted to] demonstrate to the general public an outstanding achievement in nature conservation which was simple to understand and which in its conception was legitimate because it was part of our heritage. We had been looking for so many years for something really outstanding. We were misunderstood, people did not really appreciate what we were trying to do. Here was something that could be understood by the common man in the street. This would be wildlife management on a world scale that the public would appreciate if it was presented that way.'[4]

Young birds were brought from Norway and the attempt was made to teach them to live off seabirds. But that failed and they now eat, *inter alia*, Bert Leitch's lambs. I sat in Bert's van on the rain-splashed slipway at Fishnish, while he explained that neither he nor any of his neighbours has any complaint against the golden eagles, which they have always lived with and which are not capable of taking large prey on the wing. But the sea eagle is a much bigger bird and known to do so.

Bert's main complaint, however, was not the actual livestock losses, but the arrogant, contemptuous way in which the nature bureaucracy refused to consider the Mull farmers' views on the reintroduction. People are a nuisance in the great outdoor laboratory. The RSPB, as managers of the project, have not helped matters by making a spectacularly inept choice of officer to try to pacify the restless natives.

'Roger Broad has no credibility as far as I am concerned' Bert said, referring to the Project Manager. 'He is obsessive as far as these birds are concerned, which is one of the problems. He has tunnel vision. The RSPB are far too narrow minded. They're not like the John Muir Trust who go along with the people where they can, and come to compromises. But with the RSPB it's almost like they're God: *you'll* do as *we* say.'

As so often, the problem came back to secrecy. 'Both SNH and the RSPB conceal things from us,' Bert said. 'We've had so many evasions and half-truths over the years that we just cannot have any confidence in them anymore.'[5]

Echoing Donald Kennedy, Bert also told me about the use which the RSPB is

---

4   Interview with the author, 7 May 1998. Perhaps predictably, Magnus Magnusson, the first Chairman of SNH, discusses in his book on Rum the reintroduction of sea eagles without any mention of the public relations goals which drove the project in the beginning. His wholly misleading account gives the impression that the bird was brought back to Scotland solely for nature conservation reasons.

trying to make of the presence of the sea eagles on Mull. 'I'm worried about this eco-tourism that they're starting to promote. Just now it's very free and easy. People come and go, and if you want to walk the hills, nobody minds. But if you're going to start getting organised parties, coming to see the sea eagles and the like, we're going to end up getting stuff lost. And the birds'll move away, and plants will get damaged.'

However the most unpleasant aspect of the presence of sea eagles on Mull has been the arrival of egg thieves. 'This year there were two nests definitely robbed,' Bert said, 'possibly a third. It has certainly brought a kind of undesirable element into the island, which we had never heard of before.'

'Where do these people come from?' I asked.

'South of the border,' he said, confirming the point Paul Boyer had made to me on North Uist. 'I don't like the birds, but I don't like that either.'

Bert snorted with disgust when I explained that the RSPB makes public relations capital from wildlife crime. I quoted from memory a passage from the Society's official history which has stuck in my mind ever since I first read it. This is the correct version:

> A good cops and robbers story sells newspapers and a good newspaper story sells the Society. A member recruited through misunderstanding, joining the RSPB because he wants all egg collectors shot and their children taken into care, is unlikely to do any harm and might even learn a thing or two. The Society has learned well the art of deploring publicity that it considers wide of the mark or inappropriate, while milking that publicity for all it is worth.[6]

In a sluicing, autumnal downpour I rowed back out to *Sylvia B* thinking how desperately sad it is the way the Highlands are becoming a battleground for opportunists and cynics from other parts of Britain. The thought that history might simply be repeating itself, that this was the immemorial fate of the area since the destruction of its independence in the fifteenth century, was little comfort. I ate a moody dinner by lamplight and turned in early.

---

5   I encountered Broad's evasiveness myself when, after returning home, I asked him for the Species Action Plan for the chough, another bird I had discussed with Clive Mackay on Tiree. Broad replied that he could not release the document since the Plan had been developed in conjunction with SNH and the Joint Nature Conservation Committee. I wrote to both bodies, asking for their clearance for release of the document. Both said they had no objection. I then wrote to Broad, copying the two letters I had received, saying his condition had now been fulfilled, and could I see the Plan? On 2 May 1997, he wrote to me very briefly saying, 'You will understand that I cannot comply with your request. Please note that I consider this correspondence is closed.'

6   *For Love of Birds*, Tony Samstag, RSPB, Sandy 1989, p. 124. This is a form of 'below the line' marketing which is widely used by non-commercial 'hearts-and-minds' organisations, from Greenpeace to the IRA. The occupation of the Brent Spar did wonders for the Greenpeace cash flow in 1995. Twenty years before that, Martin McGuinness famously said, 'Good operations are the best recruiting sergeant.'

Next morning I sailed for Oban under a grey and occasionally leaking sky. At least there was some wind, but it was coming from the south, which meant a lot of spray in the cockpit. It really was time to get home. Looking back at Mull I realised with sadness that, for the first time on this trip, I had no curiosity about an island I was sailing past. Somehow the shadow of militant conservationism seemed to have robbed the place of its charm.

In Oban I cheered myself up by indulging in another curry. Afterwards I went for a dram to an old haunt, the Oban Inn, where I bumped into two friends who are quite senior in 'the Forestry'. As the rain splashed in brightly-lit puddles in the streets, we discussed the problem of conservationism in the Highlands. Why has something so beautiful and wise in theory turned to dust and ashes in practice?

Jim, a forthright Scotsman, was of the opinion that it all came down to the peculiar character of the people who idealised nature, but from an emotionally safe distance. He gave the example of modern wildlife magazines which, he said, have evolved into a form of non-erotic pornography. Mother Nature is stripped of her modesty and exposed to the vulgar gaze. It is all cold, glossy, exploitative and lascivious. You may look but you'd better not touch. They are designed for what he called the dirty anorak wing of the bird-table-owning class.

John, an astute Englishman who is the senior of the two, took a thoughtful sip of his drink. His explanation was completely different. 'The fact is that in Scotland today we have a sort of one-party state,' he said. 'There is only one view of conservation issues, whether it is birds, which I don't know much about, or forestry which I know quite a lot about. This country is run by the Scottish Office so that, at a political level, it is not government and opposition, it's just insiders and outsiders, like a medieval court. It's not exactly democratic. Groups with serious lobbying power find it very easy to get the inside track, whereas others, like your crofters, find it almost impossible. The result is that power devolves to careerists, like Jim and me, who have wives, children and mortgages and work for the quangos and the big charities. Local communities didn't fight to begin with, when they might have had some effect, because they trusted us. Now we're solidly entrenched, they don't fight because they know it is hopeless. We can do more or less what we like, or should I say, what Edinburgh likes. The Scottish Office loves it.'

We ordered more drinks and I made the provocative point that in another country at another time both nature conservation and forestry had been popular concerns of a well-known authoritarian regime.[7] Himmler had conducted

---

7   See *The Environment Movement in Germany: Prophets and Pioneers 1871–1971* Raymond Dominick, Indiana University Press, Bloomington 1992: 'By 1939 at least 59 per cent of nature conservationists . . . had enlisted in the Nazi party, compared to roughly 10 per cent of all adult males . . . This indication that conservationists were overrepresented in the Nazi movement is heightened by evidence that among German professionals of all kinds, foresters had the second highest rate of participation in Hitler's party, lagging only behind veterinarians.' (p. 113)

experiments with homeopathic medicine at Dachau, where the SS ran a very profitable herb garden. Despite his compulsion to manage, order and manipulate, Himmler was a vegetarian, an animal-lover and a reader of the *Bhagavad-Gita*. Likewise Göring, the Reich Master of Forests and the Hunt, was a very serious wildlife conservationist. He had a twin-track approach: to create nature reserves and to punish wildlife crime. He pulled the eagle back from extinction, for example, by introducing the death penalty for killing one. He also established a wildlife research laboratory near Berlin, which oversaw the reintroduction of endangered species, like the otter and the beaver. He called the forest 'God's cathedral' and described his scientific culling program, gleefully but accurately, as 'conservation by rifle'. But, as the only biographer who has explored this side of Göring's character points out, 'He was capable of unparalleled callousness towards the human species, yet history shows that he introduced a tough anti-vivisection law, preceded by a broadcast warning that he would throw each and every violator into a concentration camp.'[8]

Is there a connection, I asked, between idealism and authoritarianism? Are people who do not trust others to behave as they want them to, inherently prone to ruthless compulsion in their dealings with fallen humanity? If the basic joy of life in the Hebrides is its freedom, both physical and spiritual, then the invasion of the conservationists must be the most serious threat the islands have faced since Culloden and the Clearances. All three of us were horribly conscious of the ubiquity of the nature bureaucracy in this part of the world. It was a subject too depressing to discuss. In a futile attempt to lift the gloom, we ordered another round and tried to change the subject. Twenty minutes later we did the same again. After that, my memory of the occasion rather fades.

Next morning I woke at 5.30, feeling slightly groggy, to hear the shipping forecast. The general synopsis was: 'Deep complex low, 974, moving steadily north, expected Iceland by 0700 tomorrow.' The forecast for sea area Malin was 'southerly 6 to gale 8'. High tide was at 6 a.m., which meant that if I sailed straight away I would have it with me down the sound of Kerrera and, more importantly since I intended to stop at Ardfern, through the tidal race at Cuan Sound between Seil and the north end of Luing. It was going to be a beastly day for a sail, but I know these waters well and, if I could possibly help it, I did not want to have to idle away a day or two in Oban till the gale blew itself out. I decided to go.

It *was* a beastly day for a sail. I reefed the main and rigged the working jib. *Sylvia B* is a brave little boat and we bashed and plunged into a short but steep head-sea. The wind was slightly east of south so that, close-hauled but without having to tack, we could just about make the heading down to Easdale. By then conditions would have been more accurately described as 'nasty', particularly as the strong tide that was helping us was of course ebbing into wind and producing a horrible chop. Despite being fully water-proofed, it was not long before I was

---

8   *Goring: a biography* David Irving, HarperCollins 1991, pp. 180–3

soaked from the neck to the knees and extremely cold. However, there was nothing for it but to keep going. With home coming closer as every sodden hour passed, it would have taken a hurricane to have persuaded me to turn into the safe anchorage at Puldobhrainn on the north-west end of Seil, which was my reserve plan.

By mid-morning we were past the worst. Once into Cuan Sound there was no more chop, and not too much wind in the lee of Luing. Out the other side, north-east of Shuna, the wind came back, but without the swell since the whole area is sheltered by islands and, to the south-east, the Craignish peninsula. At about lunchtime, I finally dropped anchor in Lunga Bay, just south of Craobh Haven. I took off my water-proofs, undressed, towelled myself down and put on clean, dry clothing. By the time I had a cup of hot soup inside me and a fat sandwich on the saloon table I felt a hundred per cent again. Such is the recuperative power of middle age.

I had a lot of pleasant social calls to pay in and around Ardfern, having lived there many years before. The first thing I discovered on going ashore was that on the following evening, Saturday, there was to be a birthday 'rave' for the son of a friend of mine. Since I had never been to a rave before, and since it appeared that *tout le village* was going, from Mrs My Laird up at Lunga House to the caravan dwellers scattered all over the estate, I thought I ought to stay for the big event. Conveniently, it was to be held in a marquee which had been erected on the level grass above the pier, so if the music proved unbearable, it would only be a short row out to my cosy bunk.

For a day and a half I went walkabout, ending up having a dram with the laird, Colin Lindsay-MacDougall of Lunga, after he had kindly offered me a bath and the use of his laundry facilities. I had lived in Lunga many years before while working as the literary secretary to Mathilda, the late Dowager Duchess of Argyll, who had been a tenant of his. We discussed old times and acquaintances, including one of the more colourful characters that Mathilda used to keep up with socially, the Dowager Lady Selby who lived on the island of Shuna, just opposite Lunga. Colin said that now that Lady Selby was dead, it might be time to start telling some of the funnier stories about the old dear, whom he had known since boyhood and had always thought good fun.

One concerned an occasion when Lady Selby's very wealthy mother came to visit. Since the drink had been flowing freely for some time in Shuna Castle, it was hoped that the old lady would be so gracious as to leave a large cheque to keep the good times rolling. The house was tidied up, the grass cut and all the empty gin bottles disposed of. Lady Selby's two prep school-aged sons were dressed in their smartest school uniforms and told they must be on their best behaviour for Granny. Then Lady Selby set off for Oban to meet the train bearing the critical cheque book and its authorised signatory. Shuna being an island, the whole journey took a long time. Added to that, the train was late. Then Lady Selby thought that the prospects for a goodish-sized bung would be increased if she gave her mother a slap-up tea in a respectable hotel in Oban.

Naturally the boys back on the island soon got bored waiting, and began discussing what they might do to enter into the spirit of the occasion and help impress Granny. After a bit of thought and wandering about, one of them found to his surprise that a clump of rhododendron bushes near the back door of the castle was almost entirely filled up with a vast heap of empty gin bottles. Between them they decided that it would be nice for Granny if they were to decorate the path up from the jetty to the front door by lining it in her honour with these attractive green bottles. They set to work and by the time Granny stepped ashore from the estate launch, several hours later, they had completed their task. They proudly showed their display to the Fairy Grandmother as she set off up the path. Catastrophe! Granny took one look at the bottles, thought, 'My hat, they must be in the money these days' and put her cheque book away. Mission aborted. Boys in Coventry. Lady Selby seething thirstily for weeks afterwards.

Colin is an excellent raconteur and there were more stories in that vein before it was time to leave him to his dinner and start making my way to the rave. As I wandered down the path to the pier, in the last of the light, I saw Shuna a mile away across the Sound. While working for Mathilda I had several times visited the island, being left to wander about while she went up to take tea, and possibly gin, with Her Ladyship. It is a beautiful, unspoiled place, well wooded with birch, rowan and oak. In later years, I also knew a charming girl from Seil who worked as the teacher for Lady Selby's young grandchildren. The happy memories of Shuna began to dispel the horrible gloom that still lingered from Mull.

The rave was actually good fun. A roebuck was roasted on a spit, and the good-natured crowd spilled down to the beach, enjoying the windy but dry night. To my amazement, some of the most vigorous ravers, who thrashed away all night with glazed eyes and jerky, broken-robot movements, were a group of clean-cut young lads neatly dressed in Mid-Argyll Rugby Club jerseys. I really am getting old, I thought. The music was much as I feared, being about as melodious as a steamhammer. But I was told that was how it should be, the better for the late-night chemicals to act upon what was left of the brain after the early evening dose. I said to one lad I know that I did not particularly like 'this kind of music'. He replied, 'It's not music. It's sound.' I was told later that the bass notes could be heard at the Kilmelford Hotel, four miles away.

By 4 a.m. I had had enough. I wandered out into the night, and was met with a spectacular skyscape. The full moon was shining over the Corryvreckan, casting the vast bulk of Scarba and Jura into black shadows. A stiff breeze was whipping in from the west, chasing the scattered clouds past at an amazing rate, their billowy edges back-lit with a silvery glow. The clouds were flowing in two layers, at differing altitudes, and the continually shifting effect of moonlight and shadow was sinisterly theatrical. This was the hunter's moon, the first after the autumnal equinox and said to be the brightest of the year. The marquee was not visible from the shore, and there was not a single artificial light to be seen anywhere in the vast and coldly illuminated landscape. We could have been in the Stone Age.

The beach was empty of ravers by then, but I found a couple of other elderly refugees from the 'sound' who were sitting on the edge of the pier drinking cans of beer and admiring the wild beauty of the night. As I looked at the clouds, it occurred to me that this was 'a cavernous, a wind-picked sky', a phrase I remembered from the poem 'Sad Steps' by Philip Larkin. For the benefit of my seated friends I declaimed what I could remember of it. 'Groping back to bed after a piss/I part thick curtains, and am startled by/The rapid clouds, the moon's cleanliness . . . The moon dashes through clouds that blow/Loosely as cannon-smoke . . . High and preposterous and separate – Lozenge of Love! Medallion of art/O wolves of memory!' And then there's something about the 'far-reaching singleness of that wide stare', but the rest, I had forgotten.

We mumbled our goodnights quietly, almost reverently, in this huge, empty theatre of the sky. I padded round to the pier, slipped the painter from the ring above the steps and rowed out to the dark shape with a mast on it which rocked back and forth out on the choppy, moonlit sea. O wolves of memory!

Morning brought hail in a storm so fierce I thought for a silly, confused second after waking that the coach-roof might be smashed. Then it passed and peace descended. It was too late to sail for Islay that day, so I thought on a whim I would visit one last island, my curiosity about the private, infolded world of insular living by now largely restored.

After a slow breakfast, I started the outboard and pottered over to Shuna. For an hour or so I meandered about, looking at the woods and taking a photograph of one of the cottages encircled by a brilliant rainbow immediately after another hailstorm passed over. I also keeked in through the windows of the Castle. Everything was wrecked, the building having been abandoned after Lady Selby's death ten years before. It is a huge structure, with fake battlements and turrets at each corner. It was built in Edwardian times by an architect from down south who gave the building a flat roof which, in the Argyllshire rain, leaked intolerably. Endless internal damp and unsourceable drips finally defeated the efforts of the family to maintain the building in habitable condition – another fascinating Highland ruin.

I motored back to Lunga and walked over the hill to Ardfern, where the current Lord Selby lives, and knocked on his door. It was like starting the voyage again: everything was suddenly interesting and new. I was curious to hear his version of the gin bottles story, he having been one of the boys who placed them. But he is a chartered accountant, and I feared he might give me some facts which would ruin Colin's wonderful account. Instead I asked him how his family had come to own the island.

'I see, you want a sound-bite,' Lord Selby said briskly. 'I'm not sure I can help you, but I'll try. In 1940, the Canadian Army had been given our family house near Canterbury. At the end of the war, my mother went back. She took one look at the house and went straight up to John D. Wood's in London and said, "Sell it. Now. And by the way," she said, "if you have any idyllic islands off the west coast of Scotland for sale, I might be interested." The man behind the desk said, "Yes, my Lady, one came on the books this morning." At that time, you were entitled to fairly substantial war-damage compensation, and my mother got a government valuer in, and he said, "You are entitled to £X, but I'm afraid the government are only paying out 50 per cent of £X at the moment so we'll have to put in for double." The government paid, and with the money we bought Shuna.'

Lord Selby had grown up on the island, which he told me he regarded as 'heaven on earth – we couldn't imagine anybody wanting to live anywhere else.'

'What are your plans for the place now that your mother no longer lives there?' I asked.

'We're going to burn the big house down,' he said, matter-of-factly, 'but otherwise keep things going much the same.'

'Burn it down?' I said incredulously.

'Yes, it's not safe,' Lord Selby said briskly. 'We have Keep Out signs all over the place, but people pay no attention. We don't want some daffy tourist getting clobbered by a falling beam. We did think of renting it out to a film company so they could blow it up. We could make a couple of bob out of that. We can always use the cash. But we haven't decided yet.'

My spirits now totally restored, I raised anchor at 7 a.m. next morning for the last leg home. It was a day of breathtaking beauty and stillness. Apart from a wisp on the top of Scarba, there wasn't a cloud in the sky. The sea was like a mill-pond and, after the storm of the day before, the air was incredibly clear and sharp. From about nine o'clock I would have the ebb tide with me down the Sound of Jura, so I motored slowly out past the south end of Shuna, and then Luing. While the autohelm steered, I cooked a big breakfast down below, then ate it on deck as we passed the eastern entrance to the Corryvreckan. By the time I had Crinan abeam on the port side, I had washed up and settled down to a pint of coffee.

Soon Barnhill on Jura was visible to starboard and, like most passing yachties, I thought about George Orwell writing *1984* there. Looking at the white-painted farmhouse reposing peacefully in the mid-morning sunshine, I wondered what moral the great man would have drawn from the experiences I had had since leaving Islay two and a half months before. Orwell was a life-long believer in the ideals, but not necessarily the realities, of socialism. He famously said, 'The problem with socialism is socialists.' My feeling now was equivalent: 'the problem with conservation is conservationists.' Maybe it is a general truth that those who do most damage to the world are those who try to improve it.

By lunchtime I was off the Skervuile lighthouse, just to the north of Craighouse on Jura, and the sky was beginning to cloud over. A little wind had got up, from the south-east, and the air was turning chilly. The forecast at 1.50 p.m. warned of days of bad weather to come. I was only 20 miles from Lagavulin, and completely determined that I would get in that evening and finish for a season with all this wind and rain and cold and shitting in plastic buckets.

By mid-afternoon the tide had turned and our progress slowed dramatically.

In the distance I could see fishing boats up the Sound of Islay, and thought I could recognise some of the colours and shapes. Darkness fell not long after I had rounded Ardmore Point on the south-east tip of Islay. I could almost see Lagavulin. But the clouds were coming in thick and the wind getting up. I could picture home, with my wife and son roasting in front of a coal fire. Every mile was an effort now. With no moon, the skerries which dot the whole south coast of Islay, between Ardmore Point and Lagavulin, were invisible. There were lights on the land, but nothing could be picked out in between. This was an increasing worry. I did not want to waste time by tacking too far out to sea, but equally, I had to avoid the rocks on which from time to time I could hear, and occasionally see, surf breaking.

But I was in safer hands than I knew. During the afternoon, I learned later, messages had been coming and going between the Port Ellen fishing boats which I had sighted in the distance as I passed the southern end of the Sound of Islay. My progress was being observed.

An hour later I had the Iomallach – in English, the 'edge marker' – somewhere ahead, hopefully fine on the starboard bow. This is a rock which stands outside all the other skerries, and after which (if you are coming from the east) you can turn to starboard and steer more or less directly into Lagavulin. But the Iomallach is completely black and rises no more than ten feet out of the water. I had no chance of seeing it from more than a few yards off. I could only lay a course by dead reckoning outside it and hope I was navigating accurately. Normally, I would never attempt such a passage in the dark, but this was not 'normally'. Home was near.

Then I saw lights astern, and inside of me. It was a fishing boat coming up fast, making a similar course to my own. I could not identify it, but was comforted by the thought that it was inshore of me. But had it seen me? Suddenly I thought with a horrible dread that I had not the speed to get out of the way if it had not. I flashed a torch on the mainsail continuously, and even tried the radio briefly, though I got no answer.

Slowing noticeably, the boat drew alongside and I recognised the beamy, high-prowed shape of the *Intrepid,* out of Port Ellen. I did not know it but at that moment an argument was in progress on aboard. The crew had been on the radio all afternoon and knew I was in home waters. They had been keeping a lookout for me all evening. Having seen my lights up ahead, half a mile or so short of the Iomallach, they had slowed and steered inside to keep me safely to seaward of the rock, whose relative position they could track easily on their radar. 'Big Asher', the mate, was all for throttling back totally and escorting me round the rock. But the other two on board, John the skipper and Donald the deckhand, took the view that 'Ian knows what he's doing' and that anyway we were nearly past the dreaded rock. So they wallowed by at, for them, a sluggish six knots or so. I quickly realised what they were doing. Suddenly the throaty boom of their 300 h.p. diesel was the friendliest, most comradely sound I had ever heard. What a lovely gesture! I said so a few days later to Donald in the pub. But he would not accept the compliment, saying, 'Admit it, Ian. If you'd been in our position, you'd've done the same.'

Soon we were past the Iomallach and they were powering ahead into the darkness. For the last time on this voyage, with mingled feelings of elation and exhaustion, I pulled the helm up and eased the sheets. The lights of the distillery glowed in Lagavulin Bay. The rain came on heavily but I was past caring now. Fifteen minutes later, I sailed through the perches which mark the entrance to the Bay. I steered down between the distillery moorings, turned hard to port and luffed up. As the sails lost their drive and started slatting, I went forward, waited for a moment till the boat lost way then hurled the anchor overboard and listened with a joy almost amounting to ecstasy as the chain rattled up through the hawse pipe and out over the bowhead for the very last time. I was home, and safe.

I took the sails in, snugged everything down on deck and inflated the dinghy. I went to sit down below for a minute to gather my strength and gear. I did not realise it but I had been spotted by our neighbour. Should my wife be phoned and told that I was in the bay? In the end the decision was against: what could she do? Would she not prefer a surprise? There was no risk now anyway.

I packed everything I thought I might need for the next three days, all of which I intended to spend indoors doing absolutely nothing but taking it easy: eating, sleeping, bathing and shitting in comfort. With my camera-bag over one shoulder, my precious notes and recordings over the other, and two suitcases to carry, I clambered into the dinghy and rowed gingerly in to the distillery pier. I lashed the dinghy well out of the water and picked up my baggage. I regret to say that once on dry land I did not give a single backward glance at my loyal friend and protector, *Sylvia B*. Feeling outwardly laden but inwardly light, I walked up through the village in the rain to my own bright hearth, and a family reception so warm and beautiful I could not begin to describe it.

AFTERWORD:
FIVE YEARS ON

IT IS FIVE YEARS SINCE I set sail from Lagavulin Bay on *Sylvia B*. What has changed in the islands since then? Quite a lot, is the short answer, one that I can give with confidence because so many of the people featured in the book have kindly written to me since publication, adding further details to stories I told, or letting me know of subsequent developments. Others whom I have spoken to have all, with the single exception of the RSPB, been helpful with information. I am grateful.

The saddest thing to report is that quite a few of the nicer people I talked to on the trip are no longer with us. Tex Geddes is probably the most memorable. He died of a stroke in April 1998 on returning home from a piping competition. Col. Lachie Robertson of Elgol told me recently, 'It was because he went onto the wine. He'd 've been alright if he'd stayed on the whisky.' Seven months earlier, Tex's Orkney friend John Flett also died. The obituary in *The Herald* noted that the tune, 'Flett from Flotta', was played at President Kennedy's funeral.

In the same year, Robert Sturgeon of Coll died, as did Lord Selby and Clive Murray, the relatively youthful head gardener at Inverewe. So too did Dr John Morton Boyd, my valued advisor on the history of conservation politics in Scotland. It was Morton, as he liked to be called, who gave me the first clues to some important political realities. 'The RSPB spends a disproportionately high proportion of its substance servicing public opinion and a disproportionately low proportion servicing wildlife,' the famous conservationist said. 'There is no evidence whatsoever that membership of the RSPB helps keep the robin at the bird table.'

A year later I reviewed Morton's autobiography, *The Song of the Sandpiper*, for *The Herald*. The central dichotomy of the book seemed to me that, though self-consciously Christian, he thought of himself as an evangelist for another, quasi-religious faith: nature conservation. I wrote that 'his hero was Fraser Darling, the Christ to his St Peter'. If Darling had supplied the sacred texts, it was Morton who had built the Church, namely the bureaucratic structure of authoritarian conservationism. The religious metaphor met with approval from a surprising quarter, Morton's own son Alan, a Gaelic-speaking resident of the Uists, and an office-bearer in the newly formed Free Church (Continuing).

As a teenager, Alan had been introduced by his father to the great man. His impression was of a 'charlatan' and 'a big ego merchant'. He found Darling 'very flat, not charismatic; he was dull, almost lethargic and, as I later discovered, an arch-adulterer'. Alan's main point was that, though his father had been an Elder in the Church of Scotland, his belief that all of creation is part of God and God an element within all creation was closer to Hinduism than Christianity as he understood it. 'In the Free Church at any rate, we worship the Creator not His creation,' Alan said.

The sanctity of the natural world was the underlying axiom of Morton Boyd's moral conservationism – remember that in following Darling's footsteps onto Lunga, he said he felt he 'had trodden hallowed ground'. That sanctity is what is supposed to raise man's relationship with nature above either squalid utility or careless amenity. But it is a compulsory sanctity if, as current conservation legislation implies, a legal 'duty' has in effect been laid on landowners to act as stewards of biodiversity rather than simply as owners of a territorial asset. This is where moral conservationism tips into authoritarianism. Bureaucratic control of the countryside is not an unfortunate aberration but the inevitable consequence of messianic Darlingism. Alan's point attacks this structure at its root. No-one else whom I talked to about *Isles of the West* went to the heart of the matter so directly.

Alan Boyd was not the only reader of this book to react positively to the iconoclastic portrait of Fraser Darling. A Mr Astle wrote to me from Cheshire enclosing a copy of a monograph of his which included an eight-page description of the great man in Africa, where he was employed as a consultant by the British government in the late 1950s. Though Darling spent a mere five months in Northern Rhodesia (now Zambia), his influence appears to have been considerable. Astle reports that he arrived with 'pre-formed and strongly held views on Africa and Africans . . . [He was] authoritarian and dogmatic . . . He did not meet African villagers . . . He appeared not to appreciate the fact that the Administration could not rule by diktat.'[1]

As in the Highlands, Darling wanted to create wilderness areas by frustrating the natives' attempts to develop their local economy. His main recommendation was a compulsory livestock de-stocking programme. Darling even went so far as to suggest that Africans should not be paid wages until they had been taught how to spend them. Undermining local economic autonomy simply increased the need to attract external finance. This, of course, was more readily available for 'noble' causes like wildlife conservation than it was for social welfare or infrastructure development. Of course, much of the cash flowed into the pockets of those people, like Darling, who administered the noble causes. Astle, a first-hand witness of these developments, wrote that:

> Darling's consultancy was the first, and typical, of others which followed in the next decade in which very eminent people and 'experts' would appear and pronounce instant solutions to local problems about which it was only too obvious they had little understanding . . . Current policy regarding Game Management

1   *A History of Wildlife Conservation in the Mid-Luangwa Valley, Zambia* (Research paper #3), British Empire and Commonwealth Museum, Bristol, 1999, p. 90.

Areas appears to be strongly influenced by the readier availability of expatriate funding for wildlife projects compared with that on offer for other aspects of rural life. Why should local people have to rely on wildlife for development funds?[2]

One of the most enthusiastic reviewers of the first edition of this book, the eccentric explorer Redmond O'Hanlon, took the 'colonial' point. In the *Times Literary Supplement,* O'Hanlon, himself a member of the RSPB, wrote, 'The RSPB not a wholly good thing? Blasphemy! But Mitchell makes his case . . . Every staff member of the hallowed organisations he attacks should read it. And mend their ways.' Though the RSPB had the book examined by their lawyers with a view to suing me for libel,[3] that appears to be as far as the reading has gone. Certainly there has been no appreciable mending of the ways, either in that organisation or elsewhere in the conservation establishment. Exactly the opposite has happened. Acting on SNH advice, and under pressure from the RSPB and other such bodies, the Scottish Environment Minister recently announced plans to tighten up the regulations on SSSIs, to declare more of them and to make it a criminal offence to disturb 'recklessly' – as opposed to intentionally – any feature of wildlife interest. No longer will the legal test be whether you *did* know that the nest you walked past was that of a Schedule 1 species, but whether you *ought to have* known. Ignorance of the bureaucratic agenda will have criminal consequences. In extreme cases, jail sentences are proposed.

This will hurt both productive and recreational land users, the latter being the main cash generators in the Highland economy. But, like Darling's blacks, they do not appear to count. The allegation against the pre-devolution administration of Scotland was that it was colonial. This implies two general features: first, that the administrators are not native; and secondly, that they are not responsible to the natives. In the conservation world, the new Scottish parliament has brought little change. The Chairman of SNH comes from Lancashire and his Chief Executive from Leicestershire. The RSPB's Director for Scotland grew up in south London. The President of the Scottish Wildlife Trust comes from a distinguished Yorkshire family and the Chief Executive from a yet-to-be distinguished Lancastrian one. The Chairman of the National Trust for Scotland hails from Sussex and his Director from Yorkshire. Looking more widely, the Director of the Scottish Landowners' Federation is English, as is the Chairman of the Deer Commission and the majority of the Board of the government's official Biodiversity Group. So is the Head of the Ecological Advisory Department of the Scottish Executive. Even the Director of the only Institute for

---

2   *Ibid.,* p. 93. Astle wrote to me saying, 'The situation you describe [in Scotland] was replicated all over Africa. For example, in 1986 in the Luangwa Valley there were 13 4.W.D vehicles engaged in "Save the Rhino" projects and one battered pick-up in a "Save the Children" project.' (20 January 2000)

3   David Minns explained their failure to do so by saying that the RSPB 'decided that to [sue me] would be wasteful of the Society's resources'. A member told me that Dr Rhys Green, the RSPB's corncrake expert, wrote to him explaining that decision by saying, 'The RSPB would not normally consider taking an individual to court for criticising us; there is little to be gained from this route.'

Environmental History within a Scottish University – and incidentally
Historiographer Royal in Scotland – comes from Cambridge.

By contrast, the top officers of the main associations that are trying to develop
the local economy – the Crofters Commission, the Scottish Crofters Union, the
National Farmers Union of Scotland, the Scottish Fishermen's Federation and
Highlands and Island Enterprise – are all Scottish. This split in national origins
of the two groups is so striking that it calls for comment.

Different countries have different ideas about how their natural heritage should
be used and about what constitutes misuse. The purpose of conservation is to
protect what people see as worthwhile in the environment their society has
inherited (or feels it should have inherited: hence reintroductions like the sea-
eagle). Consequently it is a largely atavistic impulse. But different countries have
different attitudes to the past, which is why the Germans have extensive forests
and the Americans dude ranches. The English paradigm is of a lost Eden which
hovers somewhere between the worlds of J.R.R. Tolkein and Henry Williamson.
Both were fierce opponents of modern industrialism. They saw virtue in a happily
old-fashioned rural society which had not broken its ties with the soil. Even the
most cursory glance at an RSPB corncrake leaflet shows that modern
conservationists look at Hebridean crofters in a similar way.

The nationality distinction is important since the incredible resources directed
towards 'saving' the corncrake from local extinction are, in the eyes of many
Hebrideans, wasted. Since the corncrake is not a globally threatened species, the
bird's importance is largely symbolic. By far the most frequently quoted example
of the corncrake as a symbol is Stanley Baldwin's speech to the Royal Society of
St George, celebrating St George's Day 1924, when he mentioned the bird in
Anglocentric terms.

> The first thought that comes to my mind as a public man is a feeling of satisfaction
> and profound thankfulness that I may use the word 'England' without some fellow
> at the back shouting out 'Britain' . . . To me England is the country and the
> country England. And when I ask myself what I mean by England, when I think
> of England when I am abroad, England comes to me through my various senses.
> The sounds of England, the tinkle of the hammer on the anvil in the country
> smithy, the corncrake on a dewy morning, the sound of scythe against
> whetstone . . .[4]

So long as it does not tip over into racism, there is nothing necessarily wrong
with patriotic, arcadian nostalgia. Many a Hebridean would sympathise with
Baldwin's obviously sincere sense of place. But it is vital to appreciate that the
Scottish view of natural heritage is quite different from the English view.

No Scottish poet has written in elegiac terms, as Thomas Gray did, of
ploughmen homeward plodding their weary way. Likewise, no English poet has
written, as Burns did, that his heart was in the Highlands 'a-chasing the deer'.

---

4 *On England*, Rt. Hon. Stanley Baldwin, Philip Allen, London 1926, pp. 6–7. It is
   ironic that the pipe-smoking 'countryman' Prime Minister's large personal fortune
   derived from a steelworks in the most filthily industrialised part of the west Midlands.

Even in the late eighteenth century, there were easier ways to get food than by 'chasing the wild deer', but few so romantic and so free. Gray's English ploughman would have been roughly contemporaneous with Burns's Lowland dreamer, but two images of 'man in nature' could hardly be more different.

The effect of all the bureaucratic ploughmen who have plodded north to run rural Scotland has been to take the joy out of the fresh air experience. To make something beautiful into work is to destroy it. The real tragedy of the modern Highlands is that the culture is being killed by people who do not understand it, and for reasons which most locals see as trivial. So what if there are a couple more corncrakes in Lewis?[5]

A second important difference between the administrators and the natives is related to this work/leisure dichotomy: there is an almost puritanical solemnity about the conservationists which is rare in the locals' attitude to nature. Hugh Mackinnon said of the Coll of his youth, 'You got a laugh at every door.' But where is the wit, where is the sense of joy, in the tens of thousands of pages of books, research reports, theses, surveys, minutes, appeals, colloquia, press releases, interviews, media transcripts or profile-raising educational leaflets produced annually by the conservationists? Their publications are like the Bible in the sense which Robert Graves meant when he observed that there is 'not a smile from Genesis to Apocalypse'. It would appear that if we are not terrified into glumness by the latest corncrake statistics, we are infidel.

Readers of *Private Eye* will be familiar with the precise way in which the word 'bore' is used in that magazine. In his biography of Richard Ingrams, *Lord of the Gnomes*, Harry Thompson says, 'Ingrams, and also Auberon Waugh, use the word "bore" in a very distinctive way. They don't really mean someone who bores you by talking about knitting or how to get on to the M11, they mean someone who threatens you with moral reproach. Bores are people who have convictions, who passionately believe in something and try to persuade you to their viewpoint [and who] cannot be deflected with a joke.' Thompson goes on to observe that such people are more than dull, they are dangerous. Having quoted a journalist who once jeered that 'Ingrams would justify the Second World War by saying it repelled bores', Thompson concludes, 'Bores are extremists, whether they be tiresome and unimportant or powerful and frightening. In that sense, yes, the Second World War did repel a bore, the most terrifying, humourless bore that ever passionately believed in his own convictions.'

The Nazis were the ultimate conservationists since they considered, in theory at any rate, that land was a communal resource which should be managed exclusively for the public good by land users who had explicit duties to the State. Rebadged as 'stewardship of biodiversity', this view is being introduced into

---

5   In 1996, when I made my trip, there were 583 calling male corncrakes recorded in Scotland, out of a total world population of about 2.5 million. In the last summer before this writing the Scottish total had risen to 591, an increase of eight birds. That increase was bought at a cost of about £300,000 per annum, or £1.2 million over the four-year period. This equates to £150,000 per new bird.

Scotland by people from England. People will not be allowed to act in what they judge as a responsible balance of private and public interest, but in what the administrators see as the pure public interest. The fear is that the Highlands and Islands will be turned into a giant National Park, with the community themed into humiliating self-parody, while local economic activity is confined to whisky, history and wildlife tourism operated by immensely rich, state-supported charities. *Kash durch freude.*

How have the people I talked to on my trip fared in the past five years? Starting where I made my first landfall, on Colonsay, Bill and Annie Lawson still trade at Seaview. But the island's population has dropped further, and Lord Strathcona has handed over management of it to his son, Alex Howard, who has managed to extract £100,000 from the public purse to pay for a rhododendron-eradication programme. Since it was his family which introduced this botanical scourge to the island, the gift illustrates the fact that 'the polluter pays' principle tends to be enforced selectively.

Oronsay hasn't changed much with four years of intensive RSPB management: there were three corncrakes in 1996, now there are four; there is still only one breeding pair of choughs. On Coll and Tiree, corncrake numbers have not increased much on RSPB ground, though on Tiree they have risen substantially off it. Clive McKay's career with the RSPB stalled on Islay and he has now left the organisation. Donnie Campbell moved from Tiree to Islay, but in his case to be promoted to Head Teacher of the Islay High School. He is now a neighbour and tells me that the Tiree goose shooting scheme is going splendidly, though not so splendidly as the geese themselves, which are said to be increasing at the staggering rate of nearly 20 per cent per annum. Many of them have, like him, moved recently to Islay.

On Coll, Pat Graham continues to harry SNH and the RSPB, as do Colin Kennedy, who briefly moved off the island, and Kirsty Macleod, who comes back to it from Lochaber whenever she can. Kirsty has closely monitored what she calls 'the creeping environmental manipulation of the island's future', and the locals' response to it. 'The much vaunted European designation for the corncrake was universally condemned at a public meeting,' she says, 'while schemes for a scientific base, thinly disguised as a "heritage centre" in Arinagour, were kicked into touch last year by a newly awakened community.'

Martin Lunghi eventually managed to swap the social confines of Coll for the wider horizons of Mull, while Major MacLean-Bristol has published the second volume of his historical trilogy, *Murder Under Trust: the Crimes and Death of Sir Lachlan Mor MacLean of Duart 1558–1598* (Tuckwell, 1999). Though hard at work on volume three, wildlife problems still beset him. 'We've more geese than I've ever seen in my life,' he says today. 'There's nothing left for the sheep.'

Rum continues its long sleep, with no discernible progress, either in disburdening the state of its expensively under-utilised natural asset or in caring for its magnificent artificial monument. A £1 million SNH scheme, started in

1998, to increase the island population collapsed in embarassing failure when the local doctor diagnosed most of the incomers as suffering from stress. 'SNH do not know how to communicate with the residents,' said the local councillor, Charlie King.[6] In the space of a year, more than twenty people left the island. One of those was Anne Taylor, who married Derek Thompson, but left both him and the island because, she told the press, 'I had simply had enough of everything. I had to get away.' Now Derek himself is being evicted from his house by SNH, who will not rehouse him on the island. The worst of the old-style Lairds seldom behaved as nastily as SNH.

The corncrakes seemed just as reluctant to live on Rum as the human beings. As on Canna and Eigg, the other two publicly-owned elements of the Small Isles, not a single bird has arrived to breed. By contrast, the tiny but privately owned Isle of Muck last year increased its total to three calling males.

The Eigg buy-out succeeded so the island is now owned by the Isle of Eigg Heritage Trust, in which the major partner is the Scottish Wildlife Trust. But that really means SNH, since that organisation now provides all the core funding for SWT after it fell on hard times in 1998. An independent consultant, called in to investigate the Trust's conduct of its affairs, concluded that it had been guilty of the common trick among conservation charities whereby charismatic species are used to take from the public money which is then used for other purposes. The Trust has kept this report secret. When the money ran out, SNH stepped in. Acting as the donor of last resort, SNH now bankrolls the Trust, last year to the tune of £406,000. But still there is a large cash shortfall.

In 1998, the SWT lost a libel action after being sued by Keith Schellenberg over a fund-raising advertisement for the Eigg purchase, which it had published in 1995. The text implied that he had taken 'little interest in the conservation of this precious island'. The Trust knew this allegation to be false. On 16 May 1994, Professor Aubrey Manning, the then Chairman, had written to Schellenberg saying, 'I am very aware of the efforts you have put into managing the island in the past and your constant concern for its wildlife.' Since the Appeal letter saying exactly the opposite was also signed by Professor Manning, the case was open and shut. Despite this, none of the money taken by the Appeal – over £1 million – was ever returned to donors who might have been misled by the Trust's advertisement.

The John Muir Trust is one of the few bodies untainted by that sort of allegation. Nonetheless, on Skye it has expanded its territories substantially at public expense (and also acquired Ben Nevis), and has seen its Director of Land Management appointed Chairman of the Deer Commission, an important position in the world of mountain management. The cosy interweaving of the public and charitable sectors of the conservation industry is something which leaves private landowners at a disadvantage, as the residents of Soay have found to their cost.

---

6 *The Scotsman* 2 April 2001

Recently the last pupil left the Soay Primary School, so it closed. Not content with putting the building on a 'care and maintenance' basis, which would cost only a few thousand pounds a year, the Highland Council decided to sell it, in order to save money. Since building a new school, should an island woman fall pregnant in the future, would be prohibitively expensive, this parsimony will probably mean the end of schooling on the island and, in due course, the end of a living community there, since anyone with children of primary school age will have to move away. It is relevant to observe that at no time has the lack of children for the school on Rum resulted in the threat of a sale of the school house by the same Council.

On the Uists, Digger Jackson continues to observe dunlin and hedgehogs. Recently a three-year joint RSPB–SNH project for the erection of electric fences to create 'exclusion zones' was initiated. Phase I of this scheme is expected to cost £300,000. Subject to European approval, the birds will also benefit from an SNH mink-eradication programme at a cost of £1.7 million.

Bill Neill had a lucky escape in connection with my visit. I have been told I was correct in my suspicion that RSPB HQ had instructed the likes of Sean Morris and Alison Maclennan not to talk to me. What I did not know was that Bill Neill was also contacted. Had he defied even an informal warning from the RSPB, he would have risked excommunication from the Darlingist Church. But as it happens the message arrived the day after he and I met, so he does not have to take the rap for his helpfulness. He can hold up his hands and say with a clear conscience, 'Your warning came too late!'

'John Love is a very quiet man,' a reader from Uist subsequently told me, 'but the only time I have seen him with a pepper up his backside was when your book was mentioned.' John's sparring partner on North Uist, Ena McNeil, is no longer on the Western Isles Council, but she is still active in the fight against the future she fears: 'all geese and no crofters.' She has published articles in the broadsheet press about the problem, which is a new departure for her. Sadly, though, she has never written the children's books we talked about.

Another aborted development has been the Lingerbay superquarry, which was turned down by the Scottish Environment Minister nearly ten years after the first application. Donnie Rodel, therefore, has had his dreams of wealth shattered. Or has he? Moves are afoot to reactivate the original quarrying consents which were granted in 1965 and 1981. I asked him recently if he thought this was now a long shot. 'I have never thought that it would be a long shot,' Donnie replied. 'I just thought it would take some time. I still believe there will be a quarry at Lingerbay.' More immediately, Donnie will be the proprietor of what he calls 'a singing, dancing, new hotel' by the middle of this summer.

Two other establishments which have done well since I visited them are Scoraig and Sabhal Mòr Ostaig. Scoraig now has its own high school, with two teachers and a roll of six. The community has expanded and there is talk of a regular ferry to the mainland. Topher Dawson has turned his woodworking talents to the manufacture of ultra-light, hollow, plywood-skinned propeller blades which, at

90 feet long, are capable of driving the 6 kW wind turbines made by the firm he supplies in Kilmarnock. Sabhal Mòr Ostaig has expanded physically, and vastly increased its student roll, now that it has been selected as the principle Gaelic campus of the University of the Highlands and Islands.

Nearby on Sleat, Sir Iain Noble stood unsuccessfully for the Scottish parliament as an Independent. Though he recently retired from his bank, Noble & Co, he is far from idle. He has started a new 'business angel' company in Edinburgh, and is also actively engaged in 'teasing' SNH, as he puts it, about their species policy.

'They tell us that we are not under any circumstances allowed to plant Scots pine trees on the grounds that they are not indigenous to Skye,' Sir Iain says. 'I have pointed out to them that the peat bogs are absolutely full of them so they obviously were around once. "Ah," they say, "that was before the last Ice Age so it doesn't count." But, I say, if they do believe in only having indigenous species around, why don't they have a few more indigenous people around in their own organisation? We did an SSSI agreement with them back in 1978 over some woodland. One of the clauses would be that they would use their best endeavours to use Gaelic-speaking staff for operations which were in anyway concerned with that woodland. But from that day to this, Gaelic has never been mentioned. Now I wonder if they are in breach of their agreement. If they do believe in indigenous species, why don't they use indigenous people for their own workforce?'

Getting closer to home, Bert Leitch is now paid for his sea-eagles and Shona House has yet to be blown up. Ardfern doesn't change, and Barnhill still catches the morning sun. Finally, the crew of the *Intrepid* are now the crew of the larger, more elegant and powerful *Village Belle*, on which I have had some memorable summer days out scalloping and photographing the gannets.

Having summarised, all too briefly, the more interesting human developments, I cannot avoid mentioning one very sad item of marine news. In pitch darkness, at 4 o'clock in the morning of Tuesday 10 November 1998, as the tail end of Hurricane Mitch lashed the southern Hebrides with winds reaching over 100 mph, *Sylvia B* was torn off her mooring in Lagavulin Bay and wrecked.

Lagavulin, April 2001